a political sociology of transnational europe

Edited by
Niilo Kauppi

ecpr PRESS

First published by the ECPR Press in 2013

The ECPR Press is the publishing imprint of the European Consortium for Political Research (ECPR), a scholarly association, which supports and encourages the training, research and cross-national cooperation of political scientists in institutions throughout Europe and beyond.

ECPR Press
University of Essex
Wivenhoe Park
Colchester
CO4 3SQ
UK

Typeset by ECPR Press
Printed and bound by Lightning Source

British Library Cataloguing in Publication Data
A catalogue record for this book is available from the British Library

Hardback ISBN: 978–1-907301–34–6

www.ecpr.eu/ecprpress

ECPR – *Studies in European Political Science* is a series of high-quality edited volumes on topics at the cutting edge of current political science and political thought. All volumes are research-based offering new perspectives in the study of politics with contributions from leading scholars working in the relevant fields. Most of the volumes originate from ECPR events including the Joint Sessions of Workshops, the Research Sessions, and the General Conferences.

Other books in this series

Europeanisation and Party Politics
ISBN: 9781907301223
Edited by Erol Külahci

Interactive Policy Making, Metagovernance and Democracy
ISBN: 9781907301131
Edited by Jacob Torfing and Peter Triantafillou

Perceptions of Europe
ISBN: 9781907301155
Edited by Daniel Gaxie, Jay Rowell and Nicolas Hubé

Personal Representation: The Neglected Dimension of Electoral Systems
ISBN: 9781907301162
Edited by Josep Colomer

Political Participation in France and Germany
ISBN: 9781907301315
Oscar Gabriel, Silke Keil, and Eric Kerrouche

Political Trust: Why Context Matters
ISBN: 9781907301230
Edited by Sonja Zmerli and Marc Hooghe

Please visit www.ecpr.eu/ecprpress for up-to-date information about new publications.

contents

Part III. Citizens Imagining Europe

| list of figures and tables

Figures

Tables

| list of abbreviations

AALEP	Association of Accredited Lobbyists to the European Parliament
AER	Assembly of European Regions
AHELO	The Assessment of Higher Education Learning Outcomes
AIDS	Acquired Immune Deficiency Syndrome
ALTER-EU	Alliance for Transparency and Ethics Regulation-European Union
ATTAC	Association for the Taxation of Financial Transactions
BMIR	Benzecri's Modified Inertia Rate
CEDAG	European Council for Non-Profit Organisations
CEFIC	European Chemical Industry Council
CEO	Corporate Europe Observatory
CHERPA	Consortium for Higher Education and Research Performance Assessment
CoE	Council of Europe
CSCG	Civil Society Contact Group
CWTS	The Centre for Science and Technology Studies, Leiden University
DDR	Deutsche Demokratische Republik
DG	Directorates-General
ECFR	European Charter of Fundamental Rights
ECHR	European Convention for the Protection of Human Rights and Fundamental Freedoms
ECJ	European Court of Justice
ECSC	European Coal and Steel Community
ECtHR	European Court of Human Rights
EEC	European Economic Community
EESC	European Economic and Social Committee
EPC	European Policy Center
ESF	European Social Forum
ETI	European Transparency Initiative
ETUC	European Trade Union Confederation
EU	European Union
FOEE	Friends of the Earth Europe
GDP	Gross Domestic Product

GJM	Global Justice Movement
GMO	Genetically Modified Organism
HEEACT	Higher Education Evaluation and Accreditation Council of Taiwan
HEI	Higher Education Institution
HIV	Human Immunodeficiency Virus
IGO	International Governmental Organisation
IMF	International Monetary Fund
INGO	International Non-Governmental Organisation
INTUNE	Integrated and United: A Quest for Citizenship in an Ever Closer Union
IRA	Irish Republican Army
ITF	International Transport Forum
MCA	Multiple Correspondence Analysis
MEP	Member of European Parliament
NGO	Non-Governmenatl Organisation
OECD	Organization for Economic Cooperation and Development
OMA	Optimal Matching Analysis
PLWA	People Living with AIDS
POS	Political Opportunity Structure
REACH	Registration, Evaluation, Authorisation and Restriction of Chemical Substances
SA	Sequence Analysis
SEAP	The Society of European Affairs Professionals
SES	Socioeconomic Status
SJTUIHE	Shanghai Jiao Tong University Institute of Higher Education
SMO	Social Movement Organisation
TCE	Treaty establishing a Constitution for Europe
THES	Times Higher Education Supplement
TSMO	Transnational Social Movement Organisation
UK	United Kingdom
UN	United Nations
UNHCR	United Nations High Commissioner for Refugees
UNICE	Union of Industrial and Employers' Confederation of Europe
UNICEF	United Nations Children's Fund
UNWTO	United Nations World Tourism Organization
US	United States
WTO	World Trade Organization

| contributors

DIDIER BIGO is Professor at King's College London, Department of War Studies (part time) and Research Professor of international relations (maître de conférences des universités) at Sciences-Po Paris, CERI/FNSP. He is Director of the Center for the Study of Conflicts (Centre d'études sur les conflits) and editor of the quarterly journal *Cultures & Conflits* published by l'Harmattan. He is founder and former co-editor, with Rob Walker, of the International Studies Association journal *International Political Sociology*, published by Blackwell. He works on critical approaches to security in Europe and the relationship between internal and external security, as well as on the sociology of policing and surveillance. He analyses the relationships and tensions between international relations, politics and sociology. Bigo has been responsible for the WP1 of the FP7 'INEX' research programme on internal and external security and has been the scientific coordinator of the FP6 'Challenge' research programme.

PHILIPPE BLANCHARD is Senior Researcher at the IEPI, University of Lausanne. He works on political sociology, political communication, and methods for social and political sciences: sequence analysis, content analysis, questionnaire surveys, interviewing, correspondence analysis and other descriptive multivariate statistics. He is presently conducting research on political biographies: AIDS activists in France, party members in Morocco, Swiss trade unionists, and European corporate elites. His current research projects also include the socioeconomic roots of parliamentary voting in Switzerland and the public controversy about nuclear energy in France. He is currently preparing a book on sequence analysis, to be published by Palgrave Macmillan and the ECPR Press.

DONATELLA DELLA PORTA is Professor of political science at the Istituto Italiano di Scienze Umane (on leave of absence) and Professor of sociology in the Department of Political and Social Sciences at the European University Institute. She has directed the Demos project, devoted to the analysis of conceptions and practices of democracy in social movements in six European countries. She is now starting a major ERC project 'Mobilizing for Democracy' on civil society participation in democratisation processes in Europe, the Middle East, Asia and Latin America. She is co-editor of the *European Political Science Review* (ECPR-Cambridge University Press). In 2011, she was the recipient of the ECPR's Mattei Dogan Foundation Prize in European Political Sociology for distinguished achievements in the field of political sociology. Her main fields of research are social movements, the policing of public order, participatory democracy and political corruption. Among her recent publications are *Mobilizing on the Extreme Right* (with M. Caiani and C. Wagemann) (Oxford, 2012), *Meeting Democracy* (ed. with D. Rucht) (Cambridge 2012), *The Hidden Order of Corruption* (with A.

Vannucci) (Ashgate 2012), *Los movimientos sociales* (with M. Diani) (CIS 2011), *Democrazie* (Il Mulino 2011), *L'intervista qualitativa* (Laterza 2011) and (with M. Caiani) *Social Movements and Europeanization* (Oxford 2009).

TERO ERKKILÄ is University Lecturer of political science at the Department of Political and Economic Studies, University of Helsinki. His research interests include transnational governance, public institutions and collective identities. He has published on accountability, transparency, public information management, governance indices, higher education rankings and EU concepts. His recent publications include 'The making of a global field of higher education: actors, institutions and practices' (with N. Kauppi) in *International Political Sociology* (2011) and 'Alternatives to Existing International Rankings' (with N. Kauppi) in *UNESCO World Social Science Report* (2010). His book *Government Transparency: Impacts and Unintended Consequences* is forthcoming by Palgrave. Erkkilä directs 'Transnational Governance of Higher Education', a research project funded by the University of Helsinki Network for Higher Education and Innovation Research (HEINE).

OLIVIER FILLIEULE is Professor in political sociology and member of the CRAPUL Research Center on Political Action at the University of Lausanne. He is also Research Professor at CNRS, Paris I Sorbonne (on leave). His work focuses on social movement and political activism, anti HIV/AIDS and global movements. He has recently published (with D. Tartakowsky) *La manifestation* (Presses de Sciences Po 2012) and co-edited (with E. Agrikoliansky and I. Sommier) *Penser les mouvements sociaux: Conflits sociaux et contestations dans les sociétés contemporaines* (La Découverte 2010), (with L. Mathieu and C. Péchu) *Dictionnaire des mouvements sociaux* (Presses de Sciences Po 2009), (with P. Roux) *Le sexe du militantisme* (Presses de Sciences Po 2008), (with E. Agrikoliansky and I. Sommier) *Généalogie du mouvement altermondialiste en Europe* (Karthala 2008), (with P. Favre and F. Jobard) *L'atelier du politiste* (La Découverte 2007) and (with D. Della Porta) *Police et manifestants. Maintien de l'ordre et gestion des conflits* (Presses de Sciences Po 2006).

DANIEL GAXIE is Professor of political sociology at Paris I University (Panthéon-Sorbonne) and a member of the European Centre for Sociology and Political Science (CNRS). He is presently doing qualitative (in-depth semi-structured repeated interviews) research on ordinary citizens' attitudes towards politics. He has recently participated in a comparative survey on attitudes towards European integration of representative samples of political, economic, media, and trade-union elites of 18 European countries (INTUNE Program). He has also been in charge of a comparative qualitative research project on ordinary citizens' perceptions of European integration. The main findings of this research have been published in *Perceptions of Europe: A comparative sociology of European attitudes* (ECPR 2011).

NICOLAS HUBÉ is Associate Professor of Political Science and Deputy-Dean of the Political Science Department at the University of Paris 1 Panthéon-Sorbonne. He is also Research Fellow at the European Center for Sociology and Political Science (CNRS). Apart from his involvement in the INTUNE project (FP 6), his research interests include the use and misuse of polls in political life and communication in EU institutions, political sociology and comparative journalism. He is a member of the Network of European Political Communication Scholars (NEPOCS). He has recently published in *Perspectives on European Politics and Society* (2010) and was co-editor (with D. Gaxie and J. Rowell) of *Perceptions of Europe: A comparative sociology of European attitudes* (ECPR 2011).

NIILO KAUPPI is Research Professor at the National Center for Scientific Research (CNRS, France) and Associate Director of the Center for European Political Sociology at the University of Strasbourg. He teaches political sociology and social theory at Sciences Po Strasbourg, the University of Lausanne and the University of Luxembourg. His research interests range from European integration and reforms of the European university, to intellectual radicalism and social theory. His publications include *Democracy, Social Resources and Political Power in the European Union* (Manchester 2005) and *Radicalism in French Culture: A sociology of French theory in the 1960s* (Ashgate 2010) and articles in *Comparative European Politics, Scandinavian Political Studies, Politique européenne, International Political Sociology* and *Theory and Society*. A member of the Executive Committee of the ECPR, Kauppi is co-convenor of the ECPR Standing Group in Political Sociology.

THERESA KUHN is a Post-doctoral Research Fellow at the Department of Politics and International Relations, University of Oxford. She is also a member of Nuffield College. In 2011, she obtained a PhD from the European University Institute. Currently, she is working on a book project entitled *Experiencing European Integration: The effect of individual transnationalism on European identity*. Her research interests are at the intersection of political sociology, European studies and comparative politics, and focus on collective identities, democratic legitimacy, transnationalism, cosmopolitanism, solidarity and border regions. Her work has appeared in *European Journal of Political Research* and *European Union Politics*.

MIKAEL RASK MADSEN is Professor of European law and integration, focusing on international law, courts and society, and Director of iCourts, the Danish National Research Foundation's Centre of Excellence for International Courts, Faculty of Law, University of Copenhagen. Trained in both law and sociology, his research concerns the globalisation of law and the creation of transnational legal fields with a particular focus on the interface of agents, typically legal agents, and the emergence of institutions and law.

HÉLÈNE MICHEL is Professor of political science at Science Po Strasbourg where she teaches the sociology of the European Union and European public policies. A member of the Institut Universitaire de France, her research deals with European interest groups, especially with the sociology of lobbyists and the analyses of their practices. She has published *La cause des propriétaires* (PUF 2006) which is an historical and sociological analysis of the evolution of housing policy and landowner and real estate agent lobbies, and she has edited *Lobbyistes et lobbying de l'Union européenne* (PUS 2005) and *La fabrique des 'Européens': Processus de socialisation et intégration européenne* (PUS 2010). She conducted a large quantitative and qualitative research project PRESSURE on the representatives of European interest groups. Currently she is interested in the litigation strategies of interest groups and their political uses of European law and rights ('The Construction of a European Interest through Legal Expertise: Property Owners' Associations and the Charter of Fundamental Rights', in J. Rowell and M. Mangenot (eds), *The Political Sociology of the European Union: Reassessing constructivism*, Manchester 2010).

LOUISA PARKS completed her PhD, a comparative study of the impacts of social movement campaigns in the European Union, in 2009 at the European University Institute in Florence. She is currently mapping recent social movements in Italy, as well as working as an editor and academic translator.

ETTORE RECCHI is Professor of political sociology in the University of Chieti-Pescara, Italy. He holds a PhD (with distinction) in Social and Political Sciences from the European University Institute (EUI). His main research foci are migration and mobility (in its different forms), social stratification, elites, and European integration. Currently he coordinates two international projects funded by the European Commission – EUCROSS (www.eucross.eu) and MOVEACT (www.moveact.eu) – on the 'Europeanisation of everyday life' and the 'Political behaviour of European mobile citizens'. Among his recent publications are 'Social Mobility and Spatial Mobility' (with A. Favell), in A. Favell and V. Guiraudon (eds), *Sociology of the European Union* (Palgrave 2011), 'Crossing Over, Heading West and South: Mobility, Citizenship, and Employment in the Enlarged Europe' (with A. Triandafyllidou), in G. Menz and A. Caviedes (eds), *Labour Migration in Europe* (Palgrave 2010) and *Pioneers of European Integration: Citizenship and mobility in the EU* (co-editor with A. Favell) (Elgar 2009).

STEFAN SEIDENDORF is Researcher in political and social sciences at the Franco-German Institute (DFI) in Ludwigsburg, Germany, where he heads the European Politics department. His PhD-thesis (*Europäisierung nationaler Identitätsdiskurse? Ein Vergleich französischer und deutscher Printmedien*, Nomos, 2007) analyses the 'Europeanisation' of French and German identity discourses (1950–2000). Other major publications concern the use of history in European politics and the constitutive role of discourses in national debates on Europe.

JONATHAN WHITE is Reader in European politics at the London School of Economics and Political Science. His research interests lie in the fields of political sociology and political theory, with a focus on contemporary European democracy and the European Union. Prior to joining the LSE, he was an Alexander von Humboldt Research Fellow at the Humboldt University in Berlin, and a doctoral researcher at the European University Institute in Florence. His publications include articles in *American Political Science Review, Journal of Politics, Political Studies, British Journal of Political Science, and Journal of Common Market Studies*. He is the author of *Political Allegiance after European Integration* (Palgrave 2011).

| acknowledgements

This book project started after the Potsdam European Consortium for Political Research (ECPR) General Conference in August 2009. As the organiser of the political sociology section, I was asked to publish a selection of the interventions from the political sociology panels. The idea was to publish some new European political sociology as contributions to European political science, and to contrast these contributions to American political sociology. In Europe, political sociology was quite invisible in the disciplinary landscape. In the US, apart from a few scholars involved in European studies, political sociologists were removed from the concrete transformations that were taking place in Europe. For these reasons I felt there was a market niche for original research on transformations in European politics from a political sociology perspective.

In 2009 only a few studies existed on political sociology and European politics, but in the next few years several volumes came out that dealt with political sociology and European integration. The manuscript at hand then found itself in a new competitive situation. The editors still felt that the collection proposed something new to an understanding of European politics both at theoretical and empirical levels. Political and economical developments in Europe also played their role in the final shaping of the volume. They highlighted the fragility of the European nation-state, one of the central themes of this book.

My greatest thanks go to all the authors who have patiently responded to my numerous queries and especially to Michael Kull, Mikael Rask Madsen, Ettore Recchi, Stefan Seidendorf, David Swartz and Jonathan White for many critical comments as well as for ideas concerning the overall framing of the volume. I also wanted to thank series editors Dario Castiglione and Vincent Hoffmann-Martinot as well as Mark Kench, Peter Kennealy, Sharleni Inbanathan and Laura Pugh from ECPR Press for their support. Without the constant encouragement of my dear wife Anne all of this would not have been possible.

Niilo Kauppi
Strasbourg, April 2012

part i. from the grassroots to brussels: making voices heard

chapter one | introduction: political sociology and 'second-wave' european studies

Niilo Kauppi

A new political science is needed for a world altogether new
(Tocqueville [1835] 1986: 44, my translation)

I will begin this introduction by briefly discussing the current state of European political sociology, then present some features of established approaches in European studies to finish with the presentation of the main ideas developed in this book.

Max Weber remarked that in order to understand German domestic politics, one had to grasp the global state of political affairs (Gerth and Mills 1991). Although conceived within the context of his analysis of colonialism, Weber's notion of a global competition for resources is an even more defining feature of our age. It is through these global processes that large portions of political power have been transferred from the nation-state level to both the supranational and regional levels. The European nation-state has been reshaped and our concepts of democracy challenged (Habermas 2001). However, these transformations cannot be explained by simple Europeanisation whereby there would be more 'Europe' and less 'nation-state'. National public policies are not just downloaded from a European level (for critical discussions see, for instance, Fligstein and Mérand 2002; Beckfield 2009). Social transformations processes are fundamentally complex, often non-linear, even contradictory.

Since the 1950s, significant changes have also taken place in the relationship between political science and sociology. While political sociologists such as Robert Dahl, Seymour Martin Lipset, Robert Putnam and Stein Rokkan produced some of the classical works in political science, political sociology has since the 1970s, been eclipsed by the expansion of other sub-disciplines such as political economy and international relations, and the institutionalisation of a core set of political science objects and methods that favour institutional and quantitative approaches. These developments have been simultaneous with a recentering of political science on comparative politics (Eckstein 1991). The result has been a shift in the status of political sociology as a scholarly specialty. In the US, Anthony Orum (1996) observes that by the mid-1990s there is no longer a coherent paradigm in US political sociology. David Swartz underlines a shift away from behavioural studies of parties, voting, political participation, political attitudes, etc. toward an increased interest in social institutions, particularly the welfare state and social movements (Swartz 2013).

European political sociology has had difficulty responding in a creative manner to complex Europeanisation, in part because of divergent endogenous developments, and in part because of different national traditions. The institutional position of political sociology as an academic discipline, in different national contexts, has also played a role. In some academic settings such as the Finnish academic field, following American disciplinary divisions, political sociology has been integrated into sociology departments, creating a clear split between political science and political sociology (for an overview see Nedelmann and Sztompka 1993). In the Finnish political science repertoire one finds studies on political institutions with a strong quantitative emphasis, whereas political sociology is considered a sub-discipline of sociology, and features research on nationalism and social identity for instance. This disciplinary division corresponds to a political one: political science is on the right, sociology on the left. Consequently, the extra-academic networks in which these disciplines are embedded are distinct. Political scientists will have institutional ties with the Foreign Ministry and the Ministry of Finance, whereas sociologists will be in regular contact with the Ministry for Social Affairs. In other national settings such as the French academic field, political sociology plays an important role in political science, a relatively weak discipline in the French context. French political science has been rooted in the universities and in the Instituts d'études politiques that are professional training schools for civil servants. This division of political science between the university (and other institutes of higher education) and the Instituts d'études politiques is still today a major dividing line in the profession. French political science has been heavily influenced in a first phase by law, and in a second phase by sociology. Sociological theories and approaches have developed to such extent that some foreign observers wonder if French political science is really political science or sociology (Klingemann 2007).

This diversity in the academic status of political sociology makes communication between different national representatives of political sociology difficult. A Finnish political scientist will have serious problems in understanding the approach and logic of a French political scientist, versed in political sociology, and vice versa. Conversely, a Finnish sociologist will have no problem understanding French political science debates. A symptom of this multiplicity in the institutional situation of European political sociology, the division of labour between political science and sociology, the conventions of scholarly discourse and the transnational coordination problems that follow, is that until the mid-2000s political sociology has been absent in the sub-disciplinary landscape of professional organisations such as the main European political science association ECPR (European Consortium for Political Research) or the EUSA (European Union Studies Association)[1].

---

1. See the website of the ECPR Standing Group in Political Sociology, established in 2010, http://www3.unil.ch/wpmu/ecpr-polsoc/ and the website of the Political Sociology Section of the European Sociological Association ESA, created in 2008, http://www.europeanpoliticalsociology.eu/About-us.php.

If endogenous constraints have prevented the development of a common *prob-lématique* for European political sociologies, shared exogenous transformations have enabled new ideas to develop. In reaction to a rapidly changing political and social landscape, a new generation of European scholars has begun, since the second part of the 1990s, to develop alternative approaches to political phenomena. Globalisation and European integration have caused fundamental transformations in the traditional objects of political science research such as sovereignty and the nation-state. Political science tools no longer seem sufficient to make sense of a rapidly changing political and economical reality and growing competition among scholars in political science has led to the importation of concepts and methods from disciplines such as economics and sociology. The aim of this volume is to bring together some of this research and to present an overview of some of the exciting and innovative work now under way in European political sociology. Inspired by authors such as Pierre Bourdieu, Robert Gamson, Robert Merton and Charles Tilly, these scholars seek to combine qualitative and quantitative research techniques in a theoretically informed research perspective that unites macro- and micro-levels. Central to their work are redefinitions in traditional objects of political sociology research such as civil society, the nation-state and citizenship in the face of a growing denationalisation and transnationalisation of both politics and societies. In Europe, these broad symbolic and material transformations have also led to a demand for scholarly work that explores ordinary citizens and their relationship with political institutions and politics more broadly (see for instance Cotta and Best 2007, and the chapters by Gaxie and Hubé, Recchi and Kuhn, and White in this volume). '[T]he social conditions making for democracy' (Lipset 1960: 1) have also put into question traditional institutional political science perspectives drawing on normative concepts such as sovereignty and autonomy (for a critique, see Adler-Nissen 2009, see also Bigo and Seidendorf in this volume). A more and more interdependent global landscape and increasing mobility of social groups and ideas, requires a scholarly vocabulary and methodology that are less tied to the nation-state and its official or normative science (as expressed in the German concept of *Staatswissenschaft,* literally 'state science').

Political sociology has undergone a revival as several published English-language edited books witness (for a recent theoretical overview of the political sociology of the EU see Zimmermann and Favell 2011)[2]. In contrast to these volumes, the book at hand seeks to present a series of cutting-edge, theoretically am-

---

2. Adding to existing works like Rumford's pioneering *The European Union: A political sociology* (2002), Janoski *et al.*'s (eds) *Handbook of Political Sociology* (2005) and Nash's *Contemporary Political Sociology* (2007), Mitra and Pehl's edited volume *Political Sociology: The state of the art* (2009) presents updated research inspired by the classics of political sociology, but leaves out international and transnational processes that are key to understanding developments in European societies. Contributors to Rowell and Mangenot's *The Political Sociology of the European Union* (2010) offer a collection of valuable empirical studies. In a slightly different vein, Favell and Guiraudon in their edited volume *Sociology of the European Union* (2011) propose a panorama of sociological approaches to issues of interest for scholars working in European studies.

bitious studies in political sociology that deal with some of the major challenges European societies and politics are currently facing. These transformations can be boiled down to the loosening of the social ties between institutions, individuals and political action. As the studies in this volume demonstrate, supranational institutions like the European Commission, the European Parliament, social movements, interest groups, parapublic organisations, elites and 'ordinary' citizens all grapple with changing political circumstances and seek to redefine the legitimate parameters of political identity and action by challenging, in different ways, existing political hierarchies and values. These attempts to solve the contradictions between archaic descriptions of reality and political dynamics, explain the often messy and opaque developments in European politics. The studies in this volume seek to clarify these changing circumstances by methodological and conceptual innovations such as sequence analysis (SA), multiple correspondence analysis (MCA), field theory and the study of space sets for instance, to analyse the symbolic redefinitions of political action. They share a contextual analysis of politics through scrutiny of configurations of groups, representations and perceptions. In contrast to more institutional approaches in political science, a dynamic transnational perspective that seeks to avoid methodological nationalism is present in all the studies of this volume. These endeavours are taking place against a background of more established scholarly approaches.

A science of the european supranational state

As a political reality, the European Union is Janus-faced. On the one hand, the EU is a networked, emergent system of governance. On the other hand, it is a new power centre that more traditional powers have to reckon with. Until the 1990s, two scientific approaches dominated scientific discourse on the European Union. The state-centric model emphasised the role of nation-states to strengthen their power. From the viewpoint of this state-centric, high-politics scenario, first developed in the 1960s by prominent scholars like Stanley Hoffman, it is a fundamental mistake to downplay the role and strength of the European nation-state, the only really democratic instance in the EU. Alan Milward (1994) has controversially stated that European integration saved the European nation-state. From this government perspective several scholars have produced stimulating works. Andrew Moravcsik's *The Choice for Europe: Social purpose and state power from Messina to Maastricht* (Moravcsik 1998) argued that what really matters in the European Union are the high level negotiations between key players, the heads of the larger member-states and the European Commission. This approach became more popular among scholars when, after the Luxembourg compromise of 1966, it became clear that the member-states were crucial in any kind of supranational experiment in Europe. In this approach, that is reminiscent of the neorealist model in international relations, states have power interests that they pursue despite transformations in the larger political and economical landscape. A second model, propagated by a variety of scholars, has been called a multi-level governance model. In this governance scenario, nations are losing ground in the face of growing

supra- and transnationalisation of, decision making. This process is complemented by a regionalisation of political decision making. Liesbet Hooghe's and Gary
Marks' *Multi-Level Governance and European Integration* (Hooghe and Marks
2000) has become the standard reference reflecting this approach.

Since the mid-1980s, scholars have devised a variety of alternative neo-institu-
tional approaches to European regional integration. In their path-breaking article,
James March and Johan Olsen (1984) develop an institutional account of politics
arguing that institutions are the missing link that unites individual and society. In
their view, political science had until then assumed that the relationship between
the individual and the political system was more or less direct. Institutionalism
was also introduced into the study of organisations by sociologists Walter Powell
and Paul DiMaggio (1991). A variety of different types of institutional approaches have developed, labelled rationalist, historical and sociological approaches.
Institutions are most often understood as rules and shared meanings that enable
social interaction. It is from this background that a sociological version of institutionalism started to emerge in the mid-1990s. In his seminal work, *Social Theory
of International Politics*, Alexander Wendt (1999) challenged the classic neorealist work of Kenneth Waltz (1979) by introducing a sociological perspective to
international relations. In addition to the structuration theory of Anthony Giddens
(1984), Wendt also drew inspiration from a plethora of sociological works, such as
those of George Herbert Mead and Erving Goffman, while remaining in a framework of international politics and not, for instance, global politics. In this way,
sociological institutionalism opened new paths of research on topics such as socialisation and more broadly, the processes of social construction of reality, following Berger and Luckmann (1966). The purpose was to take a resolutely low
politics point of view to European integration. According to some developers of
this approach (Christiansen, Jørgensen and Wiener 1999), the aim was to examine
relatively neglected, but crucial aspects of integration, rules and norms, identities,
ideas and language. Since the end of the 1990s, sociological institutionalists have
published numerous studies on the role of intersubjective meanings, cultures of
national security and symbolic politics. By emphasising the role of social interaction in the process of European integration, they have been able to re-examine the
structure of the European and international order, as well as the crucial interaction of nation-states and the international system. This way sociological institutionalists have also contributed to research not just on European integration but
also on global politics. If the process of construction of scientific objects is rarely
examined in either political science or economic research on European integration, there are many sociologically inspired approaches that will emphasise the
complexity of scientific construction. A growing literature has emerged on social
scientific instruments of analysis, ranging from concepts and definitions to statistics and indexes (see for instance Hood 1983; Desrosières 1998). Despite its clear
merits, the 'sociological turn' in political science and international relations had its
limits. For many pioneers, 'social' meant in reality 'cultural' which was not taken
as a power resource but as a system of norms and identities. They reproduced, in a
slightly modified form, established political science and IR dichotomies. Perhaps

because of the right dose of radicalism and conservatism, social constructivism has become one of the leading research perspectives in European studies and IR.

The reasons for the success of these discourses in European Studies are complex. The obvious fact is that they were the first studies in this area. The broader questions are what are the links between political action, scholarly discourse and the definition of political reality? How does scholarly discourse participate in the construction of political reality? What is the connection between contemplation and action in European studies? Political agents involved in European politics apply certain symbolic structures (national-European, political-technical, executive-legislative, etc.) in their political practices that, in turn, reproduce specific power relations. For instance, by repeatedly displaying open contempt towards the European Parliament and its elections national ministers reinforce the public perception that the political influence of the European Parliament is weak. This type of political action delegitimises certain social resources – in this case transnational legislative political resources – and reinforces the view of the EU as simply a battlefield of national leaders in control of the political game. This delegitimation plays into some politicians' hands, and allows these same politicians, with important executive political resources, to have 'common sense' on their side. The principles of their actions resonate with a common sense perception of politics reproduced by the media. In this map of reality the real decision makers are heads of governments congregating in important meetings under the camera-lights. The role of non-governmental and private actors is minimised. The national is strictly separated from the trans- and international or European, as is more broadly the inside from the outside, internal affairs from foreign policy and so on. 'European' is the opposite of 'national', and the relationship between the two is a zero-sum game. All the way from identity issues to public policies, more 'European' means less 'national', and vice versa.

Scholarly discourse plays a day-to-day role in the production and reproduction of the European political order. Legitimised by some academic theories like intergovernmentalism (see for instance Moravcsik 1998), reproduced in the European media, sustained by journalistic practices, the common sense conception of European politics is not merely a detached description of a state of affairs. As a description and a prescription it is an integral part of European political and economic reality, a key element in the legitimation and reproduction of the European political order. Together with other European elites such as lawyers and civil servants, academics working in the area of European studies are implicated in the social (re- and de-) construction of the European Union and the European nation-state. Academics influence, to varying degrees depending on their positions in expert networks or in public debates and their social capital, the form these will take. Some take part in powerful networks uniting elite institutions of higher education and top professional reviews. In many ways their academic careers depend on broader developments. For a long time, European integration has been for European political and economic elites, the only viable political project for the foreseeable future. The politically thinkable has thus been severely constrained. Until recently, it seemed the dice had been cast, the future of the European Union and, through it, of the continent had already been decided. The economic crisis of 2011–12 is only beginning to seriously shake this political confidence. The vast and sophisticated system of symbolic and material rewards that European Union institutions have set up over the years (Jean Monnet chairs, Marie Curie grants, research framework programs, Erasmus student mobility grants etc.) has provided the financial infrastructure for empirical, policy-oriented European Union research. Most European funding is directed to research that can provide a European added value: it is not research funding in the traditional sense of the term, subjected to only scientific criteria. This observation does not mean that all research financed by the European Union is necessarily favourable to European integration. But this significant sponsorship certainly legitimises, by its mere activity, certain topics and research problems, this way guiding broader European social scientific orientations.

If we are to believe sociologists of knowledge, as systems of knowledge evolve, they become more self-reflexive (Collins 1998). Until now, the relationship between scholars studying the European Union and the object of their investigations has been unmediated and unproblematic, in part because the epistemological assumptions of this type of research transpose scientific models from the so-called hard sciences (or certain interpretations of these sciences) to the social sciences. Social scientific discourse is supposed to record what the scholar observes, that is reality as it reveals itself, effortlessly. Recent developments in academic material and symbolic reward systems have contributed to important changes in academic work. In many European member-states the budgets of social scientific research have been cut in most research areas, and numerous scholars have converted to the study of European integration and public policies, one of the few growth areas. There are few alternatives if one wishes to stay in the profession. It is in this context of the profound restructuring of European social scientific research that scholars have developed new approaches to European studies. Research has evolved from direct analysis of political phenomena to more complicated approaches that are increasingly self-reflexive about the conditions of production of scientific discourse and its political effects. The scientific pretensions of traditional approaches now look like 'baroque fantasies' (Ball 2006) that hide a naïve relationship to the European Union, that sustains a scholarly illusion in the neutrality of the discourse in question. Political scientists inspired by the studies of scholars like Alexander Wendt and Thomas Christiansen have introduced a more critical perspective. For many trained in constructivist and interdisciplinary traditions (working in such diverse domains as sociology, history, philosophy and anthropology) the construction of the research object – a minor concern for more traditional approaches – is, in fact, one of the main research questions. Until now, scholarly discourses that resonated with dominant political strategies have succeeded in getting the upper-hand, and alternative academic visions of the driving forces behind European integration have been delegitimised (for a stimulating discussion of these mechanisms see Rosamond 1999). Scholars are busy developing discourses that will enable them to objectify the evolving political reality while, at the same time, not to naïvely legitimise political agendas that seek to instrumentalise scholarly discourse to further their political goals. In this sense European studies might be at a threshold.

Moving beyond traditional paradigms: a 'second wave' of European studies

The authors of this volume seek to move beyond more established approaches to European politics and societies. In contrast to the practices of institutional political science or international relations, their terminology is more independent from the traditional normative vocabulary (sovereignty and independence for instance) used in describing the European nation-state. Terms such as *field* and space-set are analytical tools that can be applied within any area of research and any national context. This relative independence from nation-state terminology is coupled with another advantage, namely that political sociology investigates not only institutional structures but also, perhaps most significantly, systems of meaning or cultural/symbolic structures. This goal requires combining ethnographic fieldwork (using interviews and participant observation for example) with statistical analysis, for instance, and a more general investigation of cleavage structures and structures of symbolic domination. In this way, the micro-level can be analysed from a macro-perspective and vice-versa. In this Weberian way, political sociology provides analytical tools for entering into perhaps the most difficult aspect of the study of European societies– their analysis in relation to the cultural/symbolic role of the European Union. This is a dimension that is frequently missing in existing social scientific work focusing primarily on formal institutions and decision-making mechanisms. This area is avoided because analysing meaning structures requires a great deal of familiarity with the cultures under scrutiny.

The transformations induced by European integration and globalisation are not only quantitative but – indeed, more importantly –qualitative. This is precisely what makes them difficult to grasp. Several political sociologists have examined European institutions such as the European Commission and European Parliament through analysis of social resources and the mechanisms of their usage (including conversion into other resources) (Georgakakis 2000; Kauppi 2005; Beauvallet and Michon 2010). In this perspective, political groups, such as European Commissioners, MEPs (Members of the European Parliament) and other European *berufspolitiker* to paraphrase Max Weber, political careers, European parliamentary elections and their campaigns, and civil society (the media, intellectuals…) are the primary objects of scrutiny. These studies have shed light for instance on the transformative effects of European Parliament elections in national political fields. They show that the value of a political investment in the European Parliament is variable from member-state to member-state, and from party to party. In France, for example, small parties such as the Communist Party and the Front National have found in the European Parliament, a strategy of political survival. Had the Parliament not developed in the way it has, these parties might not exist today. Gaining a seat in the European Parliament is not only a way to secure political resources, however. For some, like political novices, a seat in the European Parliament provides a 'back door' opportunity to access national politics. The Finnish European Parliament elections demonstrated how political novices are provided with an opportunity to convert cultural resources (such as

media fame) or economic resources (especially private wealth) into political resources. These novices link political representation and group interests in a new,
creative way. Labelling these elections as of second or third order – as is the reflex
of most political scientists (see the seminal article by Reif and Schmitt 1980)–
does not clarify their political status and uses (for analysis see Kunz 2012). On the
contrary, it devalues their political functions and prevents us from seeing qualitative changes in political fields. What is required is a 'phenomenological' study
of European Parliament elections in different national political fields. Similar in-
sights can be achieved by using the same approach in other contexts, such as in the
analysis of the European Commission.

   The links between state and society (to simplify) as well as the social arrangements which structure power and produce forms of domination (see for instance
Michel in this volume) are at the core of European politics. Identity and citizenship
are key elements in the development of new forms of political power (see contributions by Recchi and Kuhn, and White in this volume). The analysis of social resources links political action to society in the broad sense of the term. For instance
in the French case, the role of social movements such as the 'Hunter's' movement
for instance, and the political strategies of the French Communist Party, as they
try to reinvent themselves through the European Parliament, both illustrate specific uses of transnational institutions. The struggles over the political status of the
European Parliament in the public space are determined by such strategies relying
on social resources. It is especially through the analysis of European Parliament
party campaigns that the links between 'Europe' as conceived and Europe as a
new political system, are crucial in explaining party political strategies. In other
words competing perspectives are too limiting. We need to study a broader range
of power relations in order to make sense of the transformations that are taking
place and to draw a new political roadmap.

   The constitution of transnational, mobile political spaces has been one of the
key innovations in the development of European societies in the past decades
(Favell 2008; Aradau *et al.* 2010; Mau 2010; Sigalas 2010; for a critique Berezin
and Diez Medrano 2005). The denationalisation of the European nation-state has
led to the development of transnational power bases and resources as well as
groups that use these assets to further their political agendas (see Knudsen 2009;
DeBardeleben and Hurrelmann 2011; Kauppi and Madsen 2013, for further analysis). Donatella della Porta and Louisa Parks push further, the limits of research on
social movements by introducing three new recent developments. First, they underline the cultural and symbolic dimensions of social movements. Second, they
develop a more dynamic vision of protest by examining the social mechanisms
that intervene between macro-causes and macro-effects. And third, they combine
analysis of the effects of protest on policy outcomes with its effects on protest
itself. This reflexive aspect of the research process links with other studies that
underline the cognitive dynamics of political action (see for instance Kauppi and
Madsen 2008 and Madsen 2011, White in this volume). Hélène Michel draws on
extensive fieldwork among European interest groups. Her research debunks the
numerous false perceptions that actors and observers alike have concerning EU

lobbying. She shows how European institutions have actively encouraged interest groups to participate in policy making and why these incentives have worked. The role and influence of social movements is also structurally linked with the social characteristics of their members and constituencies. Drawing on a variety of sociological work and sequence analysis (SA), Olivier Fillieule and Philippe Blanchard conceptualise the contribution of internal personal processes to the transformation of social movements, and the continuities and changes within protest groups. This perspective combined with sequence analysis enables them to scrutinise the duration and intensity of activists' commitment as well as the complex mix of structural attributes and their ordering along time.

The denationalisation of the European nation-state has led to its transnationalisation, to its insertion in a multitude of global networks and power relationships. The chapters in Part 2 discuss a key facet of this development, the redefinitions of the European nation-state and attempts to redefine the symbolic boundaries of political action. These transformations have led to new challenges in terms of security and liberty of movement, one of the founding blocks of European integration. No longer the symbol of freedom, mobility has become a threat to security. Didier Bigo's critical analysis points to the conceptual contradictions of existing definitions of borders and offers a way out of them. However, his contribution amounts to much more. In effect it is a fundamental critique of normative conceptions of statehood. In reality, these normative concepts do not correspond anymore to observed empirical reality. The European university, a key public institution in the historical development of the European nation-state since the nineteenth century, has also had to reinvent itself. In dominant ranking lists of global universities, European universities do not fare well, forcing them and their financers to adapt to an increasingly unified global field of higher education. Tero Erkkilä and Niilo Kauppi investigate some of the challenges facing the university and research, and the European Commission's strategies to legitimise radical changes in a context of global competition. Since the 2000s, the European Commission has become the key actor in the coordination of reforms in European national higher education systems. To succeed in this, it has created various policy instruments like a new multidimensional global ranking of institutions of higher education with which it seeks to challenge dominant ranking lists such as the so-called Shanghai list (for further developments see Kauppi and Erkkilä 2011 and Harmsen and Kauppi 2013). The interaction between the national and the global is also very clear in the dramatic 'turn to human rights' and its significance for European societies and citizens, further weakening the already fragile, sovereign juridical basis of the European nation-state. By addressing the *longue durée* of human rights in Europe, Mikael Rask Madsen further explores the reintegration of the two 'Europes' in the post-Cold War era and its ramifications for human rights in law, politics and society. Studying the interface of human rights and European integration provides a way to explore the internationalisation of the European nation-state (see Madsen 2004) and its normative-political foundation. Human rights have clearly been one of the political-legal pillars of European integration.

The chapters in Part 3 demonstrate that the political cultures of European societies and polities have undergone dramatic transformations since World War II. Due to European regional integration as well as to globalisation, geographical mobility has legitimised new political, European and cosmopolitan identities such as those of the highly educated free movers and the various seasonal labour migrants (see Recchi and Favell 2009). Using multiple correspondence analysis (MCA) completed by a cluster analysis, Daniel Gaxie and Nicolas Hubé compare the opinions and attitudes of four kinds of elites (political, economic, media, and trade-union) to European integration and institutions (see the project website INTUNE 2009). By crossing two dimensions, the degree of support and the coherence of opinions, Gaxie and Hubé are able to provide a 'map' of elites' attitudes toward European integration and EU institutions (for analysis see also Diez Medrano 2003; Feron, Crowley and Giorgi 2004; Best 2008; Gaxie *et al.* 2011). Expanding on the theme of the perceptions citizens have of European integration, Ettore Recchi and Theresa Kuhn scrutinise the transformation in Europeans' perceptions and practices of geographical mobility. Drawing from the classical work of Robert Merton and his concept of social set, they introduce the new concept of 'space-sets' as representations of physical sites where individuals spend their social existence. They hypothesise that there is a correlation between the widening of Europeans' space-sets and the political legitimacy of the European Union (see also Aradau *et al.* 2010).

If, for European citizens, European integration has not led to the development of a separate European identity (Sigalas 2010), it has become easier to compare one's economic and social situation with individuals and groups in other European countries, thus creating common spaces of symbolic reference. Jonathan White approaches the political sociology of citizenship in contemporary Europe by examining how processes of transnational integration present new opportunities for the practices of social comparison. By generating diverse social encounters, new information resources, and an extension in the scope of common legislation, these processes invite citizens to compare their daily experiences with those of people living elsewhere in Europe and to evoke reference groups outside their country of residence. Jonathan White shows how citizen self-understanding in the contemporary, transnationalising age can be approached without undue reliance on concepts such as 'identity' as applied to their study in the nation-state context. If the various processes of denationalisation have weakened the European nation-state, attempts have also been made to create transnational political identities by rewriting European history and collective memory. One example examined in this part is the creation of a binational secondary school history textbook. Stefan Seidendorf approaches the issue of transnational political subjects from the perspective of the creation of a Franco-German history textbook. Can the teaching of history in school, traditionally one of the 'engines of integration' of citizens into nineteenth century European nation-states (see for instance Harp 1998), take on a similar role in today's Europe? Why and under what conditions? The methodological approach involves content analysis of schoolbooks and analysis of teachers' and students' experiences.

Going deeper in the analysis of European politics requires questioning established conceptual dichotomies and the 'taken for granted' that goes with them. Paradoxically, the 'national' is often the condition of existence of the 'European'. National policies have served and continue to serve as a basis for the creation of European policies. Before integrating within the European Parliament, politicians have national careers, and return to them after their term in the European Parliament. The interaction between categories such as 'national' and 'European' is the key to an understanding of the dynamics of European politics. As the contributions to this volume demonstrate, objectifying transnational patterns of social interaction reveals new structures of political domination and legitimisation. These are not visible if one approaches them using more traditional research perspectives that separate from one another realities that should be examined together. What characterises the contributions to this volume is a sensitivity to these shifts in the politically possible at all levels of social lifeworlds, including social practices and conceptions of political legitimacy. It is precisely because it arrives late at the EU ball, to paraphrase George Ross (2011), that political sociology is able to provide fresh and sometimes disturbing questions about developments in European politics and societies.

References

Adler-Nissen, R. (2009) 'Late sovereign diplomacy', *The Hague Journal of Diplomacy,* 4: 121–141.

Aradau, C., Huysman, J. and Squire, V. (2010) 'Acts of European citizenship: A political sociology of mobility', *Journal of Common Market Studies,* 48(4): 945–965.

Ball, P. (2006) 'Baroque fantasies of a peculiar science', *Financial Times,* October 29.

Beauvallet W. and Michon, S. (2010) 'Professionalization and socialization of the members of the European Parliament', *French Politics,* 8(2): 145–165.

Beckfield, J. (2009) 'Remapping inequality in Europe: the net effect of regional integration on total income inequality in the *European Union'*, *International Journal of Comparative Sociology,* 50(5): 1–24.

Berezin, M. and Diez Medrano, J. (2005) 'Distance Matters: Place, Political Legitimacy and Popular Support for European Integration', paper presented at the ASA meeting, Philadephia, August 13th.

Berger, P. and Luckmann, T. (1966) *The Social Construction of Reality,* Harmondsworth: Penguin.

Best, H. (2008) '*The Europe of Elites: Determinants of Europeaness of European Political and Economic Elites'*, available at *ttp://www.allacademic.com,* accessed January 6, 2012.

Christiansen, T., Jørgensen, K. E. and Wiener, A. (1999) 'The social construction of Europe', *Journal of European Public Policy,* 6(4): 528–544.

Collins, R. (1998) *The Sociology of Philosophies: A global theory of intellectual change,* Cambridge: Harvard University Press.

Cotta, M. and Best, H. (eds) (2007) *Democratic Representation in Europe: Diversity, change, and convergence,* Oxford: Oxford University Press.

DeBardeleben, J. and Hurrelmann, A. (eds) (2011) *Transnational Europe: Promise, paradox, limits,* Basingstoke: Palgrave.

Desrosières, A. (1998) *The Politics of Large Numbers: A history of statistical reasoning,* Cambridge: Harvard University Press.

Diez Medrano, J. (2003) *Framing Europe,* Princeton: Princeton University Press.

Eckstein, H. (1991) Regarding Politics: Essays on political theory, stability and change, Berkeley: University of California Press.

Elias, N. (1978) *The Civilizing Process,* Vol.1. *The History of Manners,* New York: Pantheon Books.

Erkkilä, T. (2012) *Government Transparency,* Basingstoke: Palgrave.

Favell, A. (2008) *Eurostars and Eurocities.* Basingstoke: Palgrave.

Favell, A. and Guiraudon, V. (eds) (2011) *Sociology of the European Union,* Basingstoke: Palgrave.

Feron, E., Crowley, J. and Giorgi, L. (2004) *The Emergence of a European Political Class,* Paris: European Deliverable D3, CIR-Paris and ICCR.

Fligstein, N. and Mérand, F. (2002) 'Globalization or Europeanization? Evidence on the European economy since 1980', *Acta Sociologica,* 45: 7–22.

Gaxie, D., Hubé, N. and Rowell, J. (eds) (2011) *Perceptions of Europe*, Colchester: ECPR Press.

Georgakakis, D. (ed.) (2000) *Les métiers de l'Europe politique,* Strasbourg: Presses universitaires de Strasbourg.

Gerth, H. H. and Mills, C. W. (eds) (1991) *From Max Weber: Essays in sociology*, London: Routledge.

Giddens, A. (1984) *The Constitution of Society*, Cambridge: Polity.

Habermas, J. (2001) *The Postnational Constellation: Political essays*, Cambridge: The MIT Press.

Harmsen, R. and Kauppi, N. (eds) (2013) *The Europeanisation of Higher Education and Research Policy: The Bologna Process, the Lisbon Agenda and beyond*, Amsterdam: Rodopi.

Harp, S. (1998) *Learning to be Loyal: Primary schooling as nation building in Alsace and Lorraine*, De Kalb, IL: Northern Illinois University Press.

Hood, C. (1983) *The Tools of Government*, London: Macmillan.

Hooghe, L. and Marks, G. (2000) *Multi-level Governance and European Integration*, Boulder: Rowman and Littlefield.

INTUNE (2009) Project site http:www.intune.it, accessed 12.1.2012.

Janoski, T., Alford, R. R., Hicks, A. M. and Schwartz, M. A. (eds) (2005) *Handbook of Political Sociology: States, civil society and globalization*, Cambridge: Cambridge University Press.

Kauppi, N. (2005) Democracy, *Social Resources and Political Power in the European Union*. Manchester: Manchester University Press.

— (2010) *'The political ontology of European Integration'*, *Comparative European Politics,* 8(1): 19–36.

— (2011) 'EU Politics', in A. Favell and V. Guiraudon (eds) *Sociology of the European Union*, Basingstoke: Palgrave, pp.150–171.

Kauppi, N. and Erkkilä, T. (2011) 'The struggle over global higher education', *International Political Sociology,* 5(3): 314–326.

Kauppi, N. and Madsen, M. R. (eds) (2003) 'Institutions et acteurs: rationalité, réflexivité et analyse de l'UE', *Politique européenne,* 3: 87–113.

— (eds) (2013) Transnational Power Elites: The new professionals of governance, law and security, London: Routledge.

Klingemann, H.-D. (2007) *The State of Political Science in Western Europe*, Opladen: Barbara Budrich.

Knudsen, A.-C. L. (2009) *Farmers on Welfare: The making of Europe's Common Agricultural Policy,* Ithaca: Cornell University Press.

Kull, M. (2008) *EU Multi-level Governance in the Making: The Community Initiative LEADER+ in Finland and Germany,* Helsinki: Acta Politica.

Kunz, Y. S. (2012) 'European Elections as a "Back Door" to National Politics: The Case of the French Greens in 2009', in B. Crum and J.-E. Fossum (eds) *Practices of Inter-Parliamentary Coordination in International Politics: The European Union and beyond*, Colchester: ECPR Press.

Le Roux, B. and Rouanet, H. (2004) *Geometric Data Analysis: From Correspondence Analysis to Structured Data Analysis*, Dordrecht: Kluwer.

Lipset, S. M. (1960) *Political Man: The social bases of politics*, New York: Doubleday.

Madsen, M. R. (2004) 'France, the UK and "Boomerang" of the Internationalization of Human Rights (1945–2000)', in S. Halliday and P. Schmidt (eds) *Human Rights Brought Home: Socio-legal perspectives on human rights in the national context*, Oxford: Hart Publishing.

— (2011) 'Reflexivity and the construction of the international object: the case of human rights', *International Political Sociology*, 5(3): 259–275.

March, J. and Olsen, J. (1984) 'The New Institutionalism: organizational factors in political life', *American Political Science Review*, 78: 734–749.

Mau, S. (2010) *Social Transnationalism: Lifeworlds beyond the nation-state*, London: Routledge.

Milward, A. S. (1994) *The European Rescue of the Nation-State*, London: Routledge.

Mitra, S. and Pehl, M. (eds) (2009) *Political Sociology: The state of the art*, Opladen: Barbara Budrich.

Moravcsik, A. (1998) *The Choice for Europe: Social purpose and state power from Messina to Maastricht*, Cornell: Cornell University Press.

Nash, K. (2007) *Contemporary Political Sociology*, London: Blackwell.

Nedelmann, B. and Sztompka, P. (eds) (1993) *Sociology in Europe: In search of identity*, Berlin/New York: Walter de Gruyter.

Orum, A. M. (1996) 'Almost a half century of political sociology: trends in the United States', *Current Sociology*, 44(3): 108–131.

Powell, W. and DiMaggio, P. (eds) (1991) *The New Institutionalism in Organizational Analysis*, Chicago: University of Chicago Press.

Recchi, E. and Favell, A. (eds) (2009) *Pioneers of European Integration*, Cheltenham: Edward Elgar.

Reif, K. and Schmitt, H. (1980) 'Nine second-order national elections: a conceptual framework for the analysis of European election results', *European Journal of Political Research*, 8: 3–44.

Rosamond, B. (1999) *Theories of European Integration*, London: Palgrave.

Ross, G. (2011) 'Arriving Late at the EU Studies Ball', in A. Favell and V. Guiraudon (eds) *Sociology of the European Union*, Basingstoke: Palgrave, pp. 215–44.

Rowell, J. and Mangenot, M. (eds) (2010) *The Political Sociology of the European Union*, Manchester: Manchester University Press.

Rumford, C. (2002) *The European Union: A political sociology*, London: Blackwell.

Shore, C. (2000) *Building Europe: The cultural politics of European Integration*, London: Routledge.

Sigalas, E. (2010) 'Cross-border mobility and European identity: the effectiveness of intergroup contact during the ERASMUS year abroad', *European Union Politics*, 11(2): 241–265.

Smith, A. (ed.) (2004) *Politics and the European Commission: Actors, interdependence, legitimacy*, London: Routledge.

Swartz, D. (2013) *Symbolic Power, Politics, and Intellectuals: The Political Sociology of Pierre Bourdieu*, Chicago: University of Chicago Press.

Tocqueville, A. de [1835] (1986) *De la démocratie en Amérique: Souvenirs. L'ancien régime et la révolution,* Paris: Robert Laffont.

Waltz, K. (1979) *Theory of International Politics*, Boston: Addison-Wesley.

Wendt, A. (1999) *Social Theory of International Politics*, Cambridge: Cambridge University Press.

Zimmermann, A. and Favell, A. (2011) 'Governmentality, political field or public sphere? Theoretical alternatives in the political sociology of the EU', *European Journal of Social Theory*, 14(4): 489–515.

chapter two | contentious eu politics: a comparative analysis of protest campaigns

Donatella della Porta and Louisa Parks

Contentious politics addressing the european union: political opportunities, movement strategies and their effects

This chapter addresses two (quasi) silences in social movement studies: the effects of protest and contentious politics targeting the European Union (EU). Social movement studies, like other areas of the social sciences, have been late to address phenomena of Europeanisation, and are still in search of adequate methods, concepts and theories to address them. Research on political parties and interest groups shows a similar pattern.

Much research, often within a comparative perspective, has in fact investigated the role of national political opportunities, defined as properties of political institutions as well as those of a more contingent political system that influence the channels of access available for challengers in the polity (Tilly 1978). Historical sociology has also stressed that the modern repertoire of protest emerged with the creation of the nation-state (Tilly 1984) and social movements have in fact played an important role in the development of (national) citizenship rights and the first democratisation processes (Marshall 1992 (1950); Bendix 1964). Social movement organisations (SMOs), considered as the main actors in the mobilisation of protest within social movement studies, were also studied mainly at national level. This was especially the case for the principal historical social movement, the labour movement, but continued to apply for the so-called new social movements (NSMs).

Notwithstanding its relevance, and not only for scholars, research on the effects of social movements has been hampered by the double difficulties of conceptualising and operationalising successes and failures, often given vaguely defined objectives, as well as of tracing successes back to specific inputs to the complex process of policy transformation (Giugni *et al* 1999; della Porta and Diani 2006, chap. 8, for a review of the literature). In the late 1990s and the 2000s, more attention to both transnational issues and effects was brought about by the encounter of social movement scholarship with international relations scholars, who were studying the contributions of Non-Governmental Organisations (NGOs) to international norms (e.g. Risse and Sikkink 1999), and normative theorists, who were reflecting on the contributions of a global civil society to global democracy (e.g. Marchetti 2008). Some systematic research on the outcomes of social movements developed at cross-national (Giugni *et al* 1999) and transnational levels (Silva 2008; Alcalde 2009; della Porta and Caiani 2009; Parks 2009a).

When Europeanisation emerged as a field of study bridging comparative politics and international relations, the first contributions by social movement scholars tended to look at this new emerging object by adapting the dominant categories in the field. The assumed characteristics of political opportunities, mobilisation processes and action strategies at EU level, were singled out through a sort of 'lumping' exercise. On the bases of the little research available, political opportunities were described as formally closed, even if some openings were found in the consensual diplomatic culture dominant in EU institutions, and social movement organisations active in the EU were assessed as particularly civilised International Non-Governmental Organisations (INGOs), used to lobbying strategies more than being active in the streets. Deprived from main channels of access to institutional decision makers and disruptive repertoires of action, it was expected that European social movements would have little effect.

As we will see in the following, further research—including our own—allows us to move from lumping to splitting distinct political opportunities for specific institutions, as well as the different strategies used by the various social movements active at EU level during the various steps of their campaigns. Also at the transnational level it was observed that:

> movements promoting different goals not only vary with respect to the actors they mobilise and in their degree of formal coordination, but also face different political opportunities in national, intergovernmental, and trans-governmental decision-making arenas, and these factors influence the strategic choices they make (Smith, Pagnucco and Chatfield 1996: 59).

The emerging research in the field allows us to develop hypotheses about the conditions under which protest campaigns are more likely to be successful. As for research on national protest campaigns, exogenous conditions (especially political opportunities) as well as endogenous ones (in terms of resources that may be mobilised by social movements) were mentioned. Besides using the concepts and hypotheses developed in social movement studies to understand effects at the transnational level, we want to reflect on the need for the adaptation of these concepts and hypotheses when transferred from the national (or local) level to the transnational one. In this direction, we will present and discuss knowledge that addresses the following (very established) concepts: political opportunities; organisational networks; collective framing; repertoire of actions.

We shall, however, also take into account two recent developments in social movement studies, plus add a new one. First of all, there has been a growing attention to the cultural and symbolic dimension of social movements (Goodwin, Jasper and Polletta 2001; Flam and King 2006). Second, a more dynamic vision of protest has been promoted, with attention paid to the social mechanisms that intervene between macro-causes and macro-effects (McAdam, Tarrow and Tilly 2001). Third, we will combine the analysis of protest campaign effects on policy outcomes, with that of effects on protest itself. Notwithstanding the relevance of protest events for social movements, they have mainly been studied as aggregated collective action (e.g. in protest cycles). In social movement studies, protest has in fact been mainly considered as a 'dependent variable', and explained on the basis of political opportunities and organisational resources. In this analysis, we want instead to stress the emergent effects of protest on the social movements themselves, by focusing on what, inspired by the historical sociologist William H. Sewell (1996), della Porta (2008) has called 'eventful protest'. We shall in fact suggest that transnational protests tend to be particularly 'eventful' as, first, they require long preparation; second, they usually involve broad coalitions; and, third, they have a particular emotional tension.

The research design: case selection and research methods

In this chapter, we shall develop some hypotheses on protest effects on the basis of the analysis of four protest campaigns targeting[1] the EU, as well as from the development of the European Social Forum (ESF) as an arena for encounter and a tool of mobilisation for social movements addressing claims to multilevel institutions of government, with a particular focus on the EU.

After presenting our methodological choices, we shall address the operationalisation of the effects of protest campaigns which we want to understand, continuing then with parts devoted, respectively, to the dimensions we find could help to assess successes and failures: political opportunities, organisational networks, frames and strategies. We shall focus in particular on the EU as a context and target of transnational protest campaigns. Considering the EU as a complex, multi-centred cluster of transnational institutions, we shall look at the opportunities that different EU institutions (in particular, the Commission, the Parliament and the Council) offer to social movements. The campaigns are selected purposefully in order to have cases of success and failure, as well as variance in terms of the issues addressed.

In all four campaigns, research is based on in-depth interviews with activists, government officials and observers, as well as the analysis of social movement and official documents. A total of 24 semi-structured interviews were carried out with relevant representatives of the organisations forming the core of each campaign for the four EU campaigns, providing information to corroborate and add to the pictures gleaned from the documentary analysis.

Another part of the research addresses the counter-summits targeting the EU as well as the ESF that, since the first gathering in Florence in 2002, has brought together tens of thousands of people and thousands of social movement organisations from all over the EU and beyond to discuss proposals for 'Another Europe' (see della Porta 2009a and 2009b). For this part of the analysis, we relied on

---

1.   This is the first step in a project in which we then plan to systematically compare EU protest with that addressing other institutions such as the WTO (World Trade Organization) and the UN (United Nations).

information from the Democracy in Europe and the Mobilization of Society project (Demos), coordinated by Donatella della Porta. Focusing on six European countries (France, Germany, Britain, Italy, Spain and Switzerland), and the transnational level, we analysed conceptions and practices of democracy in the Global Justice Movement's (GJM) interactions with institutional politics, the organisations involved with the GJM, and individual activists. The research combined different sources and methods of data collection and data analysis including the study of websites of 266 selected social movement organisations (SMOs); the fundamental documents produced by 244 of them; semi-structured interviews with about 220 of them; and the patterns of political activism, the democratic visions and practices of GJM activists on the basis of a survey of more than 1000 activists conducted at the ESF in Athens in 2006.

Operationalising protest outcomes

Our research aims at explaining social movement outcomes at transnational level. Even though work dealing with issues of movement 'success' are more numerous than many think (Giugni 1999), studies that systematically assess the effects of campaigns on institutions identify numerous problems to be overcome, and are relatively scarce.

A first difficulty that this research has to address, is the operationalisation of social movement outcomes, which have variously been termed as effects, successes, or impacts. In our research we have been mainly concerned with assessing if the outcomes of the protest, in terms of institutional decisions, indeed went in the direction called for by the campaigners.

Our definition therefore points at effects, but assesses them on the basis of the claims of the protestors. Looking at the effects, and following the influential distinction presented in Gamson's *The Strategy of Social Protest*, we distinguish 'new advantages' (as the achievement of specific aims) and 'acceptance' (where an actor is recognised to be representative of a specific group's claims) (Gamson 1990). To this we added another aspect, singled out by Schumaker (1975) in his fivefold typology: agenda, that he defines as a movement capacity to spark a debate on a previously ignored subject (he also suggests looking at output, as the effective implementation of legislation relating to a movement's goals, and impact, as the actual consequences of a policy change – e.g. where an agency is established, does the latter have any real power?). Differently from Gamson, we shall however look also for unintended consequences (Giugni, McAdam and Tilly 1999). In particular, we consider the importance of taking the likelihood of complex paths into account when investigating issues of movement consequences. Keeping this in mind, we decided not to use the term 'success', but nevertheless to assess consequences on the basis of movement claims. Of the various possible outcomes of a protest, we selected policy changes and access, as most suited to our main focus of study, the EU. Some of these consequences may entail one another – for example a policy change may also imply recognition and thus access responsiveness. Although other similar typologies distinguish consequences according to broader categories,

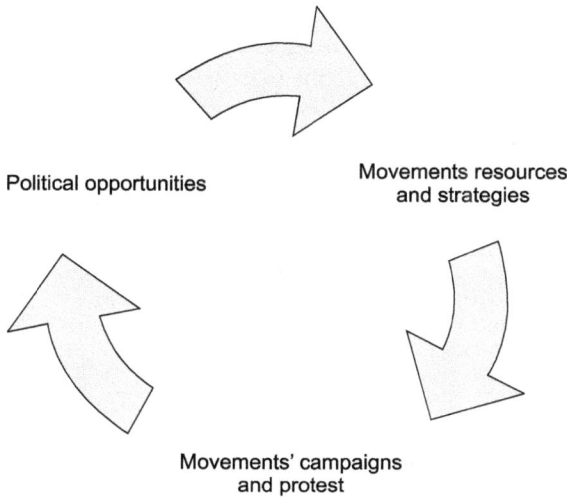

Political opportunities

Movements resources
and strategies

Movements' campaigns
and protest

Figure 2.1: Explaining social movement effects

we decided to focus our analysis on policy change. Following a quite established model in social movement studies, when analysing the campaigns we assess the effects of the political opportunities available, as well as some SMO resources and strategies, and the outcomes of the campaign in terms of agenda, access to policy makers and policy changes (see Figure 2.1). We shall, however, also use the research on counter-summits and ESFs and how they produce effects on the movements themselves, affecting their organisational networks, framing and repertoires of contention, finally producing emerging new European actors.

With this model in mind, we have assessed the degree of convergence versus divergence of outcomes in relation with protest claims, taking account of stated aims, even though the perceptions of protest campaigners and other actors have also been analysed. Campaigns were also split into different phases, allowing us to increase the effective 'n' of our study. Our results are synthesised in Table 2.1 below.

Of the four specific campaigns targeting the EU, two were concerned with environmental/public health issues, and two concerned broadly defined (as they are in EU institutions) social issues. The first of the environmental/public health campaigns focused on the coexistence of genetically modified and conventional crops. Beginning in 2003, against the background of the adoption of far-reaching EU legislation on Genetically Modified Organisms (GMOs), this campaign, by an ever broader coalition of environmental NGOs, regional organisations and governments, and farmers' organisations, called, at first, for EU legislation on the issue. As the campaign moved on and the realistic chances of such legislation being adopted receded, the groups moved to calling for the legalisation of 'GM-free zones' which they had in any case already created. The second campaign took place around the passage of EU chemicals legislation, known as REACH, and saw another broad coalition of environmental, women's, consumer's, public health and other groups pitted against a strong chemical industry lobby campaign that was able to dominate the framing of the issues raised. Both of the environmental/public health campaigns failed to secure their ultimate objectives, although some smaller-scale outcomes were secured in the GMO case.

Table 2.1: Summary of campaigns and their effects by phase

Campaign	Phase	Effects	Type
GMOs and Coexistence	1 (Publication of Commission communication on coexistence February 03 to publication of recommendations July 03)	Idea that concerned parties should pay for protective measures dropped by Commission.	Policy outcome
	2 (Publication of recommendations to publication to Commission communication March 05)	Recognition of the Network of GM-free Regions by the Commission	Access outcome
	3 (Publication of Commission communication to WTO ruling May 06)	None – failure to secure legislation or recognition of GM-free zones	No outcome
REACH[2]	1 (White Paper February 01 to publication of draft legislation October 03)	None – failure to amend draft	No outcome
	2 (First reading October 03 – July 06)	None – failure to secure new measures	No outcome
	3 (Second reading July 06 – December 06)	None failure to secure new measures	No outcome
Lisbon agenda mid-term review	1 (only phase February – March 2005)	Presidency conclusions reaffirm social pillar Social Platform sought by Council President	Agenda outcome Access outcome
Services Directive	1 (publication of draft directive January 04 to Barroso announcement February 05)	Barroso announcement that Commission will conform with EP vote	Policy outcome
	2 (Barroso announcement to second reading vote February 06)	Watered down version of the directive	Policy outcome

---

2. Although the REACH issue saw one of the closest instances of coalition campaigning ever seen at the EU level, even if in the end it was not enough to secure the desired policy outcome. For the groups taking part in the campaign, both at European and national level, this was seen as an important learning experience, and an incentive to carry on working on EU issues with national level groups. This is also, therefore, an important outcome of the campaign, falling into the category of the effects of protests on movements as discussed earlier.

The two social campaigns concerned the Lisbon agenda and the Directive on Services in the Internal Market, better known as the Bolkestein directive, after the relevant Commissioner. The first was a short, sharp campaign against a proposed change to the structure of the EU's Lisbon agenda, which saw groups affiliated to the Social Platform (an EU umbrella group for social NGOs) campaign to save the social aspects of the policy. The campaign was launched in reaction to a communication by President Barroso of the European Commission intimating that the Lisbon agenda, as part of its mid-term review, should concentrate more on issues of growth and jobs. The campaigning groups feared this would mean the neglect of the original agenda's emphases on social protection and sustainable development, and sought to convince the European Council to reiterate its support for the original version. Notably, they launched a web-based no logo petition and exploited well-attended demonstrations arising from the contemporary furore around the Bolkestein directive. The second was a more prolonged campaign, and saw an unprecedented wave of mobilisation over an EU issue across the member states, spearheaded by the trade union movement and culminating in two demonstrations in Strasbourg in February 2006. Importantly, this campaign capitalised on the parallel issue of the Constitutional Treaty, playing a role in the French 'no'. Both of the social campaigns secured their ultimate objectives (or at least the immediate stated objectives of their campaigns – whether they had any effect on what they perceived as the ultimate neo-liberal direction of the EU can certainly be debated), balancing the case selection in terms of successes and failures, as well as in terms of targets (each subject category is made up of one legislative and one policy case) and subject area.

Multilevel opportunity structures

Political opportunities are fundamental for defining the chances of success of transnational movements. In any case, the concept was originally created for a national context and, for this reason, when adopting it for a multilevel political opportunity structure (POS) its dimensions need to be adapted. This has been done first of all through the idea of a multilevel POS that refers to the different contexts at different levels that can be favourable to collective action.

The reflection on multilevel opportunity structures for multilevel social movements was developed in one of the first edited volumes on transnational activism (della Porta, Kriesi and Rucht 1999, expanded edition 2009). The introduction to the volume (della Porta and Kriesi 1999), as well as some of the chapters (e.g. Marks and McAdam 1999; Passy 1999), reflected, in particular, on the specificities of International Governmental Organisations (IGOs) as offering political opportunities (and constraints) for social movements addressing domestic as well as global problems. In this sense, two main paths of transnationalisation were singled out: social movements with domestic political concerns (especially in authoritarian regimes) searching for external, international allies (in what Keck and Sikkink 1998: 12–13 define as the 'boomerang effect'); and social movements addressing their own governments, in order to influence international political decisions (in what Putnam 1988: 427 calls double level games). Later on, research on European integration and Europeanisation increasingly addressed the role of civil society. First, if the building of the European institutions as oriented to the creation of a common market explains the dominance of producers' interests in the EU lobbying system, with the progression of market-making legislation (from the European Commission, the Council, but also the Court), then there was also an increase in demand for market-correcting policies (with mobilisations by consumers, environmentalists, and so on). Moreover, in recent times, the debate about good governance and the democratic deficit has induced the Commission to reflect about the involvement of civil society and, especially after Maastricht, to look for broader social acceptance of EU policies (e.g. the White Paper on Governance) as well as for allies in the power-play with the Council. The development of campaigns targeting diverse IGOs stimulated further reflections on the range of opportunities that various international institutions offered to social movements.

The reflection on the effect of political opportunities on protest at transnational level developed in two steps, which we can define as lumping and splitting. In the very beginning, some general characteristics of IGOs were singled out, extending the concepts of political opportunities as it had developed at national level to international institutions. Especially in view of campaigns addressing the United Nations (UN), the presence of IGOs was initially considered as offering additional leverage to transnational protest. In this sense, Passy (1999) argues that the existence of quasi-supranational power centres, such as the EU and the UN, offers new political opportunities to social movements. The main observation is that IGOs tend to be formally closed (lacking electoral accountability), but informally open (thanks to the bargaining culture of diplomacy). As for the configuration of power, nation-states tend to represent potential allies and opponents, occupying the role that is usually played by political parties at the national level.

With our research we want to move from lumping to splitting, by looking at the different opportunities and constraints offered by different EU institutions. As decentred institutions (Bohman 2007), IGOs present different channels of access to different societal actors. Our research aims at building upon this accumulated knowledge, distinguishing however the characteristics of different IGOs and IGO institutions, and therefore the strategies successful in addressing them, looking especially at formal access, informal access and the configuration of friends and foes (Passy 1999). First, some international institutions give *formal access* to some NGOs by granting them consultative status to take advantage of their resources, especially in terms of specialised and local knowledge. Social movement organisations are important pools of resources, especially in terms of knowledge (Haas 1990, 1989, 1992; Rosenau 1998). These NGOs, in turn, tend to adapt their skills and forms to exploit these opportunities of access. However, IGOs vary considerably in terms of formal access. The UN institutions have traditionally been considered as formally more open, while the EU has been considered more and more so in light of its creating channels of access for civil society organisations. Some international institutions have incorporated organised sectors of civil society in international negotiations. For example, since the early 1990s, the number of organisations allowed to participate in UN activities has grown and their role in such activities has gained in importance (Smith 1997). At the other end of the spectrum, however, the World Trade Organisation (WTO) offers limited and minimal relationships to social movement organisations.

Additionally, it is also important to note that IGOs are complex and fragmented institutions, composed of different bodies that provide external actors with differentiated channels of formal access. Some UN bodies, such as UNICEF, UNDP or UNHCR, are much more open than others to collaboration. Additionally, in complex multilevel international organisations access may differ widely at different geographical levels. For instance, the Work Bank collaborates with NGOs at the country level while the headquarters remain inaccessible. Looking at the EU, social movements target the council, the commission, the parliament and the courts, but their degrees of openness vary.

The Commission, as the institution that drafts EU legislation, is the logical first port of call for all organisations that seek to influence the EU (Greenwood 2003: 33). Influencing policy and legislation at the drafting stage makes sense, since in general, large portions of the text passed to the Parliament and Council remain, when legislation is adopted. The Commission works hard to create an appearance of openness, encouraging 'civil society' involvement (e.g. Commission 2001) through consultation meetings in many shapes and forms. However, the opportunities for involvement the Commission provides also imply a series of constraints on social movements who wish to take advantage of them. The information the Commission seeks and will consider most pertinent when drafting legislation, is costly to procure, and often the institution requires fresh information. Therefore, movements who wish to take part in Commission consultation procedures must be more institutionalised, with permanent members of staff working to produce such information.

In addition, the Commission represents further constraints as a result of its highly fragmented nature, where the cultures and interests of each separate DG may often be played off against one another in internal power struggles. Finally, many SMOs active in the European arena feel that despite their best efforts, the messages they convey to the Commission fall on deaf ears, and that this institution is merely paying lip service to ideas of consultation and inclusion (Parks 2009b). These ideas find some confirmation in the work by Michalowitz (2002). In her study of the pluralist and corporatist qualities of interest representation in the EU, Michalowitz found that the Commission displays both, but at different stages of their consultation procedures. In a first, more pluralist step, a wide variety of parties is consulted for their opinions on a particular legislative initiative. In a second step however, where the drafting of the legislation proper is undertaken, consultation is restricted to privileged partners who have secured seats in the Commission's labyrinthine network of committees – in other words those organisations with the most resources to devote to such activities. Some movement organisations thus prefer to concentrate their efforts on tactics more traditional to their genre, which are more invited by the other European institutions.

In this sense, the European Parliament, as the most traditionally democratic of the EU institutions, does invite more unconventional actions, such as letter-writing and e-mail campaigns and exhibitions, although it is not a magnet for protest on the scale of the Council of Ministers or the European Council (Lahusen 2004). Although it is seen as the most open of the EU institutions in terms of political opportunities (Parks 2009b), the fact that the Parliament also invites conventional lobbying techniques as a legislative body capable of amending texts also entails that SMOs must produce the kind of information needed by resource-poor MEPs involved in several issues at the same time. Once again, this requires permanent staff and expertise not only on the subject in hand, but also on the Parliament's structure and working patterns, and the ideological make-up of the institution. The Parliament therefore offers opportunities for both conventional and unconventional actions, although both are usually required in successful campaign as we will outline below. Finally, the Council of Ministers and the European Council are the most secretive institutions of the EU, working behind closed doors and closed to lobbying actions from third parties. These institutions, composed by high-profile national leaders, form the best targets for protest since they usually receive decent levels of media coverage. The long record of counter-summits at European Council events pays testament to this (della Porta 2009a).

To sum up, the upshot of all of this in terms of political opportunities for SMOs in the EU is that multiple access points, as well as complex legislative procedures and the relatively distinct separation of powers at work in this organisation entail a heavy burden of knowledge and expertise. SMOs seeking to influence EU policies must be able to judge the appropriate tone and aim of each action that forms their European level campaign, considering the political leanings or roles of their targets, the information that they want, and the timing for releasing that information. They must also be able to anticipate the entire European level process with enough time to launch national level campaigns that will allow them to mobilise enough protesters to influence the Council.

Moving on to discuss more *informal possibilities,* different movements can have a more difficult or an easier life in finding access to specific institutions within broader IGOs. The extreme openness of UNHCR and UNICEF in involving NGOs in research formulation and policy consultations has been related to the fact that these institutions have a relatively high number of staff members who have themselves previously worked in NGOs, or are at least sympathetic to many transnational coalitions' values. The Oslo Process that banned cluster munitions was also facilitated by the fact that some of the main players on the governmental side had a background in civil society organisations (Alcalde 2009).

At EU level, overlapping membership (or at least the presence in the administration of former NGO leaders) has been mentioned when distinguishing between sympathetic and unsympathetic Directorates General (DGs) in the EU, or opposing powerful DGs (Ruzza 2004; Balme and Chabanet 2008; Alcade 2009). When looking at our EU campaigns, we therefore considered the aspect of the 'natural partner' as a condition for more fruitful dialogue with the Commission. According to Ruzza (2004), in many DGs in the Commission the staff employed tends to share a certain ideology, or at least a sense of the importance of their particular policy area, often as a result of their previous work outside the institutional arena. This means that some institutional actors are 'naturally' sympathetic to the ideas of certain groups. This can be theorised as an opportunity for a campaign, or, in the opposite situation, as a hindrance. It should be noted, however, that those DGs that are more friendly to movements are often less influential within the Commission. As Bieler puts it, 'The DG for Competition and the DG for Economic and Financial Affairs are more decisive within the EU. Together with the DG Internal Market and DG Trade they are the hard core of the Commission' (2005: 469). The more general theoretical point arising from these considerations, is that it is crucial to consider the Commission as a group of smaller organisations jostling for power and influence amongst themselves, rather than as a unified, single institution. Since social movements are usually active on issues such as labour rights, environmental issues, women's and minority rights and the like, their institutional allies in the context of the Commission, are not always the most powerful.

Informal possibilities can be argued to play an important role in EU campaigns, yet our evidence suggests that these possibilities are usually available (or even, more available) to other actors, especially business lobbies. Members of SMOs involved in the GMO and REACH campaigns expressed suspicions of informal access leading to unfair advantages and the disempowering of official consultation procedures. Here, interviewees felt that business lobbyists ignored official consultation forums because they knew that these were toothless and were exploiting informal possibilities to influence processes (Parks 2009a).

Third, the *configuration of allies* and indeed that of enemies may expand or narrow the opportunities for action and lobbying by activists. For certain questions, states become social movements' allies by facilitating their lobbying, by signing resolutions drafted by organisations, by disseminating their reports, by orienting political debates so as to favour the organisations and by exerting pressure on other states. But states may also try to do their best to exclude activists by reducing their speaking time, by excluding them from international conferences or by asking for the right of censorship over their statements. In this sense, the configuration of allies and opponents forms a relational opportunity structure of the totality of actors in the international system. The distribution of ties is however relatively flexible and changes over time. Contingent factors or transforming events (such as the Chernobyl nuclear disaster in 1986, and the attacks in the US on 11 September 2001) can change this distribution, by reconfiguring the alliances. In social movement parlance, they are sometimes known as 'suddenly imposed grievances' (Walsh 1981:18).

In the context of the EU, allies and enemies come in a variety of guises, but with varying levels of influence. The campaigns we studied showed that allies were indeed extremely important in securing outcomes, as is in line with numerous previous studies (see, e.g. Tarrow 1990). However, they also suggest that the position and influence, that is the power of the ally is also paramount, as is that of enemies. To illustrate, both of the environmental cases showed similarities in terms of important political threats – these came from hostile elites (DGs within the Commission), and from open – to the point of becoming endless – dialogue with third parties. Comparing these circumstances with the more effective campaigns in the social cases, hostile elites were also a factor for both of these, although obviously to a lesser degree. More interestingly, if we concentrate less on the *presence* of hostile elites and more on the *lack of elite allies*, then we can note that in the two (successful) social cases elite allies were indeed present, even if hostile (though less powerful) elites were too, whilst the reverse is true of the (failed) environmental cases.

More explicitly, in the environmental campaign, hostile DGs in the Commission proved formidable threats to each other because the Commission had an important role in both. Elite allies, on the other hand, were, where present, not in a position to 'fulfil their promises', in other words they did not dispose of the power to decide the outcomes of the campaign. In the two social cases, hostile elites were also powerful: the Commission President in the Lisbon case, and Commissioner Bolkestein in the case of the same name. However, allies were present in the institutions that mattered more for the outcomes of each of these campaigns: the presidency in the Lisbon case, and the socialist group in the European Parliament (as well as this institution more generally) in the Bolkestein case. In terms of the 'natural partner' consideration and the idea that the latter may lend a helping hand to a campaign, these findings suggest a more complex situation that takes account of the relative roles of allies in different contexts. The cases show that a hostile DG in the Commission can sometimes kick start a national-style campaign with effective results, thus transforming the presence of political threat in the form of an elite enemy into an opportunity where other powerful targets are available, underlining the importance of the *perception* of political opportunities and threats. Following the ideas presented by Gamson and Meyer (1996: 283–7), the presence of a hostile elite can allow those arguing the benefits of a more extra-institutional approach to a campaign, to frame their case more strongly – as the elites are already hostile, more will be lost by doing nothing extraordinary than may be lost by doing so.

Our campaigns thus confirmed that the political opportunities offered in the EU, as well as the different institutions within it, do not determine the success or failure of protest campaigns, but certainly influence the choice of the (combination of) strategies used to address them. In the social EU campaigns, as seen above, strong institutional opposition in the form of institutional foes blocking access and other opportunities led the European trade union organisations in particular, to adapt little seen (at the EU level) protest tactics to great effect. Combined with well-planned and tireless lobbying through the institutional channels that remained open in the European Parliament, these strategies secured the policy outcomes the campaigners sought.

European contentious networks

The resources that social movement organisations can mobilise in multilevel arenas certainly influence their effectiveness. In past research, attention was paid to the resource exchanges between transnational social movement organisations

(TSMOs) and IGOs (Smith 1999; Lahusen 1999; della Porta and Kriesi;1999, Rucht 1999). The exchange of knowledge as well as a reciprocal potential legitimation was singled out as well as the potential of vicarious activism to sensitise public opinion to global problems. At the same time, the difficulties in protesting beyond national borders were stressed, by looking at different data (Imig and Tarrow 2001; Rucht 1999). In the EU, these difficulties were judged to be compounded by its openness to conventional lobby tactics, particularly the Commission (Marks and McAdam 1996, 1999). Similarly, empirical research in international relations has addressed the birth of international non-governmental organisations (INGOs), pointing at the recent increase in their numbers, membership, and availability of material resources, as well as their influence on policy choices. The related concept of TSMOs was coined to define the INGOs active within networks of social movements. While domestic non-governmental organisations and social movements developed as national politics grew, the formation of INGOs and TSMOs have been seen as a response to the growing institutionalisation of international politics. This is also the case in the EU. In particular, after the extension of the EU's competences that came with the Single European Act in 1986, the number of recognised European public interest groups greatly increased (Mazey and Richardson 1993; Lahusen 2004).

Focusing on the interactions between these actors and IGOs (initially especially the UN, and later the EU), the first studies emphasised especially their capacity to adapt to the IGOs' rules of the game, preferring a diplomatic search for agreement over democratic accountability, discretion over transparency, and persuasion over mobilisation in the street. Some of these actors have been highlighted as having not only increased in number, but also strengthened their influence in various stages of international policy making. Their assets include an increasing credibility in public opinion and consequent availability of private funding, as well as a specific knowledge, rootedness at the local level, and independence from governments. Finally, they are said to enhance pluralism within international institutions by representing groups that would otherwise be excluded, and by focusing attention on transnational processes, making the governance process more transparent. In the EU the Commission explicitly seeks the expertise of civil society, which it sees as conferring them with some borrowed legitimacy (Parks 2009a).

Research indicated however that, in contrast to business organisations and other economic actors, the actors of global civil society are usually loosely-organised and poorly staffed, consisting mainly of transnational alliances of various national groups. Their inclusion in international politics has also been selective: only those organisations that adapt to the 'rules of the game' obtain some access, though usually of an informal nature, to some IGOs. Finally, rootedness at the local level and independence from governments are variable. The NGOs have also been criticised for their internal decision making, often accused of being non-transparent, unaccountable and non-representative. Our research indicates that the specific forms of these networks have a particularly relevant influence on the chances of success of various campaigns.

Networks in cases of positive outcomes were marked by specific macro characteristics not shared by the networks in the cases of no impact. The networks are extremely dense, with a low average distance, and with a high degree of compactness. This confirms the major findings in the relevant literature in which so-called 'non-segmented', 'optimised', or 'dense' networks are the most effective in terms of political impact (Diani 1995; Caniglia 2002; Diani and McAdam 2003; Anheier and Katz 2005). In fact, networks with the above characteristics appear to favour an optimised flow of information and resources, which cannot but enhance the effectiveness of its actions.

At the European level, such dense networks were seen in the social cases with positive outcomes. The key to these dense networks here appears to be the permanent and long-standing coalition structures present among the trade union and social groups respectively. For the latter, the European Platform of Social NGOs (the Social Platform), set up in 1995 with funding from the European Commission, brings together many different kinds of social NGOs working on many different issues – poverty, humanitarian aid, and the representation of minorities, for example. Despite numerous problems during its early days, when members found it difficult to define the common ground on which they could work, and procrastinated over the issue of the institutionalisation of the coalition (see Cullen 2005: 71–75), the Social Platform now maintains a permanent secretariat in Brussels. Its main functions are to facilitate information exchange and dissemination, to facilitate common campaigns on those broader issues allowing common positions, as well as some capacity-building work and facilitating access to the European institutions for its members.

For the trade union movement, the European Trade Union Confederation (ETUC) is a federation of national Trade Unions. Founded in 1973, long after the formation of a similar federation by employers, the body only began to come into its own as a vehicle for representing workers' points of view on European level legislation in 1991. This owed much to the activism of the Delors Commission, who provided large sums of funding for the ETUC (for a summary of the ETUC's history, see Martin and Ross 2001). Nevertheless, divisions between member Unions, ranging from Christian to Communist, have often formed an obstacle to the development of transnational positions in the organisation (Balme and Chabanet 2002: 66). In 1991, the ETUC became an official legislative player alongside the Union of Industrial and Employers' Confederations of Europe (UNICE, now Business Europe) in the Social Dialogue. In addition, these two collective actors also have regular and institutionalised contact with one another, exchanging information and coordinating positions. In the social EU campaigns, these two umbrella organisations were useful in diffusing information quickly and efficiently not only among EU level groups, but also among national and local players, and in coordinating messages and actions. The case for the utility of such permanent coalition structures is also reinforced if we consider that the equally dense, but temporarily-based, network present in the GMOs and co-existence case, did not end in any effects on EU legislation (although highly effective in imposing de facto solutions).

To sum up, the higher the density of the network, the higher the number of linkages and, therefore, the more (alternative) paths for the different actors to exchange resources and information (knowledge, expertise, competences) with other actors. The lower the average distance is, the shorter the paths through which information and resources have to flow, and, thus, more resources are saved and resources and information flow more quickly. The more compact the network is, the more easily resources and information will be diffused and shared among *all* the nodes and not only by those closer to each other.

On the contrary, highly segmented networks have very few possibilities of surviving simply because their actors have difficulties exchanging the information and resources necessary to foster their cooperation. Building a new linkage is not a costless task since it requires an effort to establish and maintain it. If the network structure is not able to 'return' these costs in terms of cooperation enhancement, the network risks collapsing with respect to its very *raison d'être*, its capability to establish linkages among actors. Once again we can turn to our EU campaigns to demonstrate this. The REACH case is a good example of a highly segmented network, where problems in disseminating information and encouraging mobilisation persisted despite the constant efforts of European-level groups. Lacking any well-established, permanent and active umbrella group at the European level (the alliances in place cannot be compared to the permanent structures exemplified in the ETUC and the Social Platform), the groups that came together for the REACH campaign found that their various networks were not sufficient to raise the levels of engagement necessary to impose their message effectively in the EU institutions. Involving national groups through each of the separate organisations of the coalition necessarily depended on the internal structure of each, and these varied greatly from the hierarchy of Greenpeace, to the network of independent groups of Friends of the Earth, to the strong national but weak European presence of Women in Europe for a Common Future. The immature network seen in the REACH case was thus a work-in-progress, with groups dedicating time and resources to its development, rather than being able to draw on an already strong and dense network for their campaign. Their work may bear fruit in the future, but here highlights the necessity of dense networks.

Positional analysis, – which looks at the position within the networks of specific actors/nodes – has also proved valuable in explaining patterns of impact. Data available fleshed out the intimate overlapping between the concepts of 'powerful nodes', 'network leaders' and 'political reach' by showing that those actors that are the most powerful according to the network scores, were also those primarily involved in the causal mechanisms leading to social movements' political impact.

Actors that score high in the different measures of power are said to have a more favourable structural position. This favourable structural position is classified in different ways according to different ideas such as number of connections, powerful friends and bridging roles. Actors that are powerful according to these measures are those that can exploit their structural position. Since they have less potential constraints and better exchanges, they can have greater influence on other actors of the network. This is why network literature stresses the frequent correspondence, often empirical, between powerful nodes and network leaders (Diani 1995).

Now, leadership in a network also often translates into an external visibility in the public and political sphere. An organisation that is powerful or a leader in the network is more likely to also be a spokesman to the media and the public, and generally is often the one to present the network's demands and goals vis-à-vis institutions. The more a node acts as a representative of the whole network towards third parties, the more its leadership role in the network is strengthened (Diani and McAdam 2003). If leaders are those who are more likely to talk to the public, the media, and to lobby policy makers and other relevant actors, leaders are, so the argument goes, those that by exploiting the force of the network are in the best position to influence the political and public spheres. Our analysis tends to support the several empirical studies (Caniglia 2002; Diani 2003; Ansell 2003; Anheier and Katz 2005) that stress how the favourable and predominant position of certain actors can be capitalised on behalf of the whole movement translating into an effective political influence.

In our campaigns these multilevel, flexible and decentralised networks emerged as all the more important when, during the social campaigns, informal access to EU institutions was hampered, or at least countervailed by the presence of influential opponents and/or the competence of movement-hostile DGs, and when decision making moved to the intergovernmental level (the Council).

Research on EU counter-summits and the ESF allowed us to look at the effects of campaigns on the social movements themselves. At the turn of the millennium, the Global Justice Movement has proposed different organisational strategies, more grassroots and network based (della Porta 2007). Protest at EU level helped the convergence of local, national and transnational organisations from different social movements in a series of roundtables, nets, and coalitions that were very often not limited to one national state. *Netzwerke, reti, redes, coordinadoras, tavoli*, nets and forums are in fact frequent terms in the names of new organisations that allow not only for overlapping memberships of different organisations by individual activists, but also for the convergence of organised actors. The ESF has in fact been defined as a space for the encounter and networking of a loose network of organisations and individuals, engaged in collective action of various kinds, on the basis of the shared goal of advancing the cause of justice (economic, social, political and environmental) among and between peoples across the globe (della Porta 2007). These networks have seen the involvement of INGOs together with grassroots oriented groups, also contributing to the spread of new organisational conceptions and resources.

Framing europeanised claims

Framing processes are relevant for the success of mobilisations; they are even more relevant at the transnational level, where identities often have to be rethought and negotiated from scratch amongst different groups with specific aims and historical trajectories. Various concepts can assist in making sense of framing processes. First, there is the classic categorisation into diagnostic, prognostic, and motivational frames (Benford and Snow 2000). Second, the diffusion of frames (both passive and active) amongst groups and into the wider public sphere is a useful concept. Finally, bridging[2] is also crucial to the investigation of framing in transnational protest coalitions. Framing is an ongoing process including reactions to new inputs and outside information. The methodology of the frame analysis used in our analyses is sensitive to these aspects, and produces a dynamic, cross-time analysis based on documents by key coalition members at different territorial levels and at different key stages of protest campaigns. This continuous analysis of documents addresses the common criticism by many academics that although framing is described as an ongoing process, analyses tend to 'freeze' frames, taking them as fixed (Oliver and Johnston 2000). By taking 'snapshots' of frames at different points in time, we may avoid such a static representation of the frame.

In terms of the political opportunities afforded by the EU, strong frames can help groups exploit these by contributing to their network density (while the latter also contributes to strong frames), as well as by allowing them to pool all the kinds of resources needed to exploit the different opportunities of different institutions – financial resources, knowledge, and expertise. Strong frames allow organisations to achieve this because they build a unified, shared response to a perceived problem. More specifically, the frames used in making claims at the European level can also help react to threats that may be characterised as more discursive in their character. Indeed, a separate strand of literature often critical of the political opportunity approach focuses instead on *discursive* opportunities (see in particular Koopmans and Statham 1999 and Goodwin and Jasper 1999). These opportunities and threats arise precisely from the (in our cases political) discourses that arise during campaigns, for example by different institutions, individual actors, or opposition campaigns. How well groups can build frames together that are strong and relevant to these discourses affects their chances of securing campaign outcomes.

Framing processes have been addressed in a transnational perspective. Research has analysed the cross-national diffusion of movement frames (Snow and Benford 1999), as well as of strategies of public order control (McCarthy, McPhail and Crist 1999). With the development of transnational campaigns, calls for international norms on issues such as human rights and environmental protection have been put forward. In particular, the Global Justice Movement has contributed to the definition of global issues, such as global justice or global democracy. If the symbolical reference to the globe is considered by some scholars as nothing really new – referencing the traditional internationalism of the workers' movement or the transnational campaigns against slavery – others have instead stressed the centrality of the global dimension today. It is however an open question to what extent strategies of 'thinking small'—or at least 'focused'—versus thinking global do facilitate mobilisation.

---

2.   'Frame bridging refers to the linking of two or more ideologically congruent but structurally unconnected frames regarding a particular issue or problem' (Benford and Snow 2000: 624).

Our campaigns offer contrasting evidence on the question of the role of frames in mobilisation, as, for instance, the mobilisations on the broadly defined 'social issues' were more capable of reaching positive outcomes at the EU level than the more narrowly defined anti-GM campaign, which failed to secure its legislative goals. Defining the goal in concrete and feasible messages emerged in some of our campaigns as a facilitator of success – for example in the short campaign over the Lisbon agenda at the EU level. In this brief mobilisation the main actions consisted of a web-based petition – 'Save Our Social Europe', and a large demonstration. Both of these actions contributed to the development of simple, slogan-like frames throughout the campaign. These were of course backed by more detailed explanations in other, more conventional actions, but the momentum of the protest campaign owed much to the mobilising power of these simple, yet memorable and meaningful frames. Similarly effective and slogan-like frames were seen in the extremely strong Bolkestein campaign (most memorably the 'No Valentine for Bolkestein' frame used in the final demonstrations and the 'Stop Bolkestein' web-based petition).

Another dimension of the framing process that emerged clearly as fundamental for policy success in the context of the EU was the capacity of a protest coalition to develop shared frames. Aside from their efficiency, frames, or understandings of problems, solutions, and enemies, must be shared by different coalition actors in order to make it possible for them, whether local, national or transnational, to join together to mobilise and carry out common campaigns. Where the different groups in a campaign coalition share frames this also means they will present a coherent message and demands, making it easier for institutions to respond to them, and for them to respond to institutions with a united front. They are therefore the glue that holds a coalition together, and a strong coalition is an obvious requisite for policy success, particularly in transnational policy arenas saturated by interest groups jostling for the attention of powerful institutions. In the Bolkestein campaign, for example, the organisations that had come together to campaign against the draft proposal consolidated their main frames of opposition around the ideas of 'social dumping' and 'a race to the bottom' (in terms of social protection). Despite the obvious intricacies of the issues at stake in the legislation, the campaigning groups were able to agree to focus on these particular, more basic messages, which were in turn useful in coalescing the organisations in mobilisations throughout Europe, as mentioned above.

As already hinted, frames which are strong, as they resonate with institutional discourses, public opinion, and discourses within social movements, and are shared among the campaigners, are very much connected to the density of networks. The EU social campaigns in part owed their ability to develop their frames to their existing, dense networks. Indeed, the evidence from our European campaigns suggests that without the backing of a dense network, which serves to ensure the diffusion and quick construction of strong shared frames, these alone do not lead to policy success. The co-existence campaign was the only one of our campaigns to display evidence of frame building work, particularly through the bridging of different frames. However, it seems that the time and effort spent building these frames contributed to the campaign's eventual loss of steam before a formidable political threat in the shape of a WTO ruling, if we consider that the social campaigns were able to sustain their levels of mobilisation despite facing political threats themselves. The main difference between the campaigns was the resources and time spent in building frames in the co-existence case, rather than the ability to draw on long-standing relationships and shared understandings, in the social cases.

These points on the importance of strong, shared, and easily accessible frames are further bolstered if we consider the campaign on chemicals legislation. Here again organisations spent a great deal of time negotiating frames that focused on detailed points in the legislation – their overall message of opposition was thus lost in the fine print and their campaign suffered as a result. This concentration on the 'fine print' was the consequence of an extremely strong industry campaign, based on the kind of dense networks described as important in gaining positive outcomes. The industry campaign dominated the discursive field, forcing the weaker REACH network to respond to, rather than control the terms of the debate. The broad and heterogeneous character of the temporary coalition in this campaign made it difficult to take a strong position on the main issues at stake – as indeed has been observed in much other literature (for example Helfferich and Kolb 2001:149; Rucht 2001: 137; Lahusen 2004; Cullen 2005).

For a protest coalition to be effective, therefore, dialogue must take place between groups at different territorial levels in order to build these shared understandings and allow mobilisation – yet this takes both time and effort. Groups must meet frequently to build relationships of trust and thrash out the more thorny issues that may cause friction within a coalition if left untouched. This can be complicated in transnational coalitions despite the opportunities afforded by modern communication technologies as a result of the sheer breadth of some groups, and the difficulties they are confronted with in involving and aggregating the interests and opinions of local members spread throughout the globe. Time is therefore an all important factor in framing, and our own investigations have shown that where groups are constantly in contact through some more or less formal framework, they are able to build common frames that can then be quickly activated for the purposes of single-issue campaigns, allowing them to react quickly and in unison to the various actions of transnational policy institutions.

The importance of strong and shared frames is thus closely tied to the importance of dense networks. The observations laid out above point to the conclusion that building new coalitions for every new and separate campaign is far less effective than drawing on more permanent coalition structures that in turn, denote dense networks. The environmental groups that spent more time on building coalitions and developing arguments did not do so well as the two campaigns that drew on existing coalitions based on many years of work towards developing shared understandings. Looking at the evidence in this light, it can be said that shared frames are in the end important for outcomes, but not so directly as is often hypothesised. The years of work that the social groups put in to forming their permanent coalition structures provided them with important resources that helped secure their desired campaign outcomes. Because they did not need to spend time building frames, they were able to mobilise quickly and effectively when faced with threats. Overall then, shared frames are important in securing outcomes – strong frames throughout the campaign were factors common to all three of the cases displaying outcomes, and dialogue enabling multi-level campaigns was present for two. It rather underscores the fact that shared understandings that can be quickly and simply tapped into seem to be more useful.

Once again, the counter-summits and ESF experiences have contributed to the development of shared frames on Europe and Europeanisation that, in their turn, provide a cognitive and emotional basis for further campaigns. During these events, there was indeed a cognitive linkage between different themes in broad transnational campaigns (frame bridging). In the 1980s, social movements had undergone a process of specialisation on single issues, with 'new social movements' developing specific knowledge and competences on particular sub-issues. The Global Justice Movement, on the other hand, has bridged together a multiplicity of themes related with class, gender, generation, race, and religion. Also at the EU level, different concerns of different movements were bridged in a lengthy, although not very visible, process of mobilisation around the symbols of 'another Europe', defined as social, inclusive and 'from below'. Protest campaigns developed around 'broker issues' that tied together the concerns of different movements and organisations. In all these campaigns, to different degrees, fragments of diverse cultures – secular and religious, radical and reformist, younger and older generations – have been linked to a broader discourse with the theme of social (and global) injustice as an adhesive, while still leaving broad margins for separate developments. Beyond specific claims, the discourse on 'Another Europe' developed around values such as equality, justice, human rights, and environmental protection. Although emphasising pluralism and diversity, in the discourse of the movement a common master frame developed based on a definition of the self around a European dimension.

In parallel, the enemy is singled out in neoliberal globalisation, which activists perceive as characterising not only the policies of the international trade and financial organisations (the World Bank, IMF, and WTO), but also the free-market and deregulation policies by national governments and the support lent to them by an EU-sponsored 'negative' Europeanisation, based on the free-market and competition. These choices are considered not just regulatory (challenging the EU search for efficiency-driven legitimacy) but also as politically wrong, and responsible for growing social injustice, with especially negative effects on women, the environment, the global South, and other groups. Alongside social justice (a social Europe), the search for a Europe from below has emerged as a central concern. If the development of a global governance with the increasing influence of (private) global economic actors challenges traditional democratic legitimacy through electoral accountability, the most widespread claim is not the return to the nation state but the requests for the development of democratic global institutions. Although still deeply rooted in the national political systems and corresponding movement families, cosmopolitan activists tended to bridge the local with the global and vice versa. In doing so, they are contributing to the development of a multilevel political system as well as multilevel collective identities. At the EU level, the very strength of EU institutions has pushed the construction of alternative European identities forward.

The forms of european activism

Action strategies are clearly a fundamental choice for social movements. At the transnational level, studies on INGOs and TSMOs have highlighted that many had become increasingly institutionalised, both in terms of acquired professionalism and in the forms of action they employ, devoting more time to lobbying or informing the public than to marching in the street. Protest event analysis has repeatedly concluded that concerns about transnational decisions have mainly been expressed at the national level, where elected political institutions are considered more accountable to the citizen-electors. Using data on protest collected mainly from newspaper sources, studies stress the paucity of protests directly targeting IGOs. Using Reuters World News Service and the Reuters Textline, Doug Imig and Sidney Tarrow found a very limited number of protests addressing EU institutions, explained in Marks and McAdams' view to a great extent by the institutions' open attitudes to consultation with third parties (1996, 1999). Protest events addressing international institutions emerged as constantly marginal (or even of declining relevance) in research projects on single countries (e.g. in Germany), alongside specific issues such as migrant rights or environmental protection.

Nevertheless, in more recent times, specific forms of transnational protests (among which counter-summits, global days of action and social forums) have been invented and spread. With time, indeed, frustration with the results of the more polite forms of interactions brought about the development of broader coalitions, including religious groups, unions and social movement organisations, who combined pressure with petitions, marches and even direct action (Reitan 2007; Smith *et al.* 2007). Since Seattle, the 2000s have seen an escalation of interactions between protestors and the police during the contestation of international summits (della Porta, Peterson and Reiter 2006). If previous research had stressed, as mentioned, the taming of social movements with a shift from the street to the lobbies, recent studies, addressing the Global Justice Movement in particular, pointed instead at a growth of disruptive transnational forms of protest. Especially since the protest against the third WTO conference in Seattle in November 1999, Global Days of Action, and transnational Social Forums have contributed to build awareness of and interest in transnational activism. These protests developed from a number of campaigns that networked various organisations against the North American Free Trade Agreements (NAFTA); against the Multilateral Agreement on Investment; for the cancellation of poor countries' foreign debt (among others, in the Jubilee 2000 campaign); or for a more social Europe (for instance, in the European Marches against Unemployment and Exclusion). Within these campaigns, new frames of action developed, symbolically constructing a global self, but also producing structural effects in the form of new movement networks.

If our campaigns confirm that protest strategies are relevant for policy success as well as the production and reproduction of protest actors, they nevertheless point at the fact that different opportunities require different strategies. The EU has only recently become accustomed to being contested in the street, as observers started to notice that the structuring of interest mediation practices were disrupting the initial informal access that environmentalists or unionists had enjoyed. In the EU campaigns we have studied, the majority of organisations active at this level complained that the EU paid only 'lip service' to the idea of real consultation, and stated that going back to their roots, that is back to the streets (or at least trying to), was sometimes the best way of driving their messages home to greater effect, albeit in combination with other more conventional methods.

Dwelling in more detail on the role of protest in the EU, the evidence provided by the social campaigns that ended in positive outcomes points to the idea that the most important political opportunities in the EU are still essentially provided by national actors within member states (an idea also expressed by many other scholars, for example Lahusen 1999: 190; Rucht 2001: 135; Imig and Tarrow 2001: 18; Helfferich and Kolb 2001: 156; Tarrow and McAdam 2005: 121), and that more traditional mobilisations, in particular when carried out at different territorial levels, are therefore the most effective where the Commission's role is smaller. As already mentioned, when we look at the four cases together they seem to provide some evidence overturning the idea that the EU arena, with its Commission so open to dialogue, means that campaigns directed more towards lobbying actions and the Commission will be more effective in the EU arena (Marks and McAdam 1996; della Porta and Kriesi 1999), although it should be stressed that overall, the cases do not suggest that protest is a tactic used as an alternative to lobbying – on the contrary, all interviewees stressed that both tactics may be useful, but neither on its own will secure an impact (see also della Porta and Caiani 2009). A wide range of tactics are used in the campaigns studied here,[3] thereby challenging the view of defined types of actions for different kinds of groups put forward by Balme and Chabanet (2002: 89). Yet it should still be noted that lobbying is still the major tactic used at the EU level (e.g. Marks and McAdam 1996, 1999; della Porta and Caiani 2009), where levels of protest are low, albeit slowly increasing (Imig and Tarrow 2001; Balme and Chabanet 2002: 52).

This highlights that it is wrong to assume that national targets are purely national, and not sometimes part and parcel of the European or indeed the wider

---

3. 'A closer look at campaigns reveals that their action repertoire is much wider. Depending on the campaign's stage, they may focus on providing information, bargaining, lobbying, or seeking alternative solutions – a wide range of activities that cannot be subsumed under the label of protest. Research attention must be paid to the full array of activities in which the campaigners are involved' (della Porta and Rucht 2002: 8). The campaigns included in this study aim to pay attention to all the activities of the campaigning groups, even if conclusions about the role of protest are especially interesting.

transnational level itself. The cases, particularly Bolkestein, demonstrate that national protests and debates can in reality be a coordinated part of wider actions that are European in nature and scope. This lesson can equally be transferred to the environmental cases, where the open attitude of the Commission and the resources sunk into engaging with the latter in various dialogues, pulled groups away from their networks and grassroots members, and into highly technical arguments hard to use when attempting to mobilise at the local and national levels. More pessimistically, it could be suggested that the Commission purposely appears to be open in order to stifle more public voices in semi-closed discussion forums, pulling them away from grassroots activities and thus ensuring that they seem to listen to all whilst really following their own agenda (i.e. the 'lip service' view).

The cases may also be said to begin to reveal a split between campaigns focussing on more technical issues at the EU level – i.e. the two environmental cases – and those focussing on more politically charged (in the sense of traditional 'high' politics affecting the distribution of goods) issues – i.e. the two social cases, in that they show some kind of pattern in types of actions for each of the categories. In the 'technical' campaigns, convincing various actors is seen as a matter of science rather than politics – many interviewees were careful to underline the fact that the subject matter was beyond left and right. This is certainly the case for the coexistence campaign, where the main target is the supposedly non-political Commission, but also for the REACH case where the main target is the European Parliament. Here, interviewees stressed that the real challenge in convincing MEPs was not their political affiliation, but their committee affiliation. While those sitting on the environment committee were seen as more or less on side, no matter their ideological leanings, those from the internal market and industry committees were seen to be more sympathetic to arguments related to economic threats than human health or environmental ones. Both environmental campaigns featured the heavy use of scientific reports in campaigning efforts, rather than the more political tools of demonstrations and petitions.[4] The two campaigns studied here may offer an additional explanation for the relative lack of protest seen at the European level by environmental groups (Rucht 2001), one that differs from the usual array of constraints also experienced by social and other types of groups.[5] These are all valid obstacles to protest at the EU level but, as Rucht himself points out, are not restricted to the experiences of environmental groups.

---

4.   It is interesting to note that the split between working on technical EU policy and working on campaigning is often reproduced in the staff structures of EU environmental groups – those working on policy do not campaign, those who campaign do not work on policy. In light of the conclusions drawn here, this raises the problem of reconciling these two crucial aspects.

5.   Rucht lists these as, among others, the continuing importance of national channels for mobilisation (also acknowledged here), the appropriateness of lobbying in the EU arena as opposed to protest (discussed above), financial support from the Commission, the career ambitions of lobbyists, the difficulties of transnational coordination, lack of material resources, the opacity of the EU system to 'ordinary' people, the lack of a pan-European public sphere, and the non-immediate threats posed in questions of European legislation (Rucht 2001: 135–9).

However, the technical nature of legislation is not restricted to environmental issues. The real contrast lies in the fact that the social campaigns both sought to target more traditional political actors at both the European and national levels. The Lisbon agenda campaign concentrated its efforts on governments in the sense that its main target was the European Council. Tellingly, the tools it used to achieve this were very much linked to the national level.[6] The Bolkestein campaign, on the other hand, is a highly interesting (although not a common) example of political work at both European and national levels together. Interviewees stressed that since the socialist group in the European Parliament could be more or less relied upon to support trade union positions, much lobbying work was directed to convincing the centre and centre-right groups of the Parliament. At the same time, political parties as governments were targeted from the national level, and the European Council from the EU level, in various demonstrations. Thus, both of the most successful campaigns presented in this paper were careful to mirror the structure of the EU itself – a structure in which the member state, and by knock-on effect the political party – is still perhaps the most powerful entity.

In a nutshell, it would appear that where the EU issue in hand is to do with 'low' politics, i.e. more technical issues, it is difficult for EU social movement organisations to exploit the mobilisation opportunities offered by the national arena. Or, it may be that the national level is more easily exploited in social campaigns because of previous social mobilisations at the national level on related issues, using similar types of actions. The strong trade union movement traditions in some western European countries spring immediately to mind here. The same mobilising potential does not exist – or at least not to the same extent or manner, where more 'technical' campaigns are concerned (these being mostly the preserve of the more recent and qualitatively different 'New Social Movements'). Other high-profile campaigns that have known a high impact have also targeted the intergovernmental aspects of the EU, such as the integration of a gender equality clause in the Treaty of European Union, which also saw 'multilevel action coordination' (see Helfferich and Kolb 2001). A broader conclusion than observing that the most important opportunities are still offered by the member state level could thus be that social movement campaigns at the EU level are shaped (more than any other factor) by the institution that is the most powerful or active on the subject concerned. Sikkink (2005) posits a similar conclusion in her finding that domestic structures continue to shape transnational interaction, while Tarrow and della Porta (2005) also note that international opportunities can be expressed in domestic arenas.

Our research indicates that, generally speaking, what facilitates a positive outcome, is a co-existence between street politics and lobby politics, whose balance is influenced by protest cycles, as well as the specific issue addressed and

---

6.   In this sense, the social campaigns also seem to disprove the impression that 'EU social policy is notable for its commitment to social dialogue, its promotion of social partnership and the involvement of civil society actors' (Daly 2006: 464). They seem to provide further proof of the ETUC's new role as a more contentious EU actor as suggested by Bieler (2005: 479) rather than the co-opted social partner (Martin and Ross 2001).

international institution targeted. Coexistence of strategies was, for example, the approach (successfully) adopted during the WTO Ministerial round in Cancun in 2003, where 10,000 people invading the streets were 'complemented' by civil society organisations accessing the conference venue via accreditation and participation in national delegations. And the same can be noted about the anti-Bolkestein campaign. It is the ability to judge the right combination of protest and lobbying, disruption and cooperation, and at the right time, that leads to policy outcomes.

Once again, research on counter-summits and ESFs singles out the retrospective effects that protest has on the Europeanisation of social movements. As mentioned, at EU level, counter-summits and ESFs developed as macro-regional counterparts of global events. One main new form of transnational protest is the *counter-summit*, defined as the encounter of transnational activists in parallel to official summits of international institutions (Silva 2009). In the 1990s, the end of the Cold War opened opportunities for movements in the form of UN-sponsored Conferences, but also autonomous networking, especially against the war in Iraq and former Yugoslavia, and in solidarity with the Zapatistas movement. In the 2000s, confrontational counter-summits developed with the contestation of IGOs such as the World Bank, the IMF, the WTO, the G8 and even the EU. Prominent counter-summits include marches as well as direct actions against the International Monetary Fund (IMF) and World Bank meetings in Washington and Prague in 2000 and 2001; against EU summits in Amsterdam in 1997, Nice in 2000, and Gothenburg in 2001; against the World Economic Forum in yearly demonstrations in Davos; against the G8 summit in Genoa in 2001. Since the Seattle protests in 1999, there has been an escalation of conflicts between protestors and police during the contestation of international summits. Together with counter-summits, *global days of action* brought activists together to march, on the same day, in many countries. In what was defined as the largest mass protest ever in the world history, millions of people joined the international day of protest against the Iraq war on February 15, 2003, marching in thousands of cities around the world. Most recently, the diffusion of a protest model that recalls these have been seen in the *Occupy* and *indignados* protests throughout the global North, more or less in English-speaking and non-English speaking areas respectively. This protest model, aimed against widespread austerity measures in the wake of the latest global economic crisis, and perceived as targeting the poorest whilst leaving the richest (blamed for unleashing the crisis in the first place) untouched, thereby exacerbating already serious gaps between the richest and the poorest, has spread like wildfire in the last year, and at the time of writing, is ongoing.

Since 2001, transnational networking intensified in the World Social Forums, as well as its many macro-regional and national versions. In general, Social Forums have been innovative experiments promoted by the GJM. Distinct from counter-summits, which are mainly oriented towards protest, a Social Forum is a public space of debate among activists. In yearly editions, World Social Forums as well as European Social Forums have provided arenas for encounters and debates for thousands of organisations and tens of thousands of activists from different countries.

Not only have supranational events increased in frequency, they have also constituted founding events for a new cycle of protest that has developed at the national and sub-national levels on the issue of global justice. Even though transnational protests remain a rare occurrence, they (in the forms of global days of action, counter-summits or social forums) emerged as particularly 'eventful' in their capacity to produce relational, cognitive and affective effects on social movement activists and social movement organisations (della Porta 2008). A global language developed during the protest itself, together with intensified interactions during the mentioned transnational events and a growing acknowledgement of the roles and responsibilities of IGOs. Although still deep-rooted in national political systems and movement families (della Porta 2007), cosmopolitan activists do, as mentioned above, tend to bridge the local with the global and vice-versa (della Porta and Tarrow 2005). In doing this, they contribute to develop a transnational political system, as well as transnational identities (Tarrow 2005; della Porta and Caiani 2009).

Summarising

The aim of this paper was to map some hypotheses that emerge from a first comparative look at research on four protest campaigns targeting the EU, plus other transnational protest events. In terms of social movement studies, we locate our contribution within a shift from 'lumping' to 'splitting' in research on transnational contentious politics (see Table 2.2).

We have looked at outcomes, defined on the basis of the capacity of protest coalitions to achieve (or approximate) their aims, and have considered the impact on them of some exogenous and endogenous characteristics. In the presentation we have used some well-established concepts in social movement research, trying to adapt them to the characteristics of transnational politics. In particular, we have observed:

(a) *Multi-level political opportunities*. Political opportunities have emerged as important and varied. First, even though political opportunities do affect successful strategies, they do not seem to determine success and failure.
Additionally, as there are very different political opportunities at national levels, so there is also great variance at the EU level, where different EU institutions offer different types of chances and threats. We stressed in fact the different degrees of formal accessibility, not only between different IGOs, but also within them, between their different bodies. Additionally, we pointed at the role of potential allies, both within the administrative staff (overlapping memberships) and among representatives of member states.

(b) *Protest networks*. While previous research insisted on the bureaucratisation of transnational social movement organisations, our research pointed at the characteristics of the networks of very different types of movement organisations. In particular, (positive) outcomes seem facilitated by high network density, with low average distances between nodes and high degrees of compactness. We also noted the particularly important impact of the strategic choices of the 'powerful nodes' in influencing campaign strategies and, in turn, outcomes.

(c) *Global framing.* While previous research tended to consider 'thinking small' as the most promising of framing strategies, we noted that outcomes were positively influenced not only by a concrete and clear language and a resonance with the official discourse of some IGOs, but also (and even more) by elements such as the bridging capacity of some frames and the degree of frame sharing within the coalition. A process of frame bridging contributed to a politicisation of the image of EU institutions, as well as to the development of visions of a social Europe and Europeanisation from below. Framing processes were also seen to be closely linked to network density.

(d) *The forms of transnational activism.* While previous research stressed the taming of TSMOs repertoires of action, our analyses point at the importance of coexistence between more and less disruptive strategies, and of their dosage and timing. Additionally, we noted that protest tends to favour the development of networking and frame bridging, helping to build new resources for protest, in a process of 'acceleration'.

Table 2.2: Strategies for adapting the study of transnational contentious politics

The social movement studies agenda	Applying it to globalisation: Step 1. Lumping	Applying it to globalisation: Step 2. Splitting
POS	TPOS	Multilevel governance
SMOs	TSMOs	Multi-networks
Framing	Cross-national diffusion	Global identities
Repertoires	Lobbying	Multiform campaigns
Strategies	Boomerang	Domestication, externalisation and transnationalisation

References

Alcalde, J. (2009) *Changing the World: Explaining successes and failures of international campaigns by NGOs in the field of human security*, PhD Thesis, European University Institute.

Amenta, E. and Young, M. P. (1999) 'Making an Impact: Conceptual and methodological implications of the collective goods criterion', in M. Giugni, D. McAdam, and C. Tilly (eds) *How Social Movements Matter,* Minneapolis: University of Minnesota Press, pp. 22–41.

Anheier, H. and Katz, H. (2005) 'Global Connectedness: The structure of transnational NGO networks', in H. Anheier, M. Glasius and M. Kaldor (eds) *Global Civil Society 2005/2006*, Oxford: Oxford University Press.

Ansell, C. K. (2003) 'Community Embeddedness and Collaborative Governance in the San Francisco Bay Area Environmental Movement', in M. Diani and D. McAdam (eds) *Social Movements and Networks: Relational approaches to collective action,* Oxford: Oxford University Press, pp. 123–146.

Balme, R. and Chabanet, D. (2002) 'Introduction: Action collective et gouvernance de l'Union européenne', in R. Balme, D. Chabanet and V. Wright (eds) *L'action collective en Europe*, Paris: Presses de Sciences Po, pp. 21–120.

——— (2008) *European Governance and Democracy: Power and protest in the EU*, Lanham, MD: Rowman and Littlefield.

Balme, R., Chabanet, D. and Wright, V. (eds) (2002) *L'action collective en Europe*, Paris, Presses de Sciences Po.

Bendix, R. (1964) *Nation Building and Citizenship*, New York: Wiley and Son.

Benford, R. D. and Snow, D. (2000) 'Framing processes and social movements', *Annual Review of Sociology 26*, 611–39.

Bieler, A. (2005) 'European Integration and the transnational restructuring of social relations: the emergence of Labour as a regional actor?', *Journal of Common Market Studies* 43(3): 461–484.

Bohman, J. (2007) *Democracy Across Borders: from Dêmos to Dêmoi*, Cambridge, Mass., MIT Press.

Boli, J. and Thomas, G. M. (1999) *Constructing the World Culture: International Nongovernmental Organizations since 1875*, Stanford, CA: Stanford University Press.

Caniglia, B. (2002) 'Elites Alliances and Transnational Environmental Movement Organisations', in J. Smith and H. Johnston (eds) *Globalizaton and Resistance*, Lanham: Rowman & Littlefield, pp. 153–172.

Commission of the European Communities (2001) *European Governance: A White Paper*, COM(2001) 428.

Cullen, P. P. (2005) 'Conflict and Cooperation within the Platform of European Social NGOs', in J. Bandy and J. Smith (eds) *Coalitions Across Borders: Transnational protest and the neoliberal order*, Oxford: Rowman and Littlefield, pp. 71–94.

Daly, M. (2006) 'EU Social Policy after Lisbon', *Journal of Common Market Studies* 44(3): 461–481.

Della Porta, D. (ed.) (2007) *The Global Justice Movement: Cross national and transnational perspectives*, Boulder, CO: Paradigm.

— (2008) 'Eventful protest, global conflict', *Distinktion, Scandinavian Journal of Social Theory* 17: 27–56.

— (ed.) (2009a) *Another Europe*, London: Routledge.

— (ed.) (2009b) *Democracy in Social Movements*, London: Palgrave.

Della Porta, D., Andretta, M., Mosca, L. and Reiter, H. (2006) *Globalization from Below*, Minneapolis: University of Minnesota Press.

Della Porta, D. and Caiani, M. (2009) *Social Movements and Europe*, Oxford: Oxford University Press.

Della Porta, D. and Diani, M. (2006) *Social Movements*, Oxford: Blackwell.

Della Porta, D. and Kriesi, H. (1999) '*Social Movements in a Globalizing World: An introduction*', in D. della Porta, H. Kriesi and D. Rucht (eds) *Social Movements in a Globalizing World*, New York, Macmillan, pp. 3–23.

Della Porta, D., Kriesi, H. and Rucht, D. (eds) (1999) *Social Movements in a Globalizing World*, New York, Macmillan. Expanded edition 2009.

Della Porta, D., Peterson, A. and Reiter, H. (eds) (2006) *The Policing of Transnational Protest*, Aldershot: Ashgate.

Della Porta, D. and Rucht, D. (2002) *'Comparative environmental campaigns'*, *Mobilization*, 7(1): 1–14.

Della Porta, D. and Tarrow, S. (eds) (2005) *Transnational Protest and Global Activism*, New York: Rowman and Littlefield.

Diani, M. (1995) *Green Networks: A structural analysis of the Italian environmental movement*, Edinburgh: Edinburgh University Press.

— (2003) *'Networks and Social Movements: A research programme'*, in M. Diani and D. McAdam (eds) *Social Movements and Networks: Relational approaches to collective action*, Oxford: Oxford University Press, pp. 299–318.

— (2005) *'Cities in the World: Local Civil Society and Global Issues in Britain'*, in D. Della Porta. and S. Tarrow (eds) *Transnational Protest and Global Activism*, New York: Rowman and Littlefield, pp. 45–67.

Diani, M. and McAdam, D. (eds) (2003) *Social Movements and Networks: Relational approaches to collective action*, Oxford: Oxford University Press.

Flam, H. and King, D. (eds) (2006) *Emotions and Social Movements*, London, Routledge.

Gamson, W. A. (1990) *The Strategy of Social Protest*, Belmont: Wadsworth Publishers.

Gamson, W. and Meyer, D. S. (1996) *'Framing Political Opportunity'*, in D. McAdam, J. D. McCarthy and M. N. Zald (eds) *Opportunities, Mobilizing Structures, and Framing*, New York/Cambridge: Cambridge University Press, pp. 275–90.

Giugni, M. (1999) 'How Social Movements Matter: Past research, present problems, future developments', in M. Giugni, D. McAdam and C. Tilly (eds) *How Social Movements Matter*, Minneapolis: University of Minnesota Press, pp. xiii-xviii.

Goodwin, J., Jasper, J. M. and Polletta, F. (eds) (2001) *Passionate Politics*, Chicago: University of Chicago Press.

Greenwood, J. (2003) *Interest Representation in the European Union*, New York: Palgrave Macmillan.

Haas, P. (1989) 'Do regimes matter? Epistemic communities and Mediterranean pollution control', *International Organisation*, 43 (3): 377–403.

— (1990) *Saving the Mediterranean: The politics of international environmental cooperation*, New York: Columbia University Press.

— (ed.) (1992) 'Knowledge, power and international policy coordination', *International Organisation*, Special Issue, 46 (1): 1–390.

Helfferich, B. and Kolb, F. (2001) 'Multilevel Action Coordination in European Contentious Politics: The case of the European Women's Lobby' in D. Imig and S. Tarrow (eds) *Contentious Europeans: Protest and politics in an emerging polity*, Lanham: MD: Rowman and Littlefield, pp. 143–161.

Imig, D. and Tarrow, S. (eds) (2001) *Contentious Europeans: Protest and politics in an emerging polity*, Lanham: MD: Rowman and Littlefield.

Kaldor, M. (2003) *Global Civil Society: An answer to war*, Cambridge: Polity Press.

Keck, M. and Sikkink, K. (1998) *Activists Beyond Borders*, Ithaca, NY: Cornell University Press.

Koopmans, R. and Statham, P. (1999) 'Ethnic and Civic Conceptions of Nationhood and the Differential Success of the Extreme Right in Germany and Italy', in M. Giugni, D. McAdam and C. Tilly (eds) *How Social Movements Matter*, Minneapolis, University of Minnesota Press.

Kriesberg, L. (1997) 'Social Movements and Global Transformation', in J. Smith, C. Chatfield and R. Pagnucco (eds) *Transnational Social Movements and World Politics: Solidarity beyond the state*, Syracuse, NY: Syracuse University Press, pp. 3–18.

Kriesi, H. (1996) 'The Organisational Structure of New Social Movements in a Political Context' in D. McAdam *et al.* (eds) *Comparative Perspectives on Social Movements*, Cambridge: Cambridge University Press, pp. 152–184.

Kriesi, H., Koopmans, R., Duyvendak, J., and Giugni, M. (1995) *New Social Movements in Western Europe*, London: UCL Press.

Lahusen, C. (1999) 'International Campaigns in Context', in D. della Porta, H. Kriesi and D. Rucht (eds) *Social Movements in a Globalizing World*, New York, Macmillan, pp. 189–205.

— (2004) 'Joining the Cocktail Circuit: Social movement organizations at the European Union', *Mobilization*, 9(1): 55–71.

McAdam, D., Tarrow, S. and Tilly, C. (2001) *Dynamics of Contention*, Cambridge: Cambridge University Press.

McCarthy, J., McPhail, C. and Crist, J. (1999) 'The Emergence and Diffusion of Public Order Management System: Protest cycles and police response', in D. della Porta, H. Kriesi and D. Rucht (eds) (1999) *Social Movements in a Globalizing World*, New York, Macmillan, pp.71–96.

Marchetti, R. (2008) Global Democracy: For and against, London, Routledge.

Marks, G. and McAdam, D. (1996) 'Social Movements and the Changing Structure of Political Opportunity in the European Union', in G. Marks *et al.* (eds) *Governance in the European Union*, London: Sage Publications, pp.95–120.

— (1999) 'On the Relationship of Political Opportunities to the Form of Collective Action: The Case of the European Union D. della Porta, H. Kriesi and D. Rucht (eds) (1999) *Social Movements in a Globalizing World*, New York, Macmillan, pp. 97–111.

Marshall, T. H. (1992) 'Citizenship and Social Class' (1950), in T. H. Marshall and T. Bottomore, *Citizenship and Social Class*, London, Pluto Press, pp. 3–51.

Martin, A. and Ross, G. (2001) 'Trade Union Organizing at the European Level: The dilemma of borrowed resources', in D. Imig and S. Tarrow (eds) *Contentious Europeans: Protest and politics in an emerging polity*, Lanham, MD: Rowman and Littlefield, pp. 53–76.

Mazey, S. and Richardson, J. (eds) (1993) *Lobbying in the European Community*, Oxford: Oxford University Press.

Melucci, A. (1996) *Challenging Codes*, Cambridge/New York: Cambridge University Press.

Meyer, D.S. and Tarrow, S. (eds) (1998) *The Social Movement Society*, New York: Rowman and Littlefield.

Michalowitz, I. (2002) 'Analysing structured paths of lobbying behaviour: why discussing the involvement of "civil society" does not solve the EU's democratic deficit', *Journal of European Integration*, 26(2): 145–173.

Oliver, P. and Johnston, H. (2000) 'What a good idea! Ideologies and frames in Social Movement research', *Mobilization* 5: 37–54.

Parks, L. (2009a) In the Corridors and in the Streets: A comparative study of the impacts of Social Movement campaigns in the EU, PhD Thesis, European University Institute.

— (2009b) 'Improving Accountability in the European Union: The potential role of NGOs' in S. Gustavsson, T. Persson and C. Karlsson (eds) *The Illusion of Accountability in the European Union*, London: Routledge, pp.155–169.

Passy, F. (1999) 'Supranational Political Opportunities as a Channel of Globalization of Political Conflicts: The case of the rights of indigenous people', in D. della Porta, H. Kriesi and D. Rucht (eds) (1999) *Social Movements in a Globalizing World*, New York, Macmillan, pp. 148–169.

Piven, F. F. and Cloward, R. (1992) 'Normalizing Collective Protest', in A. Morris and C. McClurg Mueller (eds) *Frontiers in Social Movement Theory*, New Haven, CT: Yale University Press, pp. 301–25.

Putnam, R. D. (1988) 'Diplomacy and domestic politics: the logic of Two-Level Games', *International Organization*, 42(3): 427–60.

Reitan, R. (2007) *Global Activism*, London: Routledge.

Risse, T. and Sikkink, K. (1999) 'The Socialization of International Human Rights Norms into Domestic Practices: Introduction', in T. Risse, S. Rapp and K. Sikkink (eds) *The Power of Human Rights International Norms and Domestic Change*, New York: Cambridge University Press, pp. 1–38.

Rosenau, J. (1990) *Turbulence in World Politics*, Brighton: Harvester Wheatsheaf.

— (1998) 'Governance and Democracy in a Globalizing World', in D. Archibugi, D. Held and B. Kohler (eds) *Re-Imagining Political Community: Studies in cosmopolitan democracy*, Cambridge: Polity Press, pp. 28–57.

Rucht, D. (1995) 'The Impact of Anti-Nuclear Power Movements in International Comparison', in M. Bauer (ed.) *Resistance to New Technology*, Cambridge: Cambridge University Press, pp. 271–91..

— (1999) 'The Transnationalization of Social Movements: Trends, causes, problems', in D. della Porta, H. Kriesi and D. Rucht (eds) (1999) *Social Movements in a Globalizing World*, New York, Macmillan, pp. 206–222.

— (2001) 'Lobbying or Protest? Strategies to Influence EU Environmental Policies', in D. Imig and S. Tarrow (eds) *Contentious Europeans: Protest and politics in an emerging polity*, Lanham: MD: Rowman and Littlefield, pp. 125–142.

— (2002) 'The EU as a Target of Political Mobilisation: Is there a Europeanisation of Conflict?', in R. Balme, D. Chabanet and V. Wright (eds) *L'action collective en Europe*, Paris, Presses de Sciences Po, pp. 163–194.

Rucht, D. and Neidhardt, F. (2002) 'Towards a "movement society"? On the possibilities of institutionalizing social movements', *Social Movement Studies*, 1(1): 7–30.

Ruzza, C. (2004) *Europe and Civil Society, Movement Coalitions and European Governance*, Manchester/New York: Manchester University Press.

Schumaker, P. D. (1975) 'Policy responsiveness to protest-group demands', The *Journal of Politics*, 37(2): 488–521.

Sewell, W. H. (1996) 'Three Temporalities: Toward an eventful sociology', in T. J. McDonald (ed.) *The Historic Turn in the Human Sciences*, University of Michigan Press: Ann Arbor, pp. 245–80.

Sikkink, K. (2005) 'Patterns of Multilevel Governance', in D. della Porta and S. Tarrow (eds) *Transnational Protest and Global Activism*, New York: Rowman and Littlefield, pp. 151–73.

Silva, F. (2008) *Do Transnational Social Movements Matter? Four Case Studies Assessing the Impact of Transnational Social Movements on the Global Governance of Trade, Labour and Finance*, PhD Thesis, European University Institute.

— (2009) 'Transnational Forums and Summits', *International Encyclopaedia of Civil Society*, Springer.

Smith, J. (1997a) 'Characteristics of the Modern Transnational Social Movement Sector', in Smith, Chatfield and Pagnucco (eds), pp. 42–58.

— (1997b) 'Building Political Will after UNCED: Earth Action International', in Smith, Chatfield and Pagnucco (eds), pp. 175–194.

— (1999) 'Global Strategies of Social Protest: Transnational Social Movement Organizations in World Politics', in della Porta, Kriesi and Rucht (eds).

Smith, J. and Johnston, H. (eds) (2002) *Globalisaton and Resistance*, Lanham: Rowman & Littlefield.

Smith, J., Chatfield, C. and Pagnucco, R. (eds) (1996) *Solidarity Beyond the State: The Dynamics of Transnational Social Movements*, Syracuse, NY: Syracuse University Press.

— (1997) *Transnational Social Movements and Global Politics*, Syracuse, NY: Syracuse University Press.

Snow, D. A., and Benford, R. (1988) 'Ideology, Frame Resonance and Participant Mobilization', *International Social Movement Research*, 1: 197–219.

— (1999) 'Alternative Types of Cross-national Diffusion in the Social Movement Arena', in della Porta, Kriesi and Rucht (eds), pp. 23–39.

— (2000) 'Framing Processes and Social Movements: An Overview and Assessment', *Annual Review of Sociology*, 26: 11–39.

Tarrow, S. (1990) 'The Phantom at the Opera: Political Parties and Social Movements of the 1960s and the 1970s in Italy', in Dalton, R.J. and Kuechler, M. (eds), *Challenging the Political Order: New Social Movements in Western Democracies*, Cambridge: Polity Press, pp. 251–73.

— (1996) 'States and Opportunities: The Political Structuring of Social Movements' in McAdam, D., McCarthy, J.D. and Zald, M.N. (eds) *Comparative Perspectives on Social Movements*. New York. Cambridge University Press, pp. 41–61.

— (2005) *The New Transnational Contention*, New York/Cambridge: Cambridge University Press.

Tarrow, S. and McAdam, D. (2005) 'Scale Shift in Transnational Contention', in D. della Porta and S. Tarrow (eds) *Transnational Protest and Global Activism*, New York: Rowman and Littlefield, pp.121–150.

Tarrrow, S. and della Porta, D. (2005) 'Conclusion: "Globalization", complex internationalism, and transnational contention', in D. della Porta and S. Tarrow (eds) *Transnational Protest and Global Activism*, New York: Rowman and Littlefield, pp.227–246.

Tilly, C. (1978) *From Mobilization to Revolution*, Reading, MA: Addison-Wesley.

— (1984) 'Social Movements and National Politics', in C. Bright and S. Harding (eds), *State-Making and Social Movements: Essays in history and theory*, Ann Arbor: University of Michigan Press, pp. 297–317.

Walsh, E. J. (1981) 'Resource mobilization and citizen protest in communities around Three-Mile Island', *Social Problems*, 29: 1–21.

chapter three | eu lobbying and the european transparency initiative: a sociological approach to interest groups

Hélène Michel

Many scholars maintain that with more and more regulation and an ever-widening scope, EU lobbying is the consequence of European construction. European interest groups would come to Brussels in order to put pressure on the European institutions that would then take into account their demands. I argue that this view is simplistic and wrong because it ignores the process of co-production of EU lobbying. In this chapter, I show how interest groups and European institutions work together to set up a European system of interest representation. Interest representatives and EU staff are not so different as they are said to be. Geographically and sociologically, they are close. They often have the same background and they share a same idea of European governance. In this context, regulations like the European Transparency Initiative (ETI) (COM 2006) are a means and a result of this co-production and not, as presented in the literature, a tool to tackle the lobbying issue.

In this chapter I will focus on the European Transparency Initiative as it was launched in the spring of 2005 and discussed in the Green Paper consultation in 2006. But my aim is not to follow up on this consultation. I leave this task to the Secretariat General of the European Commission in charge of civil society relations (COM 2007) and to those who wish to advise the European Commission in its dealings with European lobbying. As I demonstrate in the first part of my chapter, scholars use the ETI to re-launch their studies and to be listened to more by the EU institutions on lobbying issues. Unlike these scholars, my aim is to study ETI consultation as a collective mobilisation process, shaping EU lobbying, where actors find a position according to their financial, human and social resources, enabling them to meet the expectations of the European administration. In the second part of this chapter, at odds with the view that interest groups pressure institutions that are open and look for inputs on policy making (Mazey and Richardson 1999), I show that it is actually the European Commission that generates, selects, dismisses or promotes organisations that are involved in the functioning of European governance. The ETI process reveals the role played by EU institutions in selecting the actors of European governance and shaping interests. In the third part of my chapter, I focus on the responses to the consultation to show how the conceptions of the ETI, and the role of lobbying in European governance, relate to the positions occupied by the organisations involved in EU lobbying and to the positions of their members within this field.

By closely studying the process of production of position papers in various organisations from the perspective of those who are in charge of drafting them, I demonstrate that identifying a political stand with an organisation is simplistic. Interest representatives are not only involved in several embedded organisations, but the same interests can also be expressed by different organisations in the absence of a consensus. In other words, the differences between the positions published during the consultation process are not to be found between different organisations, the nature of the interests, and the nationality of the groups. These factors are more akin to forms of 'presentation of the self' (Goffman 1959) for these organisations in relation to the expectations of European institutions. Rather, differences in positions and stands are due to the sociological properties of interest representatives, regarding both their position in the EU field and their professional and activist paths. Studying the contributions and the contributors together shows other dividing lines among these papers, and makes us understand, for instance, why proposals by CEO (Corporate Europe Observatory) prevail, even though the organisation actively fights lobbying. Quite well integrated in European institutions, these activists support the 'new European governance' (Georgakakis and de Lassalle 2007) and adopt the rules of the game just as they pretend to denounce them: they form interest groups and lobby to defend the right for activism in Europe.

How the ETI relaunches studies on EU lobbying

Much has been written about the European Transparency Initiative (ETI) launched in 2005 by Siim Kallas, then Commissioner for Administrative Affairs, Audit and Anti-Fraud, in the first Barroso Commission. As is often the case with the EU, two types of publications greeted the launch and the implementation of this program, which, among other things, aimed at regulating lobbying and scrutinising the use of Community funds.

The first set of reactions came from the 'European lobbying world' (Michel and Courty 2012), directly targeted by measures liable to change the 'rules of the political game' in the EU (Bailey 1969). Indeed, by proposing a code of conduct for lobbyists, the registration of interest representatives, the publication of lists of clients, of office holders and of sources of funding, the European Commission faced much criticism from professionals who felt accused of acting covertly and having suspicious practices (because of their secrecy). In the professional journals (such as the *Journal of Public Affairs*), in the European press (*Euractiv.com, European Voice, Europolitique*), in professional organisations (EPACA, SEAP) and other forums (Notre Europe, Confrontation Europe, Toute l'Europe...), they pointed out that transparency had always been a core concern in deontology and in practice (Harris and Danny 2001) and dismissed the new EU imperative as one more slogan used by EU institutions to restore their image at the expense of lobbyists (Billet 2007). In the process, they were responding to activists supporting transparency and regulation in lobbying, who, through NGOs such as CEO and ALTER-EU (The Alliance for Transparency and Ethics Regulation), denounced the 'dangerous liaisons' between industrialists and European authorities (Balanyá *et al.* 2000) and called for more regulation (Wesselius 2005) to end them. Acting as arbiters of the conflict between these two sides, the administrative leaders in charge of this reform programme emphasised the need to further legitimise EU institutions in the eyes of the citizens (Legris and Lehmann 2008; Lehmann 2009). To them, transparency is a means to 'bring Europe closer to its citizens' (COM 2001), a longstanding preoccupation with which specialists of European governance are quite familiar (Lodge 1994; Peterson 1995). They believe that trust in the institutions entails regulating lobbying and moralising the profession, in order to silence criticism and, more broadly, fight Euro-scepticism.

The ETI was also the impetus for a second type of publications by specialists of European interest groups, who are all the more involved in this debate as they are often called to contribute to it by EU institutions and professional organisations alike.[1] This provided an opportunity for them to reinvest in the field of European governance studies, in which they had been somewhat eclipsed by specialists of 'European civil society' (Kohler-Koch and Rittberger 2006). The promotion of a 'civil society', considered virtuous because it comes directly from citizens and defends disinterested causes, was indeed no longer on the order of the day. While the ETI drew from the debate on good European governance, it nonetheless revealed a shift in perspective that cannot be boiled down to a mere rhetoric change (Jobert and Kohler-Koch 2008). By introducing the idea of regulating lobbying, even if the latter was considered as a 'legitimate part of the democratic system' (COM Green Paper 2006), the European Commission put the question of the relationship between EU institutions and interest groups back into the limelight. In new terms and under the guise of a new issue – transparency – the old debate on the development of interest groups and the role of lobbying in policy making was relaunched (Greenwood 1998, 2007; Balme and Chabanet 2008; Chabanet 2009). For the academics specialised in the subject, the transparency initiative proved an excellent opportunity to pick up their research on interest groups and the managing of European lobbying (Coen and Richardson 2009). Some, in the interest of taking transparency seriously (Naurin 2008), discussed the measures introduced to regulate lobbying (Dinan and Miller 2006; Janos 2009). Some made recommendations on what can and should be done to regulate lobbying and thereby increase transparency, while others stuck to observing and assessing the options chosen (Basilien-Gainche 2009; Greenwood 2011). Yet others, replacing the ETI within a broader EU policy towards interest groups, focused on the development of lobbying at EU level. They pointed out that the 'lobby boom' should be studied in the light of the transformations of European governance (Kohler-Koch and Eising 1999), which was extended to other Member States (Blavoukos and Pagoulatos 2008) and developed with increasingly wide competencies in different

---

1. David Coen was heard by the Parliament and the AFCO Committee on 8th October 2006; Christine Mahoney spoke before the SEAP on her comparative survey on the American Congress and the European Union (Mahoney 2008).

areas (Eising 2009). To them, if the profusion of interest groups is inevitable in a democratic regime, it can – and must – be managed to such an extent that not only institutional agents can make the best possible use of the interest groups' 'inputs', but also that the measures aiming at increasing transparency do not worsen the inequalities in terms of access to the institutions and the available resources. Thus, they endeavoured to show how each institution, and even each Commission DG, developed its own policy towards interest groups. They emphasised the differences between groups according to their legal status (consultants versus non-profit organisations), the nature of the organisation (NGOs, trade unions, business associations), the type of interests defended and their geographic presence (European, national, local, international), in order to account for the great heterogeneity of the positions towards the ETI. These academics suggested taking all these elements into account in implementing the European transparency policy (Obradovic 2009). These publications thus contributed to the administrative and political debate on how to deal with interest groups and how to implement transparency.

Ultimately, however, these publications tell us nothing about the ETI, which is used as a pretext to stipulate, in a manner that is more normative than analytical, how European governance works or should work. Worse yet, they tell us nothing new about interest groups and European lobbying, as Jan Beyers recognised when he concluded a special issue on the subject by 'much we study, little we know' (Beyers, Eising and Maloney 2008). Indeed, interest groups are always considered as outside the EU institutions, which have to face them and deal with them. The ETI is thus seen as one more measure taken towards interest groups. Yet, aren't interest groups also produced by these policies? Aren't they outputs of policies?

Unlike those scholars, I think that European interest groups deserve to be studied further, as long as we adopt a perspective that breaks from current scientific routines and that the question of our research does not merely echo the practical questions faced by the European administration. I also argue that the ETI is an excellent area to conduct a structural sociological analysis (Kauppi 2005) of interest groups and to address two main questions that are unfortunately often overlooked by the mainstream literature. The first question is that of the genesis and enduring development of interest groups at EU level. The second one lies in the study of the effects of the various regulations on lobbying activities as well as the structuring of interests and the way organisations work.

Regarding the first question (how are these groups formed and how do they manage to endure?), I contend that the rational explanations provided in most studies are inadequate for two reasons. Firstly, they are Euro-centred and reduce the EU political field of power to the European institutions and, secondly, they confuse the goal put forward by the organisations (exerting pressure on EU institutions) with the reasons of their constitution. Other hypotheses can be formulated (Grant 1998) that take into account on the one hand the 'moral entrepreneurs' (Becker 1963:9) who work to keep the groups alive by mobilising supporters and organising activism (Salisbury 1969), and on the other hand, the competing configurations in which they are involved, both in Brussels and in national political fields (Michel 2009). In this manner, we can show that if so many interest groups are active in Brussels, it is not only to influence European legislation, but also to show off their economic and logistical power and therefore improve their standing (Schattschneider 1960; Salisbury 1990). We may also find that while some national and international organisations would have objective reasons to come to Brussels and specialise in European matters, not all of them are able to do so (Smith, Maillard and Costa 2007). Their financial resources matter, and so do their staff, depending on their skills, know-how, beliefs and personal activist experiences (Dezalay 2007). On this dimension, my research converges with studies on collective mobilisations and activist trajectories (see della Porta and Parks, as well as Fillieule and Blanchard in this volume). The ETI is an excellent observatory of the plurality of the motivations for organisations to act, and of their unequal abilities to respond to such a consultation.

Regarding the second question (the effects of these policies towards interest groups), it does not suffice to say that the European Commission's policies aimed at interest groups, structure interest representation (Coen and Richardson 2009) and produce an 'elite' representation (Eising 2007). One must show how these normative frames inform practices of representation and defence of interests. In order to do so, it is necessary to study the plurality of the tasks carried out by interest representatives in a very concrete manner (Michel 2005). Only this way we will be able to understand that constituting an interest group and organising its activities is a very specific task, which not only requires skills to mobilise and manage members, draft position papers, produce common positions, but also a specific notion of what an 'interest group' must be, a definition as close as possible to that of the European Commission agents'. In interactions with EU institutions, there is a process of selection, not so much of the interests represented, but of the forms of expression and representation of these interests. The 'interest group' form is preferred to unions or social movements, because it gives the administration stable and long-term interlocutors, who provide figures and expertise, respond to online consultations, can make constructive proposals, get involved through their networks with the processes of implementation and legitimation of measures, and so on. The 'interest group' form thus constitutes a 'repertoire of contention' (Tilly 1993: 757–63) generated and institutionalised both by the EU institutions, who seek inputs and legitimacy, and by those who defend and represent interests in Europe. In this respect, the geographic (Brussels) and social (similar academic and professional paths) proximity between institutional agents and interest representatives contributes to the sharing of views in constituting and dealing with 'problems' (Campana, Henry and Rowell 2007). Analysing the ETI is an excellent means to show that, on the one hand, in order to do politics in Europe, it is necessary to adopt commonly used repertoires of action such as interest groups, and on the other hand, that claims are more likely to be taken into account if they are defended by people who are sociologically close to the agents of EU administration, who share the same 'referential' (Jobert and Muller 1987:63–74), that is a similar conception of European governance.

The co-production of EU lobbying

On the 3rd May 2006, the Commission published the European Transparency Initiative Green Paper (COM 2006) and launched an online consultation, opened until the 31st August 2006.[2] More than just a time period for opinions on lobbying to be voiced, the consultation was an opportunity for lobbying involving very different actors identified, deliberately or not, as being 'lobbyists'. Indeed, whether they refused or accepted the term, called themselves 'professionals' or 'actors of civil society', they were part of the ETI, and beyond, of the making of EU lobbying. EU lobbying consists of a set of relationships between, on the one hand, the European Commission and organisations, and on the other hand, between the organisations themselves. One of the key effects of this consultation was that it led to establishing relationships, however indirect, between the organisations involved in lobbying.

Identifying and disclosing european lobbyists

for the Commission, writing to the 'stakeholders' was quite a deft way not to set the boundaries of the respondents and let them designate themselves by participating in the consultation. Yet, the Green Paper explicitly defined 'lobbyists' as

> persons carrying out with the objective of influencing the policy formulation and decision-making processes of the European institutions [...and] working in a variety of organisations such as public affairs consultancies, law firms, NGOs, think-tanks, corporate lobby units ('in-house representatives') or trade associations. (COM 2006).

Table 3.1: The categories and sub-categories of the European Commission

Public Sector (18 contributions) C1: National Governments and Public Bodies (8) C2: Regional and local interests (10)	Private Sector (73 contributions) C3: EU-level bodies (34) C4: National bodies (31) C5: Local and regional (3) C6: Individual companies (5)
Non-Governmental Organisations (50 contributions) C7: EU-level bodies (30) C8: National bodies (19) C9: Local and regional bodies (1)	Citizens C10: Citizens' contributions (17) Others C11: Others contributions (7)

2.   Source: http://ec.europa.eu/transparency/eti/index_en.htm.

It might seem strange to use such a broad definition. Indeed, some were quick to question the well-foundedness of a concept that put heterogeneous actors (businesses, industrial sectors, professional groups, groups of citizens, etc.) that did not share the same motives (lucrative or not), pursue the same goals (defending ideas or interests) or defend the same interests (private vs. public) on the same level. As was the case for 'civil society', the actors involved tried to impose their definition of what civil society should be (Michel 2008).

Yet, this definition seems to have suited the diverse actors who took part in the consultation. All types of organisations participated: governments at various levels, professional organisations, unions, companies, consultancies, associations of public affairs professionals, associations of European lawyers, an environmentalist NGO, an ad hoc coalition, a consumers' organisation, and even a think tank (European Policy Centre [EPC]) and an association of regions (Assembly of the Regions [AER]). The Secretariat-General staff that received the contributions was thus able to fill all the available categories on the consultation follow-up.

Admittedly, the number of respondents remained low compared to the number of organisations registered in the CONECCS database[3] or to the participation observed in other consultations. With 174 contributions, the ETI was far from the mobilisation around sector consultations on legislative projects, such as the REACH regulation (Persson 2007). However, it has to be said here that the respondents were networks of NGOs or platforms writing on behalf of an entire sector, or even of several public policy sectors. Due to the generalist dimension of the consultation, there were no reactions from sector-based organisations that, on the one hand, did not see the point in mobilising around such a broad issue, and on the other hand, did not have the time or the skills to discuss a subject that concerns the functioning of the EU as a whole. Specialised organisations were thus de facto excluded. They could only participate in the consultation through wider networks of which they were members. These networks (Social Platform, Civil Society Contact Group, ALTER-EU…) and cross-sector organisations such as professional organisations of consultants (SEAP, EPACA…) amounted to most of the respondents. They acted as spokespersons for all those who could have responded but did not do so because the definition of the interests they defend, and therefore of the scope of their activities, was insufficiently generalist.

Accordingly, before they got around to addressing the questions explicitly asked by the Commission, all contributions started with an appreciation of the definition of lobbying and lobbyists put forward in the Green Paper. Accepting (or refusing) this definition amounted to accepting (or not) the 'external scrutiny' and the 'integrity rules' that the Commission sought to impose on lobbyists. This was an important issue, and one that went beyond the merely rhetorical argument suggested by some who argued that the derogatory term of 'lobbying' should be

---

3.   The Register of Interest Representatives/Lobbyists replaced the CONECCS (Consultation, the European Commission and the Civil Society) database in 2009. It included only civil society organisations active at the EU level, not the consultancies.

replaced by 'public affair' or 'advocacy'. All had to formulate a stance on this denomination. While the Commission's assertion that 'lobbying is a legitimate part of the democratic system' (COM 2006) was unanimously approved, cleavages nevertheless appeared.

Those who could claim a different identity and did not feel directly targeted by the proposals for regulation, even though they might have to deal with them in the course of their activities of representation, merely opposed the terminology used. This was the case of the European Trade Union Confederation, which, comforted by its status as 'social partner', argued that 'ETUC and its member organisations are not pressure groups; they are actors (recognised in the Treaty and by institutional actors) of European construction, notably in the social domain' (my translation from the French). UNICE, the European employers' association and the other 'social partner', expressed a similar view, although they admitted that they did 'lobbying' in certain cases. This was also the case of think tanks like the European Policy Center (EPC), which emphasised the distinction with pressure groups:

> Under the Commission's definition, think tanks are classified as lobbyists. However, a number of these, including EPC have very broad aims, such as promoting the broad concept of European integration. This is quite different from traditional lobbying organisations whose typical purpose is to promote specific or sectoral interest or even to represent the views of a single organisation.[4]

Likewise, the lawyers of the Council of Bars and Law Societies of Europe refused to be treated as lobbyists even though the intervention of lawyers 'before institutions in the framework of the legislative process [...] is likely to be considered as lobbying under the definition of the Green Paper'.[5]

Yet, not all the respondents had such a well-defined status to oppose the Green Paper's definition. Most of the NGOs had to take a stance against a definition that they ascribed to the business world. For instance, the European Council for non-profit organisations (CEDAG) reasserted its allegiance to 'organised civil society' as opposed, precisely, to interest groups. Implicitly criticising the institutional definition of civil society, CEDAG, in its contribution,

> question[ed] the content of the Green Paper, which seems to treat all actors of the organised civil society on an equal footing, as well as to confuse between social and civil dialogue [...] Those platforms [of European NGOs] cannot be considered as mere lobbyists, because they ground their actions as intermediate bodies, whose actions are based on a vision of citizenship which is based on participation.[6]

4. Contribution 95 of EPC.
5. Contribution 167 of CCBE, p.2.
6. Contribution 87 of CEDAG.

Other organisations shared this conception of civil society as focused on public issues and mobilised by disinterested causes (Weisbein 2007). Brought together within the Civil Society Contact Group (CSCG), they were all genuine interlocutors of the EU institutions, particularly of DG Employment, Social Affairs and Equal Opportunities, which constantly called for their expertise and included them in elaborating and implementing public policies. For this reason, they benefited from funding on specific projects, which enabled them to be present both 'in the field' and in Brussels, where their permanent representatives worked in offices located close to the Schuman Roundabout. For these representatives who, when interviewed, admitted that they did the same job as professional lobbyists, albeit with entirely different objectives, the Transparency Initiative was an opportunity to set things straight regarding slightly dubious organisations[7] forming potential threats insofar as they found themselves on equal footing with the business world. Most still refused this situation and worked to promote, and sometimes institutionalise, with the help of the European Economic and Social Committee (EESC) (Michel 2009), what they consider to be the 'real' civil society. Organisations like the Social Platform, which emphasised 'the specific role of NGO's in the promotion of participatory democracy',[8] were considered to be distinct from 'market forces'.

The NGOs brought together by ALTER-EU, however, had no objections to this common denomination. Their representatives used the term to claim recognition as 'true' lobbyists. Although the figure of the professional consultant acting on behalf of industrialists was a negative one, it did structure the representations of the profession, and beyond, the EU representation of interests (Michel 2005). Anticipating criticism on the unaccountability of NGOs that deemed themselves representatives of given categories of citizens, they called for financial transparency for all, and for the publication of their contributions in EU institutional texts. According to them, once the public found out how all the organisations working with EU institutions were funded, they would find it easier to assess their contribution to the process of elaboration and implementation of public policies. Their action against 'industrial lobbies' progressively turned into an action for 'good' lobbying, i.e., transparent and complying with certain deontological standards. In this perspective, compulsory registration and scrutiny of the organisations concerned consultants and professional organisations as well as NGOs and other European platforms. For these activists, treating all interest representatives the same way, regardless of the interests they defended and the organisations for which they worked, was good policy. Hence, the conception they defended somewhat matched that of the European Commission.

The nascent EU lobbying was, then, first a field or structured space that included heterogeneous actors sharing an ongoing 'dialogue' with the European

---

7. For instance, in July 2005, Health Action International Europe denounced the European Patients' Forum, accused of acting as a Trojan horse for the pharmaceutical industry.

8. Contribution 151 of the Social Platform.

Commission, either regarding sector-based policies under the aegis of the Directorates General, or on a broader level, such as for this consultation on European governance as a whole. But this space was not only one of bilateral relations between the organisations and the European Commission. Because the consultation addressed a general issue, and because the contributions were published online as they were received, relationships were established between the organisations structuring EU lobbying.

The constitution of relationships between organisations

The European Commission and the main stakeholders presented the ETI as an institutional response to an open letter of the Corporate Europe Observatory (CEO), and 50 civil society groups, that denounced the excessive influence of 'industrial lobbies' and their hidden ties with EU institutions. CEO asked the new Commission to take measures in order to stop two types of practices they judged anti-democratic: first, the covert actions of some lobbyists (acting on behalf of fronts or fake NGOs); secondly, the Commission's alleged privileged relationship with business affairs.[9] Effectively, a few months later, on the 3rd March 2005, in Nottingham, Commissioner Kallas spoke of the need for transparency in such matters.[10]

Yet, this presentation, which emphasised the importance of the CEO, overlooked other attempts by the same organisation, which, since its inception during the Amsterdam summit to promote with others organisations a 'Europe of the citizens' (Weisbein 1999), had ceaselessly denounced these dangerous liaisons and asked for measures to end them. Jens Nymand-Christensen, the Director in charge of civil society relations, initially replied that nothing needed to be changed.[11] However, the CEO's claims were noted and used by the European Commission, first because they matched the preoccupations of the Commissioners, Margot Wallström in charge of institutional affairs, and Siim Kallas in charge of administrative affairs, eager to 're-establish trust in Europe by bringing EU institutions closer to the citizens'. Claiming to be a 'research and campaign group targeting the threats to democracy, equity, social justice and the environment posed by the economic and political power of corporations and their lobby groups',[12] the CEO appeared as an organisation likely to support the EU's policy of communication and 'democratisation' (Kauppi 2007). Secondly, because it worked with some fifty organisations active in the EU and made concrete proposals

---

9. Letter dated the 25th October 2004, published on the CEO website and on the former website of Commissioner Kallas: http://ec.europa.eu/archives/commission_2004–2009/kallas/work/eu_transparency/index_en.htm.

10. 'The need for a European transparency initiative', speech by Siim Kallas, The European Foundation for Management, Nottingham Business School, Nottingham, the 3rd March 2005.

11. Letter dated the 17th November 2004.

12. According to the presentation of the organisation on their website: http://www.corporateeurope.org.

to remedy the excesses it denounced, the CEO showed resources that interested the EU administration. They were no longer dealing with activists organising European counter-summits or agitators. The organisation seemed structured, with networks and members able to debate with the political-administrative personnel of the European Commission in their own terms, to some extent. Thus, more than a response to claims, the ETI was a European policy that relied on organisations that were promoted as agenda setters as well as implementers. This enrolment happened of course with the complicity of the CEO leaders, who knew very well that furthering their cause entailed such instrumentalisation. They subsequently went further in the same direction by structuring their network of NGOs in a new organisation, more European in terms of the positions of its member organisations, ALTER-EU, which was founded a few months after the launch of the ETI.

This form of promotion of organisations was not specific to the ETI. All of the sectors covered by the Directorates General (DG) of the European Commission sought privileged interlocutors and therefore promoted organisations. When no interest groups seemed to exist, the Commission did not hesitate to help financially and symbolically in creating and structuring them. But in the case of the ETI, while this process occurred, it came with another process of dialogue between organisations that also generated the constitution and the structuring of new organisations. Existing organisations responded to the consultation first and foremost to react to the CEO's proposals.

Subsequently, other organisations were created, nuancing the debate and making it more complex. For CEO spokesman Erik Wesselius, it was time to shed light on some lobbyists' shady dealings and impose rules of conduct complying with the requirements of democracy. He called for a system of compulsory registration and scrutiny of lobbyists, inspired by what existed in the US and Canada, and took the opportunity to denounce the inefficiency of the code of conduct promoted by SEAP, the Society of European Affairs Professionals, which was neither compulsory nor binding. The latter, which at the time of ETI's launch was the only organisation of professional lobbyists in Brussels, answered to the CEO on all topics, relying on arguments that had already proved successful in the early 1990s, when the European Parliament and Commission had envisioned regulating lobbying.[13] For SEAP, the profession already worked with transparency and according to ethical rules, guaranteed by a code of conduct followed by its 210 members and by criminal law. Furthermore, they argued that the system of compulsory registration following the pattern of the US Lobbying Disclosure Act would not be suited to Brussels. Yet, within SEAP, some members found this position overly defensive, failing to promote the profession sufficiently. While then President Roger Chorus was striving to make SEAP mirror the diversity of interest representatives,

---

13. In 1992, the Commission published a paper on 'An open and structured dialogue between the European Commission and special interest groups'; the Parliament set up in the Rules of Procedure of the European Parliament, Rule 9 'Members' financial interests, standards of conduct and access to Parliament' and adopted a code of conduct.

whether they worked for a consultancy, a trade and business association, like him, or an NGO, these members created another association dedicated to defending lobbyists working in consultancies. The European Public Affairs Consultancies Association (EPACA) stepped into the debate and defended the specificity of consultants in the lobbying world and the difficulty, even the impossibility for them to follow the proposals for transparency. On the one hand, consultancies were companies whose clients did not necessarily wish that their recourse to professionals be known to everyone; on the other hand, the services they offered did not necessarily concern influencing political decision makers. That said, these consultancies were competing to increase their market shares and their leaders would welcome the introduction of a regulation system that would protect them from their competitors. Some, from the biggest consultancies in Brussels (Hill and Knowlton, Weber Shandwick, Euralia...), were in favour of creating a professional body, following the lawyers' model. This would be a way to regulate access to the profession and defend professional confidentiality. Others, with fewer resources, were reluctant to accept such a regulation. But the idea of a register centralising all professionals interested those who saw in it a commercial tool for developing their activities. Christian de Fouloy, a French-American lobbyist, who readily played on his double allegiance to two very distinct lobbying traditions, founded a few days after the launch of the ETI, the Association of Accredited Lobbyists to the European Parliament (AALEP). For him, the Commission's register could be a good thing, provided it would not merely amount to only registering lobbyists, as the European Parliament already did, but if it also provided information (on experience, speciality, success...) to anyone seeking the services of a lobbyist to defend their interests in order to help them in their choice. The register would work as a directory of professionals located in Brussels or other capitals, in which they could publicise the fields in which they specialise and thereby attract clients.

Hence, different points of view were defended by organisations that were sometimes created for the occasion. Indeed, in the consultation process, the Commission tended to grant more importance to the contributions sent by organisations, and among them, to those who could claim to represent a sector, a category of professionals or a cause. Failing that, the contribution was classified as an 'individual' one and did not elicit similar interest. Christian de Fouloy had first-hand experience of this, as it was only after the AALEP was created that his contribution, no longer sent in his own but now in a collective's name (Boltanski, Darré and Schiltz 1984:12), was taken into account in the debate on the ETI. The consultation thus contributed to multiply the number of organisations representing the multiplicity of points of views: this is how the Commission produced pluralism.

Organisations were also formed following another process. As the consultation was online, each stakeholder was able to have updated information on the state of the debate and the others' positions. As each organisation could only provide their input on the Green Paper once, if an organisation that had already sent its contribution wished to respond to another's arguments, it had to do so under a new entity – which was actually why many organisations waited until the last days to participate. Admittedly, the organisations responding to the consultation had busy agendas, and they needed time to debate internally with their partners to elaborate a common position. But waiting until the others have responded in order to have the last word was also a sound strategy. Accordingly, the contributions must be read as a double response: to the questions raised by the European Commission, and to the other contributions. When observing the chronological order of the contributions on the website, beyond the type of organisations that have sent them, one can clearly notice that there was a dialogue between organisations, with two clans debating under the guise of various organisations. Again, organisations were often created or reactivated for the occasion.

Indeed, if the contributions remained intentionally generalist and were written in a somewhat listless style that perfectly suits this type of public consultation, they included numerous specific attacks aimed at specific organisations as well as answers to these covert jibes. For instance, the representatives of the European chemical industry, CEFIC, sent a contribution to the Secretariat-General that admittedly responded to the three main sections of the consultation, but was actually more of an answer to the attacks made by CEO on them[14] regarding their action during the process of adoption of the REACH regulation. Accused of misinformation, they felt they had to take a stance on transparency. After pointing out their role in the 'democratic process', they emphasised their 'professionalism': 'When using results from studies, CEFIC relies on the professionalism of well known consultants. Methodologies and hypotheses are made available, allowing stakeholders to challenge the results on the basis of sound information if appropriate'.[15] As if to explain and excuse actions that may have seemed out of line, they emphasised how difficult it had been for them, when the REACH regulation was adopted, to strictly comply with the general principles of consultation applied by the European Commission. Whether they were explicitly named, such as David Earnshaw, a lobbyist with Burson-Marsteller, or indirectly targeted by accusations regarding their consultancy, such as Weber Shandwick or Hill & Knowlton, the consultants publicly concerned by the allegations posted on the CEO's website could not remain indifferent. EPACA enabled them to respond to these attacks indirectly by turning the argument around towards NGO representatives:

> EPACA believes the term 'public interest organization' should be applied in a more selective fashion, as it can run counter to the objectives of transparency and be used as a flag of convenience by those seeking a special status for their lobbying activities.[16]

---

14. See for instance, CEO's accusations about CEFIC, nominated for the Worst EU Lobbying Awards in 2006, for the organisation's alleged misinformation during the adoption of the REACH regulation (information ad published in European Voice on the 19th October 2006 (http://www. worstlobby.eu/runnersup.php). See also 'BulldozingREACH – the industry offensive to crush EU chemicals regulation' http://www.corporateeurope.org/lobbycracy/BulldozingREACH.html.

15. Contribution 75 of CEFIC, p.2.

16. Contribution 20 of EPACA.

They also took the opportunity to promote their professional code of conduct. For their part, the members of the CEO countered by attempting to demonstrate the inefficiency of self-regulation, through Friends of the Earth Europe (FOEE) and ALTER-EU, of which the CEO was a founding member. Thus, not only did the consultation allow all the organisations to make their voice heard at the European Commission, in the hope it was taken into account, it also allowed them to respond to each other, albeit indirectly, following a process of exchange and one-upmanship.

Due to the embedding of the various entities participating in the consultation and to the multi-positionality of the representatives, the contributions did not come from sources as varied as the acronyms and logos of the authors to respons-es to the Green Paper, as some would have us believe. For instance, Athenora Consulting, a consultancy that sent a contribution in their own name, was also a member of EPACA, and their director, Stéphane Desselas, was personally affili-ated with SEAP. The same went for the coalition led by CEO's Erik Wesselius, a member of ALTER-EU's steering committee, which he contributed to creating with Paul de Clerck, a representative of Friends of the Earth Europe.[17] Both very active in the transparency process, they took part in the consultation by send-ing contributions, sometimes alternatively signed CEO, FoEE and ALTER-EU. The embedding of networks and structures, far from leading to an increase of the number of positions, gave way to a form of rationalisation of the represent-atives' work within these different organisations. To make economies of scale, time and energy, those in charge of responding to the consultation within a given structure, had often already worked, or were working, on similar consultations (Convention on the Future of Europe, White Paper on European Governance, Plan D for Democracy…). For the same reasons, they were entrusted with the task of responding to the consultation in the name of another structure. This was the case for the Secretary-General of CEDAG, also a board member of the Social Platform, who, along with others, contributed to setting up the Civil Society Contact Group (CSCG) and was actively involved in the EESC Civil Society liaison group. Thanks to his many positions, he helped disseminate information and arguments from one organisation to the other. Crucially, he was the one who drafted position papers on the subject for each of these organisations, making small adjustments according to their specific identities. Indeed, the organisations strove to highlight their differences, if not among one another, at least between the different networks to which they belonged and identified themselves with: 'environmentalists', 'so-cial, charity organisations', 'industrial lobbyists'.

This formalisation of the interests was indispensable to the constitution of the organisations and their identification to a specific style and specific positions, but it should not let us overlook the fact that these organisations were first and fore-most forms of expression of interests and modes of action of their defenders. It

---

17. Created on 18th May 2005, this ad hoc coalition was the formalised grouping of all the organisations that had supported and signed the open letter addressed to Mr Barroso. http://www.alter-eu.org/

was, indeed, the European Commission that contributed to promoting this 'interest group' form and its development: the more the organisations and the stances they supported were numerous, the more the Commission could make claims to 'openness' and pluralism, two dimensions it was eager to highlight. But upon closer scrutiny, this pluralism effectively resulted more from a build-up by the interest group representatives, who were ultimately not that many. They played several parts at once, according to the organisations with which they were involved or in which they worked, to best meet the expectations of the European Commission.

Ultimately, the proliferation of interest groups did not mean so much a proliferation of interests; rather, it stemmed from strategies by both interest representatives and the European Commission to produce opinions that could be seen as the expression of interests.

Lobbying as good practice

With the consultation, two types of organisations disputed the definition of good lobbying practices and the way to promote them. On the one hand, organisations such as CEO, LobbyControl, ALTER-EU, which included among others Greenpeace, Friends of the Earth, Green Group of 10 and other associations like ATTAC all emphasised their commitment against 'market forces'. On the other hand, representatives of private interests were defended by SEAP, AALEP or EPACA, and their interests matched those of the companies or industrial sectors they defended. During the consultation, a dialogue was opened between those two sides, fighting on two main themes: first, the question of the existence and of the form of a register which would amount to closing or opening up EU lobbying; secondly, the question of the regulation of the profession, which raised the problem of the autonomy of lobbyists from EU institutions. The debate, however, did not really involve the organisations, but rather the individuals who, within them, worked on these position papers. What was expressed in these contributions were ultimately different conceptions of what Europe and European governance were – and these conceptions could only be understood in light of these interest representatives' properties, career paths and experiences of Europe.

Opening or closing up EU lobbying

the problem of the registration of lobbyists was nothing new. Since the late 1980s, the European Commission, unlike the European Parliament, had refused the system of accreditation of interest groups, preferring by far an 'open' system. For the Secretariat-General members in charge of this question, this was the only way of avoiding a selection of the organisations according to criteria that appeared to them extremely hard to define. Thus, the Commission could not risk missing any contributions that might be of interest and could use interest groups in a utilitarian, even strategist manner. With the ETI, the Commission's open policy started to evolve, as if facing the increase in the number of organisations and the – sometimes real – risk of being cheated, such an approach had found its limitations. The Green Paper then raised the question of the access, not so much to the institutions – which emphasised openness and participation as 'good governance' principles – but to the lobbyists and the organisations they represented. It called stakeholders to make proposals to map out and organise this intermediary space between the institutions as such and European citizens. In this sense, the implementation of the register of interest representatives and of the code of conduct tended to delimitate and close up this space. On these two tools, the respondents expressed contrasted reactions.

We might have expected to find that supporters of the Commission's open policy, the organisations that were used to working closely with the Commission's services, in working groups, consultative boards or ad hoc committees – be they NGO networks, professional associations or consultancies – would have supported the conclusions of the Green Paper. As they largely benefited from the current system (non-compulsory registration and non-binding code of conduct), they did not have an interest in changing the rules of the game, especially as, given their status as authorised interlocutors – virtually institutional for some – they had nothing to fear from competition by newcomers in the space of interest representation. One could have assumed that they were in favour of an open, weakly regulated system. For consultancies and other professional lobbyists, voluntary registration on a public register already occurred with the publication of the members of EPACA and SEAP. Lastly, we might have expected civil society organisations to have no interest or will to go against the European Commission's proposals, as the latter supported them financially and symbolically.

Following the same line of thought, we might also have assumed that the organisations that were on the fringes of this group, neither funded nor officially recognised as regular interlocutors, providing specialised expertise in various technical domains, would have asked for resources to stabilise and close up the competition. This could have explained the radical attitude of CEO or ALTER-EU, two newcomers in the space of representation that did not necessarily benefit from the same advantages as other NGOs in their work with the Commission. For them, a compulsory register would have been a means to limit access to this space, and consequently to limit the competition between organisations, among which the weakest (in terms of financial, human and logistical resources) would have been the first to suffer. It would also have been a means to institutionalise the barely formalised ties between institutions and interest groups and go further than the CONECCS database in the recognition of organisations. Registration would thus have amounted not only to making information on the nature and funding of the organisation public, but also to provide guarantees on its reliability and compliance with the rules of the EU game. The position of AALEP President Christian de Fouloy, would be a good illustration of this: evidently a fringe character within the profession, a 'free rider' as he defined himself, he defended the merits of compulsory, and even paying, registration. This would have proven immediately beneficial for professionals, since the public and anyone requiring the services of lobbyists could have, thanks to this register, contacted the professionals depending on their speciality and their field of expertise.

Yet, the different contributions sent to the Secretariat-General did not reflect this interpretation based on the initial reactions to the Green Paper. As the consultation went on, the space of positions grew more complex. Within non-lucrative organisations, many major platforms, quite involved in legislative work, questioned the Commission's proposal. Arguing that 'self-regulation doesn't work', they asked for compulsory registration of lobbyists. This was the case, for instance, of the Civil Society Contact Group, which agreed with the CEO and the Social Platform on this point. Conversely, representatives in weaker positions, or speaking on behalf of the weakest associations, violently opposed the setting up of a register that could help them strengthen their position. As a consultant who worked within a structure that assisted and supports associations pointed out:

> A register contributes to closing rather than opening up the debate. It would suggest that it is always the same organisations that intervene in all the consultations. This is the opposite of participative democracy and openness [...].[According to her] such measures might turn off those who might have been eager to take a constructive interest in Europe, without discouraging the small minority of crooked lobbyists they target[18] .

In the same perspective, adhering to a code of conduct in order to be able to be heard by the EU institutions,

> does not bring openness; rather it closes up the European institutions: it implies excluding those who have not signed the code, and are supposedly dishonest, even though they might not have been able to do so because their action with the EU is occasional and specific, or because their approach of the institutions is not aimed at lobbying, but at exchanging information (where is the boundary?).[19]

Among lobbyists, there were similarly contrasting positions. Some, like this member of the Athenora consultancy, pushed for the creation of a professional order as a 'useful response to the specificities of the profession, quite similar to those of lawyers: professional confidentiality, scrutiny over the compliance with deontological rules, initial and continuing training'.[20] On the strength of their professional achievements, they strove to reassert the image of their profession, considered as an occupation like any other, with specific competencies that could be attested by a degree or a certain amount of professional experience. Others, who were in the majority, defended a much more open conception of the profession

---

18. Contribution 135 from Laurence Wattier, consultant and training officer with ID's – Information Diffusion Europe Associations (my translation).
19. Contribution 135 from Laurence Wattier.
20. Contribution 163 of Athenora Consulting.

that they claimed better suited the reality of their job, consisting in developing ties between the business world and the political and administrative world. This conception did suit the lobbyists who, throughout their careers, moved between different professional spaces: between administration and interest representation, between economic sectors, between legal work and communication or between organisations with different goals and vocations. This was the case of an EPACA member, who had held managerial positions in the European Commission before he was brought into Jacques Delors' cabinet, and who in the late 1980s founded his own public affairs consultancy aimed at businesses, and who also founded a European think tank defined as reformist. Likewise, the Secretary General of a professional association initially worked in his country's administration before he went to 'the other side', but did not rule out moving on to a different industrial sector. Defining themselves first as intermediaries between different worlds that they had to connect, lobbyists favoured a system that remains loose, without compulsory registration or observance of a code of conduct.

This conception of lobbyism suited quite well those who worked permanently in the European networks of NGOs, which often had professional experience in the EU institutions before moving to work in NGOs, furthering their career from one organisation to the next. On the question of the opening up of the professional space, their appreciation of the Commission's proposals largely matched the positions of some leading members of SEAP or EPACA. This was for instance the case of some members of the Social Platform who, while they emphasised the need for compulsory registration for all lobbyists, seemed to seek out means of keeping the EU lobbying open. They favoured a self-regulated system in which the stakeholders, under the aegis of the Commission, would themselves establish the basic rules.[21]

Thus, in this debate on the registration of lobbyists and the implementation of a code of conduct, two conceptions of the profession of lobbyist squared off: the first considered that lobbying was a profession, and as such, it must organise itself with rules for access and practice, and the other considered that this was an activity of intermediaries, which must therefore remain open. The first conception tended to be defended by professionals who got most of their work from relationships established with private clients. They had often worked in business and continued their management activities within their consultancies. The second conception was promoted by interest representatives that were very well integrated into EU institutions and whose activities consisted first and foremost in working in partnership with the European Commission. Heavily dependent on the institutional agenda, of Community funding, embedded in a Brussels' activity, they were also sociologically close to the agents of the EU civil service, as they had done the same studies, socialised in the same circles and lived in the same neighbourhoods.

---

21. Contribution 151 of the Social Plateform.

The question of the autonomy of EU lobbying

Beyond the question of the register and of the code of conduct, a certain conception of the European political field and of the legitimate practices within this field was at stake. The issue of the regulation of lobbying was linked to the role played by the European Commission in structuring and organising EU lobbying.

For all respondents to the consultation, avoiding fraud and corruption was an obvious necessity. This was what the CEO inferred from various investigative surveys; consultants came to the same conclusion, as, eager to promote a good image of their profession, they reflected on their own practices, like this member of Athenora Consulting:

> We should be careful not to let techniques derived from the economic war and whose legitimacy is sometimes tolerated in the business world extend to the sphere of lobbying, which concerns public decision-making. The ongoing discussions on economic intelligence allow us to lay the groundwork by distinguishing monitoring and spying, information and propaganda, criticising and smearing, grey and black literature, reasonable use of the Internet and massive unaddressed campaigns, confusion or transparency of the interest represented...[22]

Professionals of lobbying and NGO activists thus agreed on the basics. However, they did not favour the same means to prevent and punish actions that would be considered at odds with professional ethics. Whereas professionals gathered in EPACA and SEAP proposed a system of self-regulation of the profession, with an internal supervisory committee liable to, if necessary, rule on cases reported and sanction offenders to the code, for their part, members of CEO and ALTER-EU, joined by other civil society organisations, emphasised the fact that self-regulation did not work and asked the European Commission to issue rules of conduct with which lobbyists must comply to avoid sanctions. This was, on the surface, an instance of an opposition between on the one hand the private sector, which wanted no public interference in business and dismissed any 'bureaucratisation of lobbying', to use an often heard phrase, and on the other, the public sector, which believed in the virtues of public authorities to guarantee a fair and even-handed monitoring and see that the common good was promoted.

Yet, it was not that simple an opposition. All NGOs did not ask the Commission to impose a regulation system. Some, like the European Consumers' Organisation, called for a third party, which could be the Ombudsman, to act as a regulatory and monitoring body:

> The register should be managed by an independent body, such as the European Ombudsman. This independent body should also have the responsibility

---

22. Contribution 163 of Athenora Consulting (my translation).

for monitoring that the information provided is true and correct. This should be done by undertaking regular spot checks. Obviously the register must be open to everyone to see, inspect and challenge, when appropriate.[23]

Among the consultants, all those who called for the creation of a professional order knew very well that they would not be able to do without public authorities, the only guarantors of the legitimacy and capacity for action of that order. This apparent cleavage between private and public sectors seemed to obscure another that enables us to better understand the differences in the positions, and ultimately, in what was at stake in their confrontation.

All of the contributions from NGOs in favour of a public control of lobbying referred to a State system, mostly the US with the Lobbying Disclosure Act but also Canada, whose system of registration of lobbyists was mentioned in the White Paper, and Member States such as Poland or Lithuania. None of them wished to introduce such a system at the European level. The Abramoff scandal that shook the Republican Party in the US clearly showed that a registration system did not preclude corruption or influence peddling. Their contributions were informed by a State-centred view of political power, insofar as a central authority holding a monopoly over legitimate constraint guaranteed the autonomy of the political field. Transposed to the EU level, this conception of power led them to seek a strong leadership, if not from the European Commission, at least from EU institutions, particularly in the definition of the boundaries of the political space and of the legitimate conditions to access it, such as elections or designation following criteria of representativeness for the intermediary organisations associated with the elaboration and implementation of public policy. The contribution of the European Trade Union Confederation was very clear on this point: 'This register must not be managed by private organisations. It must be solely managed by institutional actors [...] If we want to avoid pressure, conflicts of interest, only the EU institutions are liable to assume such a function.' (my translation)[24] According to its representatives, the problems with lobbying listed in the Green Paper were caused by the Commission's systematic recourse to large-scale consultations, which had failed to take into account the question of who contributes and how the contributions are taken into account. They regretted that the Commission did not intend to define criteria of representativeness for the NGOs it worked with – hence the reference to '[their] actions as European social partners [which] have always been transparent and controlled'[25]. UNICE, though it supported the idea of a voluntary register so as not to 'create unnecessary bureaucratic burdens', also seemed to be in favour of a control exerted by a public or at least external authority, as its very ambiguous response showed: 'Sanctions should only be the ultimate recourse and

23. Contribution 141 of BEUC.
24. Contribution 123 of ETUC, p.5.
25. ETUC 123: 5

in case of a serious breach of the code, the Ombudsman or a committee of wise men could be called upon, for instance'.[26] It might seem strange that the social partners, usually not prone to supporting NGOs, should find themselves alongside ALTER-EU and CEO. But their common critique – formulated for different reasons – of the culture of 'participative democracy' and the recourse to consultation it entailed,[27] promoted by the European Commission, amounted to a more global critique of 'European governance'.

Indeed, their opponents who promoted the self-regulation of 'lobbyists' also defended, between the lines, a 'governance' system characterised by the absence of a hierarchy between private actors and public authorities and by the interdependency between these various actors, from which they had largely benefited until then. Among these organisations, there were professionals of lobbying, eventually satisfied by this opening up to 'civil society' of which they had become part (see Michel 2008), but also some representatives of major NGO networks, well versed in the rules of the game of a 'governance' they had contributed to defining and promoting during the elaboration of the 2001 White Paper. They were not in the majority within these organisations who signed contributions in favour of a public scrutiny over lobbying activities. But their voices mattered and they made the organisations' claims much less radical, even quite conciliatory towards the Commission's proposals. These interest representatives had pursued careers at the European level, in various institutions and organisations of the business world and in European platforms. They seemed to have largely benefited from both the openness of the EU lobbying and the European Commission's consultation policy developed since the late 1990s. Conversely, those who had come to Brussels to continue careers as representatives, that they began at the local and/or national level, were more readily shocked by such a functioning wherein, according to them, the rules remained unclear. The question of the regulation of lobbying also brought back the question of the nature of political power at the European level, as the contribution of the European Liaison Committee on Services of General Interest (CELSIG), which criticised the liberal conception at work, suggested:

Voluntary codes of conduct, without it being clear who is in charge of enforcing them, may remind us of the attitude of the 'fox loose in the henhouse'. On their own, these codes cannot suffice. Clear, legally binding legislative rules are also necessary.[28]

But in a European field where 'governance' was no longer a matter under discussion, claims in favour of a regulation of lobbying could only lead to the implementation of a voluntary system of registration of the actors and of recommendations on their conduct (COM 2007). Indeed, for the Commission, 'better regulation' no longer entailed binding rules, but the 'accountability' of the actors of governance, which guaranteed trust between the EU institutions and the so-called

---

26. Contribution 49 of UNICE, p.2

27. On the implementation of 'civil dialogue', see Michel (2007a and 2007b).

28. Contribution 154 of CELSIG (my translation).

civil society organisations. Fundamentally, the European Transparency Initiative, and those who were involved in its process, promoted a conception of the EU, of its actors and of the way it worked.

Conclusion

Ultimately, my sociological analysis of the consultation on the European Transparency Initiative has shown how EU lobbying was co-produced by the European Commission and by interest groups eager not to be excluded from their relations with EU institutions. I have also shown under which conditions these institutions will take into account these interests. Not only do they have to be organised and traced back to an organisation and representatives, they also have to be expressed in the administrative forms favoured by the EU administration in its online consultations. Indeed, not playing the game of consultation means not being able to formalise one's claims in a position paper that addresses the key topics of the Green Paper, and thus being excluded from this set of stakeholders and more largely of the interactions with EU institutions. However, those who have the resources and the skills to meet the European Commission's expectations can be a part of it and, together with the institutions, define the rules of the game. Interest groups are then not so much organisations that try to apply pressure on institutions, as ones that are selected and shaped by these institutions to contribute to defining and managing the actors of European lobbying. This sociological perspective leads us to focus on those who, within the organisations and behind the organisations' institutional facades, shape and voice their claims (Offerlé 1998). I have shown that the same representatives can lead and represent several organisations simultaneously, be they consultants for several clients, Secretary Generals in different professional federations, or holders of positions in several NGOs. The diversity of these organisations does not necessarily match the diversity of distinct interests. I have demonstrated that their skill in producing position papers liable to elicit interest and support in members of EU institutions is related to their social, geographic and cognitive proximity with them. Despite what is said about the mobilisation led by CEO and ALTER-EU, these activists were very much involved in European affairs and shared a similar conception of the EU with the civil servants in charge of the transparency process. The consultation process of the ETI also turned out to be an opportunity to appraise and select the interest representatives who considered the European Union as constituting a European field of governance.

References

Bailey, F. (1969) *Stratagems and Spoils: A social anthropology of politics*, Oxford: Blackwell.

Balanyá, B. *et al.* (2000) *Europe Inc. Regional & Global Restructuring and the Rise of Corporate Power*, London: Pluto Press/CEO.

Balme, R. and Chabanet, D. (2008) *European Governance and Democracy: Power and protest in the EU*, Boulder: Rowman and Littlefield.

Basilien-Gainche, M. -L. (2009) 'Réflexions sur les outils juridiques de la transparence politique: une évaluation de l'Initiative européenne en matière de transparence', in P. Mbongo (ed.) *Le phénomène bureaucratique européen: Intégration européenne et 'technophobie'*, Bruxelles: Bruylant, pp. 42–57.

Becker, H. S. (1963) *Outsiders : Studies in the sociology of deviance*, New York: The Free Press of Glencoe.

Beyers, J., Eising, R. and Maloney, W. (2008) 'Researching interest group politics in Europe and elsewhere: much we study, little we know?', *West European Politics*, 31(6): 1103–1128.

Billet, S. (2007) 'The theologies of transparency in Europe: the limits and possibilities of 'fusion' in the EU transparency regime', *Journal of Public Affairs* 7(4): 319–330.

Blavoukos, S. and Pagoulatos, G. (2008) 'Enlargement waves' and interest group participation in the EU policy-making system: establishing a framework of analysis', *West European Politics*, 31(6): 1147–1165.

Boltanski, L., Darré, Y. and Schiltz, M. -A. (1984) 'La dénonciation', *Actes de la recherche en sciences sociales*, 51: 3–40.

Campana, A, Henry, E. and Rowell, J. (eds) (2007) *La construction des problèmes publics en Europe: Emergence, formulation et mise en instrument*, Strasbourg: Presses Universitaires de Strasbourg.

Chabanet, D. (2009) 'Les enjeux de la codification des groupes d'intérêt au sein de l'UE', *Revue française de science politique*, 59(5): 997–1019.

Coen, D. and Richardson, J. (eds) (2009) *Lobbying the European Union: Institutions, actors, and issues*, Oxford: Oxford University Press.

COM (2001) 428 final, European Governance White Paper.

— (2006) 194 final, Green Paper 'European Transparency Initiative'.

— (2007) 128, Communication from the Commission. Follow-up to the Green Paper 'European Transparency Initiative'

Dezalay, Y. (2007) 'De la défense de l'environnement au développement durable: L'émergence d'un champ d'expertise des politiques européennes', *Actes de la recherche en sciences sociales*: 166–167.

Dinan, W. and Miller, D. (2006) 'Transparency in EU Decision Making, Holding Corporations to account: Why the ETI needs mandatory lobbying disclosure', in T. Spencer and C. McGrath (eds) *Challenge & Response: Essays in public affairs & transparency*, Brussels: Landmarks, pp. 25–32.

Eising, R. (2007) 'The access of business interests to EU institutions: towards elite pluralism?', *Journal of European Public Policy* 14(3): 384–403.

—— (2009) *The Political Economy of State-Business Relations in Europe: Interest mediation, capitalism and EU policy making*, London: Routledge.

Georgakakis, D. and de Lassalle, M. (eds) (2007) *La nouvelle gouvernance européenne: genèse et usages politiques d'un livre blanc*, Strasbourg: PUS.

Goffman, E. (1959) *The Presentation of Self in Everyday Life*, New York: Anchor Books.

Grant, J. (1998) 'What Drives Associability at the EUropean level? The limits of the utilitarian explanation', in M. Aspinwall and J. Greenwood (eds) *Collective Action in the European Union*, London: Routledge, pp. 31–62.

Greenwood, J. (1998) 'The regulation of lobbying', *Parliamentary Affairs* 51(4): 487–599.

—— (2007) *Interest Representation in the European Union*, Basingstoke, New York: Palgrave Macmillan.

—— (2011) 'The lobby regulation element of the European Transparency Initiative: between liberal and deliberative models of democracy', *Comparative European Politics*, (9): 317–343.

Harris, P. and Danny, M. (2001) 'Understanding public affairs', *Journal of Public Affairs*, 1(1): 6–8.

Janos, B. (2009) 'Lobbying: what framework for enhancing transparency?', *Zeitschrift für Politikberatung*, 2(1): 124–132.

Jobert, B. and Kohler-Koch, B. (2008) *Changing Images of Civil Society: From protest to government*, London: Routledge.

Jobert, B. and Muller, P. (1987) *L'Etat en action: Politiques publiques et néocorporatismes*, Paris: PUF.

Kauppi, N. (2005) *Democracy, Social Resources and Political Power in the European Union*, Manchester: Manchester University Press.

—— (2007) 'Légitimation politique et espaces publics européens: la communication comme pratique et ressource', in A. Campana, E. Henry and J. Rowell (eds) *La construction des problèmes publics en Europe: Emergence, formulation et mise en instrument*, Strasbourg: Presses Universitaires de Strasbourg, pp.137–153.

Kohler-Koch, B. and Eising, R. (eds) (1999) *The Transformation of Governance in the European Union*, London: Routledge.

Kohler-Koch, B. and Rittberger, B. (2006) 'The "Governance Turn" in EU studies', *Journal of Common Market Studies*, 44: 27–49.

Legris, G. and Lehmann, B. (2008) 'L'initiative européenne de transparence et l'encadrement des activités de lobbyisme par la Commission européenne', *Revue du droit de l'Union européenne* 4: 815.

Lehmann, W. (2009) 'The European Parliament', in D. Coen, D. and J. Richardson (eds) *Lobbying the European Union: Institutions, actors, and issues*, Oxford: Oxford University Press, pp. 39–69

Lodge, J. (1994) 'Transparency and democratic legitimacy', *Journal of Common Market Studies*, 32(3):343–367.

Mahoney, C. (2008) *Brussels Versus the Beltway: Advocacy in the United States and the European Union*, Washington D.C.: Georgetown University Press.

Mazey, S. and Richardson, J. (eds) (1999) *Interest Intermediation in the EU: Filling the hollow core*, London: Routledge.

Michel, H. (ed.) (2005) *Lobbyistes et lobbying de l'union européenne: Trajectoires, formations et pratiques des représentants d'intérêts*, Strasbourg: PUS.

— (2007a) 'La démocratie participative à la Commission européenne: une chance pour les groupes d'intérêt ? Le Livre blanc sur la gouvernance européenne à l'épreuve', in C. Neveu (ed.) *Cultures et pratiques participatives: perspectives comparatives*, Paris: L'Harmattan, pp.157–173.

— (2007b) 'Les groupes d'intérêt et la consultation sur le Livre Blanc: objectivation et institutionnalisation de 'la société civile', in D. Georgakakis and M. de Lassalle (eds) *La nouvelle gouvernance européenne: genèse et usages politiques d'un livre blanc*, Strasbourg: PUS, pp 235–253.

— (2008) 'Incantations and Uses of Civil Society by the European Commission', in B. Jobert and B. Kohler-Koch (eds) *Changing Images of Civil Society: From protest to government*, London: Routledge, pp. 107–119.

— (2009) 'Le syndicalisme dans la "gouvernance" européenne. Formes de représentation et pratiques de défense des intérêts sociaux en questions', *Politique européenne* 27: 129–152.

— (2010) 'The Construction of a European Interest through Legal Expertise: Property owners associations and the Charter of Fundamental Rights', in M. Mangenot and J. Rowell (eds) *A Political Sociology of Europe: Reassessing constructivism*, Manchester: Manchester University Press, pp 128–145.

Michel, H. and Courty, G. (2012) 'Groupes d'intérêt et lobbyistes dans l'espace politique européen: des permanents de l'eurocratie', in D. Georgakakis (ed.) *Le champ de l'eurocratie*, Paris: Economica, pp 213–240.

Naurin, D. (2008) *Deliberation Behind Closed Doors: Transparency and lobbying in the European Union*, Essex: ECPR Press.

Obradovic, D. (2009) 'Regulating Lobbying in the European Union', in D. Coen and J. Richardson (eds) *Lobbying the European Union: Institutions, actors, and issues*, Oxford: Oxford University Press, pp. 298–336.

Offerlé, M. (1998) *Sociologie des groupes d'intérêt*, Paris: Montchrestien.

Persson, T. (2007) 'Democratising European chemicals policy: do online consultations work in favour of civil society organisations?', *Journal of Civil Society*, 3(3): 223–238.

Peterson, J. (1995) 'Playing the transparency game: consultation and policy-making in the European Commission', *Public Administration*, 73 (3): 473–492.

Salisbury, R. H. (1969) 'An exchange theory of interest groups', *Midwest Journal of Political Science*, 13(1): 1–32.

— (1990) 'The Paradox of Interest Groups in Washington: More groups, less clouts', in A. King (ed.) *The New American Political System*, Maryland: University Press of America, pp. 203–229

Schattschneider, E. E. (1960) *The Semisovereign People: A realist's view of democracy in America*, New York: Holt, Rinehart and Winston.

Smith, A., Maillard, J. and Costa, O. (2007) *Vin et politique: Bordeaux, la France, la mondialisation*, Paris: Presses de Sciences Po.

Tilly, C. (1993) 'Contentious repertoires in Great Britain, 1758–1834', *Social Science History Publication Info*, 17(2): 253–280.

Weisbein, J. (1999) 'Les ONG et les associations face à la CIG de 1996: naissance d'une "société civile européenne"', *Politique et sécurité internationales*, 4: 6–17.

— (2007) 'Instituer la "société civile européenne": la contribution des mouvements fédéralistes. L'expérience du Forum permanent de la société civile', in D. Georgakakis and M. de Lassalle (eds) *La nouvelle gouvernance européenne: genèse et usages politiques d'un livre blanc*, Strasbourg: PUS, pp. 51–74.

Wesselius, E. (2005) 'High Time to Regulate EU Lobbying', *Consumer Policy Review*, 15(1):13–18.

chapter | fighting together: assessing
four | continuity and change in social
| movement organisations through
| the study of constituencies'
| heterogeneity[1]

Olivier Fillieule and Philippe Blanchard

There is today a rather large consensus among social movement scholars upon the idea that most protest movements and organisations are set in motion by social changes that render the established political order more vulnerable or receptive to challenge. Indeed, these 'political opportunities' are not likely to be grasped by potential challengers in the absence of sufficient organisation (so called 'mobilising structures') and shared emergent meanings and definitions (so-called 'framing processes') (McAdam, McCarthy and Zald 1996). However, the literature is less convincing in explaining the development of social movements. The promoters of the political process model themselves admit that if 'movements may largely be born of environmental opportunities, [...] their fate is heavily shaped by their own actions'. (McAdam, McCarthy and Zald 1996: 15) 'Organisational dynamics' remain to be specified and operationalised (Fillieule 1997, 2006; Goodwin and Jasper 2003)

In this chapter, we focus on the dynamics that may help us understand continuities and changes within protest groups. We define change here along three dimensions: Change in internal modes of organisation (e.g. leadership, recruitment policy), strategic and tactical choices (e.g. repertoires of action, alliances) and formation and transformation of collective identities, i.e. the way individuals internalise a vision of the world, of the place of the group in this world and one's place in this group, the way they incorporate or resist organisational modelling (e.g. Lichterman 1995; Whittier 1995). All these contribute to fix members' shared identities (Stryker, Owens, and White 2000; Polletta and Jasper 2001). Explanations of change and continuity in social movements generally fall into two broad categories.

1. The writing of this chapter has been facilitated by the invitations of the first author for a semester at the Department of Sociology at New York University and of the second author at the Department of Sociology at Penn State University, thanks to a Swiss National Science Foundation Postdoc grant. The authors thank the participants of the 'Protest and Politics' workshop at the City University of New York where a preliminary version of this chapter was presented and especially James Jasper for his valuable comments.

Macro structural approaches emphasise that movements change in response to shifts in available resources or external conditions. One can distinguish here two complementary traditions of research. Organisational approaches stress the characteristics of organisational structure, ideology, and culture that may help Social Movements Organisations (SMOs) to mobilise resources, (McCarthy and Zald 1977; Morris 1984) and maintain members' commitment in hostile and changing environments or through abeyance phases (Taylor 1989). Political process approaches seek to explain the effects of political opportunity structures on mobilisation cycles and repertoires (McAdam 1982; Tarrow 1994; Tilly 2008).

Micro structural approaches attempt to conceptualise the contribution of internal personnel processes to the transformation of social movements, adding to the factors emphasised by political process and organisational theories, the movements' internal dynamics of recruitment, lines of cleavages and collective identity. To date, these approaches have been less developed.[2] However, since the beginning of the 1990s, many writers in the cultural tradition shifted their attention to non-organisational factors of internal cleavages, such as ideologies, identities and consciousness, among others (Fantasia 1988; Gamson 1997; Jasper 1997; Steinberg 1999; Cohen 2000; Waite 2001; Armstrong 2002; Polletta 2002).[3] Two important traditions of research can be distinguished.

Firstly, feminist theory has played a central role in defining the intersecting nature of individual structural attributes and their complex effects on the internal dynamics of social movements. By placing at the heart of the analysis of activist groups, gender relationships and their articulation with other dominance relationships, this research convincingly demonstrates that protest movements experience the same principles of classification as the societies from which they come, even if they are seeking to transform them. In that sense they have constituted a Trojan horse against an epistemology of the individual subject fed by rational choice theories and based on the model of 'white middle-class men in Western capitalist systems' (Marx Ferree 1992: 36). As a result, feminist researchers have worked at length on the relationships between multiple dimensions and modalities of social relations and subject formations. They have demonstrated that symbolic power and material inequalities are rooted in relationships that are shaped by structural characteristics that can be defined in terms of class, race, gender, age and sexuality (e.g. Mohanty 1988; Crenshaw 1989; Stockdill 2003; McCall 2005; Filleule and Roux 2008).

Secondly, generational approaches have explored the fractures generated in a protest group by the succession of generations and generation units (Mannheim [1928] 1952). The basic idea is that if the persistence of committed long-time

---

2. Indeed, until the end of the 1980s, the irreducible heterogeneity of protest movements was only considered in organisational terms through distinguishing, vertically, between leaders and the mass of mobilised individuals (e.g. Piven and Cloward 1977) and, horizontally, between 'conscience constituents' and the mass of members/beneficiaries (e.g. McCarthy and Zald 1977).

3. See Ghaziani 2008, Chapter One, for a recent review of this literature.

participants secures continuity in social movements, recruitment and personnel turnover help produce change and are often the source of internal conflicts (Gusfield 1957; Freeman 1975; Evans 1979; Gitlin 1987; Rupp and Taylor 1987; Ginsburg 1989; Whittier 1995, 1997; Zwerman and Steinhoff 2005). Such an approach is of particular interest since it aims to link the political processes that shape recruitment and cycles of protest, to an analysis of interaction in micro-mobilisation contexts and the construction of collective identity. However, most of the time, generational approaches identify heterogeneity only through common period of entry into a SMO (i.e. micro-cohorts in the sense of Whittier 1997).

In this chapter, we follow the path opened by micro structural approaches that have attempted to conceptualise the contribution of internal personnel processes to the transformation of social movements. We argue that one must carefully examine, at the micro-sociological level, the fractures generated by diverse structural char-acteristics in order to understand continuities and changes within protest groups.[4] It is not only the historical and social movement context when individuals begin activism that defines lasting common political understandings, but also the dura-tion and intensity of commitment, as well as a complex mix of structural attributes and their ordering along time.

In what follows, we offer a more complex way of identifying movements' in-ternal lines of cleavages (what we call here heterogeneity) and their dynamics, in order to understand conflict and change within SMOs. We propose a method that offers the means, perhaps for the first time with quantitative data, to build a model in which the actual profiles of activists we isolate can fully account for how inter-individual distances and proximities are combined in reality to produce complex and overlapping groups defined by multiple intersecting affinities.

We draw on a case study of Aides, the oldest and largest French SMO mobilised against the AIDS epidemic, that was founded at the end of 1984 by Michel Foucault's partner, Daniel Defert.[5] We start by outlining a dynamic model of individual activ-ism in which the heterogeneity of protest groups depends on the *multisituated* and *processual* structural attributes of its members. We then develop a new methodology to empirically describe internal heterogeneity by applying sequence analysis (SA) to our data. We build a typology of profiles characterised by distinctive structural attributes. We show how the coexistence and succession of these profiles allow us to better understand the dynamic of continuity and change within the organisation.

---

4. Very classically, by structural characteristics, we mean the individual properties that, in a given social structure, generate divisions and classification of people and, as a consequence, hierarchisa-tion. A structural characteristic is defined then always in relation to a structural location of the individual, to a given structure of power relations, and is always translated into differentiated forms of acquisition of dispositions, objective positions and role expectations. Generally speaking, all the characteristics that determine differences in material and symbolic resources are structural. Thus, the fact of being a man or a woman constitutes a structural characteristic in an androcentric world, while differences in curly or straight hair—in most of the social world—generate neither division nor hierarchy.

5. Aides was initially conceived on the self-help and caring model of the Gay Men's Health Crisis (Altman 1988; Ouellette *et al.* 1995).

A dynamic model of individual activism

Our approach is rooted in a dynamic conception of activism that has been coined 'the sociology of activist careers' (e.g. Fillieule 2001, 2010; Sawicki and Siméant 2010). Activism in this model is defined as a long-lasting social activity that involves joining, committing, and defecting, in phases. Such a model is particularly helpful as a theoretical account of activist commitments that diachronically resituates them in the whole picture of individual life histories, as well as contextualising the coexistence of various activist profiles in SMOs. The expression 'activist career' refers directly to the Chicago School's interactionist tradition[6] and more precisely to the basic theoretical assumptions of 'symbolic interactionism'.[7] The concept of career pays attention to the permanent dialectic between individual history and social institutions. It aims at rebuilding,

> 'a sequence of steps, of changes in the individual's behavior and perspectives, in order to understand the phenomenon. Each step requires explanation, and what may operate as a cause at one step in the sequence may be of negligible importance at another step. [...] In a sense, each explanation constitutes a necessary cause of the behavior. [...] The explanation of each step is thus part of the explanation of the resulting behavior' (Becker 1966: 23).

Applied to political commitment, the notion of career allows us to understand how, at each stage of a biography, attitudes and behaviours are determined by past attitudes and behaviours, and in turn condition future possibilities, thus resituating the periods of commitment in the entire life cycle.

However, contemporary studies of careers too readily forget the extent to which methodological knowledge has evolved tremendously. Fifty years ago statistical studies were anathema to interactionists; this should no longer be the case. In reality, multivariate statistical analysis can be done using observations tracked over time that take into account changing conditions. Our conceptual framework will be operationalised by means of sequence analysis (SA), an approach rooted in Abbott and his colleagues' works in the sociology of professions (Abbott 1995) which has then been applied to a larger range of topics and also further developed (Dijkstra and Taris 1995; Elzinga 2003; Aisenbrey and Fasang 2007; Lesnard 2008; Gabadinho *et al.* 2009; Gauthier *et al.* 2009). To the efficient treatment of

---

6. See Gerth and Wright Mills 1954; Strauss 1959; Becker 1966.

7. Coined by Herbert Bulmer in 1937, 'symbolic interactionism' is closely linked to the social behaviourism of George Herbert Mead. Its subsequent usage belongs less to a school of thought than to a wide array of research sharing two standpoints: a common conception of the individuals and their relation to society, deeply rooted in the philosophical tradition of pragmatism; and a way of doing research inherited from the Chicago School of sociology. More precisely, symbolic interactionism can be defined as a micro sociological and processual approach, which systematically links the individual and the study of situations to broader contextual factors and social order rules and norms.

diachronic data (Abbott 1995: 95), we add three more assets to SA: a flexible handling of missing values and ill-categorised states, which are common in all longitudinal questionnaire studies; robustness to censorship and varying lengths of sequences, which are also common phenomena due to age variations and to unfinished careers at survey time; and the possibility to adjust the time period according to available data and to the research question. Inside the SA toolbox, the present study will rely particularly on optimal matching analysis and sequence plotting so as to operationalise our model of individual activism as *multisituated* and *processual*.

Multisituated structural attributes

Differences in structural characteristics are observable in activists' different tasks and functions, and in other life spheres. Anselm Strauss's (1959: 41–43) notion of *plurality* emphasises the actors' memberships in a number of other social worlds and subworlds as part of contemporary social life. In each of these spaces, individuals are led to adopt specific roles in which they are more or less 'stuck.' These define various contexts of socialisation.

From this, the idea arises that activist organisations are also comprised of individuals belonging to a multiplicity of social worlds and subworlds. As a consequence, they struggle with a need to abide by different, sometimes contradictory norms, rules and logic. Therefore the analysis of activist commitment must proceed through the identification of the 'individual's succession[s] of phases, changes in behavior and perspectives' (Becker 1966: 64). These critical moments change the expected reward in each sphere, which covaries with other areas. It is vital that we find the means to identify, in each life sphere, these 'critical moments' as points in time, to measure the length of the 'phases,' and finally to articulate the various spheres of life, since they interact. From this perspective, while the consideration of such indicators as 'biographical availability' (McAdam 1988) for overlapping roles, it remains too rough an indicator.

Current uses of optimal matching analysis (OMA) rarely try to grasp more than one life domain. Multiple-sequence analysis, also called multichannel analysis, remains a nearly virgin territory. [8] Our perspective implies four individual careers that compose each individual *biography*. The career in the organisation under study (being in or out, degree of involvement, status) is our central career. The career in one's sociosexual identity (sexual orientation and degree of disclosure to relatives and acceptance by them) is crucial because of the link between AIDS activism and the homosexual cause (56 per cent of the sample's members claim to be homosexuals). The career in AIDS (HIV status and degree of disclosure of it) is also important because the HIV positive status of many activists has direct consequences on their involvement, its meaning, and the activities in Aides (Broqua and

---

8. We will partly follow Pollock's methodological propositions (Pollock 2007, implemented in TraMineR, Gabadinho *et al.* 2010) and Gauthier *et al.* 2009 (implemented in Saltt).

Box 4.1: Multiple sequence analysis, step by step

Sequence analysis (SA) was imported in the 1980s from bio-computing to the social sciences as a pragmatic way of representing, comparing and clustering sequences. Sequences are defined as strings of states or events. In our case, sequences are individual trajectories inside Aides, in the socio-sexual career and in the relationship with AIDS. The core tool of SA is the optimal matching algorithm (OM), which compares two sequences, state by state, and calculates an index of dissimilarity or distance.

OM first defines an alphabet of states for each of the three careers. Each alphabet contains between seven and twelve states (including missing values). In the example below, our fictitious alphabet is composed of states A, B, C and D. Then, a cost is attributed to each elementary operation of transformation of states. Here, the deletion (del) or the insertion (ins) of a state costs 1, its substitution (sub) for another state costs 2, and the match (mat) of two identical states costs 0. Real studies usually keep insertions and deletions at the same constant value of 1. The decision on substitution costs between A and B may take three main options: set as a constant, like insertions and deletions; varying according either to the scarceness of empirical moves from A to B (the more common a transition, the cheaper its cost); or, depending on objective knowledge about the social cost of moving between A and B.

Using these cost settings, the OM algorithm finds the best aligning path, that is, the sequence of elementary operations that outputs the smallest total cost between S1 and S2. In this case, the cheapest path manages to 'align' the BBBC subsequence, made of four successive matches that have the advantage of costing zero. At the beginning of S1, two As have to be deleted, and in the end, a D is substituted for a C, then two Ds are inserted in S2. The total cost is 6. Any path that would miss the BBBC subsequence would need more substitutions, deletions and insertions, and therefore would cost more than 6.

Two sequences S1 and S2

S1	A	A	B	B	B	C	C
S2	B	B	B	C	D	D	D

Comparison of S1 and S2: total cost = 6

S1	A	A	B	B	B	C	C	X	X
S2	x	x	B	B	B	C	D	D	D
Operation	del	del	mat	mat	mat	mat	sub	ins	ins
Costs	1	1	0	0	0	0	2	1	1

Multiple SA uses three sets of costs. The three careers, referring to different realities and their alphabets are different as are their costs. The process of optimisation is similar as for single SA, with three pairs being examined at the same time: S1-S2, S1'-S2' and S1"-S2". At each step of the comparison, three elementary operations are used, one for each career. The optimal path to transform S1-S1'-S1" into S2-S2'-S2" is the one that minimises the whole cost.

This process is lead for all pairs of sequences inside the sample, that is N(N-1)/2 times. The outcome is an NxN matrix of distances between individuals. This matrix is symmetric around a diagonal made of zeros, which represents the distance of each case with itself. Then it is treated by means of a clustering algorithm. In our case, an ascending cluster algorithm aggregates individuals according to their respective profiles of distances with all the others. The more similar the profiles of distances of two cases, the more chances they have of ending up in the same cluster. We chose a ten-cluster typology (Table 4.1). Each cluster gathers activists whose threefold biographies resemble one another the most.

Fillieule 2001; Stockdill 2003; Gould 2010). Professional career is our fourth individual career. However, due to the lack of sufficiently precise longitudinal data, professional status will not be added to the combined analysis of the three former careers. We will use it as a supplementary variable in the final analysis.

Contrary to traditional regression models with *a priori* causal hypotheses, OMA does not split careers between independent and dependent factors. As a more descriptive approach to statistics, OMA searches for similar patterns in different biographies. This is done by comparing all possible pairs of biographies, year by year, on the whole period under study (see Box 4.1). The more similar two biographies are, the lower their *distance*. Using a hierarchical clustering procedure, biographies that are most similar are gathered in clusters.[9] Depending on the respondent's profile, one or two of the three domains might provide a more relevant explanation of the moment of his/her commitment, his/her change of status or his/her exit. But, at the final aggregated level, if appropriately

9. To sum up the SA method in a more technical fashion: inter individual distances equal the least expensive sum of costs among all possible successions of elementary operations – insertions, deletions, substitutions – in the three careers. Substitution costs are field-based objective costs (with pragmatic minor adjustments to help maximise clusters coherence), for three reasons: we already had a good knowledge of the data, having previously studied at length the organisation; studies of other complex datasets produced good results by relying on objective costs (e.g. Pollock 2007); comparing results from competing methods (uniform costs, transition rates and computer-based costs), this one reveals itself as more efficient and better adapted to our data. Insertion and deletion costs are set at a half of the mean of all substitution costs and substitution costs from all three matrices at each step. The pair comparison of all biographies outputs a N*N positive distance matrix that is processed through ascending, hierarchical cluster analysis, with Ward aggregation criteria applied to square Euclidean distances.

weighted, all three careers significantly contribute to the final result. On all three dimensions, the clusters of biographies are both distinguished clearly and have reasonable internal coherence, each relying on specific typical *multisituated sequences* (Gauthier 2007; Pollock 2007; Blanchard 2010).

Structural attributes in a process

Identifying the diachronic formation and reformation of structural attributes presents the greatest difficulties. Individual structural characteristics evolve over time.[10] We recognise however that biographical time, in combination with historical time, determines an objective structure of social opportunities for each structural characteristic at each stage. We must therefore go beyond static analyses of structural attributes and restore the temporal order of individual experiences. Two main issues arise.

First, most structural characteristics are not bestowed upon individuals but rather are sequentially acquired, the order of which partially determines their meaning. For example, how do we interpret people volunteering in the field of AIDS declaring themselves HIV-positive, if we do not consider the date at which this occurs? It is clear that, whether this occurs before, during, or after the period of involvement, radically affects the explanatory value of this fact. Most questionnaires fail to take temporal order into account, falsely inferring a causal relationship from correlations.

Secondly, structural positions may be better viewed from a relational perspective. The value of a structural position is derived from its commonality, how it compares to the experiences of others, its synchronism (coexistence) and antecedence. The link between structural attributes and structural locations (i.e. the social settings in which individuals are circulating) significantly reduces the explanatory power of analyses that correlate activist commitment with social characteristics identified in questionnaires or structured interviews. Indeed, any social characteristic (gender, age, income level, professional status and so on) lacks explanatory capacity if we do not resituate it in the 'configuration' (in the sense articulated by Norbert Elias) in which it develops and contributes to the creation of certain dis-

---

10. Which means that we do not consider that adolescence or young adultness are the sole formative periods in individuals' lives. Socialisation is here conceived as a continuous process (Strauss 1959; Berger and Luckmann 1966: chapter three), which means that commitments in protest organisations can be transformative at any age and that individual structural properties are always susceptible to change. We fully agree with Schneider (1988) and Whittier (1997) who argue that when it comes to women and their political socialisation in women's movements, age does not appear any more as the basis for defining the climax of transformative experiences because participation in the women's movement was, at any age, a strong vehicle for building a new way of seeing the world and one's own life. Gay and lesbian movements (Armstrong 2002; Ghaziani 2008) as well as AIDS volunteer groups (Broqua and Fillieule 2002; Stockdill 2003; Chambré 2006; Gould 2009), also play such a role and offer to committed people, irrespective of their position in the life-cycle, opportunities for 'institutionalised changes' and 'biographical ruptures' aimed at both acceptance of one's own stigma and one's visibility in the social world.

positions. In other words, the social characteristics of individuals are ambivalent. Their values (and explanatory power) change in conjunction with the system of interactions in which they are found.

The diachronic complexity of our biographies is an obvious challenge to OMA. Up to now, sociologists and demographers have usually analysed irreversible states or events, like leaving the educational system, marrying or having one's first child. Some of our careers do include irreversible events (becoming HIV positive, disclosing one's homosexuality to relatives) but others are reversible and/ or recurrent, like reducing or increasing the time one devotes to the organisation. Similarly, the three-career perspective increases combinatorial complexity: a specific biographical turning point central to a given cluster has to combine similar changes in all three careers at similar moments. Nonetheless, each of the final clusters gather activists that resemble each other regarding the different aspects of time involved: the nature of experiences the activists have lived, the length of these experiences, the order in which they went through them, and the combination of these three elements across the three careers. As a result, some more complex common subsequence's emerge in clusters, like turning points and recurrent experiences.

Another shortcoming of current uses of SA is that time is strictly conceived of as the succession of standard steps in one's life. Persons of different ages are compared in a non-historical, loosely contextualised perspective. By contrast, each activist's biographical time, formally identical to the time of other activists, is embedded in organisational and historical times. Moreover, these two enveloping times result in generational structures. Fortunately, SA addresses each of these time layers: biographical and organisational times are directly processed by OMA algorithms; biological time is induced by the cost of the minority, initial period, and by insertion-deletion costs; and, significant historical events, in and/or outside of Aides, materialise on sequence plots.

Data

We rely on a secondary analysis of data collected in the framework of a research project initiated in 1998 by Olivier Fillieule and Christophe Broqua (Fillieule and Broqua 2000, 2005; Broqua and Fillieule 2001). Whereas the initial research design compared the two biggest voluntary groups mobilised against AIDS (Aides and Act Up) using mixed quantitative and qualitative methods (life history interviews and ethnographic observation), the present analysis is based exclusively on a retrospective longitudinal self-administered mail survey of members of Aides. Thanks to access to the member directory granted by the organisation, a questionnaire was sent to all 1,969 members of Aides Ile-de-France (central region around Paris) in 1998.[11]

---

11. Aides started as a small Paris-based association. Chapters were later created in the provinces. In order to study a consistent group of volunteers throughout the period, we limited our investigation to the volunteers of the Paris region.

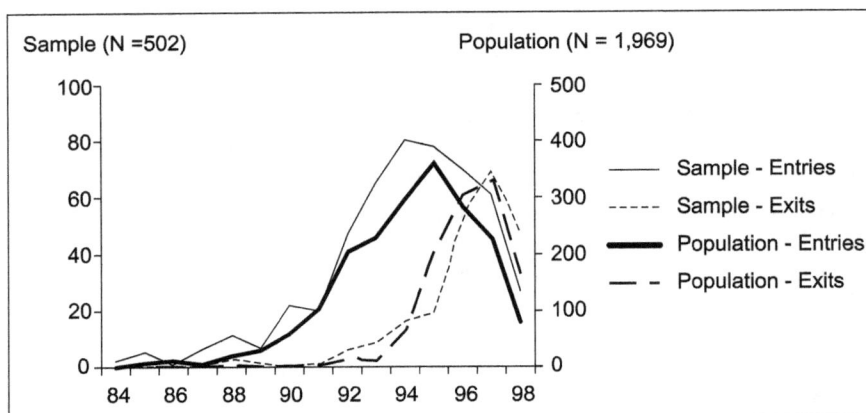

Figure 4.1: Representativity of flows of members from questionnaire sample Comparison of survey sample and population from members' directory

The response rate was decent (25 per cent, N = 502). Not only did we contact current volunteers (886 questionnaires, 289 returned, 33 per cent), we also surveyed former volunteers (1,083 questionnaires, 213 returned, 20 per cent). Their inclusion gives us a view that includes terminated, fully informed commitments, as well as unfinished, censored trajectories.

We had the opportunity to test the reliability of our sample by means of other data from Aides' archives: sex, birth year, date of entry and of exit.[12] Figure 4.1 shows the high agreement of flows of members in and out of Aides between sample and survey. All representativity tests on these four variables give satisfying results: monovariate distributions are highly tied between survey sample and population[13] and the hierarchy of bivariate correlations are similar enough in the sample and in the population.[14] Archive data are not rich enough to prove that our sample is fully representative regarding other variables like sexual orientation, socioeconomic status (SES), HIV status or positions in Aides. As a matter of fact, our questionnaire was designed

---

12. The quality of the data on members from Aides' directory is high. Missing values are only 5 per cent (birth year), 3 per cent (year of entry and exit) and 0 per cent (sex).

13. Monovariate distributions of sex S, age A, entry date E and leaving date L show Pearson correlation coefficients between the sample and population of respectively 1.00, 0.88, 0.98 and 0.94. As a consequence, none of the categories of these four variables is omitted in our survey sample.

14. The similarity of structures of correlations between the sample and the population strengthens the monovariate correlation tests (see previous note). In our case: correlations S*E and S*L are not significant in both sample and population; S*A, E*L and A*E are significant and strong in both. Only A*L is non significant in sample and significant and strong in population. Therefore, as a whole, with only one exception out of six tests, the internal structure of ties between characteristics available in both the sample and population are very close.

precisely to supply this information from respondents. Our knowledge of the organisation leads us to suspect survey response biases, particularly among more educated activists and activists in executive professions. Nonetheless, our sample can be considered reliable as to our focus on the heterogeneity of constituencies.

Our typological approach (see below) is not conditional on strong representativity as much as are linear models approaches. Surveying more members might change the typical longitudinal profiles we sketch out by providing new profiles. It would more likely impact the size of the clusters of members that we associate with these profiles, in two ways: by adding new cases which resemble the ones already surveyed; and by adding cases slightly different that would move the boundaries of clusters, but not their core. We assume that our 502 respondents drove us close enough to sampling saturation.

Biographical profiles and organisational dynamics

Optimal matching and cluster analysis produce an exhaustive, ten-group typology.[15] Each group shows high levels of internal coherence and external difference with the other groups. We use individual sequence plots[16] to describe the specific combination of experiences activists go through, not only since the creation of Aides in 1984, but from the end of the 1950s, with each biography starting at the age of fifteen. We also rely on cross-tabulations of clusters by social characteristics, with Table 4.1 summarising the most discriminating features of each cluster. Automated extraction of typical subsequences for each cluster helps characterise and name them. Finally, we illustrate graphically the ten clusters by prototypical activists (Figure 4.2), the six most representative of them being detailed in the text. The picture that emerges provides an original view of the divides between members, of the potential conflicts that result, and of the consequences of these conflicts on continuity and change.

---

15. The number of clusters is a statistically relevant cut in the hierarchical clustering tree, as the gaps between nine and ten and between ten and eleven are big enough. Also, clusters are small enough to provide a detailed insight into the diversity of profiles, without producing any marginal cluster. Choosing more (or fewer) classes by splitting (respectively, merging) some clusters, would also make sense, but would not provide much more useful information to the question of organisational change. The high variance of variables not used in the analysis (sex, education, socioeconomic status…) by cluster confirms that the biographical types we extracted by means of SA match distinct social structures.

16. For illustrations of cluster description, see Figures in the Appendix.

Table 4.1: Main features of clusters output by optimal matching and cluster analysis.

Cl.	n	Longitudinal profile of career in Aides	Multiple-career dynamics and subsequences	Other specific features**
1*	18	**Pioneers I.** Early and protracted (1984–1992) engagement, but with few managing positions. As of 1999 (when being surveyed), all have left, for personal reasons.	Mostly homosexual men with HIV+ status disclosed to relatives***.	
2	26	**Pioneers II.** Entries spread across 1984–1998. High level of commitment.	All homosexuals, of which half HIV+. HIV status not fully revealed. But lots of missing values in the sociosexual career (uncertainty about coming out) and AIDS-related career.	Mix of male and female activists. 54% >45yo (mean: 19%).
3	40	**Followers I.** Early (1987+), long term involvements, either professional (permanent positions, like administrative workers), or intense volunteering.	Only heterosexuals involved professionally, volunteers and management positions go to both heterosexuals and homosexuals. Some were HIV+ before getting involved, but many refuse to reveal their HIV status.	Only class that mixes all sociosexual statuses (50% het. women, 28% hom. men, 15% het. men, 2% hom. women) and ages (40% > 45 yo, m: 19).
4	45	**Second generation – heterosexuals I.** Volunteers all entered from 1989 and left after 2 to 8 years in Aides, mostly keeping contacts inside the organisation.	Long-term stable heterosexual and HIV- activists.	82% women (m: 40). 29% married (m: 11) and 13% divorced (m: 7). 55% >55 yo when engaging (m: 38) High affective proximity to AIDS.

Cl.	n	Longitudinal profile of career in Aides	Multiple-career dynamics and subsequences	Other specific features**
5	84	**Second generation – professionals I.** Volunteers have often been managers in Aides and then returned to volunteering.	Homosexuals with largely uncertain coming out, either really uncertain themselves or refusing to admit in the questionnaire.	Highest proportion of missing values: least robust of all 10 classes.
			Some are HIV+ activists, all of whom were + before committing in Aides, sometimes long ago.	High status in Aides: MV due to disinterest or refusal of questionnaire.
6	53	**Followers II.** Strong commitment and rapidly evolving statuses in Aides, with management (45%), and/or full-time paid (21%) positions.	Engagement following the progressive, sometimes slow, revelation of their orientation and HIV-status. Members successively hold volunteer, full-time and managing positions. They sometimes leave but maintain contact.	25% HIV+. 72% <35 yo (m: 46).
7	18	**Followers III.** Late (1992+), active involvement, mostly as managers, still in Aides as of 1999.	All homosexual men simultaneously leading coming out process, revealing their HIV+ status and engaging in Aides.	Intermediate age (25–35 yo). High proximity to AIDS.
8	98	**Second generation – professionals II.** Homogeneous 1993–1997 engagements cohort. Half of members directly held permanent-managers positions and left shortly after.	Long term stable heterosexual and HIV- activists.	Mix of male and female. 26% married (m: 11). 32% >55 yo (m: 19).

Cl.	n	Longitudinal profile of career in Aides	Multiple-career dynamics and subsequences	Other specific features**
9	42	**Second generation – heterosexuals II.** Late (1994+) volunteering with low-level engagement.	Long stable heterosexual and HIV- period before engagement in Aides.	Young heterosexual women. Low effective and affective proximity to AIDS.
10	78	**Future core activists.** Late (1994+) unterminated (still in Aides in 1999) volunteering with low-level engagement.	Engagement often embedded in slow and unachieved homosexual coming out, with stable HIV- status.	83% < 35 yo (m: 46). 80% hold only a volunteer position.

*Clusters are ordered according to their median year of entry in Aides (see Figure 4.2).

**Specific features have to be significantly higher or lower than the mean (m) of the sample of 502 activists.

***Evolving features (SES, age, education, proximity to Aides), when mentioned, are measured at the moment involvement in Aides.

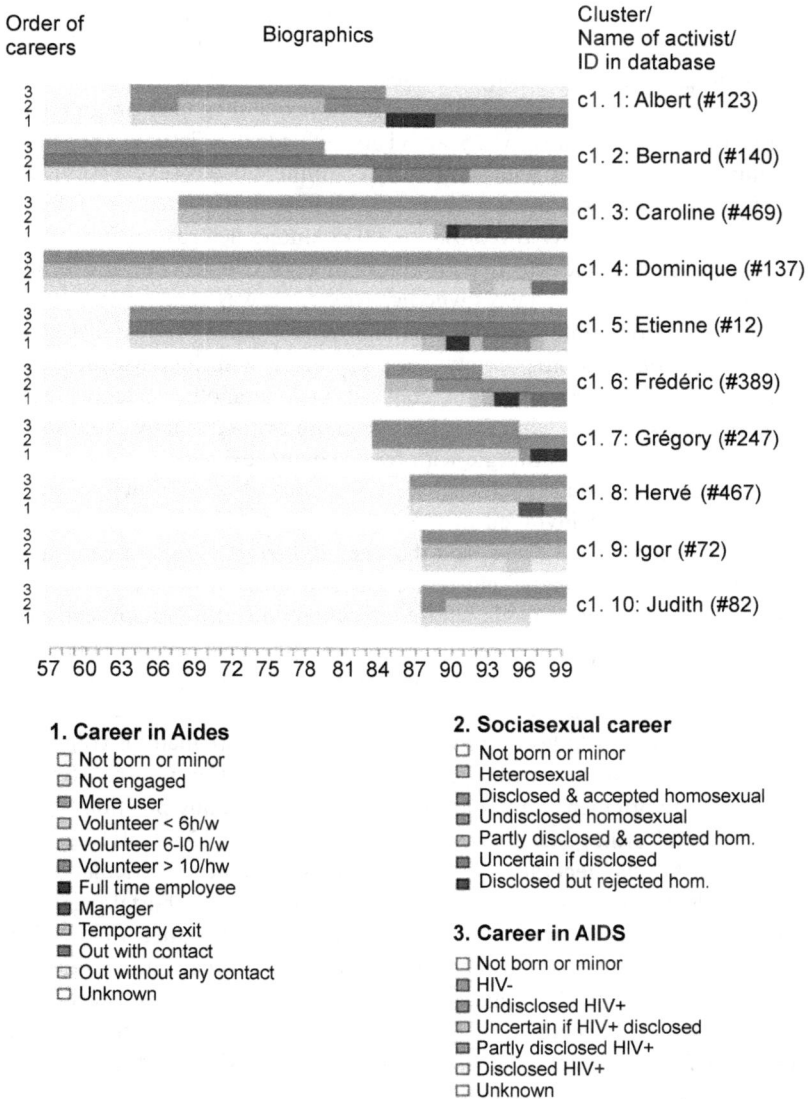

Figure 4.2: Prototypical activists by cluster

Each protypical activist is a real member of a cluster chosen for its similarity with the general description of the cluster, according to the nature, length and order of states in the biographies. Names are fabricated.

A first result is that our clusters go beyond the usual sociographic divides. By comparing activists according to their concrete, successive steps in three combined careers, sequence analysis unearths some shared biographical features that overcome strong sociosexual cleavages.

Although a coherent sociosexual group, homosexual men bear a high effective proximity to illness and mix AIDS activism with identity issues. They mingle within cluster one and three, with some early committed heterosexual women, and within cluster two, five, six and ten, with some homosexual women (see Table 4.1). In cluster one, high affective proximity to AIDS among heterosexuals works as a structural equivalent to the effective proximity of gays. Clusters one and three also include some lesser disclosed gays who use Aides as a way to act with other gays on gay issues, without professing this stigmatised activism. Their less distinctively male and homosexual profiles allow some closeness with heterosexual, female activists. Cluster two, six and ten, by contrast, include another category of gays who combine this struggle with an offensive claim of their homosexual identity. These profiles will logically mingle with female homosexuals.

Regarding heterosexual female activists, previous research usually states that they massively became involved in the 1990s, when AIDS activism became a more common, normalised cause, and that they did so in a logic of care. Indeed, this specific profile dominates clusters eight and nine, with later, less intense commitments, carried by persons whose education and SES would neatly differ from the average in Aides. But clusters three and four also include some earlier heterosexual female commitments, based on a feeling of affective closeness to AIDS, and sometimes to the homosexual cause itself at the same time. Some women would also join Aides for professional reasons, more than for volunteering purposes, and get a steady work contract in the organisation (clusters three and eight), mingling with men and homosexuals holding managing positions.

A second result is the *generation units* (Mannheim [1928] 1952: 291) that emerge from OMA within the generation of AIDS activists, and more particularly within Aides. Usually, these units would simply be created from a cohortal perspective, that is, from the year activists enter the organisation. (Whittier 1997: 762) In our case, the distribution of clusters, strictly elaborated according to similarities in individual biographical dynamics, happens to follow a clear succession in time (Figure 4.4 in Appendix). Moreover, the clusters are concentrated in time. Although successive clusters, most of the time intersect with their neighbours (by 1999, none of the groups, including the two whose entry years stop the earliest – clusters one and four, had completely left the organisation), we demonstrate here that people with various biographical profiles engaged at different periods of the development of Aides.

The distribution of entry years of clusters helps assess the impact of each of them on the dramatic changes that impinged on Aides, especially on its internal modes of organisation, its strategic and tactical choices and the formation and transformation of its collective identity. We interpret the organisational role of the clusters in a triple context: the epidemic's evolution, the pace of state intervention

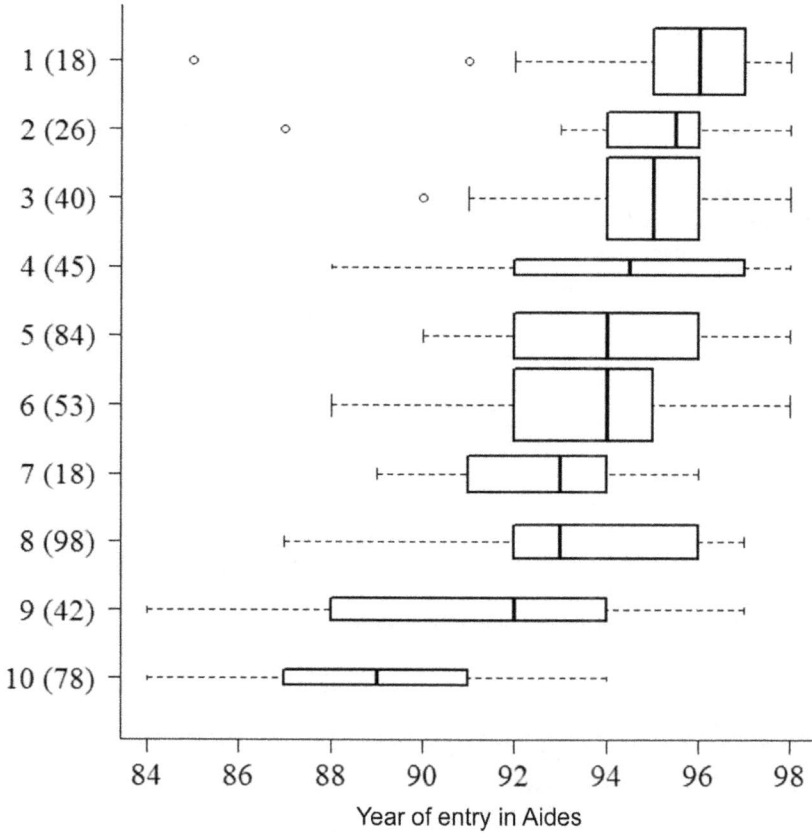

Figure 4.3: A generational perspective on biographical profiles

Boxplot of distribution of year of arrival in Aides by cluster, with size of cluster between parentheses. The median is represented by a bold dash, 50 per cent of members are inside the box, 25 per cent on the left and right of the box, circles represent outliers (>1.5 sd).

and the creation of a multi-organisational field.[17]

Clusters one and two group the pioneers of AIDS activism, those who created the association in 1984 and who developed recruitment and training procedures in 1985–1986, when the epidemic appeared in full light, the virus being better known and identified by tests. Their period of volunteering is long and intense and goes with diverse other political involvements. As a result, even the ones who left

---

17. See Rosenbrock *et al.* (2000); Pinell *et al.* (2002); and Epstein (1996) and Gould (2009) on the USA.

maintained contacts within. Since at the beginning of the fight, recruitment worked on cooptation and mutual acquaintances (Pinell *et al.* 2002), clusters one and two share a very strong social and ideological identity: they are mainly composed of gay males, in their thirties, belonging to the upper middle class. One should also note that half the members are PLWA, and were HIV positive before joining the association.

Yet, these two clusters differ in several ways. Cluster one groups the 'founding fathers' of the movement who joined before 1993, while people in cluster two joined a little later. The high exit rate in cluster one, sometimes after just one or two years, reveals two kinds of disengaging processes: either a dense, costly involvement led them to burn out or they gave up because of the direct effects of the disease itself. Members of cluster two are far more reticent than those in cluster one to answer questions about their sociosexual preferences and their serological status.[18] These differences, combined with the analysis of some open-ended questions in the survey about the reasons for joining and for exiting, as well as about the main objectives the association should pursue, indicate that clusters one and two materialise a cleavage that will be at the heart of internal conflicts in the following years, between a self-help logic, which implies a strong gay and PLWA identity and a generalist model that negates the homosexual and PLWA identity of the constituency.

A prototypical activist for cluster one is Albert. He progressively revealed his sexual orientation to his relatives at the age of twenty and made it fully public by age thirty-one. His involvement in Aides began at age thirty-six, in 1985. His primary motive was 'to appeal against an anti-AIDS policy that was ill-driven' (open question). At the time, he had a University degree and has since held a managing position at work for twelve years. The same year that he began working at Aides, he learned he was HIV+. This turning point was crucial: he simultaneously became a manager in Aides and revealed his illness to all of his relatives. The stigma of being involved in Aides was doubled by his own seropositivity. Albert fully devoted himself to the organisation and contributed to its development (open question). He completely disengaged after five years, when he joined another organisation. Albert nonetheless kept contacts within Aides.

Bernard is a prototypical activist in cluster two. He got involved right at the birth of Aides in 1984, 'because [his] lover had died from AIDS'. He gave more than ten hours per week to the organisation. He downgraded to less than six hours from 1994 on, but did not leave. As Albert, he was older than many other members (forty-three) at the time he got involved. He had a higher education diploma and worked as a manager. Unfortunately, Bernard did not answer any questions about HIV, so we have no information about his career in AIDS. This selective refusal, and the fact that he did not provide any dates for his coming out (although he admitted it was fully completed in 1999), can be explained by the generalist,

---

18. Sequence analysis proves all the more efficient by grouping these partially incomplete respondents instead of dropping them and missing a crucial point of our historical puzzle.

universalist activism he professes. He does not feel the need to tell about himself when reporting about his activism. He left Aides because it was 'not active publicly and would not deliver enough public communication'.

The divide between self-help/communitarian and generalist/universalist engagements can be detected in clusters five, six and seven. Members of cluster five show a great reluctance to reveal their sexual orientation and their serological status, reflecting the generalist ideology. People in cluster six and seven, on the contrary, defend a strong homosexual identity and are also in favor of a self-help model of the fight against AIDS.

Clusters five, six and seven form the association's backbone. The enduring cumulative commitment of individuals in these clusters during the whole period under study, supports the continuity of the movement. Moreover, they occupy the leading positions, in some ways safeguarding the association's ideological line and collective identity despite the demographic turnover and organisational upheavals. Like in clusters one and two, they declare a strong proximity to the disease, being themselves HIV positive and/or knowing persons who are.

People in clusters six and seven undertake leading organisational careers, entangled with a slow, sometimes uncertain, disclosure of both their homosexuality and their HIV-positive status. Some might use their involvement as a resource to complete their coming out.[19] The arrival of these three clusters in Aides corresponds to several contexts: the rebirth of an activist homosexual movement in France at the end of the 1980s, with new cohorts of activists, more committed to the fight against homophobia and to the defense of their civil rights, pushed by the birth of Act Up Paris in 1989, on the model of Act Up-New York (Broqua 2005; Pinell *et al.* 2002); the appearance of HAART and the decline in the mortality rate and the creation of specialised State agencies. Backed by the progressive depletion of clusters one and two, people in clusters six and seven carry along spectacular strategic and tactical changes in Aides: an increasingly visible participation of Aides in 'parallel causes' (foreigners, prisons, insurance, etc.) and first and foremost in the question of gay and lesbian civil rights (gay marriage) and the tactical rapprochement of Aides and Act Up, with the result of a certain radicalisation in the modes of action employed (joint demonstrations, radicalisation of claims).

Individuals in cluster ten shares the same structural attributes, except for the fact that, having joined Aides only recently, they do not occupy leading positions. However, one can assume that it is through this cluster that continuity of the SMO will be secured.

---

19. The high proportion of activists still in Aides in 1999 in cluster seven (89 per cent, mean: 56 per cent) again shows the robustness of SA. By gathering right-censored (unfinished) trajectories in the same cluster SA limits the spread of distortion of interpretation to the whole sample. Cluster seven (like clusters five, eight and ten) has to be read as less robust on this aspect at survey time. Conclusions about the final part of commitment in Aides and about the exit are still tentative. At the same time, dropping these respondents would literally mean censoring our sample and missing some relevant kinds of activist careers.

Daniel (cluster five) was fifty-four when he got involved in 1988. He has 'volunteered his whole life long', he likes 'helping, serving a cause'. A friend he knew for 30 years died in 1986. He had begun disclosing his homosexuality only 3 years earlier and had not completed the process in 1989. He started with three years of limited involvement in Aides. Then he took a year off and retired professionally. His educational profile is lower education, intermediate SES. He came back in 1992 with a more intense involvement, as a manager for two years, and three more as a volunteer. Daniel's trajectory illustrates the ties between sociosexual identity, biographical availability and activism.

Eric (cluster six) was thirty-two when he got involved in 1995. His case clearly demonstrates the link between the three careers. At twenty-five, all his relatives knew about his homosexuality, but most of them rejected him for that. Two years later, he tested HIV+, and soon revealed this to his relatives. He gives no less than four reasons for joining, which might explain his intense commitment: his boyfriend died three years before, he was ill himself and wanted to help before it was too late, Aides had an office close to his place and, he regretted not having used condoms to protect himself before. But, as Eric was a full time paid employee in Aides, we should not neglect, in this case, financial aspects.

Clusters three, four, eight and nine group activists who, although more numerous than in clusters one, two, five, six and seven, contribute less to organisational change. They compose a second, quite distinct wave of members, more diverse and with shorter involvements in Aides.

People in clusters three and four joined the association during the first half of the 1990s, when AIDS lost its specificity and was institutionalised. The discovery of HAART in 1996–1997 increased life expectancy of People Living With AIDS (PLWA), who refocused their attention on more day-to-day concerns. At the same time, HAART gradually shifted the image of AIDS from that of a fatal illness to that of a chronic disease, resulting in a certain social and political demobilisation and a normalisation of the cause. Clusters three and eight illustrate the professionalisation of Aides: part of their members took up paid positions for professional and/or political reasons more than in the name of a communitarian or self-help orientation. They soon clashed with the volunteers about the division of labor (and power). Other inner conflicts, between PLWA and HIV negative volunteers and between heterosexuals and homosexuals, also explain why cluster four nearly disappeared by 1998.

Clusters four and nine show the diversification of demographic profiles. Emerging after 1990, these individuals are almost exclusively composed of HIV-negative heterosexual women. Heterosexual women generally participate in a spirit of solidarity, motivated by their professional involvement in the (traditionally female) field of health and social services. They also belong to an older generation than clusters one and two. Besides, if people in cluster four still declare a strong proximity to the disease, it is experienced more through loose networks of acquaintances and professional contacts than through intimate relationships with partners or relatives. As a result, the levels of commitment are low (seldom more than six hours per week devoted to voluntary work) and drop outs quick, after two or three years (Maslanka 1996; Claxton, Catalan, and Burgess 1998; Miller 2000).

Dominique (cluster four) became involved in 1992 at the age of fifty-two, in a wish to 'give (her) anger against the affair of infected blood (non sterilised blood transfused to ill persons in hospitals in the early 1980s) a positive output'. As a volunteer she took part for two years with intermediate intensity (six to ten h./w.) then three years at a lower level (<six h./w.). Then she left, but kept contacts. She was a self-employed worker at the time of her entry and retired the same year she left Aides. This coincidence between political and professional turning points illustrates a propensity, higher in this cluster than in others, to get involved in activism according to one's family and work availability or opportunities. In her case, she was in charge of emotionally and materially supporting PLWA. She resigned with a feeling of 'shame of surviving in good health' and at the same time, chose to invest herself in a 'less desperate cause'.

Flore (cluster nine) entered Aides at age twenty-two. She had undertaken long studies at that time. She claims she wanted to be useful and express her solidarity with the victims of the epidemic. She left at twenty-six, because of lack of time, without keeping any contacts inside the organisation. Her biographical availability diminished because of several competing involvements.

Conclusions

Our analysis of clusters based on SA and OMA brings out a fairly clear picture of internal dynamics in terms of continuity and change, in conjunction with the changing context of the fight against the epidemic over time. More precisely, by focussing on the internal heterogeneity of the movement's constituencies, it contributes to the debate on the role of internal processes in the transformation of social movements at three levels. By taking into account the multisituated and process characters of structural attributes, we propose a theoretical specification of what is heterogeneity within movements. By applying SA and OMA to a questionnaire sent to former and current volunteers, we offer a new way of empirically identifying such heterogeneity and analysing its effects. And finally by exemplifying the importance of generation units to change as well as to continuity in Aides, we contribute to the vivid debate about the conditions for change and stability among SMOs.

Looking at the internal heterogeneity of the constituency of Aides usefully complements what the literature has already established about the evolution of AIDS movements (Pinell *et al.* 2002; Broqua 2005; Fillieule and Broqua 2005; Gould 2009). The increasing number of HIV-negative and heterosexual women strongly contributed to the emergence of a series of internal identity cleavages between 'treatment activists' and 'social activists' (Crimp 1992) and between HIV-negative and HIV-positive volunteers. This was due to the relative 'despecification' of the cause, which was related to the growing concern for issues like unequal access to health care for marginalised populations (immigrants, prisoners, etc) and the struggle for gay rights. In this changed internal context, different ideas about how to fight AIDS turned into acrimonious conflicts about what the group should be fighting for and about tactical and strategic choices.

Generation units enable us to grasp the factors associated with strategic and tactical changes. Belonging to specific clusters largely conditions the overall manner in which volunteers conceive of the fight against AIDS, as well as which activities are urgent or which positions are useful for their association. As a result, the growth of certain generation units has the effect of favouring changes in political orientation. Thus, for example, the rapprochement of Aides and Act Up, as well as a progressive involvement in questions of gay rights and marriage are, no doubt, related to the rise in power of cluster three within the association, in the context of a certain rebirth of the homosexual movement and, more generally, of social mobilisation around all forms of exclusion. (Fillieule and Duyvendak 1999)

However, despite the powerful centrifugal forces that could have provoked the decline and disappearance of the group, like in so many other cases (see Gould 2009 on Act Up chapters in the US), Aides did continue to develop and it still remains the biggest voluntary group fighting AIDS in France. Our analysis suggests three main explanations for that success.

First, despite the generalisation and extension of the cause from the early 1990s and the arrival of many newcomers, whose properties and collective identities were very specific, the founding group managed to maintain its grip on the association and to transmit its values and identity to new cohorts of volunteers who shared a certain structural proximity with them and were ready to take responsibilities in the association (clusters five, six, seven and ten). The maintenance of such continuity or, to put it another way, the avoidance of a generational gap, is remarkable if one considers the growing recruitments during the period and how dramatically the field of the struggle against AIDS has changed in fifteen years.[20]

Second, the expanding use of paid staff has had an effect on the maintenance of a collective identity and ideological coherence in a context of increasing numbers of new members and a correlative higher turnover. Indeed, the consolidation and professionalisation of the management of Aides in the mid 1990s generated multiple tensions around two main issues: the massive hiring of new employees, coming partly from the volunteer population, raised questions about the division of labour between professionals and volunteers and an increasingly bitter tension between volunteers and users emerged, generating feelings of non recognition, frustration, resentment and anger. However, and despite these tensions, the paid staff maintained the ideals and goals of the movement during times of expanding political opportunity and increasing volunteer activism. This is mainly due to the fact that, in the particular field of the fight against AIDS in which staffers sometimes make activism a career especially when job opportunities shrink dramatically due to the illness, paid activists do not necessarily differ from volunteers in their commitment to the cause (see also Oliver 1993) and can even be more radical and committed than the volunteers (see also Jenkins 1977). This remark is theoretically

---

20. Unfortunately, our data do not allow us to measure the effects of the introduction of HAART, which considerably modified the public image of the epidemic and certainly resulted in social and political demobilisation.

important since the literature usually insists on the positive role of paid staff only in contexts of shrinking political opportunities and decreasing activism (Rupp and Taylor 1997, and Staggenborg 1988 for an exception). Actually, our case study shows that paid staff may facilitate activism and help maintain cohesiveness during both movement doldrum and development.

This leads us to stress the importance of a series of organisational mechanisms and rules that can help the older generation maintain incumbents in positions of power, reducing the capacity of the organisation for change (Gusfield 1957; Morris 1984; Staggenborg 1988, Oliver 1993; Whittier 1997). Indeed, as early as 1986–1987, Aides established very formal and demanding rules of recruitment and training for new volunteers and different kinds of barriers for access to responsibilities within the association. These mechanisms have constituted strong means of influence on volunteers' integration and ideological formation. As a matter of fact, what Gerth and Wright Mills (1954) call the 'selection of persons' stresses how groups encourage or discourage individual commitment by means of a collection of tools for selection that comprise so many barriers to entrance into the group, or filters orienting the newcomers towards the exit or towards particular roles and tasks, rather than others. However, such mechanisms proved to be insufficient in the case of Aides, in a context of high turn-over and dramatically increasing heterogeneity. Here lies one of the reasons for the progressive broadening and diversification of activities and their more or less autonomous and segmented functioning as a way to meet internal conflicts through relative separation (see Gusfield 1957 for a similar remark in another context). If volunteers favouring a self-help logic focus on recreational activities and respond to the hotline, health professionals and heterosexual women can focus mainly on direct care to the sick, at home or in hospital. Finally, the creation of targeted prevention activities also allows volunteers to click along affinity lines (e.g. prevention in groups with male prostitutes or prevention on gay cruising areas).

To conclude, one should note that in studying the role of internal processes in the transformation of social movements, we have suggested that the coexistence and succession of generation units must not only be thought of in terms of internal conflict and dysfunction or, if one prefers, generational rupture. The question may also be looked at from the opposite perspective. To what degree does the heterogeneity resulting from the diversity of generation units contribute to foster organisational continuity? The maintenance and constant adaptation of a formal organisation, as well as that of a collective identity, occurs in reality through continuous rearrangements, most effective if spread over time. Here we can only agree with Ghaziani's idea (2008) that internal conflicts may, under certain conditions, contribute to the formation and maintenance of collective identities.

Appendix

*Figure 4.4: Example of separate graphs of the three careers (cluster 9, n = 45)
Individual career in Aides (1), sociosexual career (2) and career in AIDS (3),
from 1957 to 1999. The order differs between the 3 careers.*

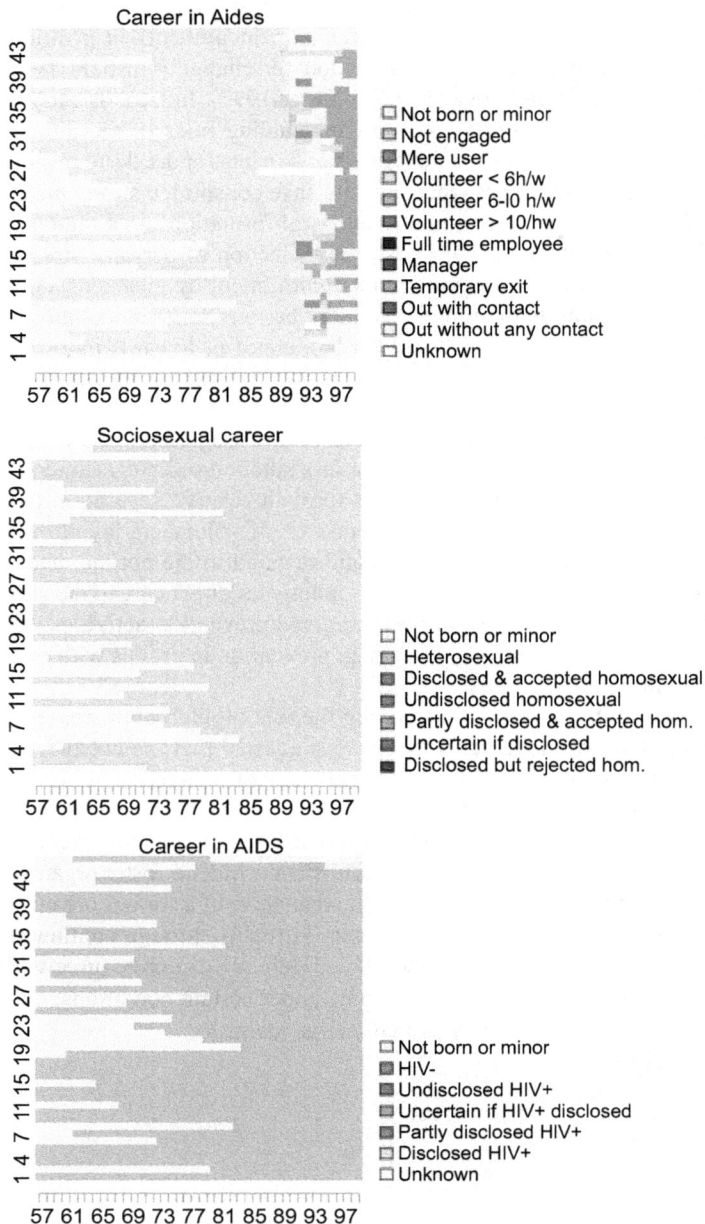

Career in Aides

□ Not born or minor
▣ Not engaged
▣ Mere user
□ Volunteer < 6h/w
▣ Volunteer 6-I0 h/w
▣ Volunteer > 10/hw
■ Full time employee
▣ Manager
▣ Temporary exit
▣ Out with contact
□ Out without any contact
□ Unknown

Sociosexual career

□ Not born or minor
▣ Heterosexual
▣ Disclosed & accepted homosexual
▣ Undisclosed homosexual
▣ Partly disclosed & accepted hom.
▣ Uncertain if disclosed
■ Disclosed but rejected hom.

Career in AIDS

□ Not born or minor
▣ HIV-
▣ Undisclosed HIV+
▣ Uncertain if HIV+ disclosed
▣ Partly disclosed HIV+
□ Disclosed HIV+
□ Unknown

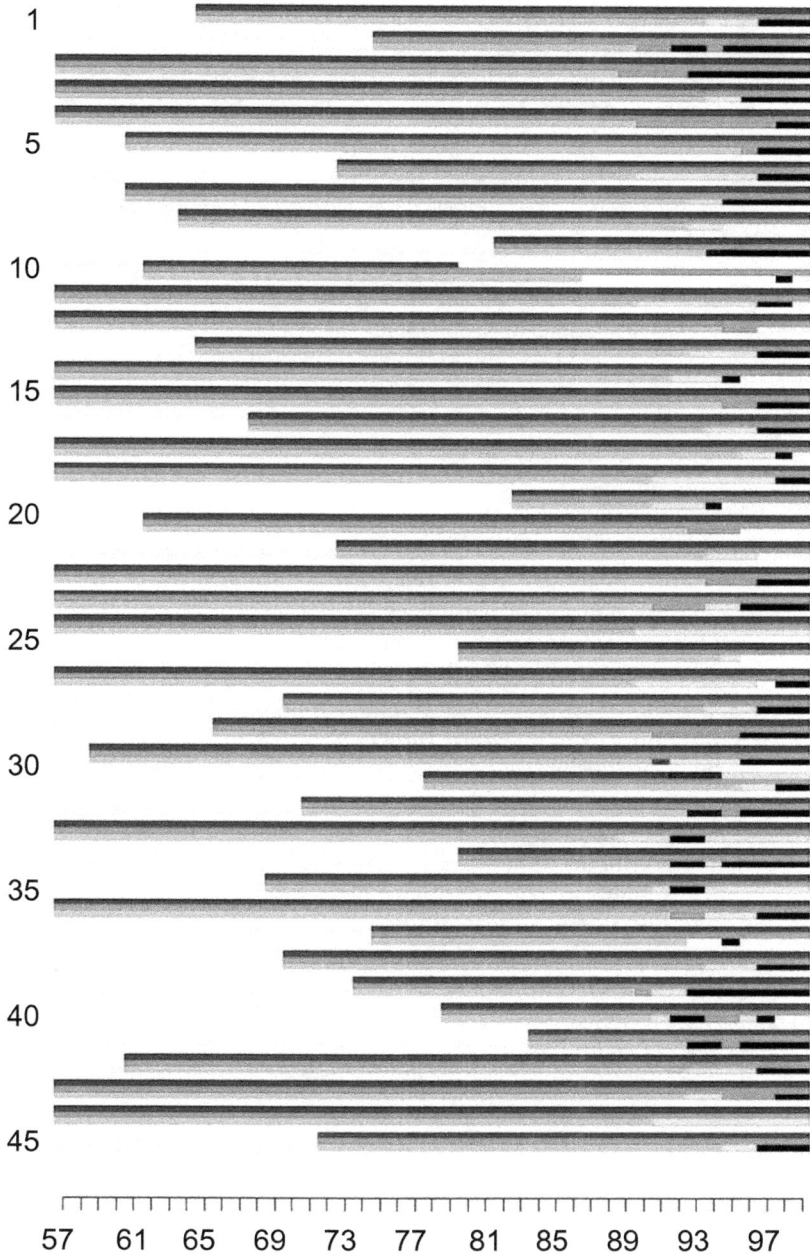

Figure 4.5: Example of biographies (cluster 9, n = 45) Combined individual careers in Aides, sociosexual career and career in AIDS (cf. legends on Figure 4.4)

References

Abbot, A. (1995) 'Sequence Analysis: new methods for old ideas', *Annual Review of Sociology*, 21: 93–113.

Aisenbrey, S., and Fasang, A. (2007) 'Beyond Optimal Matching: The 'Second Wave' of Sequence Analysis', CIQLE Working Paper, 02, August, Yale University, New Haven.

Altman, D. (1988) 'Legitimation through Disaster: AIDS and the gay movement', in E. Fee and D. M. Fox (eds) *AIDS: The burdens of history*, Berkeley and Los Angeles: University of California Press, pp. 301–315.

Armstrong, E. (2002) *Forging Gay Identities: Organizing sexuality in San Francisco 1950–1974*, Chicago: The University of Chicago Press.

Becker, H. (1966) *Outsiders*, Glencoe, IL: Free Press.

Berger, P. L. and Luckmann, T. (1966) *The Social Construction of Reality: A treatise in the sociology of knowledge*, New York: Anchor Books.

Blanchard, P. (2010) 'Analyse séquentielle des carrières militantes à Aides', available at HAL-Open Archives, http://hal.archives-ouvertes.fr/hal-00476193/fr.

Broqua, C. (2005) *Agir pour ne pas mourir!: Act Up, les homosexuels et le sida*, Paris: Presses de Sciences Po.

Broqua, C. and Fillieule, O. (2001) *Trajectoires d'engagement: AIDES et Act Up*, Paris: Textuel.

Chambré, S. M. (2006) *Fighting For Our Lives: New York's AIDS community and the politics of disease*, New Brunswick, NJ: Rutgers University Press.

Claxton, R. P. R., Catalan, J. and Burgess, A. P. (1998) 'Psychological distress and burnout among buddies: demographic, situational and motivational factors', *AIDS Care*, 10(2): 175–190.

Cohen, C. J. (2000) 'Contested Membership: Black gay identities and the politics of AIDS', in J. D'Emilio, W. B. Turner and U. Vaid (eds) *Creating Change: Sexuality, public policy, and civil rights*, New York: Saint Martin's Press, pp. 382–406.

Crenshaw, K. (1989) 'Demarginalizing the intersection of race and sex: a black feminist critique of antidiscrimination doctrine, feminist theory and antiracist politics', *University of Chicago Legal Forum*: 139–167.

Crimp, D. (1992) 'Right on, girlfriend!', *Social Text*, 33: 2–18.

Dijkstra, W. and Taris, T. (1995) 'Measuring the agreement between sequences', *Sociological Methods & Research*, 24: 214–231.

Elzinga, C. H. (2003) 'Sequence similarity: a nonaligning technique', *Sociological Methods & Research*, 32: 3–29.

Epstein, S. (1996) *Impure Science: AIDS, activism, and the politics of knowledge*, Berkeley: University of California Press.

Evans, S. (1979) *Personal Politics. The roots of Women's Liberation in the Civil Rights Movement and the New Left*, New York: Alfred A. Knopf.

Fantasia, R. (1988) *Cultures of Solidarity: Consciousness, action, and contemporary American workers*, Berkeley: University of California Press.

Fillieule, O. (1997) *Stratégies de la rue*, Paris, Presses de Sciences Po.

— (2001) 'Post scriptum: Propositions pour une analyse processuelle de l'engagement individuel', *Revue française de science politique* 51(1–2):199–215.

— (2005) 'La défection dans deux associations de lutte contre le sida: Act Up et AIDES', in O. Fillieule (ed.) *Le désengagement militant*, Paris: Belin.

— (2006) 'Requiem pour un concept: Vie et mort de la notion de structure des opportunités politiques', in G. Dorronsoro (ed.) *La Turquie conteste*, Paris: Presses du CNRS, pp. 201–218.

— (2010) 'Some elements of an Interactionist Approach to political disengagement', *Social Movement Studies* 9(1): 1–15.

Fillieule, O. and Broqua, C. (2000) 'Raisons d'agir et proximité à la maladie dans l'économie de l'engagement à AIDES, 1984–1998', in A. Micoud and M. Péroni (eds) *Ce qui nous relie*, Paris: Editions de l'Aube, pp. 283–315.

Fillieule, O. and Duyvendak, J. W. (1999) 'Gay and Lesbian Activism in France: Between integration and community-oriented movements' in B. Adam, J. W. Duyvendak and A. Krouwel (eds) *The Global Emergence of Gay and Lesbian Politics: National imprints of a worldwide movement*, Philadelphia: Temple University Press, pp. 184–213.

Fillieule, O. and Roux, P. (eds) (2008) *Le sexe du militantisme*, Paris: Presses de Sciences Po.

Freeman, J. (1975) *The Politics of Women's Liberation*, New York: Longman.

Gabadinho, A., Ritschard, G., Studer, M. and Müller, N. (2009) *Mining Sequence Data in R with the TraMineR package: A user's guide*, Department of Econometrics and Laboratory of Demography, University of Geneva, Geneva.

Gamson, J. (1989) 'Silence, death and the invisible enemy: AIDS activism and social movement newness', *Social Problems*, 36: 351–367.

— (1997) 'Messages of exclusion: gender, movements, and symbolic boundaries', *Gender & Society*, 11: 178–99.

Gauthier, J. A. (2007) *Empirical Categorizations of Social Trajectories: A sequential view on the life course*, PhD dissertation, Lausanne University.

Gauthier, J.-A., Widmer, E., Bucher, P. and Notredame, C. (2009) 'How much does it cost? Optimization of costs in sequence analysis of social science data', *Sociological Methods and Research*, 38 1 (August): 197–231.

Gerth, H. and Wright Mills, C. (1954) *Character and Social Structure: The psychology of social institutions*, London: Routledge and Kegan Paul.

Ghaziani, A. (2008) *The Dividends of Dissent, How Conflict and Culture Works in Lesbian and Gay Marches on Washington*, Chicago and London: University of Chicago Press.

Ginsburg, F. (1989) *Contested Lives: The abortion debate in an American Community*, Berkeley, CA: University of California Press.

Gitlin, T. (1987) *The Sixties*, New York: Bantam Books.

Goodwin, J. and Jasper, M. (2003) 'Caught in a Winding, Snarling Vine', in J. Goodwin and M. Jasper (eds) *Rethinking Social Movements: Structure, meaning and emotions*, Lanham: Rowman and Littlefield Publishers, pp. 3–30.

Gould, D. (2009) *Moving Politics: Emotion and ACT UP's against AIDS*, Chicago and London: The University of Chicago Press.

Gusfield, J. R. (1957) 'The problem of generations in an organizational structure', *Social Forces*, 35(4): 323–330.

Jasper J. (1997) *The Art of Moral Protest*, Chicago: University of Chicago Press.

Jenkins, J. C. (1977) 'The radical transformation of organizational goals: professionalized reform in the National Council of Churches', *Administrative Science Quarterly*, 22: 568–586.

Lesnard, L. (2008) 'Off-Scheduling within dual-earner couples: an unequal and negative externality for family time', *The American Journal of Sociology*, 114(2): 447–490.

Lichterman, P. (1995) 'Piecing together multi-cultural community', *Social Problems*, 42: 513–34.

Mannheim, K. ([1928] 1952) 'The Problem of Generations', in *Essays on the Sociology of Knowledge*, London: Routledge and Kegan Paul, pp. 276–332.

Marx Ferree, M. (1992) 'The Political Context of Rationality: Rational Choice Theory and resource mobilization', in A. D. Morris and C. McClurg Mueller (eds) *Frontiers in Social Movement Theory*, New Haven and London: Yale University Press, pp. 29–52.

Maslanka, H. (1996) 'Burnout, social support and AIDS volunteers', *AIDS Care*, 8(2): 195–206.

McAdam, D. (1982) *Political Process and the Development of Black Insurgency*, Chicago, IL: University of Chicago Press.

— (1988) *Freedom Summer*, Oxford: Oxford University Press.

McAdam, D., McCarthy, J. and Zald, M. N. (eds) (1996) *Comparative perspectives on Social Movements*, Cambridge: Cambridge University Press.

McCall, L. (2005) 'The complexity of intersectionality', *Signs*, 30(3): 1771–1800.

McCarthy, J. and Zald, M. N. (1977) 'Resource mobilization and social movements: a partial theory', *American Journal of Sociology*, 82 (7): 1212–1241.

Miller, D. (2000) *Dying to care? Work, stress and burnout in HIV/AIDS*, London and New York: Routledge.

Mohanty, C. T. (1988) 'Under Western eyes: feminist scholarship and colonial discourses', *Feminist Review*, 30 (Autumn): 61–88.

Morris, A. D. (1984) *The Origins of the Civil Rights Movement: Black communities organizing for change*, New York: Free Press.

Oliver, P. (1993) 'Formal models of collective action', *Annual Review of Sociology*, 19: 271–300.

Ouellette, S. C., Cassell, J. B., Maslanka, H. and Wong, L.M. (1995) 'GMHC volunteers and the challenges and hopes for the second decade of AIDS', *AIDS Education and Prevention*, 7: 64–79.

Pinell, P. *et al.* (2002) *Une épidémie politique. La lutte contre le sida en France 1982–1986*, Paris: PUF.

Piven, F. F. and Cloward, R. (1977) *Poor People's Movements,* New York: Vintage Books.

Polletta, F. (2002) *Freedom is an Endless Meeting: Democracy in American social movements*, Chicago and London: University of Chicago Press.

Polletta, F. and Jasper, J. M. (2001) 'Collective identity and social movements', *Annual Review of Sociology*, 27: 283–305.

Pollock, G. (2007) 'Holistic trajectories: a study of combined employment, housing and family careers by using multiple-sequence analysis', *Journal of the Royal Statistical Society,* 170(1): 167–183.

Rosenbrock, R. *et al.* (2000) 'The normalization of AIDS in Western European countries', *Social Science and Medicine*, 50 (11): 1607–1629.

Rupp, L. and Taylor, V. (1987) *Survival in the Doldrums: The American Woman's Rights Movement 1945 to the 1960s*, New York and Oxford: Oxford University Press.

Sawicki, F. and Siméant, J. (2010) 'Decompartmentalizing the sociology of activist commitment: A critical survey of some recent trends in French research', *Sociologie du travail*, 52S, 2010: 83–109.

Schneider, B. (1988) 'Political generations in the contemporary Women's Movement', *Sociological Inquiry*, 58: 4–21.

Staggenborg, S. (1988) 'The consequences of professionalization and formalization in the Pro-Choice Movement', *American Sociological Review*, 53: 585–606.

Steinberg, M. W. (1999) *Fighting Words: Working-class formation, collective action, and discourse in early nineteenth-century England*, Cornell: Cornell University Press.

Stockdill, B. (2003) *Activism Against AIDS*, London: Lynne Reinner Publishers.

Strauss, A. (1959) *Mirrors and Masks: The search for identity*, Glencoe, IL: Free Press.

Stryker, S., Owens, J. T. and White, R. (2000) 'Identity Competition: Key to differential social movement participation?', in S. Stryker, T. J. Owens and R. W. White (eds) *Self, Identity, and Social Movements*, Minneapolis: University of Minnesota Press, pp. 21–40.

Tarrow, S. (1994) *Power in Movement*, New York: Cambridge University Press.

Taylor, V. (1989) 'Social movement continuity: the Women's Movement in abeyance', *American Sociological Review*, 54(5): 761–775.

Tilly, C. (2008) *Contentious Performances*, Cambridge: Cambridge University Press.

Waite, L. G. (2001) 'Divided Consciousness: The impact of black elite consciousness on the 1966 Chicago Freedom Movement', in J. Mansbridge, and A. Morris (eds) *Oppositional Consciousness: The subjective roots of social protest*, Chicago: University of Chicago Press, pp. 170–203.

Whittier, N. (1995) *Feminist Generations: The persistence of the Radical Women's Movement*, Philadelphia: Temple University Press.

—   (1997) 'Political generations, micro cohorts and the transformation of social movements', American Sociological Review, 62(5): 760–778.
Zwerman, G. and Steinhoff, P. G. (2005) 'When Activists Ask for Trouble: State-dissident interactions and the new left cycle of resistance in the United-States and Japan', in C. Davenport, H. Johnston and C. Mueller (eds) *Repression and Mobilization*, Minneapolis: University of Minnesota Press, pp. 85–107.

part ii. renegotiating state sovereignty

chapter five | borders, mobility and security
Didier Bigo

Even if we restrict the term to its geographical meaning, the notion of 'border' has been the object of many discussions. A first set of discussions has to do with the pertinence or non-pertinence of different conceptions of what a border means. Some argue that a border is not reducible to a territory or to a political order. A second set of discussions focuses on the relationship between the technologies that are used to control mobility and the sites where identities are checked, and where the decision is taken to grant or refuse the right to visit or reside in a given state.

The first set of discussions is topological and may therefore seem to be abstract, but its political and technical implications are far-reaching. Is a border a continuous line that separates and defines solid objects or entities, or is it a transition point and the site of transformations involving an imperceptible change from one state into another, in the sense in which physics uses that term to describe how the solid, liquid or gaseous state of a substance determines the extent to which it can be separated out, or even funnelled or filtered? To put it a different way, and to adopt the language used by both political science and the military, is a border a line that can be 'armoured', a fortress or even a chain of fortresses forming a long, impenetrable wall around a 'homeland' or *patrie*? Is it, to borrow an expression from a philosopher-sailor, a series of broken or porous lines, a sort of North-West Passage for a period of global warming, when the demarcation lines that define states still exist but are constantly being modified and cannot be immobilised (Serres 1980: 11)? Is it a sign that there is an order to the world, and a real feature of a (state) order that is threatened by the new mobility, or is it the logical outcome of the *clinamen*, of change and of mobility, which are always primal causes?

To go beyond these metaphors, three possibilities emerge to conceptualise a border. Is a border a continuous line that loops back on itself and creates a distinct space that can be homogenised and purified by a power-centre? In that case the central criterion that defines it is a clear distinction between inside and outside. Or is a border like a Möbius strip, where there is a difference between inside and outside, but where the perceived difference between the two varies from one observer to another? Or is a border a series of broken lines, limits and points of contact that results in the hybridisation of heterogeneities that cannot be reduced to any unity? And, in these three alternatives, are borders subject to temporal change and are they disappearing, whatever their previous forms, and are they shrinking into the unity of a borderland or globalised border-world? If that is the case we no longer have multiple borders: we are the prisoners of one invisible border, as some sociologists have suggested by analysing globalisation as a movement destroying borders (Bauman 1998). Or is a border, on the contrary, the retroactive interpretation, in a liquid world, of differences of state and perspective between heterogeneous groups that think they see borders everywhere but that articulate them in accordance with differential logics, and thus produce a multiplicity of network-borders that are themselves shifting and uncertain? In that case, a very different way to understand globalisation emerges that is better called transnationalisation, to insist on the heterogeneity of these processes of boundary making (Appadurai 2001; Cohen, Lacroix and Riutort 2009).

The way one answers these questions will define how one understands the relationship between mobility, borders, security and freedom. Analysis will differ especially on the (il)legitimacy of attempts to control the identities of those who enter a given territory and on the effort to homogenise and integrate them into a 'citizen's identity', which can be defined in terms of equal rights or specific values and ways of living.

What we know about borders

For a long time, the notion of a border seemed to raise no problems for the various social science disciplines. Discussions centred upon territory and not upon borders. But what happens if a border is not something that encloses a territory? What if that very definition is wrong? What is a border if it is not the site where controls operate and if it is not a place of exception and sovereignty? How can one conceptualise the idea of a geographical border without immediately relating it to the processes of sovereignty and security that define a border as a state boundary and as the limits of a territory? Or, to put it another way, how can one conceptualise the idea of a border without referring to the exceptionalism of the political order and to the way nationalism produces homogeneous and profoundly different identities?

The academic community of political science seems to find it difficult to abandon its foundation myths. It admits that borders are not just barriers but, thanks to a process of occultation, it tries to go on living by believing in its myths in the full knowledge that they are not true, simply because the intellectual cost of challenging them would be too high (Veyne 1988 [1983]). We therefore have increasingly schizophrenic visions of reality that try to justify the existing relationship between border and territory, as well as the primal beliefs associated with the idea of state, order and security. Does the political's constitutive imagination require the concept of 'border' to be equated with the concept of 'territory' in order to function, and does that imply the belief that the border is the most distant point at which power can be applied, that it is the realm of the exceptional?

As geographers who take a critical approach point out, researchers have to think of borders as institutions, and not simply as the 'Roman limes' of the space occupied by a given power or as lines that demarcate territories. This implies that, rather than going on believing that these operations are naturally bound up with the existence of borders – seen as the points that are most distant from a given centre, or as peripheries – one has to take a new look at the social construction of frontiers and at how they relate to the operations of politicisation and the (in) security measures that are implemented because they are constructed around the centre. Political-discursive mobilisations constantly try to transform borders into lines of demarcation rather than places of interaction or junction. This presupposes that the extraordinary efforts that are being made by the state are inculcated into us by exhortations that become routine. As their scope increases, they become so completely integrated into the way we think that we no longer notice them. What we call our knowledge has incorporated the territorial myth and digested it to such an extent that all memory of these efforts has vanished. Except, that is, when the very banality of our practices of mobility -and especially the practices of others – seem nowadays to lead to stomach-cramps and even indigestion. One therefore has to take a new look at what we know about borders, and at the truth-value of our knowledge, even if in this short chapter, it means being extremely brief and therefore over-simplistic.

Border, territory and exception: political science, classical approaches and their critiques

Classical approaches to political science understand geographical borders to mean state borders, and a state is firstly a territorial state and only secondly, a state with a population. The territory is therefore the central element that defines the closed space that we call 'society' or even 'the nation.' It takes the form of a bubble. The sovereign state is identified with the nation, even when its federal form indicates an acceptance of the diversity of the peoples that make it. Even though the nation-state has not always existed, the nation-state form has always been crucial, as Charles Tilly reminds us in his study of the roles it has played in the political construction of Europe. It has succeeded in superimposing itself on the city-state and the empire-state (Tilly 1990). From that point on in the European trajectory and its world diaspora, nationalism used the idea of a territory to shape the social imaginary of the space in which we live and of the identities that we privilege.

Marx, Trotsky, Weber, Duguit, Giddens, Holsti and many others have theorised the territorial nation-state form in various ways. Whilst the subtle variations between their formulations obviously reveal the intensity of the debate about the spatial dimension and about it correlates with sovereign power, it seems that the notion of 'territory' gets in the way of discussions of borders (Giddens 1987; Poggi 1990; Holsti 1996). In political science's narrative, the border is nothing more than a form of 'container' that allows the state to embrace (or cage) the populations under its control and/or to protect them from enemy aggression within a given territory (Giddens 1984, 1987; Torpey 2000).

As I pointed out in my introduction, there is of course nothing natural about this relationship with the border. And many geographers, jurists and political scientists now reject the ideological notion that political entities have natural borders, the banks of the Rhine in the case of France, the Atlantic in the case of Spain and the Iberian Peninsula, and the Urals in the case of Europe. But whilst they refuse to reduce politics to a so-called natural geography or to the implications of such a geopolitics, they often define it simply in terms of the limits that apply to a sovereign entity's ability to exercise power over a population within a given space. They then argue that they have given a consensual – and scientific -definition because they reject a discourse that justifies the state's hegemony over a given space. The border then becomes the crystallisation, within a given space, of a power struggle and state borders correspond to what Michel Foucher so nicely calls 'the moment when that struggle was frozen into space' (Foucher 2004: 43). The only problem is that, whilst borders are not natural in the geographical sense of the word, they have, in this formulation, been naturalised and essentialised to the extent that they are the outcome of a balance of power that persists and occupies a space that it strives to homogenise, both by pacifying it from within and by repelling external enemies. In a word, the border is nothing more than the limit of a territory. And it is the territory that comes first.

Rather than being discussed, the almost obligatory reference to Max Weber's definition of the state becomes, paradoxically, a way of avoiding the question of the relationship between border and territory. His classic formulation is repeated in almost ritual fashion: the state is an organisation that claims, with some success, to have a monopoly on the use of legitimate violence within a given territory (Weber 1978: 78). The centre's power radiates outwards to its limits, and it does so thanks to a bureaucracy that transmits it as far as the border, but not beyond it. The border thus marks the distinction between territories belonging to different political entities, each of which can independently decide who enters and leaves its territory (Pratt and Allison-Brown 2000). The effects of this theory are well known. Weber's model fits in with the Westphalian model of the internationalists who claim that territorial borders can, like clocks, be 'set' to synchronise them with border-lines that presuppose the existence of contiguous but distinct spaces, and with a world in which there are no longer any non-sovereign territories, and in which pirates (men who are not subject to the rule of the state or of states) no longer exist (Thompson 1994).

According to this classical tradition, which was dominant from the 1930s to the 1980s, the sovereign state is defined, on the one hand, as containing a power enclosed by the borders that constitute it – the border creates the state -, and on the other hand, as an exercise of state-sovereignty that makes it possible to establish a territory with clear-defined borders that are themselves nothing more than the points which limit the expansion of that power – the state creates the border.

As Louis Sala-Molins ironically points out in his *La loi, de quel droit?* (1977), one can go in circles with tautological definitions, and construct our knowledge of the law on the basis of the myth of the state, and vice versa. This allows political science to emerge as a dogmatic discipline with a claim to being scientific. Whilst there is certainly a price to be paid in terms of our understanding, it does have the advantage of simplicity. So much so, that no candidate for authority is likely to reject it. It will certainly not be rejected, in this model, by anyone who has the authority to delineate, distinguish or purify. All we have to do is not raise the question of origins, of norms and exceptions, and above all not to question the fundamentally arbitrary nature of the institution or of its authority to draw the border and to connect every point along it, as though it was a sacred circle that had to be distinguished from the profane. The price that has to be paid for the nationalist idea of identity is absolute respect for borders, even if they are artificial and created by colonisers. The nationalist idea of identity is sacred, and therefore presupposes the existence of a sacred circle that distinguishes it and from the other (profane outsiders). A border is precisely this kind of a circle, this spherical container or bubble whose content explains its form, but whose form allows its contents to exist. A border as a line of demarcation is therefore something that cannot be questioned: the line it traces is nothing more than the expression of a power struggle that must, thanks to diplomacy, become permanent. What is at stake is a sovereign national territory and its identity within a given space. That space can expand and retract, depending upon the vagaries of inter-state relations and domestic uprisings, but it shapes a bubble that is truly watertight and airtight, even though its geometry is variable (on the notion of a bubble and, *a contrario*, of water tightness, see Sloterdijk 2002).

In the geometrically perfect world described by treatises inspired by the 'realist' theorists of international relations, ignorant of sociological practices and realities, the world is therefore a world of perfectly juxtaposed states that actually control their space and the population flows that move through them. The failure to respect the principle of the existence of the state as a watertight bubble leads to failed, weak, incomplete or fragile states. Hence the contemporary talk of their proliferation and of the chaos of the contemporary world. An inability to control population flows or to do everything possible to manage the interests of the state then becomes a sign of political failure. But that political failure becomes understandable if the contemporary world is experienced as something global, as something that dissolves borders and is therefore seen as a threat to the nation and the state because it destroys their homogeneity and penetrates its territory's every pore. From this follow, as we shall see below, the endless debates about migration and (il-)legality and the tendency of all political parties to deny the existence of transitional flows in order to maintain the illusion of an 'intact' and homogeneous 'body' that they can protect, and which demonstrates their ability to govern (Strange 1996).

This classical theory was critiqued long ago. The critique itself has not, however, really escaped the territorial vision or the idea that borders are indications of a clear radical distinction between different entities. It has not integrated the idea of the border as the logic of a transition between states (and not States), as a bubble that opens on to the world and as a drainage system. A critical theory has been developed on the basis of the inversion of the classical paradigm, in order to critique nationalism and its deleterious effects. The outcome of this critical theory is that border and sovereignty are read as being the limits or the shores of the political (Rancière 1998). And the limits of the political are analysed, in Schmittian style, as the privileged places where the exception reconfigures the norm and defines its meaning. Defined as the clear marker of distinction and demarcation, the border therefore marks the origins of power and not its limes. We have only to look at the border and the control practices that are associated with it to 'unmask' it and reveal its nature because the border belongs to the realm of the permanent exception. In this vision, at the border law ceases to apply. The rule of the sovereign administration and its monopoly on decision-making comes into application. The decision as to who is included and who is excluded is therefore taken in this peculiar site. Even though all decisions do not always go in the administration's favour and are not always detrimental to the foreigner, the appeals to the law are, by definition, weaker. The unpredictability of the moment and place of border-crossing reminds us of Agamben's homo sacer who knows that he can be sacrificed but who does not know when or by whom he will be sacrificed (Agamben 1998).

The good thing about Agambean vision is that it challenges the justifications for policies of order. It does so on the basis of a discourse that prioritises exceptionality and that reads everything in terms of a permanent exception: detention and the camp, but also the journey itself, travel documents such as passports and visa, biometric identifiers, and so on, all become signs of exceptionality. The idea of rites of passage punctuating the journey and increasing the number of barriers is obviously attractive to some extent, but whilst it leads one to conclude that the law has been abolished and that a lack of distinction in the name of sovereignty is the rule in all border areas, it offers little alternative. It simply reveals the arbitrary nature of an order that is, nonetheless, experienced as necessary because it takes decisions and makes distinctions.

As I will show below, decisions taken at the border are not in fact absolute, and are subject to appeal. The decision is usually taken not at the border, as one might expect, but elsewhere. It is taken in a consulate or a database, and it is a banal, everyday occurrence and not something exceptional. In most cases, the decision is usually just a race against time between the mobility of the body of the person who is travelling and the mobility of the data the administration has on that individual's virtual double. I will also analyse that, whilst they are autonomous from the mythical idea of territoriality, so-called enlightened controls through traceability and prevention come up against that of technology in the name of permanent exceptionality. One therefore has to question the territorial mystique and the need to defend society and 'its' identity, which still produces popular mobilisations that are hostile to mobility, and especially the mobility of others (migrants, forced migrants and even refugees). One also has to question the critique of the territorial mystique that simply reinforces its primal assumptions of a privileged locus and fails to see that the crossing of borders is commonplace.

This politics of the sovereign order and of the exception as creator of norms, reinforce the theological notion that the border is a fixed and continuous line that creates a closed (sacred) space and that, for better or worse, separate a society from another and a state from its neighbours. Insofar as it marks a territorial limit, it is the border that creates the homogeneity needed to make a national identity by creating the preconditions for a space that distinguishes foreigners from national citizens. That says it all: there is, or must be, homogeneity and continuity. There must be a self-enclosed space before the sovereign state can be deployed. To the extent that it is a political institution, the border is simultaneously a defensive line that can be secured and a line that allows a distinction to be made between inside and outside. That is its main function. Such is the implicit element of *doxa* that brings these various elements together.

The border of a territorial space obviously has other functions too. Once again, the classical approaches may differ here, but these functions also 'naturally' emerge from the (sovereign) border's function: it divides, and it homogenises that which is inside. Ultra republicans, for instance, regard the border as something that is natural and egalitarian and that applies to all. The criterion that defines sovereignty is the difference between the 'citizens' inside the border and the foreigners 'outside' it. Proximities defined in terms of a few kilometres on either side of the border are less important than distances of hundreds of kilometres inside the same borderline. Taxes, duties, redistribution and therefore solidarity are supposedly bound up with the border (in the sense of territory) (Donnan and Wilson 1999). But it is precisely this point that has been called into question by the recent financial crises, which have demonstrated that the super-rich can avoid paying tax and can relocate in an attempt to escape all appeals for solidarity.

Finally the border ensures certainty, or so claim some legal theoreticians. The logical value of a border as an 'excluder' supposedly has a certainty-value, especially when it is based upon a Cartesian logic and not the jurisprudence of precedent, which just goes to demonstrate the supposed superiority of the Napoleonic reasoning over the Anglo-American system. One is either inside or outside, and one cannot be in both places at once. The border therefore supposedly facilitates arbitration or judgement. This, the neutrality of a logical judgement, is the ultimate argument in favour of a sovereign state border. But all the practices associated with waiting zones inside airports and the legal fiction that the persons held there have not entered the territory, even though they have physically done so, would appear to contradict that argument.

To conclude this rapid overview of the classical arguments and variations on them (including critical variations), it transpires that most jurists, political scientists and internationalists share this image of a Janus-faced state whose national and territorial identity depends upon the clarity and continuity of the border that encloses it. It presupposes both the absolute contiguity of the world and the existence of clearly determined 'no man's lands' that rule out the possibility of superimpositions or ward off the threat that might be posed by conjoined twins who share organs. Coloured maps do not like superimpositions, and Andorra is still an aberrational body with two heads. The implicit metaphor of Leviathan (the collective man) is still present: the border is the epidermis or skin of the state-territory, and it can, unfortunately, sometimes be grazed or even penetrated and contaminated by flows from elsewhere.

These classic narratives whose importance was minimised in the 1970s are, as everyone knows, now resurfacing, even in neo-liberal regimes and in the writings of their critics.

Alternative approaches: a border is not a territorial membrane

Advocates of the post- 9/11 discourse on the border like to recall that it exists in a continuum with the 1930s. The claim is that it is part of an eternal discourse that goes from the present back to Carl Schmitt, and from Schmitt back to Hobbes and

Bodin. And yet this talk of a 'continuum' and a 'line' makes us laugh. Borders are discontinuous. The self-evident nature of the idea of a border began to crack in almost every domain of knowledge (with the exception of political science) in the 1960s and 1970s. Specialists in physics, biology, geography, sociology, economists, philosophers and even euro-jurists all began to think about borders without reducing them to an absolute distinction between inside and outside. One begins to wonder about the relevance of borders, or at least of material borders, when, on the one hand, the number of state borders is increasing and when, on the other hand, air travel, telecommunications media, exchanges between data bases and, at a later stage, the internet are restricting their visibility. It is increasingly unusual for a border to indicate that there is an order in the world. As in the 1930s, mobility and change once more pose a threat to the normality and immobility of order. The 'inviolability of borders' has become a slogan and not a description. The 'Westphalian' world that supposedly coincided with a centuries-old stratum of time and defined the meaning of 'international' once and for all, has itself become prescriptive. As Raymond Aron openly admits in the 1984 preface to his magnum opus, it seeks to privilege one reading of the world over all others: war and peace between nations (Aron 1984).

One also wonders whether, given the increase in the number of cultural, religious and class borders, the idea of a border can still be modelled on that of a geographical border, especially in spaces where organisational forms such as the European Union have destroyed the link between border, citizenship, territory and sovereignty and may be forging political communities that have not in any direct sense been constructed by wars, confrontations, no man's lands or lines of demarcation (Kelstrup and Williams 2000). There is no longer any necessary correspondence between the geographical border of a political entity and that of a nation state. Thanks to the Schengen Agreements, the European Union has introduced a distinction between internal and external borders. Regional groupings in Europe say that they are communities and have common borders, even when international borders whose pertinence seem to them less and less relevant, divide them.

The idea that a border is a meeting place, a place for economic transactions, trade and identity checks, that it is moveable and that it does not apply in the same way – or the same place – to every individual who wishes to cross it, therefore undermines political science's narrative and its politics of order, whilst its 'neo-liberalism' has suddenly been put to the test by economists who associate sovereignty and protection with protectionism and destruction. Their reflections upon systems and self-organisation lead them to the same conclusions as other disciplines. A border is a place for exchanges, and not for radical distinctions. A border can bring about changes of state, but it is only in very rare cases that it can close off a space, completely homogenise it, and filter everything that enters and leaves the system in any absolute sense.

A border, biologists tell us, is a broken or porous line that cannot loop back on itself because it is the exchange with the environment that creates life itself. Borders have never isolated or defined anything; at best, self-organising forms construct their own specificities because they are always exchanging information with their environment (Maturana and Varela 1980). Far from dividing and homogenising, borders 'communicate'. They are transitional places where transitions are recorded. They are rather like nodal points within a network, because the very notion of a border does imply that borders unite and divide and that there is something illusory or ideological about the idea of the global (in the sense of having no border). Here, the biologists are saying what economists and sociologists have been saying about state borders since the early 1970s, even though few listened to them (Strassoldo and delli Zotti 1982; Anderson 1996).

John Agnew (1994) was one of the first scholars on international relations to take stock of the paradigm shift that breaks the direct link between the border and the way the state uses narratives about territory, sovereignty, national identity and security to construct a discourse about itself. He demonstrates how the premises of a geography or a geopolitics that confuses border and territory, makes it impossible to think about international relations in any serious way, as it reduces them to either an inter-state order of clearly separated and contiguous entities, or a global order that appears to have no borders, constantly oscillating between these two arguments depending on the needs of the moment. Following the work of Rob Walker and his hugely important *Inside/Outside* (Walker 1993), Agnew warns us against discourses that superimpose nineteenth-century legal analyses of borders upon twenty-first century practices. All exchanges are seen as posing a threat – an attack on identity – and the discourse of contemporary globalisation, defined as a homogenous technological process, that predicts the demise of territories and states.

Many so-called alternative approaches to the concept of a border in fact simply reproduce an inverted version of the classical model based not on a discourse that critiques exceptionality, but on a discourse that eradicates borders. This critique of the notion of territory leads them to confuse a (state) territory or control over an extended political space with the notion of a border. They see globalisation as the abolition of borders and as the advent of a world in which there are no distinctions and no borders. As a result of this confusion, the development of globalisation is seen as leading inevitably to the end of territories and states, or even of a democracy that can exist only within a closed and homogeneous space that is conducive to recognition and patriotism. It therefore comes as no surprise that this alternative discourse evolves into its opposite and becomes ever more synonymous with a politics of order that seeks to ward off the threat of globalisation.

But as Agnew, Appadurai and Walker point out, globalisation increases the number of borders rather than eradicates them, and creates even more places and spaces by increasing the number of networks. The alternative is therefore not a choice between a border-line and the absence of any border, but between a border-line that goes on colonising the political imaginary and a network-border that allows us to conceptualise the contemporary as an increase in the number of border-points that are also transitional points.

In this alternative narrative, the border is not really a wall but something that has more to do with exchanges and the interaction between pressure differences. It is a liquid rather than a solid, a site of the differential and a place where identities can be labelled and traced, but not a form of blockage or of systematic controls over all transitional points and all the individuals who use them. It is still less a place where a clear distinction can be made between the categories of desirable and undesirable. If it is to function as a political institution, it has to be 'pixellated' and discontinuous, and must be a scatter of points or a broken line rather than a continuous line or circle. The intuitions of Gilles Deleuze and Félix Guattari's *Anti-Oedipus* (Deleuze and Guattari 2004) are embodied in the nomadic matrix that always threatens the state political order and its desire for immobility. That is why the border is the mark of the *hylé* (the materiality of the world) and why it functions as a triage unit that attempts to manage flows. It cannot be closed on a broad territorial scale or for any length of time, because it would have to be constantly retraced, made more dense, hardened and made continuous by the use of violence, security operations, surveillance and control. This Sisyphean task can never be completed. The fantasy of security dreams of a world in which borders can never be crossed, of a world that is homogeneous, pure and sacred, and its dream of sovereign autonomy brings violence into the world (Bigo, Bocco and Piermay 2009).

Checks on mobility and the localisation of borders

Ultimately, one is then faced with a disturbing question. Why deny the existence of practices of mobility, which are becoming ever more frequent and more banal? Why the increasingly aggressive assertion that there must be a perfect fit between border practices, the control practices of security professionals, the political desire to identify the nation with a territory, and the political desire to make that identity a homogeneous body that is different from the other entities around it and that will not tolerate any homogeneity in its make up, at a time when our knowledge of mobility and borders should make us more appreciative of mobility?

A detailed answer to this question would require an in-depth investigation into the origins of these systems of knowledge and a consideration of the way they prioritise geographical traces and law rather than history and orality. This would mean taking a new look at the genesis of the history of the mutual recognition of states, of piracy and non-recognised zones, of the colonial history of Western states, of the varied fortunes of international organisations, and of the disparity of declarations that sovereign territorial states are in theory equal. One would also have to study the practices that dominate and exploit certain territories, and analyse the perpetual declarations about (mutual) trust in the discriminatory practices of the authorities. Such studies usually end up by encouraging mutual trust between bureaucracies. However, trust implies a distrust of those who move around that quickly turns into a state of vigilance (Foessel 2010).

Although some work has been done on the genealogy of sovereignty and the constitution of the state and statehood, few scholars have been bold enough to closely examine and deconstruct the *aporia* on which international relations is based when it relies upon political science. The few exceptions are therefore precious in that they allow us to get away from classical conceptions in which political order, border and territory are simultaneously invoked in order to justify a politics of order (Walker 1982, 2006, 2009; Lacroix 1985; Bartelson 1995, 2001). They must, however, be completed by a sociology of the most everyday, routine practices of mobility. Once the border of order loses its sacred nature and once sociology demonstrates that Michel de Certeau's slogan 'We are all someone's migrant' (de Certeau and Giard 1983) is a day to day reality, it becomes impossible to see the world in terms of a distinction between the 'mobile' and the 'immobile', as a somewhat hasty reading of Zygmunt Bauman's work might suggest (Bauman 1998). We are all mobile, but we are not all mobile to the same degree, and some of us have a greater freedom of movement than others. To be more accurate, some of us can move rapidly even though we are under surveillance, without necessarily being arrested or stopped for identify checks, as I recently argued in a collective study on 'mobility under surveillance' (Bigo, Guittet and Scherrer 2010). The relationship between mobility, borders, freedom and security is a new research field, but more and more scholars are beginning to take an interest in the notion of surveillance studies. David Lyon is one of the most significant examples (Lyon 2001).

It is a commonplace to point out that inter-European travellers realise that they have changed country only when their mobile phone network (and the ring tone) changes because they travel unchecked, or because their identities were checked by the authorities of the country they are visiting at their point of departure, and not at the moment when they cross a line. Adrian Favell (2008) gives many examples of this in his work. At a deeper level, and as Elspeth Guild points out, it is increasingly rare for the forms of checks associated with borders to be actually carried out at the geographical border itself. They have been out-sourced, delegated to foreign authorities, and sometimes dematerialised. Their existence depends upon recognition by data bases and adequate software, which, in legal terms, blur the distinction between 'national' (in the nation-state sense) and 'international' by using European law to open up a different line of thought (Guild 2009).

As I have claimed in a previous study, policing now takes place at a distance all over the world. Controls take place in extra-border spaces, even if this means ceding some geographical territory, as the Australian and American governments have happily done, or 'pixellating' check points around the individual concerned by claiming that he or she has not legally crossed the border in the eyes of the law, even though that individual has landed in the middle of a space that is recognised as being that of a nation and a state, as in the case of European governments (Bigo 1996; Basaran 2010). Here, the definition of waiting areas in airports, ports or international railway stations takes us into a world where the noise of the discourse of the sovereign border forces us to turn a blind eye to these practices, or even to pluck out our eyes rather than see what happens when border and control are no longer synonymous. The territorial myth would not survive that test. Perhaps it is this, more so than anything else, that allows us to understand the emergence of electronic walls and detention centres, which cannot really be explained in terms of any geopolitical or economic rationality.

Let us be brutally clear about this. Despite the myth of the border-barrier, a whole body of historical and sociological research has demonstrated that no democratic regime has been able to apply such systematic checks. And no democratic regime can claim to have full control over the circulation of people, except in a symbolic sense. There has never been any complete checks on flows anywhere in the world, even when populations were subject to the most severe repression at the hands of Stalinist and Maoist regimes and their outposts in East Germany and Albania (Domenach 1992; Christian and Droit 2005; Pasqualinis 2009). The complete military mobilisation of all the resources available to a government can, very briefly, block transitional flows, especially if the territory concerned is small, but it can only do so for what is, in historical terms, a short space of time. The practice changes the nature of a government, or results in its self-destruction. Sealing the borders of a country is impossible. At best, it is possible to make those who cross them illegal in the eyes of the law. Controls therefore apply to the legal status of individuals and not to bodies, whatever the current rhetoric about the prevention of terrorism may say. The territory or 'homeland' cannot be made 'inviolable' and cannot be 'defended' by rigorous controls on borders that have in practical terms been transformed into barriers, and that can be crossed by those who are determined to do so and who have the economic means to do so (Ritaine 2009).

Procedures for the acceptance of foreigners by means of visas, surveillance technologies and triage mechanisms at the time of travelling, checks on air and maritime flows, the impossible Maginot line of ground crossing-points, rhetorical distinctions between 'crustacean' external borders, internal 'junction' borders, 'free circulation', all have to be discussed in terms of a disjunction between the politics of order and the practices of social change. The procedures of governmentality at a distance show us that, whilst state sovereignty can be enunciated and conceived in and by a territory and by a vision that sees borders as circles, the same cannot be said of the actual control practices that are implemented by security professionals with the agreement of politicians.

The policing-at-a distance 'dispositif' does not overlap with the sovereign 'dispositif'. It has been established on an 'alternative' basis and has already freed itself from the national myth of identity and integration of the professional politicians. It functions as an optical border that normalises majorities and categorises undesirables (Bigo 2006). The conflict between intelligence experts and border-guards tells us a lot about what appears to be a very abstract debate about the form of the border. Intelligence experts cannot and will not believe in the effectiveness of closing off territories. They want checks on mobility to be projected 'beyond' border controls. They are contemplating stationing police officers or border guards in consulates that function as outposts. This has resulted in a compromise formula with the professional politicians, and a way of reconceptualising human mobility. In order to achieve that objective, mobile human beings would have to be transformed into data that can be broken down, transferred and made available for networking by networked data bases. Electronic visas would have to be issued on the basis of the data that has already been accumulated about the individual in question, his or her family and similar-looking people, and not on the basis of his or her physical characteristics and still less those of his or her voice.

The practices of the transnational guilds described by Philippe Bonditti are spreading across Europe, Australia and the United States (Bonditti 2008). Despite the difference between those countries' political systems and their attachment to different norms, they agree about one thing: borders are becoming networks. Checks on mobility play with time, and try to anticipate which future passengers should be filtered out on grounds of 'undesirability' by using what appear to be specific categories that work with a hierarchy of fears and threats. But the actual population to which these categories apply remains ill-defined because they are not based upon any preliminary knowledge that obeys a legal logic but rather a logic of coercive preventive action and anticipated threats. No reliance upon biometrics can help resolve that confusion. In most cases, the physical individual is merely a virtual double, an object of suspicion who is actually not known to the intelligence services. The double is nothing more than a set of data collected for various reasons and over a variable period of time, and that data can be aggregated only because there is some similarity between it and an established threat-category. This is rather like trying to detect what Rumsfeld called, in almost theological terms, an 'unknown unknown' (Dillon and Reid 2001; Bonditti 2008; Guild 2009).

When it comes to mobility, the point is no longer to process the physical movements of an individual or to track that individual's travels, to check his or her biometric identity and authenticate it so as to prove that he or she has the right to enter the country. It is more a matter of reading that individual immediately at the 'molecular' level of data, of the life of his or her electronic double. Although the descriptions match, the individual is unaware of having a double. It is then possible to draw a parallel with Nikolas Rose's description of the borders of human life (Rose 2007). Human life is increasingly studied in quantum terms (molecular biology) rather than in classical terms (medicine). The same applies to the way the security of human mobility is guaranteed by defining the desirability or undesirability of the group to which an individual belongs. Managing the national myth and the myth of the border-as-order is a matter for the professional politicians. Managing the data bases and the classified profiles of our fears for the future is a matter for the (in)security professionals who have the authority to decide who is and who is not desirable. The border is no longer associated with security and political order. It has been divorced from these concerns, but mobility, which is so often identified with freedom, has now become a new challenge and the site of new threats to security (Bigo, Carrera, Guild and Walker 2010).

124 | a political sociology of transnational europe

References

Agamben, G. (1998) *Homo Sacer: Sovereign power and bare life*, Stanford: Stanford University Press.

Agnew, J. (1994) 'The territorial trap: the geographical assumptions of International Relations Theory', *Review of International Political Economy*, 1(1): 53–80.

Anderson, M. (1996) *Frontiers, Territory and State Formation*, Cambridge: Polity.

Appadurai, A. (2001) *Globalization*, Durham, NC: Duke University Press.

Aron, R. (1984) *Paix et guerre entre les nations*, 8th edn, with a new preface by the author. Paris: Calman-Lévy.

Bartelson, J. (1995) *A Genealogy of Sovereignty*, Cambridge: Cambridge University Press.

— (2001) *The Critique of the State*, Cambridge: Cambridge University Press.

Basaran, T. (2010) *Security, Law and Borders: At the limits of liberties*, London: Routledge.

Bauman, Z. (1998) *Globalization: The human consequences*, Cambridge: Polity.

Bigo, D. (1996) *Polices en réseaux: l'expérience européenne*, Paris: Presses de la Fondation nationale de sciences politiques.

— (2006) 'Le Visa Schengen et le recours à la biométrie' in X. Crettiez and P. Piazza, *Du papier à la biométrie: Identifier les individus*, Paris: Presses de Sciences Po, pp. 237–67.

Bigo, D., Bocco, R. and Piermay, J. L. (2009) 'Logiques de marquage: murs et disputes frontalières', *Cultures & Conflits* 1: 7–13.

Bigo, D., Carrera, S., Guild, E., and Walker, R. (2010) *Europe's 21st Century Challenge: Delivering liberty and security*, Aldershot: Ashgate.

Bigo, D., Guittet, E.-P. and Scherrer, A. (2010) *Mobilités sous surveillance*, Montréal: Athéna.

Bonditti, P. (2008) 'Homeland Security through Traceability: Technologies of control as critical infrastructures,' in M. D. Cavelty and K. Soby (eds), *Securing the 'Homeland': Critical infrastructure, risk and (in)security*, London: Routledge, pp. 130–52.

Christian, M. and Droit, E. (2005) 'Ecrire l'histoire du communisme: l'histoire sociale de la RDA et de la Pologne communiste en Allemagne, en Pologne et en France', *Genèses* 4: 118–33.

Cohen, A., Lacroix, B. and Riutort, P. (2009) *Nouveau manuel de science politique*, Paris: La Découverte.

De Certeau, M. and Giard, L. 'L'ordinaire de la communication', *Reseaux* 1(3): 3–26.

Deleuze, G. and Guattari, F. (2004) *Anti-Oedipus: Capitalism and Schizophrenia*, London: Continuum.

Dillon, M. and Reid, J. (2001) 'Global liberal governance: biopolitics, security and war', *Millenium: Journal of International Studies* 30(1): 41.

Domenach, J.-L. (1992) *Chine: l'archipel oublié*, Paris: Fayard.

Donnan, H. and Wilson, T.M. (1999) *Borders: Frontiers of modernity, nation and state*, New York and Oxford: Berg.

Favell, A. (2008) *Eurostars and Eurocities: Free Movement and Mobility in an Integrating Europe*, Oxford: OUP.

Foessel, M. (2010) *Etat de vigilance – critique de la banalité sécuritaire*, Paris: Bord de l'eau.

Foucher, M. (2004) 'Des fronts aux frontières en Europe et ailleurs,' in *Fronteres-Débat de Barcelona*, Barcelona: CCCB.

Giddens, A. (1984) *The Constitution of Society: Outlines of the theory of structuration*, Berkeley, CA: University of California Press.

—— (1987) *The Nation State and Violence: Contemporary critique of historical materialism*, Los Angeles: UCLA Press.

Guild, E. (2009) *Security and Migration in the 21st Century*, Cambridge: Polity.

Holsti, K. J. (1996) *The State, War and the State of War*, Cambridge: Cambridge University Press.

Kelstrup, M. and Williams, M. C. (2000) *International Relations Theory and the Politics of European Integration*, London: Routledge.

Lacroix, B. (1985) 'Ordre politique et ordre social, objectivisme, objectivation et analyse politique,' in M. Grawitz and J. Leca (eds) *Traité de science politique*, Paris: PUF, pp.356.

Legendre, P. (1974) *L'amour du censeur: essai sur l'ordre dogmatique*, Paris: Seuil.

Lyon, D. (2001) *Surveillance Society*, London: Open University Press.

Maturana, H. R. and Varela, F. J. (1980) *Autopoiesis and Cognition: The realization of the living*, Dordrecht: Riedel.

Moravcsik, A. (2009) 'Review of *The European Union and the Destruction of the Rhineland Frontier*' by M. Loriaux, *Perpectives on Politics*, 7(4): 989–90.

Musso, P. (1999) 'La Symbolique du réseau', *Quaderni*, 38(4): 69–98.

Pasqualinis, J. (2009) 'Glimpses inside China's Gulag,' *The China Quarterly* 134: 352–57.

Poggi, G. (1990) *The State, Its Nature, Development and Prospects*, Stanford: Stanford University Press.

Pratt, M. and Allison-Brown, J. (2000) *Borderlands under Stress*, London: Kluwer Law International.

Rancière, J. (1998) *Aux bords de la politique*, Paris: La Fabrique.

Ritaine, E. (2009) 'Des migrants face aux murs d'un monde-frontière', in C. Jaffrelot and C. Lequesne (eds) *L'Enjeu mondial: les migrations*, Paris: Presses de science po/L'Express.

Rose, N. S. (2007) *The Politics of Life Itself: Biomedicine, power and subjectivity in the twenty-first century*, Princeton NJ: Princeton University Press.

Sala-Molins, L. (1977) *La Loi, de quel droit?* Paris: Flammarion.

Serres, M. (1983) *Le Passage Du Nord-Ouest*, Collection Critique, Paris: Editiones de Minu

Sloterdijk, P. (2002) *Sphères, Vol. I: Bulles*, Paris: Pauvert.

Strange, S. (1996) 'The limits of politics', *Government and Opposition,* 30 (3): 291–311.

Strassoldo, R. and delli Zotti, G. (1982) *Cooperation and Conflict in Border Areas,* Milan: Franco Angeli Editore.

Thompson, J. (1994) *Mercenaries, Pirates and Sovereigns: State-building and Extraterritorial Violence in Early Modern Europe: International History and Politics,* Princeton NJ: Princeton University Press.

Tilly, C. (1990) *Contrainte et capital dans la formation de l'Europe 990–1990,* Paris: Aubier.

Torpey, J. C. (2000) *The Invention of the Passport: Surveillance, citizenship and the state,* Cambridge and New York: Cambridge University Press.

Veyne, P. (1988 [1983]) *Did the Greeks Believe in their Myths? Essay on the constitutive imagination,* trans. P. Wissing, Chicago: Chicago University Press.

Walker, R. B. J. (1982) *World Political and Western Reason: Universalism, pluralism, hegemony,* New York: World Order Models Project.

— (1993) *Inside/Outside: International Relations as political theory,* Cambridge: Cambridge University Press.

— (2006) 'The double outside of the modern international,' *International Journal of Diversity in Organizations,* 5(5): 73–82.

— (2009) *After the Globe, Before the World,* London: Routledge.

Weber, M. (1978) *Economy and Society: An outline of interpretive sociology,* Berkeley: University of California Press.

chapter six | redefining european higher education: global university rankings and higher education policy[1]

Tero Erkkilä and Niilo Kauppi

This chapter analyses the development of global university rankings, of transnational policies of higher education and European strategies to cope with macrolevel political and economical transformations in transnational higher education. In existing university rankings European universities – a building block of European nation-states – have not been able to compete with American universities. Although the general public has heard of only the dominant university rankings, a number of rankings measuring the 'quality' of higher education institutions (HEIs) have been developed in recent years. The European Commission has joined in on this activity, becoming the main defender of European universities and of their largest financers, European nation-states. The European Commission aims to create an alternative, European ranking list of world universities in which the assets of European, publicly funded universities would be highlighted. Moreover, the OECD as the organisation of the most developed nations, has also become involved in assessing HEIs, stressing academic learning results. In the following, we will analyse the symbolic logic of ranking lists in higher education, their uses, and the European Commission's and OECD's initiatives to create alternative world university classifications (see Erkkilä and Kauppi 2010).

These initiatives are political moves in a process of rapid restructuration of higher education at the global level. Rankings function as mechanisms of inclusion and exclusion with regard to actors gaining positions in the policy field. Conceptual and methodological questions are at the heart of these classification struggles: what is excellence in higher education, how should one measure it and who should do the measuring? How have the different indices been constructed, what are the criteria that have been used and to what purposes, what are the underlying premises behind higher education indices? The global landscape of higher education is dependent on the information that is produced on its objects, HEIs.

Public policy instruments such as university rankings define the relationships between HEIs and concerned governments. The first widely publicised global rankings have come to influence the policy agenda for higher education reform. The rankings that have since followed can be seen as critical reactions to these. However, evidence seems to indicate that once the global policy agenda for higher education has been initiated, it will be difficult for the actors implicated to perceive

---

1. The authors would like to thank Max Eklund for his help in collecting the data and for editorial assistance.

the policy agenda differently. The issues of concern, and ways to assess HEI, seem to have a strong continuity.

A further observation can be made about the link between European higher education policies and university rankings. While higher education has been a policy domain outside the competencies of the European Union, there are now increasing calls for European higher education policies that would limit the autonomy of individual member-states with regard to higher education. Here the policy discourse of 'European higher education' builds heavily on university rankings that now seem to define the policy problem (poor ranking of European HEIs) and its solution (increasing accountability through measurable outcomes).

In contrast to the world culture approach to modernity (see for instance Meyer *et al.* 1997), a structural approach to higher education and the policy instruments that are used, need to differentiate from one another and the specific webs of relationships they help create and legitimise. Currently, there is no single, fully structured field of global higher education, but rather a complex process of homogenisation that could be called a Global Higher Education Reform Movement where various social groups and institutions seek to impose similar, but partly differing symbolic constructions. The material and symbolic (legitimacy) resources at the disposal of these groups and institutions, the symbolic tools they produce, and the timing of their actions, condition their success.

The first part of this chapter discusses the development of the global university rankings since early 2000s. We will then turn to the responses by the European Commission and the OECD in trying to find a new form of numerical assessment that would not face as stark a political opposition as the rankings have. Finally, we will assess the new policies of the European Commission in which university rankings amalgamate higher education, economic competitiveness and European policy initiatives for higher education. Previously a national policy sector, higher education is increasingly becoming a European one with the European Commission assuming a leading role.

Global rankings in higher education: from serendipity to standardisation

In his letter of mission dated July 5, 2007, addressed to the minister of education in his newly formed government, French president Nicolas Sarkozy, declared that one of the main objectives of his government will be to have two French institutions of higher education in the world top 20 and ten among the best 100 universities in the world (reported in Bourdin 2008: 6–7). This statement not only testifies the importance given to the international classification of universities, but also the role of power of key individual actors in the setting of policy priorities. As the French presidency of the European Union had started a few days earlier, on July 1, 2007, one of the priorities set by Sarkozy was developing European higher education in the global economy. A year later, on July 3, 2008, French minister of higher education and research Valérie Pécresse, declared that she would be 'working on establishing a European-wide ranking of universities which can be used as the basis of mobility of both teachers and students' (Pécresse 2008). A few months later, in November, other powerful European elites were mobilised in other institutional sectors. Odile Quintin, director general of education in the European Commission in Brussels, participated in a European colloquium in Paris on the international comparison of educational systems, declaring that the European Commission would proceed to a call for offers for the creation of a ranking of universities that should be available in 2010.

The background for this significant initiative was; the publication of several global ranking lists of world universities, starting with the single league table produced since 2003 by the Jia Tao university in Shanghai, China, in which European universities fare poorly. The 'Brussels classification' wants to compete with the Jiao Tong classification and the list produced by the *Times Higher Education Supplement*, a journal specialised in higher education issues (see for instance Jobbins 2005). In this classification struggle over global norms in higher education, one of the motivating forces behind this policy initiative, is the growing number of mobile international students that are ready to pay for their studies. These students include students from the Third World as well as European students, for instance from the UK where a significant reform passed in 2006 has enabled institutions of higher education to charge for tuition. A growing global market, the field of higher education has also mobilised a variety of actors that are engaged in prestige competition (Weber 1968) involving global status hierarchies.

Established policy instruments such as the Shanghai list or the *Times Higher Education Supplement* list (THES), create alternative worlds by producing different maps of reality. The basic entities, universities, might be formally the same in different objectifications, but they are constructed in different ways and the relationships between universities will also differ, as they will be ordered following varying criteria. The above figures have contributed to the creation of a new 'status economy', which sets policies in higher education and innovation (Marginson 2009a).

At the beginning of the 2010s, global hierarchies and norms are reproduced, fought over and legitimised by a variety of research institutions specialising in the production of information on these hierarchies, and funded by nation-states or media corporations (see also Manners 2002). Due to their global coverage and high visibility, these lists are causing significant shifts in national policies following a similar policy script and the myth of modernity that is part of its power (Meyer *et al.* 1997). Sharing key causal beliefs and normative views, these symbolic power tools portray the world in a uniform manner. In so doing, their political nature is hidden. The figures produced and the perceptions of 'competition' that they communicate tend to lock policy actors in an iron cage, leaving little room for policy alternatives (Erkkilä and Piironen 2009).

In higher education, single league tables have provided their users (administrators, students, politicians, journalists) with objectified information in a rapidly growing international student market. Existing ranking systems represent key tools for higher education reform. The rankings became internationally policy relevant in the 2000s, due to the marketisation of higher education and increased mobility of students (Harvey 2008: 187–8).[2]

---

2. In the USA, evaluations of graduate programs started already in 1920s and a ranking of US colleges was published in 1983. The university rankings made their way to the UK in the 1990s.

For administrators and politicians, the quantitative social scientific information provided by these lists has become an indispensable part of policy planning (see for instance, Bourdin 2008; Harvey 2008). As tools of symbolic power, ranking lists reinforce, for certain users, pre-conceived ideas about university excellence and the models to emulate. For others not familiar with higher education, they present a certain state of affairs as being scientifically proven and thus inevitable, shaping this way, reality in the field of higher education.

The Chinese Shanghai Jiao Tong University Institute of Higher Education (SJTUIHE) and the British *Times Higher Education Supplement* (THES) publish the two major university rankings (see Saisana and D'Hombres 2008). With the support of the Chinese government – which wants to assess the performance of Chinese universities in comparison with the world's best universities – Jiao Tong has been producing an institutional ranking on a yearly basis since 2003. This ranking focuses on 'measurable research performance' (Liu and Cheng 2005: 133).[3] The first *Times Higher Education Supplement* entitled 'World University Rankings' was published in 2004. One of the driving forces behind the establishment of the league table was a perceived rising market demand, in the UK and globally, for advice on higher education (Jobbins 2005: 137).

In contrast to the Shanghai ranking, the THES composite index partly rests on present reputation, thereby reproducing established global reputational hierarchies (Marginson 2009b). Both the Shanghai and THES lists create a similar global order in which American universities tend to do the best, thus universalising certain research university models. In the THES ranking, UK and Australian universities fare better than in the Shanghai ranking. Continental European universities are badly positioned in both university league tables.[4]

The history of the Shanghai ranking is particularly interesting, as it is related to China's attempt at assessing where its universities stand internationally.[5] For this national exercise, the basic criteria for 'World Class University' were crafted. This example demonstrates that the way ideas are presented when the policy agenda is being shaped, format future debates, ruling out some ways of formatting policy problems (Bacchi 1999). The Shanghai ranking was a rather technical exercise to assess where Chinese universities stood vis-à-vis 'world class universities'. But having gained international attention and legitimacy, this ranking has since been uncritically adopted and emulated by policy makers all over the world.

---

3. In February 2007 the Shanghai ranking covered five disciplinary fields. It is particularly favourable to universities in English-speaking countries: they represented 71 per cent of the world's top 100 universities in 2006. US-based institutions occupy 17 of the world's 20 top ranking universities.

4. Since the launching of the Shanghai ranking a certain irritation and frustration could be detected in the statements of European political actors involved in higher education (for an example see French Minister of higher education and research, Valérie Pécresse 2008).

5. About the *Academic Ranking of World Universities* see [http://www.shanghairanking.com/aboutarwu.html]

However, it seems that the Chinese scholars were not attempting to construct the definitive global ranking of universities. Rather, it became by 'accident' a benchmark for standards of academic excellence. One explanation for its success is that the Chinese initiative caught the attention of policy makers and the media because it resonated with the timely context of global governance, where various indicators were already being created in other domains of state activities such as economic performance, corruption, government transparency, and gender equality.

While the Shanghai ranking could be seen as an anomaly, the *THES* ranking is more closely linked to the general drive for numerical policy instruments and evidence based policy making that started already in the 1960s, and which gained ground amid the New Public Management reforms of the late 1980s (Miller and Rose 1990). In a broad sense, the phenomenon of university rankings is linked to managerialist governance reforms and the emerging dynamics of global governance, where the use of rankings and indicators has become increasingly commonplace.

Ranking lists create a strong political imaginary of global competition. Moreover, the single league table presents a clear, 'objective' order, a goal to emulate, and the means to attain this goal. The top global rankings, Shanghai and THES, idealise the Anglo-American university model, which has come to dominate the policy agenda (compare Bacchi 1999). They present similar recipes for success in higher education: 'autonomisation' of universities, concentration of resources through the creation of poles of excellence, and greater funding for certain types of research through R&D investments for instance (Hazelkorn 2008). This recipe has been extensively integrated into reforms of higher education. A few examples will illustrate this. In a survey among heads of French institutions of higher education, it was disclosed that 71 per cent of respondents found the ranking lists useful, 66 per cent wanted to improve their institutions' position in the rankings, and a majority said they know how to do that (Bourdin 2008: 65). In Finland, an initiative to merge three universities used university rankings to identify the institutional characteristics of a 'top university' (Opetusministeriö 2007: 32–9).

More recently, these recipes have been codified in several World Bank publications on world-level institutions of higher education and research (see for instance Salmi 2009). These publications aim at providing governments and involved institutions clear instructions on how to proceed in establishing world-class universities.

The Politics of Higher Education Assessments and the Critique of Existing Rankings

Numerical information directs policy actors' attention to 'reality' as it is depicted by existing figures (Erkkilä and Piironen 2009). Political struggles could provide a way to escape such processes of instrumentalisation. However, at a closer look, present debates on university rankings reinforce certain ontological and epistemological *a priori*. In order to become credible players in the classification struggles, actors need to adopt the ontological and methodological views that structure these struggles. Hence even the critiques of top rankings assume the instrumental logic of numerical assessments of higher education.

It comes as no surprise that the most criticised assessments are the THES and Shanghai rankings. They rank the top rated universities consistently, but their overall correlation is only moderate (r ≤ 0.58) (Saisana and D'Hombres 2008: 11). Several scholars have pointed to their heavy use of bibliometric methods (Van Raan 2005; Gingras 2008, see also Liu *et al.* 2005). Rankings do not assess the research that is done in research institutes.[6] Moreover, they impose the norms of leading research universities (Kivinen and Hedman 2007).

The Shanghai ranking counts the Nobel Prizes awarded to an institution, which is also problematic since Nobel Prize laureates continue to influence their university's results even after their retirement or death. For its part, the THES ranking largely rests on an opinion based peer review, lacking thorough assessment. The THES ranking system offers very little information on the quality of teaching. The Shanghai ranking does not assess the quality of teaching at all.

The existing rankings also don't take into account the variations between disciplines, let alone assess the research by discipline. Furthermore, the information is presented as a fact and not as the result of a choice in terms of what to measure and how (Marginson 2006: 139). Also the academic community has called for their greater involvement in the assessments (Usher and Savino 2007).

Despite these shortcomings, university rankings have become part of the global higher education landscape. The issue has been politicised, with due institutional developments, and there is now a classification struggle over the rankings, most visible in the attempts to create new numerical assessments for HEIs. Tables 6.1, 6.2 and 6.3 show how the number of actors involved in global higher education assessment has expanded since the early 2000s. This expansion also involved a critique of existing numbers. If there was a consensus about the criteria of assessment in forming a ranking, no additional numbers would be needed. But as this is a highly contested matter among practitioners and stakeholders, there are constantly new figures that are being crafted for the purpose of evaluating the quality of HEI.

The Shanghai and THES rankings have largely set the policy agenda for future rankings (see Table 6.1). Hence, many of the knowledge products that have been produced since have commented on these two major ranking, mainly critical of their approaches. The first round of actors to produce global university rankings after Shanghai and THES were mostly academic research institutes that often claimed to possess a better approach to the bibliometric analysis used in Shanghai and the THES (Table 6.2). This is for instance apparent in the Taiwanese HEEACT ranking, as well as in the University of Twente's global ranking and the SCImago ranking.

---

6. For instance, from a European perspective, they fail to appreciate top research in Germany and France. Furthermore, they do not take into account the resources and institutional designs that are available for successful organisations.

Table 6.1: Global university rankings published in the first half of the 2000s

	Shanghai University Ranking of World Universities[7]	Times Higher Education-QS World University Rankings[8]	Webometrics Ranking of World Universities[9]	Affordability and Accessibility Comparison of Global Higher Education Rankings[10]
Publisher	Center for World-Class Universities and the Institute of Higher Education of Shanghai Jiao Tong University, China	Times Higher Education and careers advice company Quacquarelli Symonds Ltd	Cybermetrics Lab at the Consejo Superior de Investigaciones Científicas (CSIC), Spain	Educational Policy Institute (EPI), North-America
Published	2003–2010	2004–2009	2004–2010 (twice per year)	2005
Indicators	-Alumni winning Nobel or Fields medals (10%) -Highly cited researchers (20%) -Staff winning Nobel or Fields (20%) -Papers published in *Nature and Science* (20%) -*Science Citation Index* and *Social Science Citation Index* (20%) -Per capita academic performance of an institution (10%)	-Peer peer review (40%) -Publications and citations per research staff (20%) -Graduate employability recruiter review (10%) -Percentage of international staff (5%) and students (5%) -Faculty staff-student ratio (20%)	Indicators by main search engines: -Size -Visibility -Number of documents in web domain -Number of publications in Google Scholar database	Accessibility indicators: -Participation Rates -Attainment Rates -*Educational Equity Index* -*Gender Parity Index* Affordability indicators: -Education Costs as a percentage of Ability To Pay(ATP) -Total Costs as a percentage of ATP -Net Costs as a percentage of ATP -Net Cost After Tax Expenditure as a percentage of ATP -Out-of-Pocket Costs as a percentage of ATP -Out-of-pocket Costs After-Tax Expenditures as a percentage of ATP

7 http://www.arwu.org/ARWUMethodology2003.jsp   8 http://www.timeshighereducation.co.uk/
9 http://www.webometrics.info/about_rank.html   10 http://www.educationalpolicy.org/pdf/global2005.pdf

Table 6.2: Global university rankings published in the latter half of the 2000s

	Performance Ranking of scientific papers for world universities[11]	The Leiden Ranking[12]	The SCImago Institutions Ranking[13]	QS World University Ranking[14]
Publisher	Higher Education Evaluation and Accreditation Council of Taiwan (HEEACT)	The Centre for Science and Technology Studies (CWTS), Leiden University	The SCImago research group, Spain	Careers advice company Quacquarelli Symonds Ltd
Published	2007 – 2010	2008, 2010	2009 – 2010	2010
Indicators	-Research productivity (Article production indicators) (20%) -Research Impact (Citations indicators) (30%) -Research Excellence (H-index of last 2 years, articles in high-impact journals, amount of highly cited papers) (50%)	-Number of publications (P) -Size-independent, field-normalised average impact ('crown indicator' ($CPP/FCSm$) -Size-dependent 'brute force' impact indicator, the multiplication of P with the university's field-normalised average impact ($P * CPP/FCSm$) -'simple' citations-per-publication indicator (**CPP**) In 2010 also: -Size-independent, field-normalised average impact, (alternative crown indicator: **MNCS2**)	-Publication output -Cites per Document -International Collaboration with foreign institutions -Journal average importance -Scientific impact of an institution and the world average impact of publications	*-The Academic Reputation Index* (40%) *-The Employer Reputation* (10%) *-International Faculty Index* (10%) *-Citations per Faculty Index* (20%) *-Staff/student ratio* (20%)

[11] http://ranking.heeact.edu.tw/en-us/2010/Page/Indicators
[12] http://www.cwts.nl/ranking/ See also http://www.socialsciences.leiden.edu/cwts/products-services/leiden-ranking-2010-cwts.html#europe
[13] http://www.scimagoir.com/pdf/sir_2009_world_report.pdf
[14] http://www.topuniversities.com/university-rankings/world-university-rankings/2010/results

Table 6.3: Global university rankings published since 2010

	Times Higher Education – Thomson Reuters[15]	High Impact Universities[16]	The U-Multirank[17]	The Assessment of Higher Education Learning Outcomes(AHELO)[18]
Publisher	Times Higher Education and data provider Thomson Reuters	University of Western Australia	Consortium for Higher Education and Research Performance Assessment (CHERPA)	Organisation for Economic Co-operation and Development (OECD)
Published	2010	2010	Forthcoming 2011	Forthcoming 2012
Indicators	-The learning environment (30 %) -Research influence (32.5 %) -Industry income (2.5 %) -Volume, income and reputation of research (30 %) -International mix of staff and students (5 %)	-Leo Egghe's g-index for research performance[19]	Preliminary: -Performance in the dimension of teaching and learning -Performance in research dimension -Performance in the knowledge transfer dimension -International orientation -Regional engagement	Quality of teaching and learning in higher education via evaluation of student performance Indicators: -Generic skills of students -Contextual information -Discipline-specific skills

15 http://www.timeshighereducation.co.uk/world-university-rankings/2010–2011/analysis-methodology.html
16 http://www.highimpactuniversities.com/
17 http://www.u-multirank.eu/project/
18 http://www.oecd.org/
19 L. Egghe, 'Theory and practise of the g-index', Scientometrics 69(1): 131–152, Jan. 2006.

Since 2010, there have been new actors joining the efforts of HEI assessments (Tables 6.2 and 6.3). But this is only seemingly so, as for instance the QS World University Rankings is in fact the old *THES* ranking, now only separated from the *THE* brand due to a break in contract. The fact that a private company such as Quacquarelli Symonds Ltd should continue to pursue its knowledge production activities even after its contract with *THE* has ended shows the mounting economic interest in ranking universities. On the other hand, the *THES* has found a new provider for its ranking in Thomson Reuters. The above changes and the related negotiations over copyright issues, also make the actors and interests behind the figures visible. There are also recent attempts at enhancing the bibliometrical analysis, as the High Impact Universities ranking indicates.

Following a first phase of criticism that focused on quantitative indicators, a second phase of critical tones has been dealing with the qualitative aspects of evaluation (see Table 6.3). More recently, there is a clear shift towards more qualitative assessments of higher education, denouncing attempts to create a single cumulated ranking number. This is particularly clear in the European Union's activities on the matter. Another current critique is the lack of assessment of learning results, as the current rankings tend to stress the research output. The OECD's AHELO initiative exemplifies this phase.

Entering the field of global higher education assessments: the European Commission and the OECD

In 2008, the European Commission declared that it would create an alternative, European ranking list of world universities that would 'do justice'[20] to European universities. As a political actor with considerable organisational resources such as various research centres – when compared to specialised publications (*THES*) –, the Commission entered the field of global higher education with the aim of transforming its structure and criteria. This move reflects a broader competition over prestige (see Weber 1968: 910–11) that has considerable economic implications.

In 2009, at least three overlapping European Commission initiatives could be identified in the domain of higher education rankings, indicating the issue's growing politicisation. In June 2008, the European Commission appointed an Expert Group on Assessment of University Based Research. Later the same year, during the rotating French presidency of the European Union, a project on 'Design and Testing the Feasibility of a Multi-dimensional Global University Ranking' was launched. Along with these initiatives, there is ongoing work for profiling and classifying institutions of higher education. The Commission also participates in the OECD's AHELO initiative whose purpose is to assess higher education learning outcomes.[21] What is remarkable about these different initiatives, in particular

---

20. According to Director General of education in the European Commission Odile Quintin (quoted in Dubouloz 2008: 1).

21. OECD, AHELO [http://www.oecd.org/edu/ahelo].

the OECD's AHELO, is a constant opposition to an accumulated figure, a single ranking number, as formulated in the existing university rankings. Nevertheless both the European Commission's and OECD's mappings are based on the use of indicators. They merely decline to produce an aggregate number, a ranking.

The Commission's strategy reveals the logic of struggles over classification. Since European universities rank relatively poorly in all existing rankings, the European Commission resorted to a radical solution, introducing a new global assessment of higher education. However, this strategy is successful only if the European Commission succeeds in delegitimising existing ranking lists by producing credible alternative information. Depending on the interests of the commissioners, certain types of information will be prioritised. For instance, the Chinese government was mostly interested in clearly measurable information on the so-called hard sciences, whereas the European Commission is concerned about the performance of European universities. The European Commission plans to create a new type of knowledge construct, a 'mapping' of certain key qualities in higher education that would include teaching and research, and elite and mass-commercial institutions (European Commission 2008a).[22] The basic framework of the U-Multirank (see Table 6.3) is still in the works. During the pilot phase it will cover two disciplines (business studies and engineering) with a sample of some 150 (both European and non-European) universities, before being expanded to the social sciences as well.[23]

The OECD's AHELO seeks to evaluate four strands of higher education learning outcomes: generic skills, discipline's specific aspects of learning (engineering and economics), contextual factors of learning, and students' ability to improve their skills (see Table 6.3). Both projects are nominally at the stage of a feasibility study, but likely to evolve into comprehensive assessment tools.

These initiatives are as much attempts to enter the field of creating assessments of HEI as they are critiques of existing rankings. One should also bear in mind that the OECD, as an organisation producing expert knowledge on governance, is dependent on the knowledge products that it provides. Therefore its participation in the field of the numerical assessment of higher education is also a question of credibility and legitimacy in the eyes of its member countries. The ongoing classification struggles allow the OECD to enter a fast evolving field of expert knowledge by creating a new knowledge product.

---

22. Following the conclusions of the Berlin Principles on Ranking of Higher Education Institutions (written by a group of American and European experts in 2004), the aim of the EU initiative was to produce a new 'fairer' ranking system to replace the existing league tables. Berlin Principles on Ranking of Higher Education Institutions [http://www.che.de/downloads/Berlin_Principles_IREG_534.pdf].

23. The winning bid for the European Commission's open call for tender for the creation of a multi-dimensional global university ranking came from the CHERPA-Network consortium, a consortium which is headed by the Centre for Higher Education Policy Studies of the Twente University (Netherlands) and the Centrum für Hochschulentwicklung (Germany) (CHE [http://www.che.de/]).

Although all the university rankings have their deficiencies there has been an improvement in the technical qualities of these knowledge products. This has been due partly to an increased awareness of the power of these public policy instruments. But are the new rankings or classifications likely to replace the existing ones?

Future uses of higher education assessments: timing and visibility versus resources

While the EU is driven by the motives of certain powerful member states such as Germany and France, whose universities and research centres do not perform well in existing rankings, and the OECD is seeking a more prominent role for itself in a rapidly developing field of policy coordination, both initiatives testify to the growing politicisation of assessments of higher education. In the classification struggle that the different producers of rankings are now engaged with, timing the launch of their knowledge product seems crucial for visibility and influence. The Shanghai and *THES* ranking have become benchmarks, in many ways initialising the field of higher education assessments. What is remarkable in the early rankings is that they have largely come outside the realm of multilateral governance or intergovernmental decision-making. Their success might have to do with the fact that they have largely bypassed the political tensions between countries that HEI rankings highlight.

The second aspect in explaining the current hierarchies among rankings is media visibility. Again, the ability of Shanghai and THES to lead the way in numerical assessment of world class universities has put them in the spotlight. But here also the nature of the knowledge product is relevant. At present all of the actors involved in the global assessments of higher education reduce a highly complex and contentious policy field (higher education) into a data set. This can be highly problematic in terms of assessment criteria and the policy outcomes on the national level.

Nevertheless, the above problems of quantification go largely missing in the media use of the figures. Almost without exception the numbers are taken at their face value and referred to uncritically. The simplicity of the aggregate figures is an asset for gaining media visibility. The single ranking number is easy to communicate in a newspaper story, whereas the more sophisticated classifications that are now being constructed run the risk of becoming too complex to understand. They might be fairer and methodologically sounder, but they don't give easy answers, which is exactly why the league tables are likely to have an upper hand in the media. It will be a significant challenge for the developers of U-Multi-rank to explain their classification to the media and to get its results publicly mediated.

Though the new contenders in the field might be making better assessment tools the Shanghai and THES rankings are not easily challenged, since they have been internationally mediated and enjoy a wide audience globally. Though neither of these initial rankings has yet the lifespan of a full ten years they nevertheless are already perceived as institutions in the field. They profit from having gotten to 'the market' early, and thus still shaping it. They have certainly benefited from the seemingly apolitical nature of their products and from the simplicity of the league tables based on an aggregate number.

Though the EU and OECD have unparalleled resources at their disposal, the above logic of mediating expert knowledge may prevent them from gaining a hold in the field as it is now institutionalised. Looking at a possible future, it seems that the new contenders such as the U-Multirank and AHELO may simply be reserved for limited expert use, lacking the visibility to become a real challenge to the two best known rankings in media visibility. Hence, the way the policy field is structured is essential for the future debates. Moreover, as numbers can only be criticised by numbers, the multiple uses of rankings has a structuring effect on the future attempts to assess higher education. Paradoxically, while the numerical assessment tools become more sophisticated and complex, they will give the existing numbers and their media coverage an advantage. Furthermore, while creating a global university assessment tool is resource intensive, the ways in which such expert knowledge gets public attention may be more significant for settling the rank order between those who rank the universities, than the resources at their disposal.

Judging from the U-Multirank and AHELO initiatives, one would get the impression that the European Commission would be opposed to the use of rankings. Interestingly, while there have been attempts at creating alternatives to the higher education rankings, the policy documents of the European Commission increasingly refer to rankings when arguing for the resolution of European-wide higher education policy problems. Moreover, the rankings also function as a policy prescription that outlines certain elements of success in higher education. More importantly, they participate in the creation of a demand for European-wide higher education policies.

University rankings and 'european higher education'

Though global university rankings do not assess the national or regional higher education systems per se but rather HEIs, they nevertheless have geographical implications. How do German or French universities fare against British universities? What about Europe vis-à-vis the United States and Asia? According to the Chinese, the motivation for the Shanghai ranking was that Chinese authorities wanted to know how their HEIs were doing in comparison to 'world class universities'. Since the publication of the first global rankings, this concern has jumped to the agenda of all countries that wish to improve their HEI's standing in these rank orders.

For scholars, the future of higher education in Europe has been a policy problem for some time, leading to the outlining of a new European university model. Here the historical perspective is often based on the Humboldtian tradition (Paletschek 2002). Scholars treat this as a historical model that now is threatened by the Bologna process (Michelsen 2010) and the pursuit of competitiveness in a knowledge-based economy (Nybom 2003).

Though the redefining of the European field of higher education cannot be reduced to the university rankings, it is nevertheless becoming more and more apparent that the rankings have the ability to shape policy problems and the political and institutional responses to these (Kehm and Stensaker 2009; Hazelkorn 2011). The global rankings become cartographies of institutional traditions. From the European perspective, the global university rankings have created a rather mixed picture, with only few top ratings in the league tables of 'world class universities'. This has not only drawn interest to the historical foundations of European universities (cf Hobsbawn 1987) but also strengthened the policy concerns over the state of higher education in Europe.

European HEIs are now increasingly being compared to American and Asian universities. The rankings make such comparisons seemingly simple, portraying new peers and rivals. Within Europe, rankings have shown clear differences between countries and systems, such as between the British, German and French universities, top institutions in UK have gained the upper hand in existing rankings. These comparisons make the different historical models appear as policy choices that can be easily changed.

But this ahistorical policy discourse often overlooks the national institutional context where HEIs function. For instance, both France and Germany have significant research institutions outside universities, and these are not fully taken into account in current rankings. Moreover, the institutional practices that exist in a given country are not easily transferred since they are linked to a myriad of cultural and institutional practices that are often not accounted for when assessing HEIs with standardised criteria. Furthermore, universities also have to correspond to the prevailing social values of a society. For example Nordic universities have shared a model that is in line with the egalitarian value base of these societies and which emphasises broad accessibility with no tuition fees.

Nevertheless, university rankings are increasingly being used as a motivation for adopting new policies in higher education. Often in the background is the hope to gain economic benefits through higher education as a key element in an innovation system. European higher education as a policy problem, has been linked with the economic performance of the European Union, first in the Lisbon strategy and the following strategy work on 'Jobs and growth'.

Already in 2004, a report on the Lisbon strategy for economic performance cites university rankings when comparing Europe with other regions (High Level Group 2004). It points out that European universities are lagging behind and recommends recruiting 'world-class' researchers (High Level Group 2004: 20–21). The policy recommendation is revisited in the European Commission's communication 'Mobilising the brainpower of Europe', which seeks to 'enable' the European universities to 'make their full contribution to the Lisbon strategy'. The Shanghai and THES rankings are mentioned when identifying the policy problem: insufficient research performance vis-à-vis Asian and US universities (European Commission 2005a: 3). The uniformity and egalitarianism of the European university system is seen as a 'bottleneck', as is the lack of centers of excellence (European Commission 2005a: 3–4). The appendix to the above

Commission communication contains a lengthy discussion on the relationship between higher education and competitiveness, a discussion that refers to global indexes on economic competitiveness (European Commission 2005b).

The modernisation agenda is further elaborated in the context of the Bologna process (European Commission 2007). Started in 1999, the Bologna process is linked to the Lisbon process as a remedy for the poor performance of European HEIs (European Commission 2008b, European Commission 2009). There is also a link to the European Commission's support for European ranking initiatives. While this was most apparent during the French presidency in 2007, the trend has been visible ever since.

In September 2011 the European Commission published a communication on 'supporting growth and jobs – an agenda for the modernisation of Europe's higher education system' (COM(2011) 567 final). The communication refers to university rankings, with a double logic with regard to rankings. First, the existing rankings (read the Shanghai ranking) have shown that there are too few top HEIs in Europe. Second, more transparency – that is rankings – is needed to tackle this problem:

> Too few European higher education institutions are recognised as world class in the current, research oriented global university rankings. For instance, only around 200 of Europe's 4000 higher education institutions are included in the top 500, and only 3 in the top 20, according to the latest Academic Ranking of World Universities. And there has been no real improvement over the past years. There is no single excellence model: Europe needs a wide diversity of higher education institutions, and each must pursue excellence in line with its mission and strategic priorities. With more transparent information about the specific profile and performance of individual institutions, policy-makers will be in a better position to develop effective higher education strategies and institutions will find it easier to build on their strengths (COM(2001) 567 final: 2–3).

The above quote denounces the idea of a single model for excellence in higher education and instead calls for 'diversity'. But how does diversity match with quantification? The EU's U-Multirank is allegedly a new type of assessment tool that allows the user to choose the assessment criteria to be used in the rating. However, the criteria and their attributes are nevertheless defined by the developers of the U-Multirank, leaving only limited room for case-by-case consideration. Also the broader institutional context in different countries is not being acknowledged.

The attributes and the respective rank orders in the rankings shape the policies on national level. Presently, there is a strong convergence in higher education policies in Europe and globally. While the producers of ranking information possess no norm-giving authority over HEIs, or national administrations responsible for higher education, nevertheless they seem to have a major impact on higher education policies and institutional reforms in Europe. This mechanism of influence is perhaps best understood as reflexivity (Miller and Rose 1990, Erkkilä and Piironen 2009), meaning actors' compliance with a perceived norm.

Through this reflexivity, rankings create a political imaginary of competition that makes improving ones standing in the assessments mandatory. This phenomenon is also related to the numerical presentation of policy information (Porter 1996). Max Weber identified this as a general concern of modern government, arguing that statistics and bookkeeping have the ability to create an 'iron cage' which seemingly leaves no other options but to submit to its calculative logic.

As a result, rankings as knowledge products, effectively work as policy instruments. They portray a state of affairs in a given policy domain as competition between different actors, such as HEIs. They provide goals for improvement (rank order) and through their attributes they outline what to improve. The highest ranked universities become ideational models to copy. Consequently, university rankings take part in the convergence in higher education and innovation policies globally, motivated often by perceived gains in the knowledge-based economy. Higher education is valued only for its economic potential.

On one hand university rankings are a result of increasing international collaboration on higher education. So far higher education has been a subject of limited global or transnational policy work or regulation, but because of the high economic stakes that are involved, new means are been sought to assess and steer this policy domain. On the other hand, rankings reinforce and legitimise the political imaginary of competition in higher education.

In the European context the political imaginary of global competition in higher education has given the European Commission the opportunity to construct a policy problem labeled 'European higher education', that now is tightly coupled with economic competitiveness. The French Presidency of the European Union in 2007 helped identify the problem and its resolution. While the initial idea was to criticise the dominant global rankings, the logic has since then shifted into European policy initiatives that have adopted the policy prescriptions inherent in the global rankings.

The Commission has backed the development of new assessment tools for HEIs, further accelerating the Europeanisation of European higher education policy. While the U-Multirank might not become an assessment tool of global relevance, it will most certainly be an important policy instrument for the European higher education initiatives that now challenge national models of higher education. Numerical assessment tools give the European Union more influence on higher education policies than its actual competencies would imply. The political struggle around global university rankings is therefore essential for an understanding of the future development of European higher education policy.

Conclusions

Since the first global university rankings in the first part of the 2000s, competition in higher education has escalated. Specialised research institutes of various kinds and supranational institutions such as the European Commission and the OECD have proposed alternative constructions of global higher education. Consequently the information on HEI has become more specialised and diversified. It involves today, complex research institutions that are absorbed with this activity on a permanent basis. However, the European Commission and OECD have only partially politicised the issue of university rankings. The ontological and epistemological fundamentals set by the so-called Shanghai and THES lists are still either uncritically adopted or only slightly altered. Instead of abandoning the numerical instruments under criticism, the challengers have refined them. As a result of this classification activity, the global map of higher education has become more structured and ranking lists have turned into legitimate policy instruments for global governance in higher education. Despite their limitations, they continue to serve as a basis for a number of significant higher education reforms. The European Commission's activities in promoting European universities can be read as a political strategy that aims at helping European nation-states to redefine their role in global knowledge and economic competition. At the same time, it has marked an opening for European-wide policies on higher education.

To summarise, we have underlined four key points regarding the global structuration of higher education. First, public policy instruments such as university rankings create and define the relationships between HEIs and the governments concerned. Second, the contestation of the existing figures should be seen as a classification struggle, where the actors involved try to improve their position in the rankings, not only by adhering to the norms they convey but also by changing the criteria of assessment. A first phase of criticism was based on the use of 'better' bibliographical methods. A second phase of criticism brought in arguments for more qualitative assessments and inclusion of learning results. Third, the new actors wishing to influence global higher education assessments are still trapped by the logic of ranking. While there are improvements in the criteria of numerical assessment, the logic of ranking now steers the restructuration of global higher education more forcibly than ever. Fourth, looking at the future of the rankings, it seems unlikely that the Shanghai and THES ranking would be replaced any time soon. Though the EU's and OECD's classifications may be more sophisticated knowledge products, they are also increasingly complex in their presentation. Established rankings have the advantage of being known entities and of being simple enough to be used in the media and by practitioners. It might be that the new, more sophisticated assessment tools will find their main users in policy expert circles.

The European higher education field will be the main context where the new U-Multirank will be used. This implies the rising importance of the European Commission in setting the future agenda for higher education policies in Europe. While educational policies have traditionally belonged to the primary competencies of EU member states, rankings as new policy instruments have helped construct higher education as a 'European' policy issue that requires European Commission leadership.

References

Bacchi, C. L. (1999) *Women, Politics and Policy*, Trowbridge: Sage Publications.

Bourdin, J. (2008) *Sur le défi des classements dans l'enseignement supérieur.* Rapport d'information no. 422. Sénat, Session extraordinaire de 2007–2008, 2 juillet, 2008. Available /www.senat.fr/rap/r07–442/r07–4421.pdf (accessed 4 April 2009).

Dubouloz, C. (2008) 'L'Europe veut lancer son propre classement des universités', *Le Temps*, Carrières Management Supplément, 5 December.

Egghe, L. (2006) 'Theory and practise of the *g*-index', *Scientometrics* 69(1): 131–152.

Erkkilä, T. and Kauppi, N. (2010) 'Alternatives to Existing University Rankings', in *World Social Science Report*, Paris: UNESCO Publishing, pp. 239–241.

Erkkilä, T. and Piironen, O. (2009) 'Politics and Numbers: The Iron Cage of Governance Indices', in R. W. Cox, III (ed.) *Ethics and Integrity in Public Administration: Concepts and cases*, Armonk: M.E.Sharpe, pp.125–145.

European Commission (2005a) 'Communication from the commission: mobilising the brainpower of Europe: enabling universities to make their full contribution to the Lisbon Strategy', COM(2005) 152 final.

— (2005b) 'Commission staff working paper: Annex to the Communication from the Commission, Mobilising the brainpower of Europe: enabling universities to make their full contribution to the Lisbon Strategy, European Higher Education in a Worldwide Perspective'.

— (2007) 'From Bergen to London: The contribution of the European Commission to the Bologna Process'.

— (2008a) 'Design and Testing the Feasibility of a Multi-dimensional Global University Ranking', Tender no. EAC/36/2008, Brussels: European Commission, Directorate-General for Education and Culture.

— (2008b) 'Commission staff working document. Progress Towards the Lisbon Objectives in Education and Training. Indicators and Benchmarks 2009'.

— (2009) 'Commission staff working document. Progress Towards the Lisbon Objectives in Education and Training. Indicators and Benchmarks 2009'.

— (2011) 'Supporting Growth and Jobs. An Agenda for the Modernization of Europe's Higher Education System', COM(2011) 567 final.

Gingras, Y. (2008) *La fièvre de l'évaluation de la recherche: Du mauvais usage de faux indicateurs,* research note 2008–05, Centre interuniversitaire de recherche sur la science et la technologie (CIRST).

Harvey, L. (2008) 'Rankings of Higher Education Institutions: a critical review', *Quality in Higher Education*, 14(3): 187–207.

Hazelkorn, E. (2009) 'Impact of Global Rankings on Higher Education Research and the Production of Knowledge', Occasional Paper No. 16 in UNESCO Forum on Higher Education, Research and Knowledge. Online. Available /http://unesdoc.unesco.org/images/0018/001816/181653e.pdf (accessed

22 November 2011).

—   (2011) Rankings and the Reshaping of Higher Education: The Battle for World-Class Excellence, Basingstoke: Palgrave Macmillan.

High Level Group (2004) 'Facing the Challenge: The Lisbon Strategy for Growth and Employment. Report from the High Level Group chaired by Wim Kok', Luxembourg: Office for Official Publications of the European Communities.

Hobsbawn, E. (1987) 'Introduction: Inventing traditions', in E. Hobsbawm and T. Ranger (eds) *The Invention of Tradition*, Cambridge: Cambridge University Press.

Jobbins, D. (2005) 'Moving to a global stage: a media view', *Higher Education in Europe* 30(2): 137–145.

Kehm, B. M. and Stensaker, B. (2009) *University Rankings, Diversity, and the New Landscape of Higher Education*, Amsterdam: Sense Publishers.

Kivinen, O. and Hedman, J. (2007) 'World-wide university rankings: a Scandinavian approach', *Scientometrics*, 74(3): 391–408.

Liu, N. C. and Cheng, Y. (2005) 'The Academic Ranking of World Universities – Methodologies and Problems', *Higher Education in Europe* 30(2): 127–136.

Liu, N. C., Cheng, Y. and Liu, L. (2005) 'Academic ranking of world universities using scientometrics: a comment to the fatal attraction', *Scientometrics*, 64(1): 101–109.

Manners, I. (2002) 'Normative power Europe: a contradiction in terms?', *Journal of Common Market Studies*, 40(2): 235–258.

Marginson, S. (2006) 'Global university rankings: implications in general and for Australia', *Journal of Higher Education Policy and Management* 29(2): 131–142.

—   (2009a) 'Open source knowledge and university rankings', *Thesis Eleven,* 96: 9–39.

—   (2009b) 'University Rankings, Government and Social Order: Managing the field of higher education according to the logic of the performative present-as-future', in M. Simons, M. Olssen and M. Peters (eds) *Re-reading Education Policies,* Rotterdam, Sense Publishers, pp. 584–604.

Meyer, J.W., Boli, J., Thomas, G. and Ramirez, F. (1997) 'World society and the nation state', *American Journal of Sociology* 103(1): 144–181.

Michelsen, S. (2010) 'Humboldt meets Bologna', *Higher Education Policy* 23(2): 151–172.

Miller, P. and Rose, N. (1990) 'Political Rationalities and Technologies of Government', in S. Hänninen and K. Palonen (eds) *Texts, Contexts, Concepts: Studies on politics and power in language*, Helsinki: Finnish Political Science Association, pp.171–183.

Nybom, T. (2003) 'The Humboldt legacy: reflections on the past, present, and future of the European university', *Higher Education Policy* 16(2): 141–159.

Opetusministeriö(2007)'Teknillisenkorkeakoulun,Helsinginkauppakorkeakoulun ja Taideteollisen korkeakoulun yhdistyminen uudeksi yliopistoksi' [The merging of the Helsinki University of Technology, the Helsinki School of Economics and Business Administration and the University of Art and Design into a new university], Helsinki: Opetusministeriö.

Paletschek, S. (2002) 'Die Erfindung der Humboldtschen Universität: die Konstruktion der deutschen Universitätsidee in der ersten Hälfte des 20. Jahrhunderts', *Historische Anthropologie* 10: 183–205.

Pécresse, V. (2008) French Minister of Higher Education and Research, speech at the French National Assembly, Paris, 18 November.

Porter, T. M. (1996) *Trust in Numbers*, Princeton: Princeton University Press.

Saisana, M. and D'Hombres, B. (2008) *Higher Education Rankings: Robustness issues and critical assessment: how much confidence can we have in Higher Education Rankings?* Luxembourg: Office for Official Publications of the European Communities.

Salmi, J. (2009) *The Challenge of Establishing World-Class Universities*, Washington D.C.: World Bank.

Usher, A. and Savino, M. (2007) 'A global survey of university ranking and league tables', *Higher Education in Europe* 32(1): 5–15.

Van Raan, A.F.J. (2005) 'Fatal attraction: conceptual and methodological problems in the ranking of universities by Bibliometric Methods', *Scientometrics* 62(1): 133–143.

Weber, M. (1968) *Economy and Society,* Vol. II. Berkeley: University of California Press.

chapter | human rights and european
seven | integration: from institutional
| divide to convergent practice

Mikael Rask Madsen

The notion of Europe as an integrated social, political and legal entity is for most observers practically synonymous with the European Union (EU). One area, however, where the symbolic hegemony of the EU on the notion of Europe does not reflect the actual players and processes is European human rights. The formation of European human rights followed by and large a different trajectory than the one starting with the Coal and Steel Community in the 1950s. The major organisation in the promotion of human rights in European has, since the launch of European integration project, been the Council of Europe (CoE) and, more specifically, the legal institutions established to enforce the 1950 European Convention for the Protection of Human Rights and Fundamental Freedoms (ECHR). The EU was generally speaking a late-comer to human rights and only little by little did it devise a human rights policy. Likewise, the institutionalisation of human rights under the auspices of the EU was only achieved recently. Thus, very much in line with the general objective of a political sociological (re-)examination of European integration, inquiring into the role and place of human rights in European integration not only provides a case for a less well-known aspect of European integration, but it is also revealing of the much greater multitude and complexity of the evolution of European integration than what is offered by most mainstream accounts.

On the one hand, the interface of human rights and European integration provides a case for the internationalisation of the European state (Madsen 2004) in which the very *raison d'État* has been transformed and perhaps even, in the wording of Mireille Delmas-Marty, been 'reasoned' anew (Delmas-Marty 1989). On the other hand, it provides a case for the seemingly perpetual problem of European integration, namely its normative-political foundation. As will be demonstrated, human rights was very clearly one of the politico-legal pillars on which the vision of a united Europe was built and in many ways remained so, despite the institutional split between Strasbourg and Brussels/Luxemburg in the 1950s. This became strikingly clear when the EU, following the end of the Cold War, eventually embarked on scrambling together a common normative platform with the double objective of setting up criteria for access to the EU and re relegitimising the existing EU, vis-à-vis an electorate increasingly questioning the wisdom of enlargement (Madsen 2010a).

For sure, human rights featured as a foundational principle of the EEC in the 1973 Copenhagen declaration on European identity (Manners 2002: 241). But, with the exception of the jurisprudence of the European Court of Justice (ECJ) in the issue-area, the actual implementation of these legal principles would only take centre stage in the 1990s (Alston and Weiler 1999). Generally, the EU's eventual turn to human rights was facilitated by some new, more favourable conjunctures for the undertaking: a general breakthrough of international human rights law in the aftermath of the Cold War and a consolidation of the role of the European Court of Human Rights (ECtHR) as supreme authority on the definition of human rights in European states (Madsen 2007). That is, at this unique *fin de siécle* moment of European history, human rights were simultaneously being heralded supranationally and nationally, the latter via Strasbourg, as the most profound articulation of 'Europeanness' in both cultural and legal terms. This eventually led to the EU seeking to accede to the Strasbourg human rights regime as stipulated in first the Treaty establishing a Constitution for Europe (TCE) and secondly in the Lisbon Treaty (2007). Importantly, this also underlined a growing convergence, even reintegration, of the two 'Europes' of respectively, the market and human rights, which had developed into distinct paths of European integration since the 1950s.

To present this half century long story of the relationship between human rights and European integration, I draw on a series of more detailed studies of different periods and aspects of this transformation which I have conducted in recent years.[1] The chapter begins with an outline of the genesis of European human rights in the postwar period, first the drafting of the ECHR and then the protracted institutionalisation of the Convention. It then looks into the legal breakthrough of European human rights law in the 1970s both at the ECtHR and the ECJ, and how this reflected a new rationality of European law as driven by the legally (still uncertain) notion of European integration which nevertheless, became central both in Strasbourg and Luxembourg/Brussels. The next moment in focus is the 1990s, where, on the one side, the ECtHR greatly consolidated its position as supreme author of European human rights and, on the other side, the EU sought to transform its so far tentative engagement with human rights, into the institutionalised rationality of the EU. In conclusion, I highlight the particular lessons which might be drawn from this case in terms of developing further, a political sociology of European integration.

This outline of the chapter also reflects the political sociological approach applied in this analysis. Drawing on a Bourdieu-inspired logic of transnational fields (e.g. Dezalay 2004; Dezalay and Madsen 2006; Madsen 2006, 2011c; Vauchez 2008), I am interested in the various, and over time different, institutional and political investments in European human rights. More specifically, I am interested in how these investments and practices progressively helped structure institutionally, as well as legally and politically, what broadly speaking can be termed a field of European human rights. While the emergence of human rights in postwar Europe was the product of a number of interrelated social, political and legal processes and movements (for an overview, see Madsen 2010b), this analysis is limited to the more

---

1. For a more comprehensive but general account of this evolution, see e.g. (Madsen 2005) and (Madsen 2010b). In the chapter, however, I generally cite the more specialised studies I have conducted in the issue-area.

institutional dimension of the evolution of European human rights on the inter- and supranational level. I am however, not seeking an institutional analysis per se but, by deploying the logic of fields, an analysis which tracks both the micro and macro-developments which have structured the field of European rights. This analysis involves above all, an examination of the legal, political and institutional practices in light of the changing structural frameworks within which they operated.

The genesis of european human rights

Most studies of the ECJ, and EU-related European integration, tend to disconnect the initiatives related to European economic integration from the broader project of European unification, launched in the aftermath of WWII. However, among the Europeanists who assembled at the Congress for Europe in The Hague in 1948 the distinction between Europe of the market and Europe of human rights, was not overly important; it was above all about Europe. In 1949, when the negotiations of the ECHR were being intensified, many of the key players still envisaged European human rights, in the words of Pierre-Henri Teitgen, one of the key negotiators, as part of a broader 'generalisation of social democracy' (as cited in Merrills and Robertson 2001: 8). Moreover, the ECtHR was viewed by its main proponents as the Court not only for protecting human rights but for integrating European more generally (Bates 2010). Above all, the ECHR, as sustained by the ECtHR, was meant to produce a common conscience for all of (Western) Europe. Indeed, when the idea of a European Constitution was further concretised in the early 1950s, such a treaty was meant to unify the field of European law, which nevertheless had been split up between the projects under the Council of Europe (CoE) and the European Coal- and Steel Community (ECSC) (Cohen 2007; Cohen and Madsen 2007). In the following, I provide an outline of the genesis of the Strasbourg path.

As argued elsewhere, regardless of its obvious place in the showdown with the immediate past, the European Convention had above all, been drafted as a Cold War instrument (e.g. Madsen 2007). While the 1948 UN Universal Declaration of Human Rights had been presented as a utopia for all mankind, a vision enjoying a brief momentum in the aftermath of Allied victory among lawyers, intellectuals and some statesmen, the rhetoric was substituted with an unequivocal Westernised vocabulary of 'liberty and democracy' in the Treaties, establishing the Council of Europe and its associated human rights system. The founding fathers, from the aforementioned Pierre-Henri Teitgen to Sir Maxwell-Fyfe of the UK, a former prosecutor at the Nuremberg trials, had, in many ways, anticipated the crucial shift from the Utopia to the Cold War of human rights taking form during the late 1940s. The European Convention was obviously a continuation of the idea of securing human rights through international law developed at the UN. That said, the rapid drafting of the EHCR reflected above all a growing fear of, on the one hand, the rising power of the national Communist Parties, and, on the other, Soviet imperial expansionism into Western Europe.

One scholar, Andrew Moravcsik, has raised the central question why so many European States opted for signing a document which removed considerably national sovereignty in a key area of statehood and left it in the hands of supranational judges (Moravcsik 2000). Clearly, neither delegation theory nor more general principal-agent theorising provides a convincing answer to this. As already suggested, it requires rethinking the Convention in its structural geopolitical environment, that is, the emergence of Cold War bipolarity. This is in line with Moravcsik who claims that the main driver behind this bold move was an attempt at the 'locking in of democracy' in an uncertain moment of international politics (Moravcsik 2000: 226). Moravcsik seems however to overlook that the 'lock' remained practically unbolted. A closer look at the Convention with a view to the *travaux préparatoires* clearly suggests that the negotiating parties were indeed not of afraid of using the high prose of democracy and liberty. Yet, the document lacked a dimension of legal obligation on the Member States. It was virtually a 'Convention à la carte' (Madsen 2011a: 71): All the most central clauses, particularly the jurisdiction of the court and individual petition, were in fact made optional in the original Convention. Thus, signing the document did not necessarily imply a handing over of sovereignty to an uncertain supranational legal body but rather subscribing to a political agenda of growing importance, that of ensuring a free and democratic Europe in an increasingly hostile geopolitical environment.

The main objective of the 1950 European Convention was, accordingly, not the development of a detailed European jurisprudence that should substantially alter national traditions of human rights. Instead it is probably better understood as an early form of containment politics in a legal guise for which the real objective was to define the boundary of Free Europe. This dominant political dimension to the undertaking, had significant ramifications for the institutionalisation and judicialisation of the Convention. As a consequence, the institutional development of the European system was basically reversed and did not initially concern the carving out of an effective international jurisprudence on human rights; it concerned convincing the Member States to accept the central clauses which had been left optional in order to reach the political compromise of Free Europe as defined by the Convention. The outcome was, in the words of Lord Lester of Herne Hill, 'a game of cat and mouse' (Lester 2011: 100). On the legal-institutional level this resulted in the development of a conspicuous 'legal diplomacy' at the Court, a situation in which the actual jurisprudential developments had to be carefully balanced with diplomatic considerations vis-à-vis the member states in order to satisfy the twin objectives of, on the one hand , ensuring further institutional support, and, on the other hand , maintaining at least formally, the institution's role as guardian of human rights in Europe (Madsen 2011b).

The difficult institutionalisation of european human rights

Formally, for the Convention to be effective, ten Member States had to ratify. While this was achieved by 1952 with ratifications by Britain, the Federal Republic of Germany and a series of smaller states, the real challenge remained, namely to make individual petition and the court operational. The clause on individual petition stipulated that six states had to accept before it was made effective. This was achieved by 1955, which meant that the procedure was made effective in the Federal Republic of Germany and a number of smaller countries (Sweden, Ireland, Denmark, Iceland and Belgium). However, for the Court to start operating, eight countries had to accept, which only happened by 1958 when 7 smaller states (Ireland, Denmark, the Netherlands, Belgium, Luxembourg, Austria and Iceland) and the Federal Republic of Germany, had accepted its jurisdiction. What is striking is the absence of the three major European powers of France, the UK and Italy. As concerns France and the UK, their absence was by and large due to their problems in their colonies, where a growing number of activists were seeking self-determination among others, on grounds of human rights abuses by French and British colonial administrators. This absence in Strasbourg of probably the two most important European states in this regard, however, only put further pressure on the nascent Strasbourg institutions. Thereby, both the Commission and the Court were forced to make it their main objective to convince precisely these two states of both the relevance and reasonableness of its workings and jurisprudence and, thus, impose on themselves a set of checks-and-balances of a very real nature.

The fact that the UK, unlike e.g. France, had ratified the Convention meant, however, that the European system in terms of the European Commission on Human Rights was competent to receive inter-state complaints against the UK, notwithstanding that the UK had not accepted the clauses on individual petition and the jurisdiction of the Court. It was however deemed very unlikely in the British Foreign Office that this backdoor entrance to the European system was to pose a problem. This turned out to be completely wrong. In May 1956 Greece chose precisely to launch an inter-state complaint against the UK for its neglect of human rights in Cyprus, at the time a colonial holding of the UK. The fact that Cyprus was under the jurisdiction of the European Convention was due to a symbolic decision made in the 1950s to extend the reach of the Convention to most of the British Empire. The Foreign Office had basically played a double game of conveying a message to the colonies that they would benefit from the protection offered by the Convention, yet assuming that they would never use these options due to the limited access to the Strasbourg institutions. As noted by A. W. Brian Simpson, it was probably not an accident that the notification of the extension took place the exact same day that the Central African Federation came into force (Simpson 2004: 838–39). Put differently, it was the increasingly colliding high-politics of decolonisation, and maintaining imperial grandeur, that prompted the decision.

Clearly, bringing colonial conflicts to the heart of Strasbourg was not welcomed – and particularly as this was the very first case before the European human rights system. The distinguished international lawyer Henri Rollin, counsel for the prosecution in *Greece v. United Kingdom*, made this very clear in his opening speech before the European Commission:

> I am the first to admit the paradox – and personally I regret it – that by a chance of fate the first government to be brought to the bar by another government is the United Kingdom, which governs a country which surely, more than any other in Europe, has always shown concern for human rights (Simpson 2004: 322).

The point was hard to miss: European human rights were the inalienable rights of the free and civilised world and this should not be confused with some temporary problems with colonial insurrections. The outcome of this case was, if anything, telling of the system. As it became more and more clear during the proceedings that the UK had indeed breached the Convention, the matter was eventually solved by recourse to diplomacy. The case was closed with a friendly settlement – the 1959 Zurich and London agreements settlement on Cyprus – which also meant the end of the British Empire in Cyprus.

From the point of view of the European human rights system, this was probably a convenient solution as it thereby evaded having to pronounce violations, as well as it could convey the message that it was diplomatically sound. The diplomatic skills of the Strasbourg institutions were however, soon after, once again tested as yet another key case, the *Lawless* case, was making it to the Court as its very first case. It concerned the use of detention without trial in Ireland as a response to IRA insurgency. The European Commission, as well as the European Court, both found that this was not in compliance with article 5 of the Convention. Yet, the case did not ultimately lead to a judgement against the Irish government, as the court interpreted article 15 with respect to emergency situations in such a way that the Irish Government was entitled to apply these measures since the 'life of the nation' was threatened. Once again the European system drew a conclusion which calmed the Member States and underlined that it was receptive to the complexities of interior politics. And it was exactly against this background of what once again was perceived as sound judgement – or perhaps more accurately a well-developed sense of 'legal diplomacy' – that the UK, in 1966, chose to accept the optional clauses on individual petition and the jurisdiction of Court. In the early 1970s, the UK's decision to fully integrate was followed by a number of other countries, but only after some very significant geopolitical transformations with regard to human rights.

The rise of the europe of human rights

This initial phase of European human rights, which is probably best described as a prolonged negotiation of the ECHR and its institutional set-up, is a necessary historical backdrop for comprehending the subsequent development in the jurisprudence of the ECtHR, in which the Court, in a series of landslide decisions, set in motion a very significant change in both law and discourse on human rights. Not only did the European Court in 1978, in sharp contrast to the above-mentioned *Lawless* case, come to the conclusion that the emergency interrogation measures used in Northern Ireland by the British security forces could not be justified by evoking emergency arguments *(Irish Case)*, it also seemingly reinterpreted the Warren Court's famous notion of 'evolving standards of decency in a maturing society', as the European Convention being '[...] a living instrument [...] [which] must be interpreted in the light of present-day conditions [...] [and] standards in the [...] members states (para 31, *Tyrer Case*). To make things absolutely clear, a year later in 1979, the Court established in the *Airey Case* that '[t]he Convention is intended to guarantee not rights that are theoretical or illusory but rights that are practical and effective' (para 24). This suddenly more progressive or, according to some, aggressive doctrine can obviously not be explained as simply the fruit of the gradual legitimisation of the Court in the eyes of the Member States described above; nor can it be explained as the outcome of new judges being appointed to the bench.[2] While these factors are necessary conditions for the change, the transformation – or metamorphosis – of the Court, it is perhaps more particularly linked to the considerable changes in geo-political context of human rights in Europe.

The Court generally benefited from the fact that the Cold War of human rights was ebbing out and that the major European powers had succumbed to the idea of 'Empire lost' – France even ratified the Convention in 1974. Due to these two closely related processes, European imperial societies were no longer the object of criticism *par excellence* of human rights activism. In Western Europe, throughout the 1970s, most human rights activism was directed at non-democratic regimes outside the jurisdiction of European human rights: the Greek Colonels, Franco Spain and Portugal under Salazar.[3] In fact, in the optic of 1970s human rights activism, the real perpetrators of human rights were to a large extent geographically found outside Western Europe: in Latin America, South Africa, as well as Eastern Europe. During the same period, Western Europe alongside the US, sought to introduce human rights more expressly in foreign policies, most famously in the Helsinki Final Act of 1975 which triggered and eventually legitimised a series of Watch groups, including Human Rights Watch and Charter 77, as well as other Helsinki Watch committees. Intra-European developments further added to this development. If Greece, Portugal and Spain had been the trouble spots of Western Europe in the first part of the 1970s, the situation was reversing by the second part of the decade. In 1974, 1976 and 1977 respectively, they became integrated into the ECHR protection system. And, as already suggested, the initially reluctant Western European member states had all at this point turned around on the issue of institutional support to the ECtHR, thereby making it – it last – fully operational.

These important developments of the ECtHR were also part of a distinct process of Europeanisation, both in terms of integrating European society and building European law. By the mid-1970s it is striking that all member states of the

---

2. Particularly as the 1970s judges sociologically greatly resembled the judges of the 1960s (cf. Madsen 2011b).

3. Greece had withdrawn from the European system from 1970–1975, whilst Portugal and Spain only joined the system in respectively 1977 and 1978.

EEC were now also full members of the ECHR system.[4] In fact, the change in commitment to the ECtHR happened to take place at the precise moment the EEC undertook its first enlargement, when Denmark, Ireland, and the United Kingdom entered into the Community.[5] In the early 1970s, the most significant important EEC-related development in respect to human rights was however, taking place under the auspices of the European Court of Justice (ECJ). After an initial battle, in the mid 1960s, over the supremacy and direct effect of EC-Law (the seminal rulings in *Van Gend en Loos* and *Costa v. ENEL*[6]), the ECJ began developing EC-Law in terms of the fundamental rights they derived from a set of unwritten general principles of community law in the 1970s. It would take the ECJ about a decade to carefully craft a doctrine of fundamental rights. In the initial cases, *Stauder* (1969)[7] and *Internationale Handelsgesellschaft* (1970)[8] the ECJ underlined the importance of fundamental rights to the EC legal order. And, in the strikingly well-timed *Nold* decision of 1974[9], it went a step further. While predating the long awaited *Solange I*[10] decision of the German *Bundesverfassungsgericht* by some two weeks, yet eagerly awaiting French ratification of the ECHR, eleven days later it pronounced that it intended to take inspiration particularly from the ECHR and not only the constitutional rights of the member states (Scheeck 2005). Moreover, in 1975 the ECJ for the first time explicitly cited individual articles of the ECHR in the *Rutili*[11] case and again in 1979, in the *Hauer* case.[12]

What can be observed is a common orientation towards human rights of the two European courts in terms of taking human rights seriously as real legal entitlements and thus law. But it went further than that. The ECJ did not only add to the overall human rights momentum of the time; its judgements on fundamental rights and freedoms also underlined another crucial development of great importance for the ECtHR, namely that human rights did not only concern gross violations, but also ordinary citizen's more mundane entitlements under European law. In a similar way, the ECtHR cases of *Tyrer* and *Airey,* concerning issues related to corporal punishment and the access to divorce, also raised the question of human rights in respect to the evolving societal fabric of Europe; that is, dynamic interpretation was not simply teleological interpretation in respect to the *telos* of the ECHR, but in respect to European society and its evolution. While the ECJ could rely on

---

4.   With the exception of France which only accepted individual petition in 1981.

5.   Norway did not join the EEC at this occasion following a 'no vote' at a referendum. Greece joined in 1981, and Spain and Portugal in 1986.

6.   26/62 *van Gend en Loos* (1963) ECR 1 and 28/62–30/62 *Costa* (1954–64) ECR 395.

7.   29/69 *Stauder* (1969).

8.   11/70 *Internationale Handelsgesellschaft v. Einfuhr- und Vorratsstelle für Getreide und Futtermittel case* (1970).

9.   4/73 *Nold* 1974).

10. BVerfGE 37, 271 2 BvL 52/71 *Solange I-Beschluß*.

11. 36/75 *Rutili* (1975).

12. 44/79 *Hauer* (1979).

the notion of an 'ever closer Union', the ECtHR distilled its notion of 'present-day conditions' to legitimise progressive European law. In both cases, the courts not only found a common driving force in a general notion of European integration, they also took advantage of the geopolitical transformations of international human rights in the context of détente to improve their position. Thereby, they managed to put themselves on par with general social developments in Europe – and in some cases probably to be ahead of general societal evolution.

These developments were to considerably mark European human rights in the following decades. The ECtHR, building on its landslide decisions of the late 1970s, further consolidated itself and became basically the *de facto* supreme court of human rights in Europe. Although the decisions of the 1980s and early 1990s were perhaps not changing human rights law as radically as the ones of the late 1970s, the ECtHR nevertheless expanded significantly both in reach and productivity during the period. The ECtHR had in the 1970s only judged a few cases a year, but already by the mid-1980s the number was steadily climbing and by the early 1990s, it was up to 60–80 a year. The institutional and legal set-up equally changed, first with the Protocols 6–10 from 1983–92, and then most drastically with the complete overhaul of the system with Protocol 11. The latter established a new and permanent European Court of Human Rights which, by year 2000, issued close to 900 judgements a year concerning an ever larger number of member states. And these numbers would only climb even further as the impact of Eastern European enlargement made a clear mark on the case-load. Although the parallel evolution of the ECJ is not quite as striking, the ECJ did equally expand both legally and institutionally during the same period.[13] As the subject of this analysis is concerned, the ECJ effectively developed a catalogue of EC/EU rights which became only more central to the increasingly complex EU legal order. And, as will be shown in the subsequent section, it would become one of the cornerstones of the European Charter of Fundamental Rights (ECFR).

The EU's institutional turn to human rights

What this analysis so far suggests, is a massive juridical and particularly judicial impact on the construction and definition of the notion of European human rights. In this light, it is perhaps not surprising that when the EU, throughout the 1990s, increasingly turned to human rights, it bought into precisely this European legal knowledge and practice and embarked on drafting a Charter of Fundamental Rights. Moreover, the EU started arguing for the need of adhering to the ECHR protection system, thereby taking a significant step in potentially bridging the gap between the two 'Europes', developed in respectively Strasbourg and Brussels/ Luxembourg in the initial phases of European integration. In the following, this turn of the EU towards juridified and judicialised human rights is analysed.

---

13. On the institutional level, most notably the ECJ was reformed and divided into a two level jurisdiction by the introduction of the Court of First Instance (now General Court) in the late 1980s.

The German Chairmanship's instigation of the proceedings leading to the ECFR in June 1999, at the European Council Summit in Cologne, had its roots in a mixture of both national politics, markedly German controversies over neo-Nazis, and the new Green-Red German Government's objective of 'popularising' the EU (for details see Burca 2001; Madsen 2010a). The latter, they intended to achieve by an 'outreach programme' which accentuated fundamental rights and enhanced the institutional transparency of the EU. Ultimately, this should help improve the popular perception of the EU and re-legitimise its institutions in a context where the community was undergoing significant changes, most notably the beginning of the enlargement process which was already meeting resistance among the electorate. Although the product of an entirely different political epoch than the ECHR, the Charter nevertheless bore some resemblance to its famous precursor. The ECFR project reflected in many ways, an attempt to develop a moral-political justification of the EU that could serve as an instrument of further unification, internal democratic audit and, not the least, line of demarcation vis-à-vis the surrounding 'non-EU' world. Thus, a post-Cold War plan, that paradoxically echoed some of the Cold War, inspired ideas of the key drafters of the ECHR, half a century earlier.

It was generally argued that the new European political context after the fall of the Berlin Wall simply required the drafting of such an instrument – cf. the famous wording of the conclusions of the Cologne Summit: 'There appears to be a need, at the present stage of the Union's development, to establish a Charter of Fundamental Rights'. The idea of a common EU Bill of Rights was however hardly new. The long list of related initiatives and white books from the late 1980s and early 1990s, includes the Common Declaration of the European Parliament, the Council and the Commission on Fundamental Rights of 1977, the Declaration of Fundamental Rights and Liberties of the European Parliament of 1989, the so-called Pintasilgo Report of 1996 (on a Europe of civil and social rights produced by a group of wise-men) and the Simitis Report of February 1999 'Affirming Fundamental Rights in the European Union – Time to Act' drafted by an expert group (see the complete list in Braibant 2001). Also, the central question of the relationship between the Strasbourg institutions and the enforcement of a possible EU Charter had been the subject of vivid debate among both legal academics and European politicians for a period.[14] A considerable number of actors and interest groups were also mobilised prior to the initiation of the formal political negotiations, including a range of NGOs, trade unions and academics.

It was however the 1999 German chairmanship that gave the idea of an EU human rights charter the symbolic boost which was needed for the drafting of the document. Later, under the French chairmanship of the second part of 2000, the plan was equally given substantial political backing. There is little doubt that the mobilisation of the heavy French-German axis was key in this respect and helped take the idea beyond the level of mere political discourse. The Charter was in fact

---

14. It should also be pointed out that a number of studies and reports on EU constitutionalism existed which also dealt with the question of an EU Bill of Rights.

produced during a strikingly short time-span. Begun in June 1999, the process was further concretised in October 1999 at the Tampere European Council (under the Finnish chairmanship), where it was decided to establish a 62-member Convention charged with the drafting. At the Biarritz European Council on October 13–14, 2000, the draft Charter was unanimously approved. It was subsequently approved by the European Parliament and Commission on respectively November 14, 2000, and December 6, 2000, and finally signed and proclaimed by the Presidents of the European Parliament, the Council and the Commission on December 7, 2000, in Nice. In practice, it involved about 8 months of real drafting time which, according to leading Brussels lobbyists in the area, made the result practically like 'shooting and aiming afterwards'.[15]

All this would have been fine if it wasn't for the fact that the ECFR in one important way did not resemble the ECHR. In practice more similar to the Universal Declaration of Human Rights (1948), the ECFR was drafted as a political declaration, which then later could be given a treaty status, by for example including it in a new treaty. This was a particularly odd situation in light of the fact that it was repeatedly argued during the negotiation, that the Charter merely codified existing jurisprudence of the ECJ. Making things even more conspicuous, some parts of the Charter, particularly many of the rights listed in Chapters I and II on Dignity and Freedoms, as well as Chapter VI on Justice, were derived directly from the ECHR, some even duplicated the direct wording of the ECHR.[16] In other words, even if the EU did not accede to the ECHR – that was only decided after the drafting of the Charter – it would, through the Charter (if given treaty status), protect some of the exact same rights as the ECtHR, causing a number of unclear institutional scenarios for human rights in Europe. Consequently, the need for legalising the Chapter by including it in a Treaty, as well as the EU adhering to the ECHR, was in other words imperative for the undertaking to make any sense.

This would in practice turn out to be a serious problem, as the initial plan for juridicising the Charter by including it in the Constitution Treaty collapsed as the Constitution Treaty was eventually rejected at national referenda in 2005. Shortly after, the Treaty of Lisbon however came to the Charter's rescue, recognising the ECFR and granting it the same legal status as the other EU treaties. Moreover, the Treaty of Lisbon confirmed that that the EU could act as a single legal person and it should accede to the ECHR. By adding the mitigating Article 6(2) – '[The] accession shall not affect the Union's competences as defined in the Treaties' – even the UK government could eventually accept the solution. The enterprise of juridicising the Charter was, however, once again brought to a standstill when the Lisbon Treaty was rejected in a referendum in Ireland in June 2008. The decision was eventually reversed by a second referendum in 2009 and the Treaty came finally into force on the 1st December, 2009.

---

15. Interview III 27th of November 2002.

16. See for example the articles 2,4,5,6,7,9,10 and 12 of the Charter. This is however not an exhaustive list. In Chapter VI on Justice the rights are equally close to the ECHR.

Just as it had taken nine years from the signature of the ECHR in 1950 to the opening of the ECtHR in 1959, it took the Charter nine years to gain legal effect. However, for an EU system which long had operated on the premise of 'constitutionalisation without a constitution', a number of the usual (legal) suspects did not waste time and did indeed start juridifying the Charter in the meantime. Among these actors it was generally assumed that although the Charter in principle was only a political document (until 2009) it had more importance than that, also legally. It was after all solemnly proclaimed in Nice and included in both the Constitution Treaty and Lisbon Treaty. Moreover, it was to a large extent codifying existing law and jurisprudence. This was a view shared by practically all the key EU institutions, in particular the Commission and Court. Not wasting time awaiting the vote at referendums, the General Advocates of the ECJ and the Court of the First Instance began referring to the Charter (Menéndez 2002). New EU regulations also soon started citing the Charter, as well as being 'proofed' in respect to the Charter. The cited approach of European integration in terms of European constitutionalisation (without a constitution) was thus replicated in the area of fundamental rights by the EU continuing developing 'human rights without a legally binding Bill of Rights'. With the Lisbon Treaty now in force the actual implications of the fully juridified Charter on the broader field of European human rights remain nevertheless not clear. The only thing that is certain is that the protection in the area thereby, was somehow increased through a double protection, but with an opaque institutional division of labour. On a macro-level, it is however indicative of a further approximation between the two institutional regimes of the EU and Council of Europe in the area of human rights, as well as an increased centrality of human rights to European integration. That said, the implications of this increased centrality remain unclear.

Conclusion

When understood in the broader scheme of the development of human rights over the last half century, the EU's turn towards human rights, although a largely unfinished manoeuvre, remains irreversible. If the EU previously had played a more distant role as mainly the financier of human rights activism abroad, with the Charter, the EU increasingly situated itself as a potential key producer of human rights norms. If the proposed analysis of the way European law is brought about gets this process somewhat right, it also suggests that the history of the Charter is very far from finished. Its further development depends, at the end of the day, of the actual interplay of, on the one hand, the legal routinisation of the document by the major EU legal institutions and, on the other, the will at the political level to actually use it. The relative uncertainty of the Charter should however not overshadow that – with or without the EU aboard – human rights are at the heart of European integration. As argued in this paper, this is largely due to different processes of integration in which the EU was only a marginal player. Undoubtedly, the legal regime set up to enforce the ECHR in Strasbourg is the key player in this respect and most likely remains so, regardless of the new EU interests in the subject-area.

This analysis of a distinctively different path of European integration is also an attempt at challenging the orthodoxy of European studies. A great deal of the mainstream research on Europe tends to uncritically assume an overlap between the European Union (EU) and the very notion of European integration. Though common in European studies, this assumption is not only reductivist and misleading but has also contributed to a great deal of confusion as concerns the distinction between the political project of European integration of the EU, and European integration as a proper research object. The evolution of European human rights in terms of its institutionalisation, judicialisation and juridification provides in this respect, a different object which is also suitable for exemplifying the far greater complexity of European integration and its markedly different, but nevertheless simultaneously evolving political projects. Regardless of current approximations between the EU and the Strasbourg system, the fact remains that ECtHR protects human rights in a wider (and wilder some might add) Europe, which includes 47 member states and some 800 million Europeans and a jurisdictional territory that stretches as far South as the Kurdish provinces of Turkey and as Eastern as Vladivostok in Russia. Undoubtedly much can be learned about European integration, also with respect to the EU, by exploring this much larger space of European integration through law. It requires however, that the object of inquiry is predetermined to a single path of integration.

References

Alston, P. and Weiler, J. H. H. (1999) 'An 'Ever Closer Union' in Need of a Human Rights Policy: The European Union and human rights', in P. Alston (ed.) *The EU and Human Rights*, Oxford: Oxford University Press, pp. 3–66.

Bates, E. (2010) *The Evolution of the European Convention on Human Rights: From its inception to the creation of a permanent Court of Human Rights*, Oxford: Oxford University Press.

Braibant, G. (2001) *La Charte des droits fondamentaux de l'Union européenne*, Paris: Seuil.

Burca, G. D. (2001) 'The drafting of the European Union Charter of Fundamental Rights', *European Law Review* 2: 126–38.

Cohen, A. (2007) 'Constitutionalism without constitution: transnational elites between political mobilization and legal expertise in the making of a Constitution for Europe (1940s-1960s)', *Law & Social Inquiry* 32(1): 109–35.

Cohen, A. and Madsen, M. R. (2007) 'Cold War Law: Legal entrepreneurs and the emergence of a European legal field (1945–1965)', in V. Gessner and D. Nelken (eds) *European Ways of Law: Towards a European sociology of law*, Oxford: Hart Publishing, pp. 175–202.

Delmas-Marty, M. (1989) *Raisonner la raison d'État: Vers une Europe des droits de l'homme*, Paris: Presses Universitaires de France.

Dezalay, Y. (2004) 'Les courtiers de l'international: Héritiers cosmopolites, mercenaires de l'impérialisme et missionnaires de l'universel ', *Actes de la recherche en sciences sociales* 151–152: 5–34.

Dezalay, Y. and Madsen, M. R. (2006) 'La construction européenne au carrefour du national et de l'international', in A. Cohen, B. Lacroix and P. Riutort (eds) *Les formes de l'activité politique: Èlements d'analyse sociologique XVIIIè -XXè siècle*, Paris: Presses Universitaires de France.

Lester, A. (2011) 'The European Court of Human Rights after 50 Years', in J. Christoffersen and M. R. Madsen (eds) *The European Court of Human Rights between Law and Politics*, Oxford: Oxford University Press, pp. 98–115.

Madsen, R. (2004) 'France, the UK and "Boomerang" of the Internationalization of Human Rights (1945–2000)', in S. Halliday and P. Schmidt (eds) *Human Rights Brought Home: Socio-legal perspectives on human rights in the national context*, Oxford: Hart Publishing, pp. 57–86.

—— (2005) 'L'émergence d'un champ des droits de l'homme dans les pays européens: enjeux professionnels et stratégies d'Etat au carrefour du droit et de la politique (France, Grande-Bretagne et pays scandinaves, 1945–2000)', PhD Thesis, l'École des hautes études en sciences sociales, Paris.

—— (2006) 'Transnational fields: elements of a reflexive sociology of the internationalisation of law', *Retfærd* 3(114): 23–41.

—   (2007) 'From Cold War instrument to supreme European Court: The European Court of Human Rights at the crossroads of international and national law and politics', *Law & Social Inquiry* 32(1): 137–59.

—   (2010a) 'La fabrique des traités européens: Une analyse de la genèse et évolution de la charte des droits fondamentaux', *Revue française de science politique* 60(2): 271–94.

—   (2010b) *La genèse de l'Europe des droits de l'homme: Enjeux juridiques et stratégies d'Etat (France, Grande-Bretagne et pays scandinaves, 1945–1970)* Strasbourg: Presses universitaires de Strasbourg.

—   (2011a) 'Legal Diplomacy – Law, politics and the genesis of postwar European human rights', in S. L. Hoffmann (ed.) *Human Rights in the Twentieth Century: A Critical History*, Cambridge: Cambridge University Press.

—   2011b) 'The Protracted Institutionalisation of the Strasbourg Court: From legal diplomacy to integrationist jurisprudence', in M. R. Madsen and J. Christoffersen, J. (eds) *The European Court of Human Rights between Law and Politics*, Oxford: Oxford University Press.

—   (2011c) 'Reflexivity and the construction of the international object: the case of human rights', *International Political Sociology* 5(3): 259–75.

Manners, I. (2002) 'Normative power Europe: a contradiction in terms?' *Journal of Common Market Studies* 40(2): 235–58.

Menéndez, A. J. (2002) 'Chartering Europe: Legal Status and Policy Implications of the Charter of Fundamental Rights of the European Union', *Journal of Common Market Studies* 40(3): 471–90.

Merrills, J. G. and Robertson, A. H. (2001) *Human Rights in Europe: A study of the European Convention on Human Rights*, Manchester: Manchester University Press.

Moravcsik, A. (2000) 'The origins of human rights regimes: democratic delegation in postwar Europe' *International Organization* 54(2): 217–52.

Scheeck, L. (2005) 'The relationship between the European Courts and Integration through human rights', *Zeitschrift für ausländisches öffentliches Recht und Völkerrecht* 65(4): 837–85.

Simpson, A. W. B. (2004) *Human Rights and the End of Empire: Britain and the genesis of the European Convention*, Oxford: Oxford University Press.

Vauchez, A. (2008) 'The force of a weak field: law and lawyers in the government of the European Union (for a renewed research agenda)' *International Political Sociology* 2(2): 128–44.

part iii. citizens imagining europe

chapter eight | on the national and ideological backgrounds of elites' attitudes toward european institutions

Daniel Gaxie and Nicolas Hubé

Diversity of elites' positions on european institutions

The respective powers of Member States and European institutions have long been at stake in national and supranational debates. These debates are structured along several cleavages. There has been a first cleavage between federalists and defenders of national sovereignty. From the very beginning of the process of European integration, the former have advocated the construction of a supranational federal state relying on a European Defence Community and a Common Foreign Policy. The latter have relentlessly opposed European integration in the name of national sovereignty and independence of the nation-states. They have depicted European institutions as a centralised, bureaucratic and undemocratic Leviathan endangering national freedoms, cultures and identities. But European integration has also been conceived as a means to preserve and restore national autonomy and independence (Haller 2008: 80). The European Council has been established to guarantee that the heads of member-states have the last say in the main decisions. Besides proponents of a federal integration, there are also defenders of intergovernmental methods of coordination. Another debate has taken place on the level of relevant integration. As European construction has advanced, many champions of national independence have accepted more or less loose unionist models of Europe as a family of nations. Members of elites oppose and others claim for deeper integration in various domains. Some integrationists ask for transfers of national competences to a supranational, and others to an intergovernmental, European level. There have also been debates on majority voting versus unanimity within the European Council. We see that controversies about European institutions cannot be reduced to a simplistic binary opposition between supporters and opponents of European integration. Indeed, we need to distinguish many shades of federalist, intergovernmentalist, confederalist, unionist, and nationalist attitudes.

But elites' attitudes toward European institutions are also highly dependent on their views of the main aims of European integration. After the failure of the first attempts to establish a European Defence Community, the most eager partisans of European integration have mainly thought of market integration. The radical left has regarded the EU as a capitalist project endangering social protection and has long spoken for a 'social Europe'. Social democrats have also wished to protect national welfare regimes. They have proposed to co-ordinate fiscal policies and to extend EU competence in employment, and social regulations (Hooghe and Marks

2009: 16). In contrast, political and socio-economic elites attached to economic freedom have displayed cautious attitudes toward European institutions because of their regulatory functions. Green parties have come to consider European federal integration as part of their vision of a multi-cultural society (Hooghe and Marks 2009: 17). Cleavages over European institutions are thus intertwined with several ideological divides: deregulated market versus regulated capitalism, market liberalism versus social market capitalism or social regulations, and cultural liberalism versus conservative fondness for authority, tradition and national identities and cultures.

Research questions and hypotheses from the literature

Numerous hypotheses have been put forward to explain this diversity and differentiation of views on European institutions (see Gaxie, Hubé and Rowell 2011). One of the most solid results of numerous studies on statistical correlates is that education, professional skills, and income have a positive impact on levels of attachment to 'Europe' (Gabel and Palmer 1995; Gabel and Whitten 1997; Gabel 1998; Belot, 2002; Hooghe and Marks 2004, 2009; Binnema and Crum 2007). Many scholars have also insisted that European construction is an elite-driven process. We may thus expect that most members of political and socio-economic elites would share positive rather than negative views of European integration. However, some national political elites may be interested in safeguarding a national arena of decision making. As since the beginning, integration has been focusing on the economy and we may thus think that top economic elites would be more eager to support stronger European institutions. But some authors, such as Simon Hix (1999), contend that attitudes toward European integration are not only linked to individual human capital, but also to the 'location of social interest'. In his view, independently of their education, occupational skills and income, people will have different views and demands according to the economic sector they belong to. These economic sectors might include, for instance, the non-tradeable public sector, domestic producers, global producers, financial services, multinational European producers or agricultural private sectors. In this view, we should observe variations of attitudes among economic elites according to the type of economic activities they are involved in.

All these hypotheses are usually labelled as 'utilitarian'. Some scholars argue that citizens do not assess the EU according to the personal or collective benefits they expect from it. Rather, they rely on various representations, emotions and values (Bélot 2002: 29). Others acknowledge that citizens do take into account the economic consequences of European integration, but they add that conceptions of group membership also matter and may even be more powerful (Hooghe and Marks 2004: 415). Most proponents of value theories think first of territorial identities. It is often observed that positive attachment to European integration increases with the feeling of belonging to Europe (Dell'Olio 2005: 102, see also Recchi and Kuhn in this volume). According to such a hypothesis, MPs and executives who have studied and lived abroad and who speak foreign languages share a more cosmopolitan worldview, and thus a more positive conception of the European construction than those with more parochial experience.

Political and ideological explanations of attitudes toward European integration also refer to partisan membership. Europe is said to be the 'touchstone of dissent', opposing established pro-European centre left or centre right governing parties and governments, to more sceptical fringes or radical parties, factions or politicians (Taggart 1998; Szcerbiack and Taggart 2002; Taggart and Szczerbiak 2008). This kind of explanation often mixes up two distinct hypotheses. A first one is that attitudes toward European integration depend on the position in power relationships within the political system, political parties or political hierarchies. Marginal political parties which are excluded from governing coalitions, and also marginal factions and second-tier politicians within governing parties, should thus be more likely to share sceptical views of European integration (Sitter 2001). Within national Parliaments, all things being equal, we may expect backbenchers to be more critical of the EU than frontbenchers. But when scholars distinguish radical from centrist political parties, they refer to a different hypothesis. Partisan ideologies are said to be the best explanatory factor and 'extremist' political parties, whether far right or far left wing ones, are expected to oppose more 'moderate' organisations. It is also sometimes assumed that European politics is linked to class cleavages (Deflem and Pampel 1996). According to Gabel, education, occupational skills, and income are positively correlated with favourable attitudes toward European integration, because educated, skilled people are more able to adapt to the occupational competition introduced by a liberalised EU labour market (Gabel 1998). EU citizens with low incomes are generally hurt by capital liberalisation, because they depend primarily on wages for their living. Capital liberalisation reduces their welfare by making it less costly for capital to move rather than to accede to labour demands. In addition, low-income citizens are more dependent on social welfare spending, which is constrained by capital mobility and the European Monetary System (Gabel 1998: 337). We may thus presume that blue-collar workers and their political representatives worry about, and hold the EU responsible for job reductions, off-shoring, decreasing wages, declining social welfare spending and diminution in their bargaining power. Other authors have to the contrary, stressed that left and centre-left political parties are eager to strengthen the regulatory powers of the European institutions in order to fight unemployment and to protect national welfare, the environment and human and women's rights (Hooghe and Marks 2009: 16). That is one of the reasons why the EU is also perceived by some as a bureaucratic meddler, imposing excessive, pernickety and costly regulations on firms and economic actors. Liberal political parties may thus hold negative views of EU institutions.

Some authors contend that country differences in popular support for European integration are more important than individual – socio-demographic and ideological – characteristics (Deflem and Pampel 1996: 136, also Dell'Olio 2005: 96). Advocates of explanations relying on national cultural particularities argue that one cannot assume, as does a large part of the literature, that everybody perceives the European integration process and the EU the same way. They add that a correct understanding of international variations in support for European integration requires taking into account how people conceive of the process and the institutions involved (Diez Medrano 2003: 5). Citizens – and first and foremost elites – of the various Members States of the EU are supposed to have a distinct national experience of European integration, a diffuse sense of their national position within the EU, and a common view of their country's place in the wider world (Harmsen 2007: 72). National visions of Europe are construed as a product of a top-down elite-driven process. Elites, especially politicians and columnists, constantly shape and reshape their views of European construction according to various international and national evolutions and to their power interests. However, new ideas need to resonate with existing identity constructions, which define the range of options considered legitimate for nation-state identities. For example, it has been argued that from a German (both elite and mass) point of view, the European construction is a redemption for Germany's past, an alternative to nationalism, a safeguard against latent hegemonic and anti-foreigners tendencies, a means to reassure the world about their peaceful intentions, and a guarantee for democracy and a social market economy (Marcussen *et al.* 1999; Diez Medrano 2003). Italians are expected to be pro-European because of the generous allocation of cohesion funds that they received in the past, and because they consider European integration as an opportunity for the 'normalisation' of Italian pathologies (Della Porta and Caiani: 2007).

Some of these political culturalist explanations of attitudes toward European integration insist on the specificity of each Member State's perceptions in relation to its unique national history. Others try to provide a general model aiming at giving a systematic account of national attitudes toward Europe. In another culturalist perspective, De Master and Le Roy notice that statistical relationships between indicators of xenophobia and of negative views of European integration are weak when interviewees live in countries such as Belgium, Ireland, Italy, Portugal, and Spain. They add that these five countries are all Roman Catholic, and that the ecumenical nature of Catholicism may contribute to greater internationalism and dispose its adherents to be more open toward foreigners (De Master and Le Roy 2000). Likewise, some argue that because they belong to a supranational institution, Roman Catholics are more likely to support European construction. Another general model relies on the 'goodness of fit' hypothesis, which stresses the differential degrees of adaptation required of national institutions and policy frameworks to fit in with emerging European norms (Harmsen 2007). As Hooghe and Marks put it, the further a country is from the EU median (low labour coordination, relatively high business coordination), the greater the costs imposed on its citizens by EU legislation are, and the more likely these citizens are to share negative opinions on European integration (Hooghe and Marks 2004: 416). A close hypothesis is also that residents (including national elites) in countries that are net recipients of EU spending will be inclined to support European integration, while those in donor countries will tend to oppose it (Hooghe and Marks: 2004). The INTUNE elite survey gives an opportunity to test these hypotheses and to elucidate the main determinants of the elites' positions in the debates on European institutions within political and socio-economic fields (INTUNE 2009). The aim of this chapter is to provide a thorough depiction and explanation of attitudes of various national elites toward European integration. This chapter also presents a first analysis of the qualitative material of the French elite survey that explains several surprising quantitative results.

How to measure elites' views on institutions?

Our contribution to this collective book is a first analysis of the two waves of the INTUNE elite survey conducted in 2007 and 2009. These are based on pan-European elite surveys[1]. Representative samples of MPs (Members of Parliament) (N=2404), leaders of large companies (N=690), the media (N=521), and trade unions (N=262) were interviewed in seventeen countries.[2] Elites were asked to answer a set of about eighty questions on European identity, governance, institutions and future. We completed the survey with socio-biographic data. Our analysis is based on answers to twelve questions listed below, related to the institutional organisation of the EU and therefore considered as indicators of elites' views on these issues.[3] We looked for a statistical methodology that would enable us to take into account all configurations of opinions instead of the usual academic focus on only two opposite attitudes. We decided to conduct a Multiple Correspondence Analysis (MCA), because it provides a simplified representation of the distribution of answers by identifying the main dimensions of elites' oppositions on institutional issues. We have not enough room to provide the statistical evidence, but this chapter sums up the main findings of the MCA. We completed the MCA analysis with regressions, ascendant hierarchical classification and in-depth interviews. As a result we were able to identify the main determinants of the cleavages and consensus on European issues among national elites.

---

1. This research was funded by a grant from the INTUNE project (Integrated and United: A quest for citizenship in an ever closer Europe) financed by the Sixth Framework Programme of the European Union, Priority 7, Citizens and Governance in a Knowledge Based Society (CIT3-CT-2005–513421).

2. The elites came from four founding member States (Belgium, France, Germany and Italy), the first enlargement (UK and Denmark), the Southern enlargement (Greece, Portugal and Spain), the 1995 enlargement (Austria), and from the Eastern enlargement (Bulgaria, Czech Republic, Estonia, Lithuania, Hungary, Poland, Romania).

3. Analyses developed in this chapter are somewhat different from those published in the book edited by Heinrich Best, Georgy Lengyel and Luca Verzichelli (2012). It relies on the first (2007) and also on the second (2009) waves of the INTUNE elite survey. It therefore takes into account the reactions of MPs interviewed in 2007 and 2009, business leaders, and media and trade-union elites. The cluster analysis conducted for this chapter takes into account questions on the relevant level of governance for various policy domains included in the 2007 and 2009 questionnaires, as well as several new questions on institutional issues added in the 2009 questionnaire. It thus provides a more complex depiction of various attitudes towards European integration.

Twelve indicators of elite's attitudes towards European institutions (INTUNE 2009)

Seven questions are indicators of attitudes toward the institutional setting of the EU:

1. How much do you agree that the Member States ought to remain the central actors of the EU ...

2. ... that the European Commission ought to become the true government of the EU

3. ... that the powers of the European Parliament ought to be strengthened?

Please tell me on a score of 0–10 how much you personally trust:

4. the European Parliament...

5. the European Council of Ministers, ...

6. and the European Commission,

   to usually take the right decisions. (0 means that you do not trust an institution at all, and 10, means you have complete trust)?

7. Are you very attached, somewhat attached, not very attached, or not at all attached to the EU?

Two questions are related to debates over the transfer of National States' powers to the EU institutions:

1. Thinking about the European Union over the next 10 years, can you tell me whether you are in favour of a single foreign policy toward countries outside the EU, instead of national policies?

2. Some say that we should have a single European Army. Others say every country should keep its national army. What is your opinion?

Three questions aim at measuring elites' opinions on the competences and the future of European institutions:

1. Thinking about the European Union over the next 10 years, can you tell me whether you are in favour or against a unified tax system for the European Union; ...

2. ... a common system of social security?

3. Some say European unification has already gone too far. Others say it should be strengthened. What is your opinion? Please indicate your views using a 10-point-scale (0 means that European unification 'has already gone too far', and 10 means that it 'should be strengthened').

Why a multiple correspondence analysis?

Preliminary descriptive statistics show that elites' attitudes towards institutions cannot be reduced to a simple binary opposition between federalists and Eurosceptics. We need a statistical methodology that makes it possible to differentiate between and take into account all configurations of opinions (Boomgaarden *et al* 2011). We conducted a Multiple Correspondence Analysis (MCA)[4] of the sample of national MPs and socio-economic elites interviewed in 2007 and 2009, because it differentiates all kind of associations between modalities of active variables without de facto ignoring those that run counter usual regressions focused on polarised attitudes. In our case it accounts for all combinations of answers to the questions, and thus helps to identify the entire diverse range of elites' convictions. MCA also distinguishes between weak and strong answers, such as 'strongly agree' and 'somewhat agree', and takes other answers, such as 'no answer', 'don't know', or 'refusals' into consideration.

As already noted, the INTUNE survey members of political and socio-economic elites responded to twelve questions related to European institutions. All respondents can be located through a definite set of answers in a twelve-dimensional space, or more precisely in a space defined by 54 modalities of answers to the twelve questions. A Multiple Correspondence Analysis provides a simplified representation of such a space by identifying the main oppositions or dimensions on institutional issues. Of course, the greater the number of questions, the lower the percentage of inertia summed up by an MCA. With twelve questions, the first axis (first opposition) summarises 53.5 per cent of the variance in all answers (Benzecri's modified inertia rate = BMIR), the second 23.5 per cent (BMIR) and the third 11.7 per cent (BMIR). Considering the number of questions taken into account, these percentages are in fact highly significant.

In order to complete the depiction and explanation of elites' European attitudes towards European integration and institutions, we have conducted an ascendant hierarchical classification (or a cluster analysis). A cluster analysis defines 'groups' whose 'members' share the same positions on European issues. These 'groups' are set up through an algorithm that minimises intra-group and maximises inter-group distances. It also gives indications on the numerical weight of each 'group' and therefore about the frequency of each type of European attitude within elites.

Dimensions of elites' european attitudes

The first cleavage (first axis; modified inertia rate = 53.5 per cent) is between partisans and opponents of European integration and supranational institutions. At one pole of the continuum, we find political and socio-economic leaders who express strong negative views of European integration and institutions. They

---

4. The MCA and the Ascendant Hierarchical Classification (cluster) analyses have been carried out with the software program R 2.8.1.

strongly disapprove of the single foreign policy.[5] They strongly disagree with the ideas that the powers of the European Parliament should be strengthened and that the European Commission should become the government of Europe. They are also strongly against a common system of social security and a unified tax system. They may be characterised as staunch adversaries of European supranational institutions and the kernel of the Euro-sceptic camp. Those who express more moderate negative opinions and say that they somewhat disagree with the idea of strengthening the powers of the EP or who are somewhat against a common system of social security, are also on this 'euro-critic' side, but to a lesser degree. They may accept limited advances in European integration through intergovernmental or unionist institutions.

At the opposite pole, interviewees express strong pro-integration attitudes. For instance they strongly agree that the Commission ought to become the true government of the EU. They think that European unification should be strengthened (positions 9–10 on the scale). They disagree that the Member States ought to remain the central actors of the EU. They are strongly in favour of a unified tax system and (to a lesser extent) of a common system of social security, etc. Such a set of answers clearly defines a pole of advocates of an increase in European integration through supranational institutions. Here again, respondents with more lukewarm but positive opinions of the EU are also located in the pro-integration camp, but to a lesser degree. They might, for instance, say that they somewhat agree that the European Commission should become the government of the Union. They are often partisans of intergovernmental integration and institutions.

A second divide (second axis; modified inertia rate = 23.5 per cent) distinguishes a majority of goodwill respondents from a minority of interviewees who balk at answering to the questionnaire. As the French survey was conducted through face to face interactions and was more qualitative with in depth interviews, we observed that the latter disagreed with the way European issues were phrased through closed-ended and too simplistic questions. Several interviewees asked if we were speaking of the 'present' European Commission when asked if they agree that it ought to become the true government of the EU. Others replied that they do not understand expressions like 'states as central actors of the EU' or 'the true government of the EU'. Questions on 'trust' in the European institutions were among the most criticised.

A third divide (third axis, modified inertia rate = 11.7 per cent) opposes respondents with strong coherent opinions to those with more lukewarm and conflicting positions. At one extreme of this axis we find, at the same time, the strongest advocates and opponents of European integration. Interviewees who say that

---

5. Answers defining the various poles of all axes are mentioned hereafter in decreasing order of their positive contribution to each factorial axis. In the present case, it means that the answers 'strongly against a single foreign policy' display the highest level of contribution to the first axis on the 'euro-critic' side.

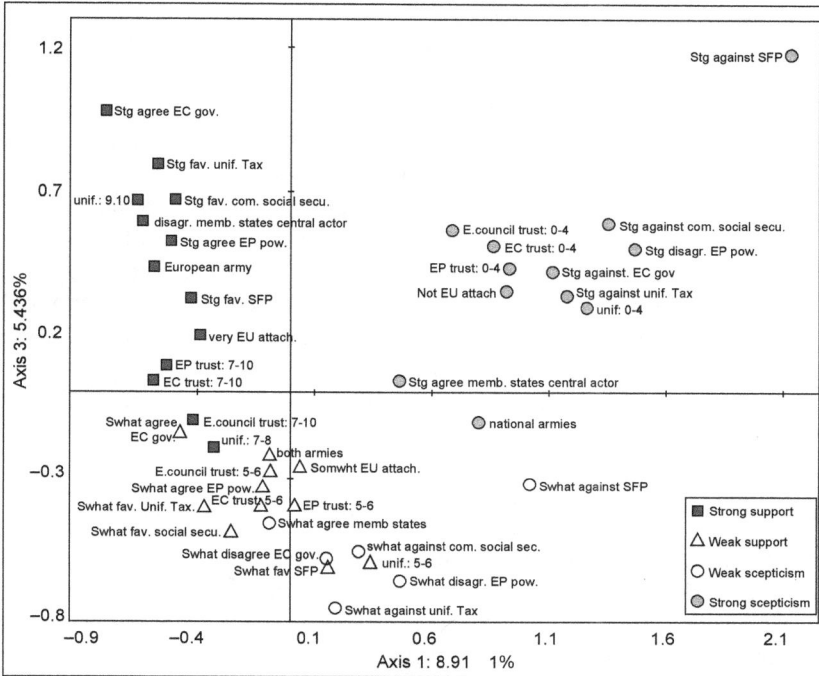

Figure 8.1: Projections of dependent variables on the factorial plan

they are strongly against a single foreign policy, as well as those who strongly agree that the European Commission ought to become the true government of the EU, are located at this same end of this third dimension. At the opposite pole, respondents express more lukewarm and somehow conflicting views, whether favourable or hostile to European construction. Those who say that they are somewhat in favour or against a strengthening of European institutions, or further advances in integration, are located there.

The second dimension is methodologically interesting because it shows some unexpected consequences of a questionnaire considered as simplistic and inadequate by a fraction of the sample. At the same time but it does not bring information about elites' attitudes toward European integration. In contrast, the combination of the first (hereafter x axis) and third (hereafter y axis) oppositions gives a clear and simple map of the distribution of European attitudes among political, economic, media, and trade union elites (Figure 8.1). Due to the statistical logic of a MCA, the first dimension equates with a synthetic index of elites' political orientations vis-à-vis European integration and institutions, based on a whole set of twelve questions/indicators. Each position on this axis may be considered as a value of a first dependent variable. This continuous variable reflects a continuum of views on European integration and institutions, from the most pro-integration and federalist attitudes on the negative side, to the most anti-integration and 'sovereignist' positions on the positive side. The second dimension of the map equates with a synthetic index of the strength and consistency of elites' conceptions of European institutions, from the strongest (negative or positive) coherent opinions on the top, to the weakest and conflicting ones on the bottom.

Not surprisingly, elites are divided not only between supporters and adversaries of supranational institutions but also between those with strong and lukewarm opinions. Strong champions of a strengthening of European integration are located in the top-left region of the map, whereas weaker or more irresolute advocates (who may also advocate intergovernmental forms of integration) are also situated in the left-hand region but in the bottom-left quadrant, closer to the centre of this first dimension. They contrast with EU-critics who are settled in the right-hand parts of the map, those with strong opinions in the top-right quadrant, and those with more moderate views in the bottom-right one, and closer to the centre of the first axis.

Main determinants of elites' views on european institutions

In order to identify the main determinants of elites' views on institutions, we placed regressions and projections of independent variables (nationality, self-location on right/left political scale, partisan affiliation, economic sector, religion, frontbencher/backbencher position in a parliament, age, gender, education) on the two axes of the map. Four main results may be stressed.

A first result is that there are few differences between different types of elite. It means that political, economic, media, and trade union elites are not homogenous groups when it comes to their European attitudes. Contrary to intuitive expectations, trade unionists (or at least those interviewed through the INTUNE survey) appear on average, as the most integrationist, even if the figures are not statistically significant. The same is true with the average location of economic elites in the pro-integration camp. A second important result is that nationality is the strongest predictor of the elites' attitudes (see Figure 8.2). On average, all elites coming from Western European countries are located in the left-hand quadrants, some in the top-left – strong partisans of European integration and supranational institutions (Italy, Greece, Belgium, and, less significantly, France and Germany) – others in the bottom left (Spain). The main exceptions are British elites who are located in the top-right quadrant (strong EU-critics) and who are the main occupiers of this quadrant. Austrian and Danish elites are also situated along the anti-integration half of the first x axis, but close to the centre of the y axis, in the moderate direction. The average locations of Austrian, French and Portuguese elites are only mildly significant. This means, for example, that Austrian elites are scattered across the four quadrants, with a tiny overall leaning toward euro-criticism. In contrast, Spanish, Italian, Belgian, and Greek elites are more homogeneous and more neatly linked to the pro-EU advocacy coalition, even if some of them may share negative feelings about European integration.

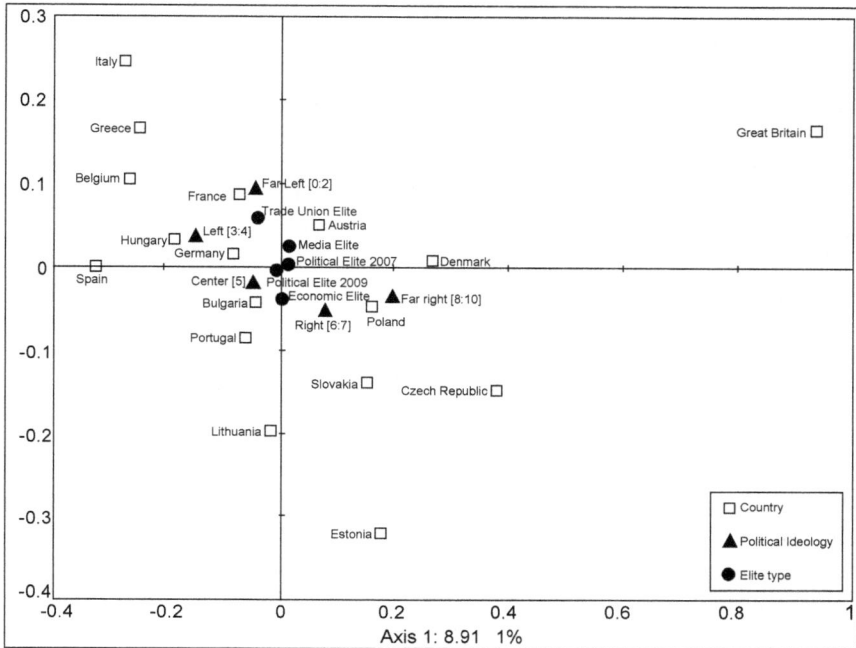

Figure 8.2: Projections of countries, political positions and elite's type on the factorial plan

Most elite members of the eastern European countries (Czech Republic, Poland, Slovakia, Estonia) are located in the EU-critical half of the map. Most of them (Estonians, Slovaks and Czechs) express lukewarm or conflicting opinions. Members of the Hungarian elite are the main exception. They are mainly situated in the EU-supporter half of the map, even if they are divided between strong and weak supporters, and are therefore located close to the centre of the y axis. The locations of the Bulgarian and Lithuanian interviewees within the pro-EU half are not very significant. One conclusion of this analysis is that when it comes to attitudes toward European integration and institutions, members of various types of elites of the same country are often closer to each other than members of the same type of elite across the EU.

A third result is that there is a close association between general ideological leanings and attitudes toward European integration and institutions. If we take the self location on a 0–10 left-right scale, we see that members of the different elites who situate themselves on the left (score 3 or 4) are more likely to be located in the top left, strong pro-integration and supranational quadrant of the map. Even more surprisingly, the same is true, although less neatly, with those who situate themselves at the far left end (0–2) of the political scale. Interviewees who place themselves at the centre of the political scale are also situated in the pro-EU half of the x axis, although closer to the centre of the x axis, which shows that they are more divided than their left-wing counterparts. By contrast, those who situate themselves on the right (6 or 7) or even more on the far right (8 to 10) positions are significantly more likely to stand in the EU-critic camp, although with mainly lukewarm and conflicting opinions. We may thus observe a left/right wing divide on European institutional issues. Such a political divide splits the political elite but also, less expectedly, other elites, including business leaders, even if the latter are more likely to stand on the right of the political spectrum. Contrary to a received idea, there is no evidence of a strong EU scepticism of the far leftists (Taggart 1998, Taggart and Szczerbiak 2008and Szczerbiak and Taggart 2002) in this survey. Political, economic, media, and trade union leaders who have answered the INTUNE questionnaire and declared far left positions, are clearly in the pro-integration camp. There is neither a linear relationship between situation on the political scale and European attitudes, nor a moderate versus radical cleavage.

We may thus observe a shift in the political bases of European integration. Elites with left and centre-left leanings are more likely to share pro-integration attitudes than those with right and centre-right preferences. Looking at MPs' partisan affiliation, it is meaningful that the Christian-Democrats, who had been the main advocates of the European construction for a long time, cannot be considered, as a whole, as members of the supra-nationalist and pro-integration camp any more. On average, they are even located in the right-hand euro-critic half of the space, more clearly on the lukewarm/conflicting side of the y axis. It means that there are more Christian-Democrats MPs on the Euro-critic side of the map than in the pro-integration camp. It is worth noticing that the 'Right Liberals' are also firmly in the anti-EU half of the map. Even if European unification is often depicted as an economic neo-liberal construction, we observe that the main advocates of economic liberalism are not the likeliest supporters of European integration. Opposition on European issues is not only associated with a cleavage between established and marginal political parties, but also rests on political and ideological divides. The established/outsiders cleavage is intertwined with the radical/moderate and left-right divisions. Nevertheless, centre-left elites seem presently more anxious to push European integration forward and to strengthen EU institutions than their right and centre-right counterparts. At this moment in the history of European unification (2007–2009), the Greens appear to be the most resolute champions of integration. Contrary to conventional wisdom that European integration is a market and business oriented process, it seems mainly supported by western elites who share left and centre-left, general, political views and who wish to increase the European dimension of welfare public policies, either through supranational institutions or intergovernmental coordination.

This is why there is a significant correlation between elites' opinions on the relevant level to deal with several public policies and their general European attitudes. Interviewees who think that public policies such as employment, crime, immigration, environment, health care, agriculture, energy and tax policies have to be dealt with at the European level, are significantly located in the top-left quadrant (strong euro-supporters). Those who believe that national and/or regional levels are more appropriate, are located in the euro-critic half of the x axis. Those who advocate a form of multi-level governance, including European and some sub-European national and/or regional institutions, are in the lukewarm pro-European camp, even if the correlations are only significant for employment, health care and tax policies. At this stage in the history of European construction, the staunchest supporters of supranational institutions and advocates of more inter-governmental forms of cooperation also back further advances in European integration and regulation. This is probably the reason why they are more numerous on the left end of the political spectrum.

The relative irrelevance of individual backgrounds

The fourth conclusion of our analysis is that there is a relative irrelevance of individual backgrounds at the elite level. Contrary to some scholars' hypotheses (for example Hix 1999), it seems that there are few relationships between the economic sector of the business leaders and their views of the European institutions. We may only observe a counter-intuitive statistically significant location of heads of public utilities in the pro-integration half of the map, which could be congruent with the previous observation. Likewise, looking at the previous sector of occupation of political, trade-unionist or media-elite, we observe that those coming from the public sector are significantly located in the pro-European half of the factorial plan and in its lukewarm quadrant.

On the whole, economic agents of the other sectors seem to be situated in the same pro-EU camp, but so close to the centre that their situations cannot be considered as significant. The main exception is the group of business leaders from trade and service companies, although, here again, the statistical relationship is not significant.

Other relationships between attitudes toward European institutions and independent variables are weak. It confirms that national and political aggregates are more homogenous than those related to individual socio-demographic variables. For instance, in most cases, correlations between the position on the first axis and religious affiliations are not significant. When they are significant, we may wonder if the religious affiliation is no more an indicator of national belonging than an independent variable.

Individual characteristics of members of the elites are poorly associated with attitudes towards European integration. There are no significant relations with gender. There are also no clear-cut correlations between the level of education of members of the elites and their European attitudes. All appears as if, at these elite levels, lower levels of formal education were neutralised by self-taught ways of bridging cultural gaps. Contrary to our hypothesis, on average, there are no differences between back and frontbenchers in parliaments, but members of governing parties are significantly positioned in the pro-European half of the first axis and those who belong to opposition parties are clearly in the opposite half.

A few individual characteristics seem however to be linked to elites' attitudes. As expected, the broader their international experience (studies and stay abroad, command of foreign languages), the more respondents are located in the pro-integration direction of the x-axis. Those with no international experience are clearly opponents, while those with strong international experiences are clearly euro-supporters. The relations with intermediate levels of experience follow the expected logic, but they are less significant. The same is true with the number of contacts with European actors and institutions. Interviewees stand all the more toward the pro-integration pole of the first axis as the frequency of their contacts increases. However, only the extreme positions (no contact last year and contacts every week) are significant on both axes. Likewise, those who say that they are considering a political or professional career at a European level are likely to be situated in the pro-integration half of the first axis.

Nationality and ideological leaning: which is the strongest determinant?

The conclusion that national belonging and political attitudes are the main predictors of attitudes toward European integration raises a new question: do these two factors have an independent impact and which is the strongest?

In fact, there is a relationship between the frequency of ideological orientations and the geographic origins of elites. Elites coming from Eastern Europe are more often far right oriented (27.9 per cent compared with 8.9 per cent for Western elites), whereas Western elites more often express left-wing political leanings (32.5 per cent and 18.2 per cent for Eastern elites). In order to observe if these two correlated variables have an independent effect, we have created a new variable by cross-tabulating elites' geographical origins and their political leanings. We have decided to split the sample into two aggregates: countries with an average location on the left part of the first x axis ('pro-integrationist countries') on the one hand, and those located on the right part of it ('anti-integrationist') on the other hand. We have cross-tabulated these sets of countries with the political leanings of the interviewees coming from each of them. The regression of this new variable on the first x axis shows a strong effect of national prevailing (positive or negative) perceptions of the EU on elites' attitudes toward integration and institutions. In each case, whether they are left, centre or right oriented, elites coming from countries with prevalent pro-EU attitudes (or those coming from countries with opposite attitudes) are systematically located within the pro-integration half of the x-axis (or on the anti-integration side). Far-right elites coming from 'pro-integration countries' may be the only dubious case, since their position in the pro-integrationist camp is not statistically significant. However, political orientations still have an effect on elites' European attitudes. The likelihood that interviewees coming from countries with a prevailing liking for European integration share such positive feelings, increases when their political orientations move from the far-right, to the right, then to the far-left, the centre, and to the left of the political scale. The relationship is even clearer for interviewees who come from countries with a leading collective scepticism about the EU, since the average position on the first x-axis is all the more further on the euro-critic half, that their political orientations move from the far-left to the far-right of the political scale.

Finally, looking at the y-axis, we see that there are fewer correlations between national European leanings and the strength and coherence of attitudes of the nationals. Left and far-left oriented members of pro-integrationist countries are located in the strong convicted part of the axis, whereas others are located in the lukewarm and conflicting part of the axis. There are no, or only weak, significant correlations for the ideological aggregates of 'anti-integration countries'.

In conclusion, we observe that national belonging and ideological leanings have distinct but combined effects on attitudes toward the EU. In many cases, we may hypothesise a leading collective national experience of European integration, more or less common to elites of a given country, which shapes the European attitudes of a more or less noticeable proportion of interviewees of each country (Diez Medrano 2003). At the same time, European attitudes are linked to ideological orientations of elites. Those who are located on the left of the political spectrum are the likeliest to express positive attitudes toward the EU, followed by those on the centre, and on the far-left. By contrast, those on the right, and, even more, on the far-right positions are likelier to display negative views. With the combination of these two factors, elites coming from countries with prevailing positive perceptions of the EU (at the elite level) are all the more likely to share more positive perceptions than if they are located towards the left of the political spectrum. Symmetrically, elites from countries with predominant negative perceptions are all the more likely to express more negative views and they are located towards the far-right wing of the political spectrum. It is not the cleavage between Western and Eastern European countries, but rather the divide between countries with prevailing collective positive or negative perceptions that structures the distribution of European attitudes among member states' elites. At the same time there is a link between the Western/Eastern cleavages and the opposition between strong, coherent and more lukewarm conflicting views of European integration.

Distribution of elites' european attitudes

In order to complete the map of elites' European attitudes toward European integration and institutions, we have conducted an ascendant hierarchical classification (or cluster analysis) that defines 'groups' whose 'members' share the same positions on European issues. These 'groups' are set up through an algorithm that minimises intra-group and maximises inter-group distances. A definite association of a selected set of parameters, taken into account by the analysis, characterises each group. Cluster analyses may thus provide information about the configurations of opinions on European institutions, and, at the same time, about the independent variables, that define the various 'groups'. That is the reason why we have introduced items not only about interviewees' opinions on European issues but also about their gender, age, education, nationality, religious affiliation, partisan membership (for MPs only) and self-location on the left-right scale. For each group, the cluster analysis provides information about the frequency distributions of the dependant and independent variables. We may observe which opinions, but also which political, national or socio-demographic characteristics are over/under-represented in a given group. At a chosen hierarchical level, we may identify and describe the whole diversity of attitudes toward European integration and institutions through the sets of opinions of the various groups. In order to have a more precise depiction of elites' opinions, we have added answers to several questions about EU institutions and policies from the first[6] and the second[7] waves of the INTUNE elite survey which are not taken into account in the MCA. As each group may be defined by over-representations of modalities of the selected independent variables, the cluster analysis also provides evidence about the main determinants of elites' attitudes toward European integration and institutions. Another reason to choose this methodology is that it gives indications about the numerical weight of each 'group' and therefore about the frequency of each type of European attitude among European political, economic, media, and trade-union elites.

Several small groups are defined by non-answers or refusals to answer opinion questions. They aggregate 329 interviewees or 8.5 per cent of the sample. At an elite level, such reactions cannot be considered as indicators of non-attitudes. There is no evidence that would lead us to construe them as an expression of a genuine European attitude. Such groups seem therefore to result from the wording of several questions of the questionnaire, especially those perceived as 'simplistic' by certain interviewees. We have thus decided to discard them. Following the cluster analysis, five main groups with distinct attitudes may be singled out. Several of them also need to be divided into sub-groups separated by nuances.

A first group (N=290, 7.5 per cent of the sample) is located in the top left quadrant of the map. It gathers the most integrationist and federalist segments of national elites. These interviewees are strongly in favour of a unified tax system and of a common system of social security. According to them, health care, employment, tax and security policies as well as European security should be dealt with at the European level. They agree to increase the powers of the European Parliament and they wish that the European Commission becomes the government of the EU. They strongly disagree that the member states remain central actors of the Union. They are strongly in favour of a common European foreign policy, a

---

6. Do you think that fighting Unemployment; Immigration policy; Environment policy; Fight against crime; Health care policy; Agriculture (second wave); Energy policy (second wave) should be mainly dealt with at regional level, at national level, at European Union level?

7. – Are you in favor or against having a president of the European Union?
– In any case, if we have it, which way of designation is most appropriate? an election by all EU citizens; an election by the EP; an appointment by the European Council?
– Which authority would be more appropriate to deal with European security? NATO, EU National governments?
– Do you agree or disagree that most important decisions concerning the EU should be taken by a majority of all European citizens via a popular referendum?
– Do you agree or disagree that Europe needs a common constitution?
– Do you agree or disagree that Majority voting should be extended in the European Council?

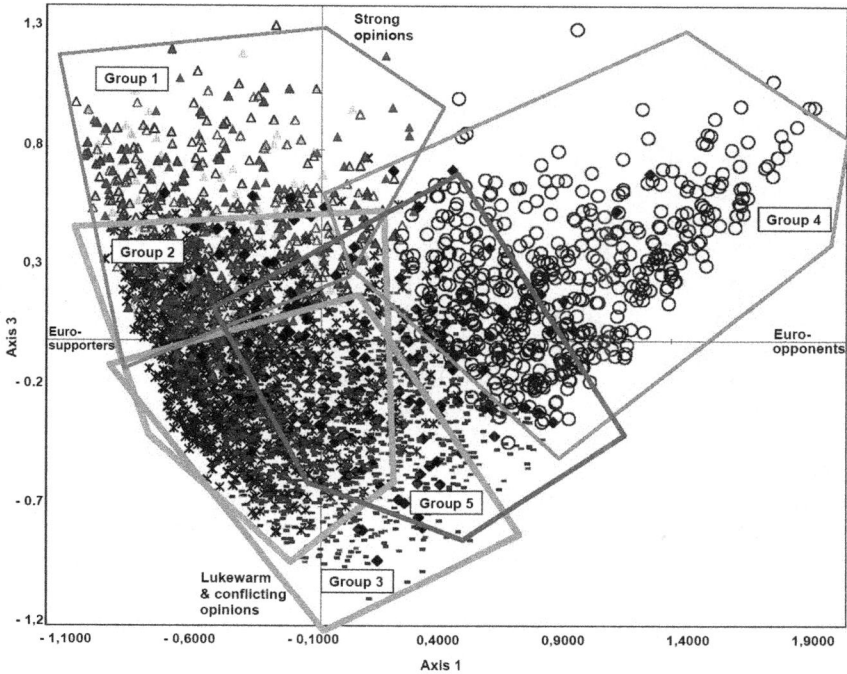

Figure 8.3: Projection of the five identified clusters

European army, a president of the EU, elected by all citizens, an extension of the majority voting system in the European Council, and a European constitution. In accordance with the findings of the MCA, Italians, Greeks, Belgians, Spaniards, members of socialist and social-democrat political parties in national Parliaments, respondents who locate themselves on the left (3–4) of the political scale, and also those with a developed international experience are over-represented in this group.

A second group gathers more tepid or less enthusiastic integrationists and federalists (N= 1283, 33.1 per cent of the sample). It is also mainly located in the top left part of the map, although closer to the centre of the two axes. A small part of the group is also situated in the bottom left quadrant but close to the centre of the y-axis. Members of this group are close to those of the first group, but they express weaker or different opinions on several issues. A first sub-group also expresses strong integrationist and federalist views on many issues, but about half of its members are only somewhat in favour of a unified tax system and a common system of social security, and agree somewhat that the European Commission should become the government of the EU. Greeks, Hungarians, members of socialist, conservative, and/or members of government political parties in Parliaments, and backbenchers are proportionally numerous in this sub-group. A second sub-group is a bit less federalist and almost as integrationist as the first group, but a large proportion of its members display a lower level of trust (5–6) in the European

Commission, the European Council of Ministers and the European Parliament. Spaniards, Italians, and members of the left are proportionally numerous in this sub-group. A third sub-group aggregates staunch integrationists and federalists who nevertheless express a surprising distrust (0–4 on the scale) of the European Institutions. French, trade union, media leaders and respondents who locate themselves on the far-left (0–2), or the left (3–4), of the political scale, are over-represented in this sub-group.

A third group is characterised by the lukewarm and conflicting views of its 1068 members (27.5 per cent of the sample). Around two-thirds of them are settled in the bottom left quadrant, others in the bottom right, but not far in the right (euro-critic) direction. All of them are well spread along the bottom part of the y axis, and are closer to the centre of the first axis. A first subgroup displays moderate conflicting opinions on European integration and on the institutional design of the EU. They declare a high level of trust in the EU institutions, and first of all in the intergovernmental Council of Ministers. They are somewhat in favour of a common European foreign policy, they agree somewhat to strengthen the powers of the European Parliament and Commission. At the same time, in a conflicting way, 54 per cent of them agree somewhat (and 45 per cent disagree somewhat) that the member states ought to remain central actors of the EU, and a majority wishes a mixed system of European and national armies. Most members of this group chose upper intermediate scores (7–8) on the unification scale. Members of this third group are proportionally more numerous in disagreeing or agreeing somewhat with the idea of a unified tax system and of a common system of social security, and thinking that employment and tax policies should be dealt with at an infra-European level. Lithuanians, Eastern elites, Portuguese, frontbenchers, members of liberal, social democrat, government political parties in national parliaments and Catholics are over-represented in this group. A second sub group is as divided as the previous one on integration issues, and a little less partisan of strengthening European unification. Members of this sub-group express even more conflicting opinions on the institutional design of the EU. Most of them are somewhat in favour of a European foreign policy, a strengthening of the European Parliament, and a European Constitution. At the same time, they are proportionally more numerous to back a mixed system of national and European armies, to agree somewhat that the member states ought to remain central actors of the EU, and to disagree somewhat that the European Commission should become the government of the EU, that Europe needs a Constitution, to increase the powers of the European Parliament, and to extend a majority voting in the European Council of Ministers. Eastern elites, especially Estonians, Poles, and Czechs, Catholics, and respondents who situated themselves on the right (6–7) of the political scale are over-represented and contribute to set this sub-group apart.

A fourth group is clearly opposed to European integration and supranational institutions. Its 203 members (5.24 per cent of the sample) are all located in the top right quadrant of the map. A huge proportion displays a very low level of trust (0–4) in EU institutions, and, a bit less often in the intergovernmental European Council of Ministers (73 per cent). Most of them are strongly against a unified tax system and a common system of social security. They think that almost all public policies should be dealt with at a non-European level. They disagree strongly with increaseing the powers of supranational institutions and they agree strongly that the member states remain central actors of the EU, and keep their national armies. Some of them may nevertheless accept some kinds of intergovernmental coordination. That is the reason why they have a less negative view of the European Council of Ministers. In accordance to the MCA, the British, Czechs, Poles, and Danes, the members of conservative political parties in national Parliaments, those who situate themselves on the far right end (8–10) of the political scale and who have no international experience are over represented in this group.

The fifth group is close to the previous one, but its 704 members (18.2 per cent of the sample) are a bit more moderate on several issues. They are all situated in the right half of the map, closer to the centre than members of group 4, and they are also scattered in the top and the bottom right quadrants, although never around the farthest positions on the y-axis. A first sub group shares almost all the views of the members of the fourth group, with only weaker positions. A second difference is that about 50 per cent of the members of this sub-group are somewhat in favour of a European foreign policy, and that more than a third agree with a moderate increase in European unification (5–6 on the unification scale). Eastern elites, especially Czechs, Poles, and Slovaks, also Austrians, members of far right wing political parties in national Parliaments, persons who mention no contact with European officials during the previous year, trade union and media elites, respondents who situate on the far left end (0–2) of the political scale, are over-represented in this sub-group. A second sub-group also gathers people with anti-federalist and anti-integrationist, but also stronger inter-governmental feelings, than the previous ones. Like the previous sub-group, they are in favour of a moderate increase in European unification (5–6 on the scale). Their main peculiarity is that many of its members express an upper moderate level of trust (5–6) in the European Commission and Parliament, and, in accordance with their intergovernmental leanings, a high level of trust (7–10) in the European Council of Ministers. British, Danes, Estonians, Protestants, members of Christian Democrat or Right Liberal political parties in Parliaments, and interviewees who choose 8th to 10th far right positions on the political scale are proportionally numerous in this sub-group.

To sum up, the cluster analysis provides evidence that European elites are divided into three broad attitudes towards European integration and institutions. Around 41 per cent of members of the sample may be located on a continuum of more or less integrationist and federalist positions; around 23 per cent share a more or less nationalist or inter-governmentalist opposition to European integration and institutions; around 28 per cent express lukewarm, conflicting, and sometimes contradictory views, which cannot be characterised as pro or anti-integration. A second conclusion is that the cluster analysis confirms that the national membership, and the general political attitudes, are the main determinants of attitudes toward European integration and institutions.

Limitations of close-ended questions: some lessons from a qualitative survey

The conclusion that elites' attitudes towards European integration are linked to distinct national experiences is descriptive. We know that nationality is the main determinant of elites' opinions on European issues, but we do not know why and how nationality shapes these opinions. We can surmise that national elites share national frames of perception of the EU, resulting from particular national experiences of the history of European integration, but we have no information about these frames and experiences. This is of course the main limitation of closed-ended questionnaires. This type of methodology can record opinions, but cannot provide indications about the reasons why interviewees express such views. For instance, we know that a given category of respondents is more likely to be in favour of, or opposed to a strengthening of European integration, but we do not know what the respondents have in mind when they express these feelings. That is the reason why, in the French case, the questionnaire was administered through a face-to-face in-depth semi structured interview. Respondents were asked to develop and explain their opinions. It is thus possible to provide a more thorough account of the motives and reasons of French elites' attitudes toward European unification. We are therefore able to observe if specific national considerations are mobilised to express these motives and reasons.[8]

Tacit references to a subjective national situation

In the French case, interviewees tacitly reason on a situation subjectively characterised, among other parameters, by a high level of taxation, social protection, state regulation, and collective infrastructure, and a well-organised and efficient public administration. These frames are mobilised by a more or less greater number of French citizens at the elite and mass levels. They result from a specific experience of European integration shared by a more or less greater number of persons. For instance, from their direct or indirect experience, numerous French people have learnt that given the high level of taxes and wages in France, many companies choose to offshore their investments, which contributes to the increase of unemployment and brings downward pressures on wages. In the circles where such issues are discussed, it is also commonly taken for granted that the high level of taxes and social protection is at odds with, and endangered by, the situation of most other European countries and of the ideological orientations of European integration, at least as it has been conducted until now. These French perceptions

---

8. We do not have enough room here to develop the analysis of the results of our qualitative surveys at the elite (INTUNE program) and mass (CONCORDE program, see Gaxie, Hubé, and Rowell 2011) levels. This analysis will be published later. In the following lines we only wish to provide a short empirical description of the French national frames of perception and assessment of European integration. Our aim is also to show how these frames are related to the specificities of the French situation within the EU, and how they may be mobilised by people with different, even opposite, ideological leanings.

may be close to other national views widespread in countries with similar situations. French citizens combine these frames of perception with convergent or divergent anticipation and expectation. For instance, many heads of French companies think that national taxes are too heavy and need to be cut. Some of them consider that it could be achieved through tax competition between EU member states, whereas others support various forms of fiscal unification or harmonisation. All in all, it is on the basis of their common national experience, screened through different and possibly contradictory aspirations, that members of various elites express views on European integration. Thus, most French economic leaders support European unification and ask for deeper integration. In their views, European Union is a way to increase economic liberalism, to curb unreasonable national public expenses and deficits, to lower national taxation, to impose greater economic discipline and to challenge excessive state regulations and social benefits. By contrast, many trade-union leaders and left wing or centre politicians see European integration as a way to promote a 'European social model', to protect the much revered national social security system, and to tighten public regulation of the economy. We may thus observe a national consensus or, at least, a prevailing attitude, in favour of European integration among French elites, and, at the same time, lasting cleavages about the aims and ambitions of this integration. On the right side of the political spectrum, many members of various elites (and some 'ordinary' citizens) support social and tax integration in order to put downward pressure on excessive French taxes and social welfare, and/or to remove distortions of competition. Elites and some citizens with left-wing leanings also wish to strengthen integration, but as a way to oppose social and tax dumping. Indeed European unification is scrutinised through a national viewpoint, which is sifted through ideological dispositions. Also, from a French perspective, at least within informed circles that are concerned with such issues, it is taken for granted that powerful states, such as France, Germany, and the UK, will not accept to be controlled, that Germany and France are 'the engine of Europe', and that France cannot accept to transfer its nuclear power to a supranational institution. Therefore when French elites ask for more integration, they are more likely to think of inter-governmental rather than federal forms of institutionalisation.

Conclusions

Multiple Correspondence Analysis (MCA) and cluster analysis confirm the diversity of elites' views on European institutions, which cannot be reduced to a simple opposition between partisans and adversaries of European construction. Indeed, there are strong and weak advocates of, and opponents to, European integration. Among the former, we may observe nuances of federalism and inter-governmentalism. Only a minority of political and economic elites shares a true federalist conception of European institutions (7.5 per cent). All euro-critics are not staunch defenders of national sovereignty. Truly Euro-sceptics constitute a small minority of national elites (5.24 per cent). Many EU-critics support a moderate strengthening of European integration through a unionist or an intergovernmental model of cooperation between member states.

European unification is undoubtedly an elite driven process (Haller 2008), but it does not entail that all members of the elites are faithful advocates of supranational institutions. Indeed, around a quarter of elites of seventeen member states of the EU appear to be more or less critical of European construction, at least as it has been conducted until now, and around 28 per cent express lukewarm reluctant support. We may surmise that national MPs fear losing some of their powers, but, contrary to common hypotheses, business elites are not more likely to be enthusiastic about the EU and trade unionists appear as the most pro-integration group. At the same time, most elites' members ask for or resign to more integration. However, in the eyes of the majority, this integration needs to be decided and conducted through intergovernmental channels.

One of the main findings of the INTUNE elite survey is the confirmation that elites of various EU member states have more or less similar views of the EU (see also Diez Medrano 2003). It is the case for the political elite as well as, perhaps more surprisingly, for other socio-economic leaders. There are no simple explanations for the variation of their perceptions. On average, elites of founding Member States are clearly in the pro-integration camp (Belgians, Italians, and, less clearly, the French and the Germans). Western elites are more likely to share positive attitudes toward European unification, whereas critics are more numerous among Eastern elites. However, Hungarians stand in the pro-integration half of the map, Austrians, Portuguese, and even more, Bulgarians and Lithuanians are not clearly situated. The British and the Danes are among the strong opponents of the EU.

Elites' European attitudes are probably a result of distinct collective experiences of European integration, more or less shared by a variable proportion of the ruling circles of each member state. More research is needed to probe into their perceptions and the reasons and motives of their appraisals. In-depth semi-structured interviews using open-ended questions is a way to observe national frames resulting from such national collective experiences of the history of European construction.

Answers to closed-ended questions are useful, but rather simplistic indicators of opinions and attitudes. It is true at the mass level, because, in many cases, not all of the citizens master the information or have the cognitive skills required to express true opinions on issues raised by a survey. It is also true at an elite level, because short answers cannot give sound expressions of the nuances and complexity of elites' views on technical, difficult matters. Contrary to closed-ended questions that artificially homogenise answers, in-depth interviews show multiple ways of reacting. Firstly, interviewees express opinions with more or less conviction. Some respondents explain for example, that they are in favour of a unified tax system but that it does not really have effect on their company, or that they do not believe that it is likely to be achieved in the foreseeable future. Secondly, elite respondents are not always willing to answer a questionnaire that they perceive as being too simplistic. Some of them turn down the wording of questions and choose to refer to their own formulation. They, for instance, say that they are not in favour of a unified, by rather of a convergent, harmonised or coordinated tax system. Thirdly, when they express views on European integration, economic leaders may speak in general terms as citizens or as economic actors referring to specific problems faced by their company or by the economic sector they belong to. It is probably one of the reasons why there seems to be no observable statistical relationship between business elites' views on European issues and their sector of activity.

At the same time, despite these methodological biases, it seems that various elites' European attitudes are strongly linked to nationality, and therefore, to national experiences of European integration. Compared with Diez Medrano's hypotheses, the qualitative surveys conducted in France bring convergent but also divergent conclusions. First, European integration is perceived and assessed through national frames. Some of them may be country specific as Juan Diez Medrano seems to presuppose, but others might be common to nationals belonging to countries facing similar situations. Second, common references to national frames of perceptions do not entail that all nationals express identical appreciations. Also, apparently converging views on European integration may result from different, and even divergent, ulterior motives. Third, national frames are rarely shared by all citizens of a state, but rather by more or less extensive groups of citizens, and in some cases, by very limited circles concerned with a particular issue.

Attitudes toward European institutions are also strongly dependent on the political leanings of the elites. The left-right cleavage contributes to explain opposition to institutional issues. Whereas European construction is often depicted as market and business oriented, it presently (2007 and 2009) seems to be mainly supported by elites who share left, centre-left, centre, and far-left general political views. Such a politicisation of European attitudes could be expected from MPs, but it is once again surprising that the same pattern can also be observed with other elites. We may thus wonder if EU institutions are not perceived as, and in some cases are not expected to be, interventionist bodies in charge of economic and social regulation instead of liberal free-market advocates? It must be noted that such trends appear in a survey conducted before and after the financial crisis of 2008. In such a perspective, Multiple Correspondence Analysis and cluster analysis confirm that perceptions of European institutions are closely intertwined with notions of their main missions. When they support or when they oppose an increase in the powers of European institutions, strong partisans and strong opponents of further European integration alike think in terms of a common foreign policy, a unified tax system, a common system of social security and a European army.

References

Bélot, C. (2002) 'Les logiques sociologiques de soutien au processus d'intégration européenne: éléments d'interprétation', *Revue Internationale de Politique Comparée* 9(1): 11–29.

Best, H., Lengyel, G. and Verzichelli, L. (eds) (2012) *The Europe of Elites: A study into the Europeanness of Europe's economic and political elites*, Oxford: Oxford University Press.

Binnema, H. and Crum, B. (2007) 'Resistance to Europe as a Carrier of Mass-Elite Incongruence: The case of the Netherlands', in J. Lacroix and R. Coman (eds) *Les résistances à l'Europe: Cultures nationales, idéologies et stratégies d'acteurs*, Bruxelles: Editions de l'Université de Bruxelles, pp. 113–128.

Bitsch, M.-T., Loth, W. and Barthel, C. (eds) (2007) *Cultures politiques, opinions publiques et intégration européenne*, Bruxelles: Emile Bruylant.

Boomgaarden, H. G., Schuck, A., Elenbaas, M., and de Vreese, C. H. (2011) 'Mapping EU attitudes: conceptual and empirical dimensions of Euroscepticism and EU support', *European Union Politics*, 12(2): 241–266.

Deflem, M. and Pampel, F. C. (1996) 'The myth of postnational identity: popular support for European unification', *Social Forces,* 75(1): 119–143.

Della Porta, D. and Caiani, M. (2007) 'Addressing Europe: How domestic actors perceive European institutions and how they try to influence them: The Italian case in comparative perspective', in J. Lacroix and R. Coman (eds) *Les résistances à l'Europe: Cultures nationales, idéologies et stratégies d'acteurs*, Bruxelles: Editions de l'Université de Bruxelles, pp. 187–210.

Dell'Olio, F. (2005) *The Europeanization of Citizenship: Between the ideology of nationality, immigration and European identity*, Aldershot: Ashgate.

De Master, S. and Le Roy, M. K. (2000) 'Xenophobia and the European Union', *Comparative Politics* 34(4): 419–436.

Diez Medrano, J. (2003) *Framing Europe: Attitudes to European Integration in Germany, Spain, and the UK,* Princeton: Princeton University Press.

Gabel, M. (1998) 'Public support for European Integration: an empirical test of five theories', *The Journal of Politics*, 60 (2): 333–54.

Gabel, M. and Palmer, H. (1995) 'Understanding variation in public support for European Integration', *European Journal of Political Research* 27: 3–19.

Gabel, M. and Whitten, G. D. (1997) 'Economic conditions, economic perceptions, and public support for European Integration', *Political Behavior*, 19(1): 81–96.

Gaxie, D. and Hubé, N. (2012) 'Elites' Views on European Institutions: National experiences sifted through ideological orientations' in H. Best, G. Lengyel and L. Verzichelli (eds) *The Europe of Elites: A study into the Europeanness of Europe's economic and political elites*, Oxford: Oxford University Press, pp.122–146.

Gaxie, D., Hubé, N. and Rowell, J. (eds) (2011) *Perceptions of Europe: A comparative sociology of European attitudes,* Essex: ECPR Press.

Haller, M. (2008) *European Integration as an Elite Process: The failure of a dream?*, New York: Routledge.

Harmsen, R. (2007) 'Is British Euroskepticism still unique? National exceptionalism in comparative perspective', in J. Lacroix and R. Coman (eds) *Les résistances à l'Europe: Cultures nationales, idéologies et stratégies d'acteurs*, Bruxelles: Editions de l'Université de Bruxelles, pp. 69–92.

Hix, S. (1999) 'Dimensions and alignments in European Union politics: cognitive constraints and partisan responses', *European Journal of Political Research* 35: 69–106.

Hooghe, L. and Marks, G. (2004) 'Does identity or economic rationality drive public opinion on European Integration', *Political Science & Politics* 37: 415–420.

— (2009) 'A postfunctionalist theory of European Integration: from permissive consensus to constraining dissensus', *British Journal of Political Science* 39(1): 1–23.

Lacroix, J. and Coman, R. (eds) (2007) *Les résistances à l'Europe: Cultures nationales, idéologies et stratégies d'acteurs*, Bruxelles: Editions de l'Université de Bruxelles.

Marcussen, M., Risse, T., Engelmann-Martin, D., Knopf, H.- J., and Roscher, K. (1999) 'Constructing Europe? The evolution of French, British and German nation state identities', *Journal of European Public Policy* 6(4): 614–33.

Sitter, N. (2001) 'The politics of opposition and European Integration in Scandinavia: is Euro-scepticism a government-opposition dynamic?', *West European Politics* 24(4): 22–39.

Szczerbiak, A and Taggart, P. (2002) 'Europeanisation, Euroscepticism and party systems: party-based Euroscepticism in the candidate states of Central and Eastern Europe', *Perspectives on European Politics and Society* 3(1): 23–41.

Taggart, P. (1998) 'A touchstone of dissent: Euroscepticism in contemporary Western European party systems', *European Journal of Political Research* 33: 363–388.

Taggart, P. and Szczerbiak, A. (eds) (2008) *Opposing Europe: The comparative party politics of Euroscepticism*, I-II vol., Oxford: Oxford University Press.

chapter nine | europeans' space-sets and the political legitimacy of the EU

Ettore Recchi and Theresa Kuhn[i]

What are space-sets and why do they matter for politics?

The legitimacy of non-authoritarian polities rests – more than on other things – on the 'space-sets' of the persons on whom they stake their claims. A 'space-set' can be defined as the complex of physical sites where individuals spend their social existence.[1] This concept is patterned after Robert Merton's concepts of 'status-set' and 'role-set', to refer to the whole of statuses and roles a person holds (Merton 1968: 422). The only difference is that while status-sets change as people quit social positions (for instance, by changing job), space-sets comprise also spatial contexts that are not occupied by an individual at present and are not continuously accessible in everyday life due to travel constraints. Space-sets stem from past and present practices, unified by remembering 'togetherness' in a geographical place.

We contend that space-sets and political legitimacy are intimately linked phenomena. All human beings have cognitively and affectively meaningful relations with space. It is when these relations are confronted with power claims, that spaces turn into 'territories' – that is, sites loaded with forms of political organisation (Sack 1986; see also Bigo in this volume). But even apart from explicit hierarchical claims, the sheer fact of 'being-in-the-world' – that is, in Heideggerian terms, being *where* one is experiencing or has experienced social relationships – tends to entail a subjective sense of compliance for situational norms, unless the situation itself is coercive (like in Max Weber's *Macht* relationships). Repeated presence in an ordered physical context breeds adaptation, familiarity, and eventually some degree of attachment to it. Which in turn substantiates the taken-for-granted nature of its institutions, thus contributing to the legitimacy of on-going systems (Popitz 1986: ch. 2). Now, legitimacy does not mean blind acceptance of all norms, procedures and incumbent power-holders. These can be criticised or contested, for the sake of the system, which can in fact be perceived as a superseding common good. Equally, this is not to deny the emergence of deviants, for whom familiarity

---

1. Merton defines the status-set as 'the complex of distinct positions assigned to individuals both within and among social systems' (1968: 434), while the role-set is 'that complement of role relationships which persons have by virtue of occupying a particular social status' (1968: 423). Elsewhere in his work, Merton paid special attention to the spatial orientation of influential people, classifying them into 'locals' and 'cosmopolitans' (1968: 447ff.). This classification is based on different 'orientations', but echoes a difference in 'the structure of social relations in which each type is implicated', thus encapsulating the intuition of different spatial references – or, as we propose to call them, 'space-sets'.

yields contempt or refusal of the established order. But they are exceptions. The rule is that social actors are likely to accept and acknowledge political orders that fit in with their space-sets. And the fit between the territory on which sovereignty is claimed and citizens' (or subjects') space-sets enhances the legitimacy of the political community.

Historically, nation-building processes were accompanied by higher human mobility out of localities of birth (Weber 1976). Indeed, a most famous (and latently functional) interpretation of these processes – such as Gellner's (1983) – holds that nation-building in modern Europe was predicated on a steep rise in population movements. Industrialisation unleashed workers from the countryside and brought them to cities, expanding their space-sets significantly. More consciously, nation-states were keen on enforcing compulsory conscription, which – apart from providing cheap manpower for their armies in case of war – took young people out of their villages, showed them different parts of the nation, forced them to mingle with peers from other provinces. At the same time, professional soldiers and civil servants were deliberately moved from one place to another during their career, instilling into them a neater sense of the national scope of their space-sets. Through all these dynamics, not only space-sets widened, but mobility made people aware of living in *one* nation. Nations fixed their boundaries as the 'natural containers' of individual space-sets and made the sense of nationhood the primary cement of collective identities in modern states.

As the above processes illustrate, before feeding back onto legitimacy, space-sets are shaped by political constraints. State policies may favour or hinder internal and international migration. Moreover, for decades modern states have structured transportation systems as state-bounded – setting up public infrastructure networks within their borders, establishing national rules and licenses for driving, limiting access to foreign railways and airlines. The conditions of the economy matter, too. A thriving marketplace may create job opportunities and attract workers from elsewhere. A burst of unemployment may foster out-migration. Prosperity can boost travelling for tourism and the purchase of second homes in distant places. Finally, space-sets are dependent on technology. Improvements in naval transportation made European mass migration across the Atlantic possible in the late nineteenth century; the spread of the bicycle was key to the expansion of marriage markets (and consequently family space-sets) in rural regions in those same decades; the organisational technology of low cost flights sustains the transnational living of many shuttle migrants between Eastern and Western Europe at the beginning of the twenty-first century.

Space-sets are like personal maps of the physically experienced world.[2] The

---

2.   While in this essay the focus is on 'physical' mobility, we do not underscore the effect of 'virtual' forms of mobility on 'personal communities' (Wellman 2001; Castells 2001). Some inquiries have found that, in fact, surfing the web does not take most people so far from home (Hampton and Wellman 2002). Still, the features and scope of virtual space-sets is a research area where, in spite of the abundance of discourse on the 'de-territorialization of social life' (for a discussion, cf. Kennedy 2010: 27 ff.), more systematic evidence is definitely needed.

width, *interconnectedness* and *salience* of these maps vary enormously across time, space and social strata. All three properties need be considered. *Width* is an objective measure: it consists of the whole of the places where individuals have been in their life (the scale of measurement may be more or less fine-tuned: by neighbourhood, city, state…). Such places can be perceived either as separate or connected contexts. *Interconnectedness*, thus, is very much subjective, even though it is normally based on factual continuities. The perception of unity between places may hinge on political, ethnic, or personal bonds. The simplest case of political connection is the inclusion of two cities of one's space-set into the same state. Typically, ethnicity sustains interconnectedness among migrants who move along diaspora lines. Personal bonds among places are common among commuters, even across continents, like the famous 'new Argonauts' between Silicon Valley and their less developed countries of origin (Saxenian 2006). Salience is subjectively defined as well. Different parts of an individual space-set are ordered by emotional relevance: the place where one lives and/or was raised sitting on top usually, sites where one has travelled occasionally being kept in the periphery of personal maps.

Again, however, politics matter, as it assigns special importance to some portions of the map. This is where the modern notion of citizenship gets into the picture. A key feature of citizenship consists exactly in the right of moving freely and having access to some privileges in given territories and not in others. Being framed as 'national', citizenship as experienced in the modern age has contributed to fit space-sets into state borders. The invention of passports (Torpey 2000) put the seal of exceptionality over potential stretches of space-sets beyond frontiers. Movements out of these 'natural containers' were framed politically as extraordinary – and still are, even in a globalising world, if one only considers that no more than 28 per cent of American citizens hold a passport (GAO 2008: 11). The existence of passports equates to a political definition of nation-wide space-sets as 'normal' space-sets.

In the light of these processes, the emergence of the European Union looks unique and path-breaking. Particularly, the cross-national free movement regime – ultimately enshrined in EU citizenship and reinforced by it – stands out as a major historical novelty. Spanning over a progressively larger number of borders, this regime shakes the foundations of modern citizenship as a state-contained bunch of entitlements. In fact, it is not the content of entitlements (voting, enjoying equal rights with other citizens) that is new in EU citizenship, but rather its territorial scope. Expanding space-sets beyond national borders does no longer translate into a penalty (being clandestine) or an extra-cost (applying for a visa, being scrutinised as alien in the host society). While a plethora of EU policies contribute to paving the way to the internationalisation of space-sets among Europeans (among others, the liberalisation of air traffic, the provision of funds to create trans-national transportation infrastructures and 'corridors', the opening of market competition among companies from different countries, the access to mobility grants for students and young workers), it is especially via free movement rights that European integration shapes new opportunities to exit the 'box' of national societies in Europe. But do EU citizens take these opportunities? Have space-sets expanded accordingly? Section 2 of this chapter shall describe the forms and sizes of the geographical mobility of Europeans since the inception of the process of European integration – that is, the underlying ingredient of the widening of space-sets in Europe. Section 3 shifts our focus from behaviours to attitudes, discussing – on the basis of existing evidence – the legitimacy of the EU among its citizens. This is a preliminary step to put to test our key hypothesis about the correlation between objective spatial behaviours and subjective cultural affiliations: that is, between space-set width and the political legitimacy of the polities insisting on them. Precisely, in section 4 we will test whether wider and more international space-sets among EU citizens associate with a stronger legitimacy of the EU.

Expanding spaces: european integration and the geographical mobility of europeans after world war two

While in the post-war decades the political history of Western Europe is marked by the rooting of liberal democracies and the deepening of the process of continental integration, one of the most significant, enduring and generalised trends in European societies consisted in the rising capacity of individual mobility. Economic growth, technological progress, urbanisation, gender equality, consumerism and secularisation – the hallmarks of social change in the second half of the 20th century – conjured to create more and more opportunities and aspirations for moving further out of places of origin. Migration, commuting, and tourism are the three different forms by which modern individuals have experienced the geographical widening of the radius of their social life. On the one hand, migration is a prime driver in the expansion of space-sets. It adds salience to the spaces involved and makes them interconnected through personal ties. Long before the concept of 'transnationalism' was forged and studied, and when means of communication were still comparatively rudimentary, migrants' lives were already revolving emotionally around *both* the host and home societies. Even their possible sense of misfit – Sayad's (1999) 'double absence' – confirms the identity salience of these two places as defining poles of migrants' space-sets. Commuterism and tourism, on the other hand, are predicated on the improvement of transportation means – that is, their higher technological efficiency and their growing affordability. As soon as infrastructures and vehicles allow them to do so, people plan to disconnect and distance their private and public life – that is, their work time and their family and leisure time. In this sense, travelling for business and travelling for vacation are fundamentally similar phenomena, whose spread led to a generalised widening of space-sets in postwar Europe.

Migration

The seeds of all these developments lie in the disaster of World War Two. In its aftermath Europeans were fewer, poorer and dislocated. Military destruction had penetrated every corner of the continent, killing more than 15 million persons, mostly civilians. Among survivors, GDP per capita had plummeted to one third that of 1939. As the 'iron curtain' was being raised and the map of Europe redrawn, an estimated 25 million people moved to ethnically and politically less hostile territories. Internal displacements were also widespread. Millions of families had their homes bombed or devastated, and were consequently forced to find shelter and ultimately settle in another town or province – if not abroad. Consequently people saw new regions, intermingled, travelled as never before – even though it was not their choice. In the 1950s, the uneven pace of economic development on the continent triggered new waves of mass migration (King 1993). Between 1950 and 1970 more than six million southern Europeans (from Portugal, Spain, Italy, Yugoslavia and Greece) headed north, where reconstruction and industrialisation proceeded at a faster pace (Livi Bacci 2010: 78). The allure of transatlantic migration – which was predominant in earlier decades of the twentieth century – was superseded by the occupational opportunities of closer European regions.[3] Germany, France, Benelux and the UK replaced the US, Argentina and Brazil as preferred destinations. The redefinition of migration projects attuned to a changing political landscape as well. On the one hand, even if less consistently, countries of origin (i.e., southern European countries) were industrialising and growing economically as well. This fact alone made returns – and hence short-term migration plans to nearer areas – a more plausible option than it was for migrants of the 1880s-1920s who used to leave for good. On the other hand, travel choices were shaped politically, as bilateral governmental agreements eased migration, initially within Western Europe and later from Yugoslavia and Turkey, while European political integration promised to make it easier to get work permits and legal protection in these destination countries.

Ironically, the introduction of free movement rights in 1968 – when Council Regulation 1612/68 and Council Directive 68/360 abolished movement and residence restrictions of member state workers and their families in the entire EEC territory – coincided with the early signs of economic downturn and the decline of mass intra-European migration of industrial workers. In the following 25 years, admission, residence and equal treatment of foreign residents from other member states were achieved through a huge canvas of piecemeal secondary legislation (for a concise overview, see Favell and Recchi 2009: 5–9). While community law and the European Court of Justice increasingly spread the matter and scope of free movement rights, the demand for foreign labour remained low and intra-European migration did not pick up, even when Portugal, Spain and Greece joined the EC in the 1980s. Symbolically, however, the most spectacular advancement in the process took place with the Maastricht Treaty (entered into force in 1993), which introduced citizenship of the European Union to 'reinforce the protection of the rights and interests of the nationals of its member states'. Concretely, EU citizen-

3. Another constraint channeled out-migration to European countries rather than to the once more popular transatlantic destinations: after the Great Depression, the United States imposed tight national quotas for immigrants. Only in 1965, did American immigration law relaxed its admission standards again.

ship consists of a set of rights allowing all European nationals to vote and stand as candidates in elections of the European Parliament in the member state they reside in, regardless of their nationality; to submit petitions to the European Parliament and appeal to the EU Ombudsman; to be protected by the consular authorities of another member state in third countries that lack diplomatic representation of one's state; and *to move and reside freely in the territory of any of the EU member states*. The first three provisions have a very small scope compared to the last – the right of free movement and settlement in the entire EU territory, that stands out as the real cornerstone of EU citizenship. Timidly, after Maastricht, slightly larger numbers of European citizens resettled in another member state. According to Eurostat, the official population of 'EU15 movers' grew from about 5.4 to 6.2 million in a decade (Recchi 2008: 203–204). Given the simultaneous demise of internal frontiers[4] and the absence of migration control on EU citizens, however, these figures fail to include a huge population of unregistered movers, contributing to differentiate the range of possible intra-EU migrant trajectories (cf. Braun and Recchi 2009). The citizenship effect on intra-EU mobility was thus likely to be larger soon after Maastricht. Even more importantly, what did definitely increase was short-term mobility, like the one epitomised by Erasmus students (whose grants last between 3 and 12 months). While this kind of mobility is almost entirely invisible to national statistics (Favell 2008), it is extremely significant as a source of Europeanisation of individual space-sets.

If we stick to Eurostat, in fact, the real jump in the number of EU citizens residing abroad in the EU occurs with the enlargements of 2004 and 2007. Even though the movement rights of the new European citizens were initially subject to temporary restrictions,[5] and only Britain, Ireland and Sweden opened the doors of their labour markets fully to newly minted EU citizens in 2004 (Finland and Sweden were the only ones among EU15 states to do the same in 2007), intra-EU migration flows from central-eastern Europe were unprecedently large. On average, between 2004 and 2008 the yearly net increase of immigrants in the EU15 amounted to about 250,000 persons from A8 (mainly Poland) and about 300,000 persons from A2 (mainly Romania) (Brücker *et al.* 2009: 23, 27). The rise of the central-eastern European population that re-settled in Western Europe immediately before and after the enlargements was beyond all scholarly expectations. Most spectacularly, Romanians in 'old' Europe were seven times more numerous in 2007 than in 2000, while Lithuanians and Slovaks became five times more numerous. Even nationals of the countries with the lowest outflows – Slovenia and Hungary – increased by more than 50 per cent in less than a decade (Table 9.1). Overall, Eurostat attests that in 2007 the EU27 member states hosted 29.1 million

---

4.   Of course, an additional key facilitation to mobility was the adoption of the Schengen system, which took place progressively in the 1980s and 1990s, eliminating passport controls between EU national borders.

5.   Such restrictions were also applied in previous enlargements, when Greece (1981), Spain (1986) and Portugal (1986) joined the European Community.

Table 9.1: Intra-EU migration in the early twenty-first century: Increase in the proportion of (forthcoming) new member state citizens residing in EU15 (2000=100)

	2000	2001	2002	2003	2004	2005	2006	2007
Czech Rep	100	125	137	168	148	168	215	246
Estonia	100	113	123	145	145	166	178	199
Hungary	100	112	116	111	108	120	125	156
Latvia	100	89	102	113	111	152	194	196
Lithuania	100	151	172	222	218	353	473	531
Poland	100	112	114	121	127	159	208	272
Slovak Rep	100	147	155	174	208	324	363	525
Slovenia	100	129	131	150	136	146	144	151
Total A8	100	115	120	129	132	167	210	266
Bulgaria	100	144	197	233	285	307	357	434
Romania	100	131	179	254	333	405	493	714
Total A2	100	134	183	249	321	380	459	645

Source: Recchi and Triandafyllidou (2010: 131)

foreign citizens, among whom 10.6 million were intra-EU migrants (European Commission 2008: 115). Such European migrants formed 2.1 per cent of the EU population, and 2.6 per cent in the EU15. About 40 per cent were citizens of new member states, the majority being Romanian (1.6 million), Polish (1.3 million) and Bulgarian (310,000). In other terms, 7.2 per cent of Romanians, 4.1 per cent of Bulgarians and 3.4 per cent of Poles exercised their free movement rights to relocate abroad in the EU (for an overview, see Recchi and Triandafyllidou (2010).

Migration is an extreme form of expansion of space-sets. Usually, only a limited share of the population moves to relocate for good or for long spells of time. In fact, most people move either in smaller portions of space or for shorter periods. That is, they commute or travel occasionally (with different purposes, the most common being business and tourism). Both forms of movements, though, are sufficient to establish some meaningful relations with other socio-spatial contexts. And both soared dramatically in the post-World War Two decades as well.

Commuting

The history of commuting is the history of urban systems in industrial and post-industrial societies. Arguably, the evolution of urban landscapes due to the rise of mechanic transportation is a key advance towards the typically modern 'liberation' of human beings from the 'ancient chains' of work-bound spaces (Gottmann 1978). While in (future global) cities like Paris and London – to limit ourselves to Europe – railroad-served suburbs blossomed already in the nineteenth century, it is not until the 1930s that the possibility of commuting decoupled public (i.e., work, study) and private (i.e., family) spaces for the large majority of the urban population, and not until the second half of the twentieth century – with mass motorisation – for people living in smaller towns and the countryside (Capuzzo 2003). As urban historians observe, 'whereas in the nineteenth century a change of work would have necessitated a residential move, in the twentieth century it could be accommodated by a longer and more complex journey to work' (Pooley and Turnbull 2000: 361–363). These authors estimate that, in Britain, over the entire twentieth century there has been a fourfold increase in the average one-way journey to work: from 3.6 km to 14.6 km. Changing transport modes explain much of this increase:

> From the 1890s to the 1930s walking to work was consistently the most common experience, and those who used public transport were quite evenly split between trams, trains and buses. From the 1930s to the 1950s the incidence of walking to work declined rapidly, but the use of buses and bicycles increased substantially. Train use remained stable, but the use of trams and trolley-buses declined almost to nothing. From the 1960s car use became dominant, with 40 per cent of those in employment commuting by car from the 1970s. Again the general trends are common to all areas and groups of travellers, but use of public transport has always been much higher in London than elsewhere; women have been consistently more dependent on walking and public transport; men were much more likely than women to cycle to work; and women switched to car travel some twenty years later than men (Pooley and Turnbull 2000: 366).

The British case is not likely to be much different from the rest of industrialised European societies. The decisive factor in this story is the spread of private cars. Statistics offer a prime cue onto the paramount change brought about by this transportation means that has re-shaped social life and landscapes dramatically (for example, it is estimated that a quarter of the London land is occupied by motor vehicles; Urry 1999: 11) (Table 9.2). The *trentes glorieuses* are marked by the exponential rise in the number of circulating private vehicles. Even in the least developed parts of Western Europe, such as Spain and Italy, the number of passenger cars increased by at least a factor of thirty between 1950 and 1973. In the course of one generation, access to the automobile turned from luxury to middle-class standard. On average, in Western Europe in the 1970s there was one car every four-five people – that is, roughly, one by household. But the rise did not end there. By the turn of the century, just one generation later, not only access but individual property has become the norm: there is a four-wheel private vehicle for every two persons (including children and other non-driving individuals). Car use has been redefined as any adults' key component of individual freedom. The huge literature on 'automobilities' has explored the multifaceted impact of the advent of the car civilisation – such as the disjunction of residence, work, shopping and leisure places, the flexibilisation of commitments, the fragmentation of time use (Featherstone *et al.* 2005; Urry 2007: 112 ff.). In our perspective, all these

Table 9.2: The irresistible spread of the automobile: private passenger cars per 1,000 residents in Western Europe, 1950–2000

	1950	**1973**	**2000**
Austria	7	203	495
Belgium	32	241	448
Denmark	28	249	353
Finland	7	190	403
France	36	282	469
Germany*	10	275	508
Italy	7	249	539
Netherlands	14	222	383
Norway	18	203	407
Portugal	7	84	471°°
Spain	3	110	454°
Sweden	36	305	437
Switzerland	31	254	486
United Kingdom	45	241	373

Sources: (Maddison 1995: 76); World Bank (2002: sparsim); Mitchell (2007: sparsim);
* Federal Republic of Germany for 1950 and 1973 data; ° 2002; °° 2003

phenomena are predicated on the expansion and personalisation of space-sets. In economically developed societies, cars are the core technology patterning almost everybody's space-sets, making it possible not only to commute for longer distances, but also to reach further away as consumers, tourists or 'explorers'. As a matter of fact, from the mid-1970s to the turn of the century, Europeans increased the radius of their daily mobility substantially. For instance, between 1976 and 1998, the average western German resident covered a 50 per cent larger number of kilometers per day (from 27 to 41), chiefly because of a larger use of automobile transport (Zumkeller 2009). While America remains the metaphorical seedbed of 'car culture' (Baudrillard 1988), European societies have equally incorporated cars at the heart of their social organisation in less than half a century.

International tourism

The social history of the automobile overlaps but does not equate with the history of mass tourism. First, and trivially, because travels and stays 'in places outside [one's] usual environment for more than twenty-four (24) hours and not more than one consecutive year for leisure, business and other purposes not related to the exercise of an activity remunerated from within the place visited – what the World Tourism Organisation defines as 'tourism' (UNWTO 1995: 14) – occurred even before the spread of private cars. Holiday taking was democratised in advanced industrial societies already in the 1930s, when the middle classes started heading to the seaside and other resort destinations by rail and coaches (for instance in Britain, see Middleton and Lickorish 2007: ch. One). Second, because technological determinism is an oversimplified account of the rise of mass tourism. As has been argued,

> the availability of new transportation systems does not simply create demand for travels: it may have to be unlocked by other developments, such as improvements in real wages or family income, the availability of consecutive free time or even paid holidays, or the development of a preference for discretionary expenditure in travel and tourism above alternative modes of leisure or consumer spending (Walton 2009: 121).

While necessary, technological advances in mobility would not have been sufficient to generate what has been called the 'globalised tourist gaze' of late modernity (Urry 2002). Such a *Weltanschauung* is, precisely, a way of viewing the world – that is, of looking at images that are projected on a large scale, beyond localities and nations. Some sort of 'distinctive contrasts', as Urry (2002: 3) notes, is searched for in the tourist experience. Travelling across borders – or 'out of the bubble' of the established contexts, encounters and routines of daily life – epitomises the inner meaning of 'going tourist' in contemporary Western culture.

Indeed, what matters particularly for our argument is not so much the quantitative widening of space-sets through a larger access to holidays, but their qualitative 'transnationalisation' (Mau 2010). In large countries like the United States or China, enhanced possibilities of travelling do not normally entail a 'leap' out of political borders. Geographical mobility can increase without imposing the experience of non-national spaces. In this respect, Europe is different. While it takes longer to drive from Los Angeles to Houston than from Naples to Amsterdam, the latter is culturally and politically a more distanced move. The attitudinal implications of international tourism are consequently likely to be more pronounced. As Mau and Büttner argue (2010: 552), 'though not all [cross-border] tourist visits will have strong repercussions on people's everyday lives, such visits may act as door-openers to other cultures and may extend people's cognitive and behavioural horizons' (see also White in this volume).

Unfortunately, comparative data on the expansion of international tourism in Europe after World War Two are scant. Statistics on the aggregate amount of air and rail traffic show an exponential growth, especially in the last forty years. The world air passenger/km figure has risen nine-fold between 1970 and 2008 (ITF 2009); total inland passenger transports (i.e., by car, coach and rail) have increased by two and a half times over the same period in Western Europe (authors' elaboration from OECD data).[6] However, we know little about the distribution of these journeys in the population. How many people do travel? And how many cross state borders? A relatively long time-series is available for Germany, where a first survey on travel behaviours was carried out in 1964. In the then *Bundesrepublik*, no more than 39.2 per cent of the population had experienced tourist travel, and 15.2 per cent had gone abroad as a tourist.[7] Ten years later, holiday travellers had increased to 50.6 per cent of the population, the majority of whom (55 per cent) had crossed national borders for more than five days. The general uptrend accelerated in the 1980s. The 1984 survey showed that 71.3 per cent of respondents had made some tourist trip the year before, and 36 per cent of the sample had moved to another country during their holidays. These proportions rose to 76.4 per cent and 51.8 per cent respectively in 1993 (this time including citizens of the former DDR as well). Finally, in the new millennium, the situation stabilised, with 76.8 per cent enjoying travel vacations and 53.9 per cent going outside Germany in 2003. Holidays and even more cross-border journeys are stratified, but age and education differences have smoothed over the decades. In 1973, only 8.7 per cent of individuals with elementary schooling travelled abroad, as opposed to 49.2 per cent of people with university education. The gap has narrowed, and in 2003 not only 77.3 per cent of the highest, but also 64.3 per cent of the lowest educated, did at least one trip over the national borders. The removal of age barriers follows this same trend very closely. As a result, the elderly and people with poorer educational credentials are no longer excluded from the lure of international tourism.

While the German case is likely to illustrate the general tendency well, its figures lie above the continental average, which has been monitored by Eurobarometer for the last two decades. In 1997 no more than 25 per cent of EU15 respondents reported that they had trespassed their national borders in the previous twelve months (Fligstein 2009: 144). Nine years later, in 2006, the proportion of EU15 citizens who declared they had visited another EU member state in the past 12 months (now, to be precise, a larger geographical area) had grown to 40 per cent. [8] Given that this question tapped visits to other EU member states only, the increase of respondents having visited any other country is likely to be somewhat bigger. Unfortunately, this raw data on tourism represents only a minimal clue

---

6. Data extracted from the OECD online statistics database (http://stats.oecd.org/Index.aspx) accessed on 17 November 2010.

7. In this section we present data taken from five surveys carried out in 1964, 1974, 1984, 1994 and 2004 in Germany and made kindly available by GESIS, Köln: *Tourismus*, DIVO, Frankfurt, 1964, ZA0098; *Reiseanalyse 1974*, Studienkreis für Tourismus, Starnberg, 1974, ZA0831; Reiseanalyse 1984, Studienkreis für Tourismus, Starnberg, 1984, ZA1427; *Urlaub und Reise 1994*, Forschungsgemeinschaft für Urlaub und Reise, Hamburg, ZA2843; *Reiseanalyse 2004*, Forschungsgemeinschaft Urlaub und Reisen (F.U.R), Kiel, 2004, ZA4268. While these surveys' scope and sample sizes are similar, their indicators of international travels are slightly different from one wave to another, allowing for only an overview of the general trend.

8. Much of the increase is due to short (less than three nights) trips, that have been made possible by the tremendous growth of low-cost flights offering new opportunities to potential travellers with limited budgets and further 'democratising' international tourism (Mau and Büttner 2010: 555).

of the internationalisation of Europeans' space-sets, as no additional information qualifies the duration, scope and subjective salience of individual trips abroad. *Faute de mieux*, we will capitalise on it in the following sections to try to assess whether our claim about space-sets width and legitimacy is empirically grounded.

The conditions of EU legitimacy: theoretical underpinnings

We turn now to the second term of our relationship between spatial behaviours and political attitudes: legitimacy. The problem of political legitimacy has spurred a plethora of writings in legal studies, philosophy, political science and sociology. Given our disciplinary approach, we leave the legal and philosophical approaches aside and concentrate on the sociological literature. In a nutshell, a 'soft' and a 'hard' version of the concept of legitimacy can be distinguished. While the 'soft version' places itself in the legacy of Max Weber's definition of legitimacy as *belief in legitimacy*, the 'hard version' tries to incorporate the characteristics of the political system in the concept. Let us explain this distinction in more detail.

It is almost imperative, in a sociological account of legitimacy, to start out with Weber's seminal use of the concept as people's belief in the rightness of power-holders' commands. Literally, Weber defines legitimacy as 'the probability that to a relevant degree the appropriate attitudes will exist [leading to] submissiveness to persons in positions of power' (Weber 1962: 74). This definition is what we call the 'soft version' of legitimacy. In such a view, a 'system of domination' – in Weber's words – is legitimate as long as those subject to it believe the claim to political power to be valid. Compliance stems from the 'dominated inwardly assent to rule', as Titunik (2005: 143) glosses. As is well known, differences in the grounds of this belief in the legitimacy of commands are then taken by Weber as the *fundamenta divisionis* of his 'pure types of authority' – rational, traditional and charismatic (Weber 1968: 215–216).

When seeking to come to grips with such an attitude in modern political systems, authors in this legacy refer to 'legitimacy beliefs' (Scheuer 2005) or to 'popular legitimacy' (Gabel 1998), defining it as 'consent and voluntary compliance of its citizens' (Gabel 1998: 7). Empirically, the focus is on the prominent role of public opinion. The 'soft version' of legitimacy is thus closely related to the concept of 'political support' (Easton 1965; Easton 1975; Norris 1999; Dalton 2004, Gunther and Montero 2006) and, as such, has been studied extensively in relation to the European Union (Franklin *et al.* 1995; Niedermayer and Sinnott 1995; Gabel 1998; Díez Medrano 2003; McLaren 2006; Eichenberg and Dalton 2007; Hooghe and Marks 2009; cf. next section for a more extensive review of the literature).

As Beetham (1991: 9) critically notes, however, this understanding of legitimacy ignores the characteristics of the political regime by looking solely at citizens' beliefs. This bears the risk of ascribing situations of low legitimacy merely to 'PR and communication problems', thus underestimating potential system-level shortcomings. The 'hard version' of legitimacy, therefore, implies a direct link to the political regime. In this perspective, Beetham defines legitimacy as 'the degree of congruence, or lack thereof, between a given system of power and the beliefs, values and expectations that provide its justification' (Beetham 1991: 11). Consequently, situations of low legitimacy are not (only) due to communication problems in elite-mass relations but should rather be imputed to the characteristics of the political system – such as its institutional design and its capacity of representation. In this sense, the 'hard version' of legitimacy is relatively close to normative-philosophical and legal approaches. This issue has been dealt with in discussions of the EU's democratic deficit (Banchoff and Smith 1999; Moravcsik 2002; Rohrschneider 2002) and Scharpf's (1997 and 1999) influential distinction between input- and output-legitimacy. While input-legitimacy claims that political decisions derive from citizens' preferences and that governments be held accountable, output-legitimacy refers to governments' 'high degree of effectiveness in achieving the goals, and avoiding the dangers, that citizens collectively care about' (Scharpf 1997: 19).

In our view, both versions of legitimacy have to do with Europeans' space-sets. First, it seems fruitful to reinterpret the 'hard version' of legitimacy in the light of Europeans' space-sets and the EU's geographical scope. An often-overlooked prerequisite of legitimate governance is the congruence between social and political spaces (Held 1995; Zürn 2000; Anderson 2002). Only if the social and political borders of a political system are congruent, all actors in a system of governance have the opportunity to actively take part in the decision-making process and thus input-legitimacy is given. Moreover, congruence is also necessary for output legitimacy to limit externalities from decisions that have been made outside one's territory (Zürn 2000: 189).

The nation state is characterised by a strong overlap between political, social and economic boundaries. Its capacity to control exits from, and entries into, its territory is among its quintessential features (Poggi 1978: 132; Rokkan 2000). However, processes of social, economic and political transnationalisation have weakened this congruence (Scharpf 1997; Anderson 2002). Individuals, corporations and organisations can now partially and fully exit the nation state (Bartolini 2005). Neo-functionalists have insisted on the fact that the 'need for human cooperation rarely coincides with the territorial scope of community' – and contemporary Europe is a case in point (Hooghe and Marks 2009: 2). While some argue that European integration is the prime cause of transnationalisation in Europe (Ross 1998; Fligstein and Mérand 2002), others see it as a reaction to more encompassing and global processes (Wallace 1996). Apart from this debate on cause and effect, few can contest that European integration entails a territorial recalibration of sovereignty (Berezin 2003). What is relevant for us is how this process relates to legitimacy. Zürn (2000) argues that, as legitimacy depends on the congruence between social and political spaces, the nation state loses legitimacy since it does not match the social spaces of the people that are subject to, or concerned by, national decision-making. First, many policies implemented by national governments create externalities, i.e. effects outside the borders of the nation state and thus concern individuals who cannot vote for these governments. Typical examples for such a lack of 'input congruence' are environmental problems spreading to other countries. Moreover, given that voting rights are mostly coupled to citizenship, the majority of immigrants cannot influence the political decision-making process by vote. Second, the lack of 'output congruence' refers to the missing overlap between the space where a decision is valid and the space where the interactions concerned by this decision are happening. In Zürn's view, the European Union, along with other institutions of supranational decision-making, compensates for the decline in legitimacy at the national level by ensuring a higher degree of input- and output congruence (Zürn 2000).

Accordingly, the issue here is not whether the EU's institutional structures and processes correspond to peoples' beliefs, expectations and values. Rather, legitimacy in this sense depends on whether the EU's geographical scope corresponds to Europeans' space-sets. Europe-wide space-sets would thus not only indicate congruence between political borders and citizens' experiences, it would also provide evidence of legitimacy as 'consent through actions' in Beetham's (1991: 12) sense.

When turning to the 'soft version' of legitimacy, we quickly come to the question of political support towards European integration. This subject has been widely studied, especially so after it became obvious that the public was not rendering the 'permissive consensus' (Lindberg and Scheingold 1970) that had been hoped for. In fact, in the aftermath of the Maastricht Treaty, evidence of survey research pointed to 'constraining dissensus' (Hooghe and Marks 2005), the most prominent explanations of which relate to utilitarian cost-benefit evaluations (Eichenberg and Dalton 1993 and 2007; Anderson and Reichert 1995; Gabel 1998), national vs. European identities (Carey 2002; Hooghe and Marks 2004; Luedtke 2005; McLaren 2006), party cues (Ray 2003; Gabel and Scheve 2006; Steenbergen et al. 2007; De Vries and Edwards 2009) and national differences in discourse frames (Díez Medrano 2003; Bruter 2005; see Gaxie and Hubé in this volume).

Rather than assessing all its explanatory factors, however, it is of interest here whether there is a relationship between Europeanized space-sets and attitudes towards European integration. People with Europe-wide space-sets should be supportive of European integration for two main reasons. First, their mobility and interaction with other Europeans should lower intergroup boundaries and make Europeans more cognisant of international interdependence. People with Europe-wide space-sets should thus support the EU for identitarian reasons. Second, people with European space-sets are ultimately those who reap the benefits of European integration. They should thus favour the integration process also for utilitarian reasons. These two arguments are consistent with the transactionalist view of European integration originally elaborated by Karl Deutsch et al. (1957) that has been revived, elucidated and tested empirically in recent years (Fligstein 2008; Kuhn 2011, Kuhn 2012). However, our emphasis is not on 'exchange relations' per se but rather on spatial contexts of personal experience, as these are deemed to have a deeper impact on individual life chances and identities. Consequently, in the next section we will seek to answer two main questions:

1) With respect to the 'hard version' of legitimacy: Do we find congruence between the EU's territorial scope and its citizens' space-sets? In other words, can we speak of Europeans space-sets or are space-sets still locked into nation-states?

2) With respect to the 'soft' version of legitimacy: does the Europeanisation of space-sets go hand in hand with citizen support for European integration? Put differently, are individuals with Europe-wide space-sets also more supportive of European integration?

Europe-wide space-sets and EU legitimacy: are they empirically related?

Eurobarometer survey 65.1, which was conducted in 2006 in the (then) 25 member states of the EU, includes a battery of items relating to Europeans' space-sets. We will therefore rely on these data in order to answer the aforementioned questions. For the purpose of this chapter, the following items will be used to operationalise the degree of Europeanisation of respondents' space-sets:

(1) *In the last twelve months, have you visited another EU country?* The answer categories were: 'yes, on several occasions'; 'yes, once or twice'; 'never'; 'don't know'. The overwhelming majority of respondents (59.7 per cent) indicated that they had not visited another EU country in the past twelve months, while 24.3 per cent declared to have visited another EU country once or twice and 16 per cent reported several visits. Only 0.11 per cent chose 'Don't know' as an answer.

(2) *In the last twelve months, have you socialised with people from other EU countries?* The answer categories were: 'yes, on several occasions'; 'yes, once or twice'; 'no'; 'don't know'. Again, more than half of the respondents (56.5 per cent) reported that they have not socialised with people from other EU countries at all in the past year, 18.1 per cent said they had done so once or twice, while 25 per cent indicated that they have socialised with other EU citizens on several occasions.

(3) A dichotomous variable combining the information of three variables that asked whether respondents *have lived in another EU member-state for three months or more to a) study, b) work or c) retire*. All respondents having answered yes to at least one of these questions (only 7.3 per cent) are coded 1, the remaining 92.7 per cent are coded as 0.

Using these three variables, we then constructed the 'European space-set index'.[9] With a mean of 1.8 on a scale running from 1 to 6, the European space-set index is highly skewed to the lower values. In other words, the majority of respondents' space-sets do not span across national borders. What is more, the index is highly stratified. In general, less educated and older people score even lower on average than younger and better educated individuals. It is also interesting to look at the mean values of European space-sets across the EU25. As depicted in Figure 1, Luxembourg is a clear outlier, followed by a group of small open economies such as Austria and the Netherlands. Evidently, residents of small countries have

---

9. The Kaiser-Meyer-Ohlin measure of scaling reliability for this index is 0.57 and testifies of a robust scale.

Mean European space-set index scores
across 25 EU-member states

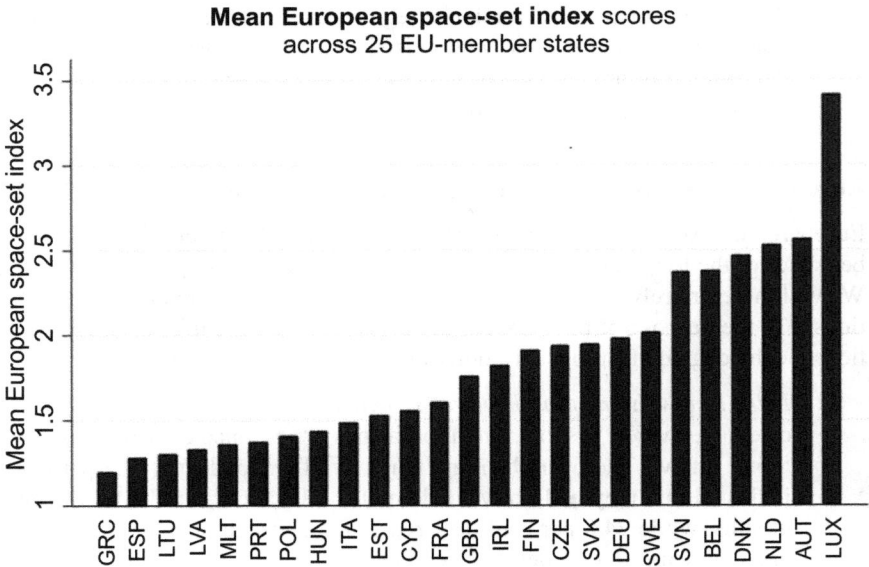

Figure 9.1: The European space-set index by country of residence

Source: EB 65.1

more opportunities to widen their space-sets across national borders (also because these are physically less distant from any possible place of residence). The bigger countries are usually situated in the middle of the range, while new member states and/or countries at the European periphery, score lowest on European space-sets.

Taking all these findings together, the prospects for the 'hard version' of legitimacy are rather sombre. The low and highly stratified scores of the space-set index indicate that only few EU citizens have widened their space-sets to the European level. Thus, the EU's territorial scope and its citizens' space-sets are so far, rather incongruent and therefore question the legitimacy of European decision-making.

We now turn to the 'soft version' of legitimacy by analysing respondents' legitimacy beliefs. To do so, we operationalise respondents' legitimacy beliefs with the membership support item, which is frequently used to measure EU support (Anderson 1998; Carey 2002; Eichenberg and Dalton 2007). The exact wording of this item is as follows: 'Generally speaking, do you think that our country's membership of the European Union is (1) a good thing, (2) a bad thing, (3) neither good nor bad, (4) don't know'. Figure 2 shows the net membership, i.e. the percentage of people indicating that membership is a good thing minus the percentage of people deeming it to be a bad thing, averaged over the EU15. The numbers are drawn from the Mannheim Eurobarometer trend file which includes a time series

EU Legitimacy Beliefs, EU-15

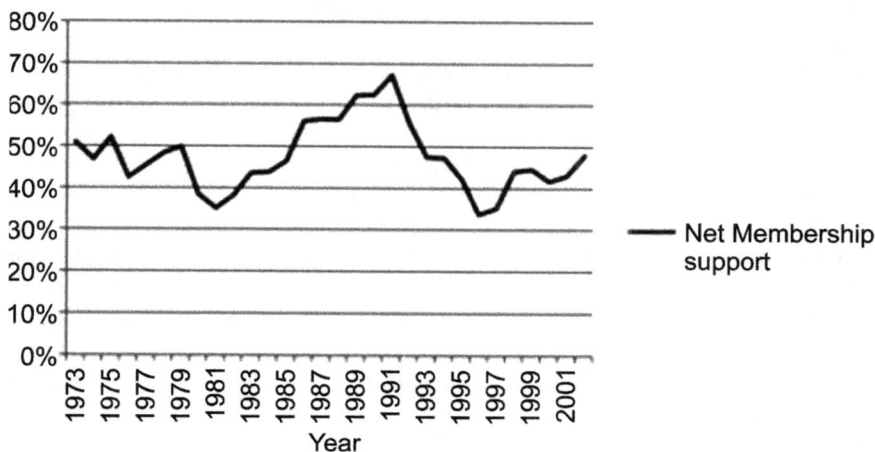

Figure 9.2: The dynamic of EU legitimacy belief in EU15

of Eurobarometer surveys from 1970 until 2002 (Schmitt and Scholz 2005). After having reached its peak in 1992, the year of the Maastricht Treaty, net support dropped considerably over the following decade. In the survey wave that we will use for the subsequent analysis of the impact of European space-sets on legitimacy beliefs, 47.5 per cent found EU membership to be a good thing, while 14.3 per cent answered that the EU is neither good nor bad and 34.1 per cent answered that it is a bad thing. The 'don't know' category was chosen by 4.1 per cent. This distribution indicates that while the majority of Europeans seem to support a governance system hinged on the EU, a substantial share of the population does not consider the European integration process to be legitimate.[10]

In a next step, we aim at testing whether respondents scoring high on the European space-set index are more likely to approve of EU membership. For this analysis, the European space-set index will be our independent variable, while the membership support question will serve as a dependent variable. Given that there is a clearly neutral category (3), this has been recoded as the middle category while all respondents having indicated 'don't know' have been omitted from the analysis. Since the dependent variable has three ordered categories ('good thing' being the highest category), and given the clustering of the data in 25 member

---

10. Note that observations for Spain and Portugal start in 1980, for Greece in 1981, for Austria, Finland and Sweden in 1995. Observations were averaged across countries.

states, we employ a multilevel ordinal logit analysis. Clearly, our aim is not to explain the full pattern of EU legitimacy beliefs but rather to outline the link between European space-sets and legitimacy beliefs. Nonetheless, given the vast amount of empirical studies on our dependent variable, we include a number of controls. One of the first, attempts to explain variation in EU support related to *cognitive mobilisation*, i.e. the intellectual capacity to grasp the complexities of a remote political system such as the EU (Inglehart 1970; Karp *et al.* 2003). We account for this by including an item referring to the habit of discussing politics and by the ability to convince friends in discussions. A prominent strand in the literature highlights utilitarian cost-benefit considerations, arguing that better educated and wealthier individuals are more likely to approve of EU membership (Eichenberg and Dalton 1993; Anderson and Reichert 1995; Gabel and Palmer 1995; Gabel 1998). Consequently, we control for respondents' *current occupation* (managers as reference category) and their level of *educational attainment*. 'Low education' relates to having left school at age 15 or younger, 'medium education' refers to having quit school between 16 and 19, while having completed formal schooling at 20 or older is coded as 'high education'. A fourth variable relates to people without any full-time education. To account for potential interlinkages between *attitudes on immigration* and EU legitimacy beliefs (De Vreese and Boomgaarden 2005; McLaren 2006; Lubbers and Scheepers 2007), we control for having indicated 'encouraging immigration of workers from outside the EU' as a measure to solve potential shortages in the labour market. *Political ideology* is measured by a 10-category item referring to left-right self-placement. Finally, we control for *gender* (male as baseline) and we include four *age categories*, the category 55+ serving as the reference category. While previous findings would suggest controlling for respondents' trust in political institutions (Rohrschneider 2002) or the exclusive national identity (Carey 2002; Hooghe and Marks 2004; Luedtke 2005; McLaren 2007), no corresponding items are included in the Eurobarometer survey wave used in our analysis.

Finally, not only individual, but also country-level characteristics are expected to have an impact on Europeans' legitimacy beliefs. First, it is frequently found that a country's macroeconomic situation influences aggregate support for European integration (Eichenberg and Dalton 1993 and 2007). Consequently, we control for GDP per capita (Eurostat 2009a), inflation rate (Eurostat 2009b), unemployment rate (Eurostat 2009c) as well as a country's share of EU trade in international trade (Eurostat 2009d). Second, given the high complexity of EU politics and institutions, Europeans are shown to rely on cues of their parties and political leaders (Ray 2003; Steenbergen *et al.* 2007; De Vries and Edwards 2009). We therefore include the country-average party positions towards European integration and the relative importance of European integration in national parties' stances (Hooghe *et al.* 2010). Each of these items was weighted by the percentage of votes the parties received in the last election and averaged for each country. Third, to account for potential differences between the 'old' and the 'new' member states, we include a dummy variable for being citizen of a EU15 member-state. We standardised all independent and control variables to range from 0 to 1 so as to make their effects comparable.

Table 9.3 shows the results of the multilevel ordinal logit analyses. As can be seen in Model 1, the European space-set index has a strong positive and highly significant effect on EU membership support. Actually, it has the greatest effect of the entire model. This is strong support for our hypothesis that people with more Europeanised space-sets are more likely to legitimise the EU. Moreover, when assessing the AIC-goodness of fit measure, we see that our model performs better than the null model. In additional analyses, that are not shown here, we estimated separate models for each variable included in the European space-set index. Each variable on its own has a significant positive effect on respondents' legitimacy belief. This again suggests that people's familiarity with the European territory has a strong influence on their legitimisation of the European Union. It is also worthwhile to discuss the effects of the control variables, which generally confirm the results of previous studies. Among these controls, high education seems to be the strongest predictor of European legitimacy beliefs, followed by having a managerial occupation, pro-foreigner attitudes and left-wing political orientations. People frequently discussing politics are also significantly more likely to support EU membership. A small negative effect was in fact found for being a woman. Among the macro-level control variables, only GDP has a strong positive effect in the null model that becomes insignificant once we include the European space-set index.

Additionally, we also estimated a ordinal logit model with country dummies (Germany serving as the baseline category) and robust standard errors. This allows us to look at the country-specific effect for each country. As shown in Table 4, some countries have a strong and highly significant coefficient. In other words, the population of these countries significantly differs from the German population in terms of their EU legitimacy belief. Especially the Austrians, the Finns and the Swedes are significantly less supportive of EU membership than the Germans. However, when including the European space-set index, the country effect for Austria further increases, while the effects for Sweden and Finland slightly decrease. This indicates that the low legitimacy of the EU among Swedes and Finns is slightly tempered by their higher than average Europeanisation of space-sets. On the other side of the spectrum are Spain, Ireland and Luxembourg, whose populations are significantly and considerably more pro-European than the German population. As shown in model one, the country effect of Luxembourg is partly due to the high scores of European space-sets among its population as it decreases once the European space-set index is included in the model. In contrast, the effects for Spain and Ireland slightly increase once 'controlling' for European space-sets.

Table 9.3: Multilevel ordinal logit models of impact of European space-sets on EU-legitimacy beliefs

	0–Model		Model 1	
	b	**Se**	**B**	**Se**
European Space–set Index			.820***	(.073)
Buy products abroad				
Ind. level control variables				
Female	−.174***	(.031)	−.156***	(.031)
Age group				
Age 15–24	.294***	(.077)	.294***	(.078)
Age 25–39	.047	(.050)	.033	(.051)
Age 40–54	−.159***	(.047)	−.159***	(.047)
Age 55+	ref.		ref.	
Education				
No full–time education	−.699***	(.199)	−.657***	(.199)
Low	−.802***	(.049)	−.749***	(.049)
Medium	−.452***	(.038)	−.421***	(.038)
High	ref.		ref.	
Occupation				
Manager	ref.		ref.	
Self–employed	−.292***	(.073)	−.283***	(.073)
White collar worker	−.286***	(.065)	−.258***	(.065)
Manual worker	−.517***	(.058)	−.465***	(.059)
House person	−.468***	(.073)	−.420***	(.074)
Unemployed	−.706***	(.076)	−.637***	(.077)
Retired	−.423***	(.065)	−.352***	(.065)
Student	−.351***	(.092)	−.311***	(.093)
Left–right scale	.509***	(.062)	.490***	(.062)
Immigrant attitudes	−.601***	(.052)	−.589***	(.052)
Convince others	.157**	(.050)	.127*	(.050)
Discuss politics	.500***	(.052)	.439***	(.053)
Country–level control variables				
EU–15 member	−.175	(.291)	−.169	(.279)
Inflation rate	.492	(.407)	.516	(.336)
GDP	1.474*	(.722)	1.290	(.719)
Unemployment rate	.496	(.387)	.607	(.409)
Intra–EU trade	.075	(.341)	−.160	(.322)
Party position on EU	−.636	(.732)	−.643	(.730)
EU salience	−.803	(.699)	−.719	(.629)
T1	−2.934***	(.811)	−2.839***	(.749)
T2	−1.065	(.810)	−.965	(.749)
Country constant	.484***	(.051)	.489***	(.048)
Log–likelihood	−17546.6		−17414.2	
AIC	35149.3		34886.4	

Source: Eurobarometer 65.1, two tailed test, * p<0.05, ** p<0.01, *** p<0.001

Figure 9.3: Predicted probability of EU legitimacy belief

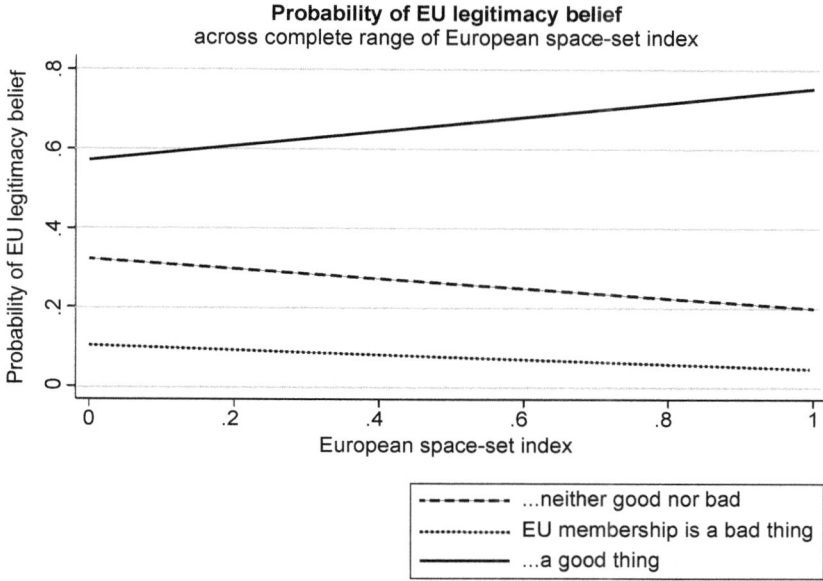

Probability of EU legitimacy belief
across complete range of European space-set index

Source: EB 65.1 (2006)

Another way to interpret the ordinal logit models shown in Table 9.3 is to calculate how the European space-set index impacts on the predicted probability of answering 'membership is a good thing'. Predicted probabilities range from 0 (perfectly improbable) to 1 (perfectly probable) and are dependent on the specific configuration of all the variables included in the model. Therefore, we calculate the change in the probability of answering one of the three answer categories across the entire range of the European space-set index, holding everything else constant. Figure 9.3 shows the change in probability of membership support across the European space-set index for a German male white-collar worker in the age group 40–55 with mean ideology self-placement, immigrant attitudes and cognitive mobilisation indicators. As shown in the figure, the predicted probability of answering membership is a good thing, moves from 0.58 to 0.76, as the European space-set index increases from the lowest to the highest possible level. In contrast, the probability of indicating that membership is a bad thing, or neither good nor bad, decreases as the European space-set index increases.

Table 9.4: Ordinal logit models of impact of European space-sets on EU legitimacy beliefs with country dummies and robust standard errors

	0–Model		Model 1	
	B	**se**	**B**	**Se**
European space–set index			.825***	(.075)
Female	−.173***	(.031)	−.155***	(.031)
Age groups				
Age 15–24	.293***	(.076)	.294***	(.076)
Age 25–39	.046	(.050)	.032	(.050)
Age 40–54	−.160***	(.048)	−.160***	(.048)
Above 55	ref.		ref.	
Educational attainment				
No full time education	−.712***	(.213)	−.669**	(.214)
15 and younger	−.807***	(.049)	−.754***	(.050)
16–19	−.454***	(.038)	−.422***	(.038)
Above 20	ref.		ref.	
Left–right scale	.512***	(.065)	.493***	(.065)
Immigrant attitudes	−.603***	(.052)	−.590***	(.053)
Occupation				
Manager	ref.		ref.	
Self-employed	−.295***	(.073)	−.286***	(.074)
White collar worker	−.289***	(.065)	−.260***	(.065)
Manual worker	−.518***	(.058)	−.465***	(.059)
House person	−.476***	(.072)	−.428***	(.073)
Unemployed	−.708***	(.076)	−.638***	(.076)
Retired	−.423***	(.065)	−.353***	(.066)
Student	−.353***	(.092)	−.313***	(.093)
Convince others	.154**	(.051)	.125*	(.051)
Discuss politics	.501***	(.054)	.441***	(.054)
AUT	−1.052***	(.091)	−1.178***	(.093)
BEL	.320***	(.090)	.262**	(.090)
CYP	.005	(.118)	.081	(.118)
CZE	−.361***	(.081)	−.352***	(.081)
DNK	−.154	(.091)	−.199*	(.092)
ESP	.887***	(.104)	.982***	(.104)
EST	−.263**	(.090)	−.189*	(.090)

	0–Model		Model 1	
	B	**se**	**B**	**Se**
FIN	−.964***	(.086)	−.950***	(.086)
FRA	−.367***	(.086)	−.316***	(.086)
GBR	−.685***	(.087)	−.674***	(.087)
GRC	−.125	(.087)	.003	(.088)
HUN	−.165	(.085)	−.098	(.086)
IRL	.879***	(.106)	.894***	(.107)
ITA	.152	(.099)	.261*	(.102)
LTU	.044	(.102)	.150	(.102)
LUX	.843***	(.129)	.639***	(.132)
LVA	−.754***	(.080)	−.656***	(.080)
MLT	−.091	(.131)	−.001	(.131)
NLD	.533***	(.090)	.464***	(.091)
POL	.037	(.090)	.133	(.091)
PRT	.077	(.096)	.143	(.097)
SVK	.145	(.081)	.145	(.081)
SVN	−.220*	(.088)	−.285**	(.089)
SWE	−.870***	(.088)	−.860***	(.088)
T1	−2.862***	(.109)	−2.672***	(.110)
T2	−.992***	(.107)	−.796***	(.109)
Log–likelihood	−17488.3		−17355.4	

Source: Eurobarometer 65.1, two tailed test, * p<0.05, ** p<0.01, *** p<0.001

Summary and conclusion

In this essay we started from two basic assumptions. The first is that space matters for politics, and especially so when the forms and contents of sovereignty are renegotiated, as occurs in the process of European integration. The second is that legitimacy represents the crucial symbolic component of 'political orders'. Few would contest these rather plain and straightforward statements. On top of these, however, we claimed that the micro-foundations of legitimacy hinge on, among other factors, individuals' relations with territories. Individuals carve spaces on the basis of their personal experiences over time, and this 'carving' – that we term 'space-sets' – defines their cognitive and affective grasp of political systems. That is, their belief in the legitimacy of such systems.

In the first part of the essay, we have shown how the history of European integration runs parallel to the dynamics of population mobility that have expanded individuals' space-sets in the second half of the twentieth century. In part, such expansion has been the outcome of a global trend towards a more mobile social life. Migration flows, commuterism, and the advent of mass tourism are not exclusively European phenomena. However, in Europe they intersected with the introduction and consolidation of the right of free movement across member states. This right stands out as the political blueprint of the growing internationalisation of Europeans' space-sets. Through its enactment – that is, through the practice of cross-state mobility – EU citizens are redefining the spatial reach of Europe's public sphere (Aradau *et al.* 2010).

In the second part of the essay, we discussed the meaning and potential operationalisation of Max Weber's concept of political legitimacy. Having singled out a 'hard' and a 'soft' interpretation of the concept, we argued that both are in fact likely correlates of citizens' space-sets congruence with polities' territorial scope. The emergence of the European Union makes this coincidence more critical than it is in well-established nation-states, where a plethora of century-old nation building processes have moulded it. Using Eurobarometer data, we found that EU citizens with Europe-wide space-sets are also significantly more inclined than the rest of the population to legitimise the European Union. When introducing an index of Europeanised space-sets in models of EU support, this factor turned out to explain more variance than all others which are highlighted in the existing literature – such as age, education and left-right orientations. Thus, our argument is empirically corroborated. Not only 'distance from the centre' affects the popular support polities manage to get, which was also found to be true for the EU (Berezin and Díez Medrano 2008), but also people's familiarity with these polities' overall space is a crucial component of legitimacy.

The implications of the nexus between Europe-wide space-sets and EU legitimacy, we surmise, are far-reaching. In a sociologically informed historical perspective, the political unification of Europe is an unprecedented and path-breaking enterprise. Like it or not, it challenges the key articulations of political power in the modern age: the state as core political organisation and the nation as its cultural underpinning. But how solid are the foundations of the European Union? While several threats to its survival and growth may certainly come from external shocks or inner structural contradictions, its Achilles' heel remains the indifference of its citizens. As is well known, the bulk of them would not regret the ship-wrecking of the integration process.[11] Even though it is true that the EU is not a nation and

---

11. Perhaps the most poignant indicator of attachment to the EU is the following Eurobarometer question: 'If you were told tomorrow that the European Union had been scrapped, would you be: *very sorry* (1) about it, *indifferent* (2) or *very relieved* (3)?' Between 1973 and 1992, the proportion of respondents worried by the possible failure of the EU (or its earlier incarnations) hovered around 50 per cent (Schmitt and Scholz 2005). Ironically the beginning of the decline of popular concern for a tragic ending of European integration (to a bottom of 28 per cent in 2001, European Commission 2005: 86) coincided with the introduction of EU citizenship – that is, the key institutional device to get the Union closer to the people. The question has apparently been abandoned in more recent Standard Eurobarometers.

its symbolic strengthening cannot naively replicate nation-building on a different scale (Marks 1997), still it is a 'political order', to borrow Weber's lexicon again, and as such it requires some form of political community that can hardly be cemented by procedural-institutional means only (Schmidt 2010). On this, a lesson can be learnt from the past. The secret formula of legitimacy in nation-states is that nationalism – mostly in its 'banal' modalities (Billig 1995) – makes 'political attachments a personal process' (Jusdanis 2001: 30). Such a 'personal process' implies participation not only to a *demos*, but also – and perhaps even more immediately – to a *topos*. Applied to Europe, the feeling of being at home on its territory could be achieved without demanding too much of an ideology: just engrained practices, as Erasmus students and other mobile EU citizens can witness (cf. Rother and Nebe 2009). More systematically, evidence illustrated in this essay proves that: a) an increasing number of Europeans are appropriating Europe's space, moving more and more out of their localities, and b) this reverberates upon support for European institutions. However, while we have shown that this process works effectively, we must also be aware that it remains circumscribed to a minority of citizens. And as long as Europe is not a familiar place to most Europeans, its political institutionalisation shall suffer from a substantial frailty.

---

[i]   This essay has been conceived by its authors jointly. However, Ettore Recchi wrote sections 1, 2 and 5, while Theresa Kuhn wrote sections 3 and 4.

References

Anderson, C. J. (1998) 'When in doubt, use proxies: attitudes toward domestic politics and support for European integration', *Comparative Political Studies* 31(5): 569–601.

Anderson, C. J. and Reichert, S. (1995) 'Economic benefits and support for membership in the EU: a cross-national analysis', *Journal of Public Policy* 15(3): 231–49.

Anderson, J. (2002) *Transnational Democracy: Political spaces and border crossings*, New York: Routledge.

Aradau, C., Huysmans, J. and Squire, V. (2010) 'Acts of European citizenship: a political sociology of mobility', *Journal of Common Market Studies* 48(4): 945–65.

Banchoff, T. F. and Smith, M. P. (1999) *Legitimacy and the European Union: The contested polity*, New York: Routledge.

Bartolini, S. (2005) *Restructuring Europe: Centre formation, system building, and political structuring between nation state and the European Union*, Cambridge: Cambridge University Press.

Baudrillard, J. (1988) *America*, London: Verso.

Beetham, D. (1991) *The Legitimation of Power*, Atlantic Highlands, NJ: Humanities Press International.

Berezin, M. (2003) 'Territory, Emotion, and Identity: Spatial recalibration in a new Europe', in M. Berezin and M. Schain (eds) *Europe without Borders: Remapping territory, citizenship and identity in a transnational age*, Baltimore: John Hopkins University Press, pp 1–32

Berezin, M. and Díez Medrano, J. (2008) 'Distance matters: place, political legitimacy and popular support for European integration', *Comparative European Politics* 6(1): 1–32.

Billig, M. (1995) *Banal Nationalism*, London: Sage.

Braun, M. and Recchi, E. (2009) 'Free Moving West Europeans: An empirically based portrait', in H. Fassmann, M. Haller and D. Lane (eds) *Migration and Mobility in Europe: Trends, patterns and control*, Cheltenham: Edward Elgar, pp. 85–101.

Brücker, H. *et al.* (2009) *Labour Mobility within the EU in the Context of Enlargement and the Functioning of the Transitional Arrangements, final report*, Nuremberg: European Integration Consortium, available at http://wiiw.ac.at/e/research_networks_lms.html.

Bruter, M. (2005) *Citizens of Europe? The emergence of a mass European identity*, Basingstoke: Palgrave.

Capuzzo, P. (2003) 'Between Politics and Technology: Transport as a factor of mass suburbanization in Europe, 1890–1939', in C. Divall and W. Bond (eds) *Suburbanizing the Masses: Public transport and urban development in historical perspective*, Aldershot: Ashgate, pp. 23–47.

Carey, S. (2002) 'Undivided loyalties: is national identity an obstacle to European integration?', *European Union Politics* 3(4): 387–413.

Castells, M. (2001) *The Internet Galaxy: Reflections on the Internet, Business and Society.* Oxford: Oxford University Press.

Dalton, R. J. (2004) *Democratic Challenges, Democratic Choices*, Oxford: Oxford University Press.

Deutsch, K. W. *et al.* (1957) *Political Community and the North Atlantic Area*, New York: Greenwood Press.

De Vreese, C. H. and Boomgaarden, H. G. (2005) 'Projecting EU referendums: fear of immigration and support for European integration', *European Union Politics* 6(1): 59–82.

De Vries, C. and Edwards, E. (2009) 'Taking Europe to its extremes: extremist parties and public euroscepticism', *Party Politics* 15(1): 5–28.

Díez Medrano, J. (2003) *Framing Europe*, Princeton: Princeton University Press.

Easton, D. (1965) *A Systems Analysis of Political Life*, Chicago: The University of Chicago Press.

—   (1975) 'A re-assessment of the concept of political support', *British Journal of Political Science* 5(4): 435–57.

Eichenberg, R. C. and Dalton, R. J. (1993) 'Europeans and the European Union: the dynamics of public support for European integration', *International Organisation* 47(47): 507–34.

—   (2007) 'Post-Maastricht blues: the transformation of citizen support for European integration, 1973–2004', *Acta Politica* 42(2–3): 128–52.

European Commission (2004) *Eurobarometer 62*, October-November 2004, TNS OPINION & SOCIAL, Brussels [Producer]; GESIS, Cologne [Publisher]: ZA4229, available at http://zacat.gesis.org/webview/index.jsp.

—   (2005) *Eurobarometer 62: Public Opinion in the European Union. Full Report.* Luxembourg: Office for Official Publications of the European Communities, available at http://ec.europa.eu/public_opinion/archives/eb/eb62/eb62_en.htm.

—   (2006) *Eurobarometer 65.1, February-March 2006,* TNS OPINION & SOCIAL, Brussels [Producer]; GESIS, Cologne [Publisher]: ZA4505, available at http://zacat.gesis.org/webview/index.jsp.

—   (2008) *Employment in Europe 2008.* Luxembourg: Office for Official Publications of the European Communities, available at http://ec.europa.eu/social/BlobServlet?docId=681&langId=en.

Eurostat (2009a) 'Gross Domestic Product in Purchasing Power Standards 2006', available at http://epp.eurostat.ec.europa.eu.

—   (2009b) 'Harmonised Indices of Consumer Prices 2006', available at http://epp.eurostat.ec.europa.eu.

—   (2009c) 'Harmonised Unemployment Rates 2006', available at http://epp.eurostat.ec.europa.eu.

—   (2009d) 'Share of Exports in the EU-25 2006', available at http://epp.eurostat.ec.europa.eu.

Favell, A. (2008) *Eurostars and Eurocities: Free movement and mobility in an integrating Europe*, Malden, MA: Blackwell.

Favell, A. and Recchi, E. (2009) 'Pioneers of European integration: An

Introduction', in E. Recchi and A. Favell (eds) *Pioneers of European Integration: Citizenship and mobility in the EU*, Cheltenham: Edward Elgar, pp. 1–25.

Featherstone, M., Thrift, N. and Urry, J. (eds) (2005) *Automobilities*, London: Sage.

Fligstein, N. (2008) *Euroclash. The EU, European Identity, and the Future of Europe*, Oxford: Oxford University Press.

— (2009) 'Who Are the Europeans and How Does This Matters for Politics?', in J. Checkel and P. Katzenstein (eds), *European Identity*, Cambridge: Cambridge University Press, pp. 132–66.

Fligstein, N. and Mérand, F. (2002) 'Globalization or Europeanization? Evidence on the European economy since 1980', *Acta Sociologica* 45: 7–22.

Franklin, M., van der Eijk, C. and Marsh, M. (1995) 'Referendum outcomes and trust in government: public support for Europe in the wake of Maastricht', *West European Politics* 18(3): 101–17.

Gabel, M. (1998) *Interests and Integration: Market liberalisation, public opinion, and European Union*, Ann Arbor: University of Michigan Press.

Gabel, M. and Palmer, H. (1995) 'Understanding variation in public support for European integration', *European Journal of Political Research* 27(1): 3–19.

Gabel, M. and Scheve, K. (2006) 'Estimating the effect of elite communications on public opinion using instrumental variables', *American Journal of Political Science* 51(4): 1013–1028.

GAO, US Government Accountability Office (2008) *Comprehensive Strategy Needed to Improve Passport Operations, Report to Congressional Requesters,* Washington DC: US Government Accountability Office, available at http://www.gao.gov/new.items/d08891.pdf.

Gellner, E. (1983) *Nations and Nationalism*, Ithaca: Cornell University Press.

Gottmann, J. (1978) 'Urbanisation and employment: toward a general theory', *Town Planning Review* 49: 393–401.

Gunther, R. P. and Montero, J. R. (2006) 'The Multidimensionality of Political Support for New Democracies: Conceptual redefinition and empirical refinement' in M. Torcal and J. R. Montero (eds) *Political Disaffection in Contemporary Democracies: Social capital, institutions, and politics*, London: Routledge, pp. 46–78.

Hampton, H. and Wellman, B. (2002) 'The Not So Global Village of Netville' in B. Wellman and C. Haythornthwaite (eds) *The Internet in Everyday Life*, Oxford: Blackwell, pp. 345–371

Held, D. (1995) *Democracy and the Global Order: From the modern state of cosmopolitan governance*, Cambridge: Polity Press.

Hooghe, L. and Marks, G. (2004) 'Does identity or economic rationality drive public opinion on European integration?', *PS-Political Science & Politics* 37(3): 415–20.

—   (2005) 'Calculation, community and cues', *European Union Politics* 6(4): 419–43.

—   (2009) 'A postfunctionalist theory of European integration: from permissive consensus to constraining dissensus', *British Journal of Political Science* 39: 1–23.

Hooghe, L. *et al.* (2010) 'Reliability and validity of the 2002 and 2006 Chapel Hill Expert Surveys on party positioning', *European Journal of Political Research* 49(5): 687–703.

Inglehart, R. (1970) 'Cognitive mobilisation and European identity', *Comparative Politics* 3(1): 45–70.

ITF, International Transport Forum (2009) *Trends in the Transport Sector*, Paris: OECD.

Jusdanis, G. (2001) *The Necessary Nation*, Princeton: Princeton University Press.

Karp, J. A., Banducci, S. A, Bowler, S. (2003) 'To know it is to love it? Satisfaction with democracy in the European Union', *Comparative Political Studies* 36(3): 271–92.

Kennedy, P. (2010) *Local Lives and Global Transformations: Towards world society*, Basingstoke: Palgrave Macmillan.

King, R. (ed.) (1993) *Mass Migration in Europe: The legacy and the future*, London: Belhaven Press.

Kuhn, T. (2011) 'Individual transnationalism, globalisation and Euroscepticism: an empirical test of Deutsch's Transactionalist Theory', *European Journal of Political Research* 50(6): 811–37.

Kuhn, T. (2012) 'Europa ante portas: Border residence, transnational interaction and euroscepticism in Germany and France', *European Union Politics* 13(1): 94–117.

Lindberg, L. and Scheingold, S. (1970) *Europe's Would-be Policy*, Englewood Cliffs, NJ: Prentice Hall.

Livi Bacci, M. (2010) *In cammino: Breve storia delle migrazioni*, Bologna: Il Mulino.

Lubbers, M. and Scheepers, P. (2007) 'Explanations of political Euro-scepticism at the individual, regional and national levels', *European Societies* 9: 643–69.

Luedtke, A. (2005) 'European integration, public opinion and immigration policy: testing the impact of national identity', *European Union Politics* 6(1): 83–112.

McLaren, L. (2006) *Identity, Interests and Attitudes to European Integration*, Basingstoke: Palgrave.

—   (2007) 'Explaining mass-level Euroscepticism: identity, interests, and institutional distrust', *Acta Politica* 42(2–3): 233–51.

Maddison, A. (1995) *L'economie mondiale 1820–1992: Analyses et statistiques*, Paris: OECD.

Marks, G. (1997) 'A Third Lens: Comparing European integration and state building', in J. Klausen and L. Tilly (eds) *European Integration in Social and Historical Perspective*, Lanham: Rowman & Littlefield, pp. 23–44.

Mau, S. (2010) *Social Transnationalism: Lifeworlds beyond the nation-state*, New York: Routledge.

Mau, S. and Büttner, S. (2010) 'Transnationality', in S. Immerfall and G. Therborn (eds) *Handbook of European Societies: Social transformations in the 21st century*, New York: Springer, pp. 537–70.

Merton, R. (1968) *Social Theory and Social Structure*, New York: The Free Press.

Middleton, V. and Lickorish, L. (2007) *British Tourism: The remarkable story of growth*, Oxford: Butterworth-Heinemann.

Mitchell, B. (2007) *International Historical Statistics: Europe, 1750–2005*, Basingstoke: Palgrave.

Moravcsik, A. (2002) 'In defence of the "democratic deficit": reassessing legitimacy in the European Union', *Journal of Common Market Studies* 40(4): 603–24.

Niedermayer, O. and Sinnott, R. (1995) *Public Opinion and Internationalized Governance*, Oxford: Oxford University Press.

Norris, P. (ed.) (1999) *Critical Citizens: Global support for democratic government*, Oxford: Oxford University Press.

Poggi, G. (1978) *The Development of the Modern State: A sociological introduction,* Stanford: Stanford University Press.

Pooley, C. and Turnbull, J. (2000) 'Commuting, transport and urban form: Manchester and Glasgow in the mid-twentieth century', *Urban History* 27(3): 360–83.

Popitz, H. (1986) *Phänomene der Macht*, Tübingen: J.C.B. Mohr.

Ray, L. (2003) 'When Parties Matter: The Conditional Influence of Party Positions on Voter Opinions about European Integration', *The Journal of Politics* 65(4): 978–94.

Recchi, E. (2008) 'Cross-State Mobility in the EU: Trends, puzzles and consequences', *European Societies* 10(2): 197–224.

Recchi, E. and Triandafyllidou, A. (2010) 'Crossing Over, Heading West and South: Mobility, citizenship and employment in the enlarged Europe', in G. Menz and A. Caviedes (eds) *Labour Migration in Europe*, Basingstoke: Palgrave, pp. 127–49.

Rohrschneider, R. (2002) 'The democratic deficit and mass support for an EU-wide government', *American Journal of Political Science* 46(2): 463–75.

Rokkan, S. (2000) *Staat, Nation und Demokratie in Europa: Die Theorie Stein Rokkans aus seinen gesammelten Werken rekonstruiert und eingeleitet von Peter Flora*, Frankfurt a.M.: Suhrkamp.

Ross, G. (1998) 'European integration and globalization', in R. Axtman (ed.) *Globalization and Europe: Theoretical and empirical investigations*, London: Pinter.

Rother, N. and Nebe, T. (2009) 'More mobile, more European? Free movement and EU identity', in E. Recchi and A. Favell (eds), *Pioneers of European Integration: Citizenship and mobility in the EU,* Cheltenham and Northampton: Edward Elgar, pp.120–155.

Sack, R. D. (1986) *Human Territoriality: Its theory and history*, Cambridge: Cambridge University Press.

Saxenian, A. (2006) *The New Argonauts: Regional advantage in a global economy*, Harvard: Harvard University Press.

Sayad, A. (1999) *La double absence*, Paris: Seuil.

Scharpf, F. (1997) 'Economic integration, democracy, and the welfare state', *Journal of European Public Policy*, 4(1): 18–36.

Scharpf, F. (1999) *Governing in Europe: Effective and democratic?*, Oxford: Oxford University Press.

Scheuer, A. (2005) *How Europeans see Europe: Structure and dynamics of European legitimacy beliefs*, Amsterdam: Universiteit van Amsterdam.

Schmidt, V.A. (2010) 'The European Union in Search of Political Identity and Legitimacy: Is more Politics the Answer?' Institute for European Integration Research, Working Paper (5/2010), Vienna.

Schmitt, H. and Scholz, E. (2005) *The Mannheim Eurobarometer Trend File 1970–2002. Data Set Edition 2.01*, Mannheim: GESIS, available at http://zacat.gesis.org/webview/index.jsp.

Steenbergen, M. R., Edwards, E. and De Vries, C. (2007) 'Who's cueing whom? Mass-elite linkages and the future of European integration', *European Union Politics*, 8(1): 13–35.

Titunik, R. (2005) 'Democracy, Domination and Legitimacy in Max Weber's Political Thought', in C. Camic, P. Gorski and D. Trubek (eds) *Max Weber's Economy and Society: A critical companion*, Stanford, CA: Stanford University Press, pp. 143–184.

Torpey, J. (2000) *The Invention of the Passport: Surveillance, citizenship and the state*, Cambridge: Cambridge University Press.

UNWTO (1995) *Collection of Tourism Expenditure Statistics*, Madrid: World Tourism Organisation.

Urry, J. (1999) *Automobility, Car Culture and Weightless Travel: A discussion paper*, Lancaster: University of Lancaster.

— (2002) *The Tourist Gaze*, 2nd edition, London: Sage.

— (2007) *Mobilities*, Cambridge: Polity.

Wallace, H. (1996) 'Politics and policy in the EU: The challenge of governance'. In H. Wallace and W. Wallace (eds), *Policy-making in the European Union*, Oxford: Oxford University Press, pp. 3–36.

Walton, J. (2009) 'Histories of Tourism', in T. Jamal and M. Robinson (eds) *The Sage Handbook of Tourism Studies*, London: Sage, pp. 115–129.

Weber, E. (1976) *Peasants into Frenchmen: The modernisation of rural France, 1870–1914*, Stanford: Stanford University Press.

Weber, M. (1962) *Basic Concepts in Sociology*, New York: Kensington Press Books.

— (1968) *Economy and Society*, Berkeley: University of California Press.

Wellman, B. (2001) 'Physical place and cyberplace: the rise of personalized networking', *International Journal of Urban and Regional Research* 25(2): 227–252.

World Bank (2002) *World Development Indicators*, Washington: The World Bank, available at http://data.worldbank.org/indicator.

Zumkeller, D. (2009) *The German Mobility Panel, 2004*, University of Karlsruhe, available at http://mobilitaetspanel.ifv.uni-karlsruhe.de/en/downloads/englische-und-franzoesische-unterlagen/index.html.

Zürn, M. (2000) 'Democratic governance beyond the nation-state: the EU and other international institutions', *European Journal of International Relations* 6(2): 183–221.

chapter ten | parallel lives: social comparison across national boundaries

Jonathan White

One way to approach the human world is in terms of a distinction between *system* and *social* integration.[1] Theorists have made it in various forms, so let us delineate it as follows. *System* integration evokes a world whose emergence and reproduction is not reducible to the intentions and understandings of individual actors within it. It is the world of structures and institutions, including the market, the law and the industrial-technological complex, all seen from an observer's perspective. *Social* integration by contrast, evokes a world of actors, and of human relations recognisable and meaningful to those immersed in them. It is the world of allegiances, conflicts and mutual concern.[2] Ultimately, system and social integration may be considered two different methodological responses to the same challenge – that of rendering the world and its patterns intelligible – and one need not suppose the existence of two separate spheres. The appeal of the distinction lies in its ability to highlight tensions and contradictions, e.g. between functionality and legitimacy. In contemporary EU scholarship, system integration is the prime focus of various strands of institutionalism and political science, legal studies and political economy, where system-evoking notions of 'adaptational pressure', 'goodness of fit' and 'incentive structure' are commonplace. Social integration meanwhile has been attended to in research on 'European identity', cross-border trust and the study of the EU's politicisation. Perhaps the standard interpretation is that the contemporary European sphere, when approached in terms of system integration, is considerably more densely enmeshed than when approached in terms of social integration, but that this situation cannot persist indefinitely without destabilising consequences – indeed, that its consequences may be fatal when the EU hits times of crisis.

This chapter focuses on social integration, with the aim of exploring one of its less familiar forms – practices of *social comparison*. Its purpose is to show how changing popular perceptions can be conceptualised differently from the 'identity'

---

1.   The author thanks Adrian Favell and Maurice Fraser for written comments and participants of the EU seminar at Sciences Po in Paris for oral feedback in July 2011.

2.   For the distinction in its original form (Lockwood 1964: 371). For overviews of various reworkings (Delanty and Rumford 2005; Mouzelis 2008; Joas and Knöbl 2009). In European studies, the relation between system and social integration was one of the main themes of debate amongst functionalist, federalist and neo-functionalist observers of post-War Europe as well as interested actors themselves. Often these debates were framed in terms of the relative significance of economic integration on the one hand, and political-cultural integration on the other, an articulation liable to create an overly strong distinction between the economic as the domain of material interests and system imperatives, and the political-cultural as the domain of beliefs and ideas.

problematic commonly favoured in EU studies, and – as a contribution to political sociology and social psychology – to theorise in some detail, the structure and wider implications of social comparison. One of the paper's themes however, is the interplay between this form of social integration and the wider context of system integration in contemporary Europe. Developments associated with the latter – rights to cross-border movement, for instance – provide opportunities and stimuli for new social relations, as well as perhaps depending, for their long-term existence, on the development and consolidation of these relations.

Social comparison in the sense we shall discuss it entails a human subject's evocation of relevant others for the purpose of a relative appraisal of conditions. It involves positing the existence of those parallel to the self who, as judged against a certain criterion, may be deemed to resemble (more so or less so) that self.[3] These relevant others may be distant in space, and only in some cases encountered. The prospect, which institutional developments in Europe raise – especially sharply perhaps, but not unlike wider processes of globalisation – is that relevant others come increasingly to be perceived cross- as well as intra-nationally, thus entailing a widening of social horizons as new figures fall within attentive range. Unlike more familiar forms of social integration, such as a convergence of identities, norms and values or a deepening of interpersonal trust, social comparison need not produce generally harmonious social relations. In some cases it may spur a sense of common predicament, and thus the basis for ties of solidarity. In others it may produce an affirmation of difference, prompting indifference or hostility and possibly social upheaval. Accordingly it will have feedback effects for system integration, consolidating it, reforming it, or placing it in question.

Methodologically, social comparison is best treated as an interpretative heuristic – a way of making sense, in idealised form, of how others in turn make sense of the social world. Rather than to postulate hard psychological laws governing beliefs and behaviour, the goal is to suggest patterned ways of thinking which, though likely to recur in some contexts especially, take a variety of forms and can produce more than one outcome, due to the way they combine unpredictably with secondary factors. Social theorists use the concept of *mechanisms* to capture this mix of regularity and indeterminacy (Elster 2007).[4] Practices of social comparison and their socio-political consequences are usefully approached as such, sensitising us to general tendencies of likely significance whose articulation and impact in the particular instance will still need to be analysed by historical, i.e. contextual, means. By elaborating such mechanisms, we sharpen our eye for the trends of the present, and give orientation to future research.

---

3. As we shall note, the perception of similarity is only one possible outcome, and even where present it is domain-specific. Parallel lives are not convergent lives – the subjects retain their distinctiveness.

4. Some approaches to social mechanisms (e.g. Hedström and Swedberg 1998) invoke them as a means to give precision to an explanatory account. Here we do not wish to explain determined outcomes – the practices we describe remain half-formed, and their ultimate consequences as yet opaque – but instead to identify some important current trends, to chart future trajectories, and develop the building-blocks from which explanatory accounts might proceed.

Varieties of social comparison and their significance

The concept of social comparison has its origins in social psychology (Festinger 1954; see also Masters and Smith 1987; Suls and Wheeler 2002; Guimond 2006). Early discussions presented it as a kind of *need*, grounded in the functional importance to the individual of accurate self-appraisal. In order to navigate life's demands, particularly in a complex society, individuals require knowledge about their relative strengths and weaknesses, and about which features they share with others and which are distinctive – knowledge achievable only through juxtaposition with the opinions and abilities of others. Comparison thus offers the subject a means of orientating and understanding themselves. More recent approaches, while continuing to focus on motivation, have located the impulse in a need to *evaluate*, in particular to accord positive evaluation to the self. In this perspective, comparison offers possibilities for enhancing self-image, especially where subjects deliberately pursue 'downward comparison' by matching themselves against an inferior (Suls and Wheeler 2002). Researchers' ongoing focus on cognitive motivation clearly has much to do with the disciplinary focus of psychology. But related research agendas more social and political in their focus have emerged also, notably the study of 'relative deprivation' (Runciman 1966).

Let us first consider social comparison from a formal perspective, before thinking about its contemporary manifestations. Clearly not all comparison is 'social'. While a human self of some sort is always present – the author of the comparison – the elements of which the comparison itself is composed may be entirely intrapersonal or non-human. For example, one can make a cross-temporal comparison with past selves (the 'younger me' with 'today's me'), comparison with an ideal standard ('beauty', 'intelligence', 'morality'), or comparison with a counter-factual self ('me as I am' with 'me as I might have been', or 'me as I experience things *here*' with 'me as I would experience things *there*'). Comparison can also involve inanimate beings (a comparison of one law with another). What then is *social* comparison? As we shall understand it, social comparison has the following structure: it involves a human subject (X) being matched against a target person or persons (the comparator, Y) for assessment according to a particular dimension (Z). While the author of the comparison will not always make these terms explicit[5] – a degree of interpretation tends to be required – it should generally be possible for the observer to narrate the comparison act in these terms.

Probably the first of these terms is the most straightforward. X denotes a human actor of some kind. Evidently it need not include the author of the comparison him /herself. The comparison may be composed entirely of third persons, as when a law-maker considers which of two potential recipients of scarce resources is most deserving, or when a citizen chooses which party to vote for.[6] First-person

---

5.   Indeed, there may be cases when one wants to speak of *tacit* comparisons – those not given explicit articulation at all, yet seemingly implicit in certain acts and utterances.

6.   One of the biases of psychology-informed approaches to social comparison is the way the self and self-esteem tend to be placed centre-stage as a matter of course.

comparisons will be our focus, since they have an immediacy and emotional involvement not present when the author detaches him / herself, but they are only one variety of several. Note also that the subject may appear in singular or plural form – as an 'I' or a 'we'. Note further that subjects may come with a certain category attached, e.g. 'we as women', 'we as black people', or 'I as a Muslim'. We shall return to some of the implications of this later.

Next in our formal sequence is the comparator, Y (sometimes termed the 'comparative reference group' – Runciman 1966: 11). It may be useful to conceive three guises in which the comparator may appear. First (Type 1), it may be an individual who is closely familiar to the subject, probably as a result of repeated encounters. In such cases the subject will have a sizeable body of information about this person, enabling a variety of comparisons, and is likely to think of this person first as an individual and only secondarily as the representative of a social group.[7] Examples would be friends, family members and work colleagues. Second (Type 2), the comparator may again be a really-existing person, but one encountered only briefly or occasionally. The subject therefore has limited information about them, and they remain largely a stranger. They may be associated primarily with a single context and treated either as a category-type or, where their individuality is affirmed, as a distantly remembered 'name'. One's hairdresser or bank manager might be examples. Third (Type 3), the comparator may be an idealised social type who is simply imagined by the subject. With this comparator there are no moments of co-presence, and they are necessarily thought of in generic terms (and also, therefore, as members of a group rather than as separable individuals). Their existence may be suggested to the subject on the basis of publicly available information (e.g. in the media, in official data, or in political discourse), anecdotal knowledge or 'popular wisdom', mixed in with ingrained memories of past experiences. In this case the subject is dependent on their imagination and on narratives and knowledge resources external to their own conscious experience.

If one accepts these as analytical distinctions – and clearly there will be empirical instances whose correct assignment to one class or another will be a matter for debate – then one can accord them different kinds of significance. The first kind – based on repeated co-presence – is the most private scenario, and its significance is likely to be local. Regarding the comparator in this way does not involve treating them as a manifestation of a larger context (the point is exactly that the individual is seen as *transcending* their circumstances) and so the implications of the comparison act are likewise for the subject as an individual. As regards the second kind – based on rare co-presence – much is likely to depend on the contact situation (Pettigrew 1998). There will be contexts in which the comparator's individuality is highlighted, and others where they appear primarily as categories: for example, when there is a clear mediating role relationship (a waiter serving a customer, a boss addressing an employee) which invites the situation to be experienced in stereotyped terms, or sharp markers of difference (e.g. language), or when the

---

7.   On the way personal ties may foster comparison practices, see Gartrell in Walker and Smith 2002.

encounter is entirely new, with no previous interaction to refer to. Different situations will invite different forms of aspect perception. While in the first case the situation becomes analogous to that based on comparison with familiars, in the latter cases it moves closer to the third kind – comparison not grounded in co-presence. Here, with the comparator knowable only as a category (e.g. the 'worker', 'the Frenchman'), we have arguably the most political scenario. Politics in many of its forms requires people to think of each other in categorical terms – that is, to look beyond the peculiar characteristics of individuals and beyond whatever private connections one might have to them so as to place them in a larger scheme.[8] Comparisons of this kind facilitate the abstraction which politics requires. They are also political in the sense that they are the site of power relations, since they are peculiarly susceptible to manipulation, not being dependent on the subject's personal experiences.[9]

We have introduced X and Y as persons, real or imagined. It is worth emphasising however that, even in those cases where they are real, it is not persons in their entirety which can be the currency of social comparison. Given the complexity of any individual, they can never be apprehended with equal regard for all dimensions of their existence: comparison involves singling out a certain aspect on which to focus. This brings us to the third of our terms, Z, the dimension or criterion of comparison. This may take various forms: it may relate for instance, to a person's circumstances (e.g. their problems or privileges), their skill in a certain task, or their opinions on a certain topic. Where the comparator, Y, is simply an imagined social category, the criterion of comparison may be largely self-evident, since that category may have few dimensions of public significance. Where the comparator is evoked with greater specificity and complexity, and thus permits a wider range of comparisons, the subject will need to exercise discrimination in the dimension they choose. Note that Z can be anchored with respect to an ideal, such that X and Y are compared for how closely they approximate a transcendental standard, be it a positive one such as 'the moral life' or a negative one such as 'brutality'. Alternatively it can be strictly relative, such that X and Y are compared, e.g. for the length of their hair, with no embedded notion that there is an ideal length.

Clearly, some dimensions of comparison will be of greater interest to the political sociologist than others. Facebook invites users to compare their 'friends' according to their looks and their smell, while daily life offers many opportunities to compare personal possessions such as mobile phones. While these practices are interesting in a number of ways, particularly from a social-psychological perspective, their political implications are indirect at best. More interesting in this regard

---

8. This is not to overlook that efforts to encourage people not to think in category terms, and instead to personalise or privatise a situation, may themselves be political in character. Consider for example the use of first names by British politicians when referring to their colleagues – a strategy presumably designed to increase perceptions of them as accessible people rather than career politicians.

9. Like all forms of common sense, social comparison is both a source of power (the power to normalise) and that which is shaped through power.

is when the criterion of comparison concerns such non-trivial life circumstances as employment, living conditions, security, relative purchasing power, and so on – dimensions we shall return to shortly.

It is worth emphasising that the act of comparison may lead to varied outcomes. It may produce the affirmation of sameness or equivalence (an outcome our language usage may lead us to expect, in that when we term things 'comparable' we imply not only that they can be compared but that a comparison will lead us to conclude similarity), and a tendency to *assimilate* X and Y. Alternatively the outcome may be to affirm difference between the subject and the comparator, and thus to *contrast* X and Y – although such a conclusion still supposes the same metric can be applied to both, and therefore implies a second-order resemblance. In either case, the outcome can be treated as something positive, negative or neutral: it will be ascribed a certain valence. Furthermore, the conclusions drawn may focus on what the comparison indicates about the nature of X (the subject) or the nature of Y (the relevant other). Note, finally, something implicit in what we have said so far (and in the social-psychological distinction between 'upward' and 'downward' comparisons): not all acts of comparison are open-ended in the sense that they have no preconceived outcome. Some are loaded in advance, such that X, Y and Z are chosen so as to affirm something the comparison-maker wishes to affirm.

These points may be summarised in tabular form:

Table 10.1: Overview of social comparison

Elements of social comparison	X – the subject	Y – the comparator	Z – the dimension of comparison	Outcome
Characteristics	Here: the first-person pronouns, 'I' or 'we'	Type 1: a real individual, familiar due to repeated exposure Type 2: a real individual, but known through limited and context-specific exposure, hence associated with just one or a small number of roles Type 3: an imagined entity, approached as a social category	Normative (i.e. connected to an ideal) or relative	Affirmation of similarity or difference … Given positive, negative or neutral evaluation

Why though does social comparison matter? What are the reasons to study it? Arguably it has an intrinsic interest as a distinctive form of social practice, one irreducible to related notions such as 'identity'. Yet its significance goes beyond this. Indeed, much of human understanding has a comparative dimension. This includes, first, an understanding of oneself and one's predicaments. How an individual sees their own experiences will depend in part on how far they have the ability and inclination to place these in a larger context and see them as replicated elsewhere, or how far conversely they see these experiences as mainly specific to themselves. For instance, it matters greatly for a person's self-understanding whether they perceive certain economic difficulties as mainly a distinct, personal challenge or whether they see them as shared, and if the latter with whom they see them as shared and with whom not at all, or less so. This may influence the extent to which they see these challenges as 'normal' or unusual, and how far they see them as appropriate targets for collective address or a matter for individual adaptation. Note, second, that practices of social comparison may have important implications for the meanings commonly given to concepts with a relational dimension. Notions for instance of poverty, equality, security, risk, quality of life (including living conditions, health, work-leisure balance and the quality of nutrition) and of geographical location (including the status of being peripheral or central) are all to some degree – even if not entirely – relative. What constitutes poverty depends on how one delimits the social field. This has, furthermore, implications for how people distinguish between what is just and unjust, insofar as some types of justice-claim refer to the *relative* deprivation of groups of citizens rather than to the absolute condition of the individual (Feinberg 1974).

Practices of social comparison may take place even where there is no generalised sense of shared subjecthood, e.g. an overarching territorial identity such as that implied with terms such as 'national' or 'European identity', or issue-specific relations of solidarity such as the 'class for itself'. Thicker forms of social integration of this kind are one possible outcome of social comparison, but they are not the same as it. Indeed, there may be places where ties of empathy and solidarity are quite weak – e.g. in the former Yugoslavia – yet where practices of comparison are common. Likewise, as a practice of interpretation rather than a material fact, social comparison cannot be assimilated to a positivist conception of shared identity or of the 'class in itself' (both of which take us back towards the realm of *system* integration).[10] Social comparison is a distinct category of practice and merits its own investigation.

Social comparison in the transnational setting

What impact might the institutional changes associated with European integration have on practices of social comparison? Without itemising these system changes in detail – their particularities are in any case in flux – we can make the guiding assumption that they create new opportunities for social comparison and increase the likelihood it will sometimes take cross-national form. In the most general sense, this

---

10. For a typology of forms of collective subjectivity, see Domingues 1995. Note the configurations evoked through social comparison cannot be subsumed within any one of the types provided, though elements of several may be involved.

is because conditions of instability and change are always likely to be those which prompt recourse to comparison, since such conditions are disorienting and place the traditional scheme of things in doubt. It is when people become uncertain of their circumstances and status that they may be most impelled to seek reorientation through comparison. But there are also more specific grounds for seeing these processes of change as conducive to social comparison. Let us examine a few of them.

First, these processes of system integration generate new kinds of social encounter, and thus new situations inviting social comparison. They contribute to many of the 'mobilities' identifiable amongst contemporary Europeans (Urry 2007: 10–11). Prominent amongst these are those associated with temporary employment migration, tourist trips, family visits, the adventure-seeking travel of young people, travel for the purpose of seeking medical care, and long-term relocation for employment or retirement reasons. Some such movements can lead to in-depth cross-national acquaintanceships of the kind that invite Type 1 social comparisons. Think for example of a chance encounter between students while Inter-Railing, developed into stronger attachments as a result of time spent travelling together, and later kept alive using a virtual network such as Facebook. Think likewise of the Erasmus exchange.[11] As noted, these may not be the source of the most politically interesting forms of social comparison, insofar as they generate mainly personal connections, but they are stimuli nonetheless. Of course, many such forms of mobility will not result in thick, repeated interactions but in one-off or occasional moments of co-presence: in this sense they may be conducive to Type 2 social comparisons. Modern life in general affords many such sites of encounter where strangers are brought together, from the metro carriage and the bus-stop to the shopping mall and the museum (Urry 2007: 37). Transnational integration, insofar as it intensifies cross-border movement, heightens the centrality of sites bringing together a potentially even more diverse set of strangers: the hotel, the airport, the beach, the carriage of the trans-continental train, the bars and clubs favoured by travellers and stag-nights, the (internationalised) university library and canteen, the football stadium, and the passport control queue.

One must be cautious in conceiving the wider significance of such encounters. For the guise in which people appear to one another in such sites may be quite site-specific: e.g. as the fellow passenger, the fellow shopper, the fellow drinker. Insofar as comparisons are provoked, they may be specific to the social categories associated with these situations: for instance, the beach may invite comparisons of beachwear, body shape and suntan, and the football stadium those of intensity of support and richness of chants – criteria potentially of little relevance to other social settings. But one can assume that such sites provoke other comparisons whose significance is transferable: a comparison of what fellow commuters are reading with one's own reading matter may lead to wider assessments of the

---

11. Encounters stemming from the Erasmus programme certainly need not lead to a heightened sense of 'European identity' – cf. Sigalas 2010 – but may still contribute to a broadening of the scope of social comparison.

relative sophistication and awareness of ones fellows, comparisons of considerable significance for the individual's understanding of the world around them and their own placement within it. Likewise the passport control queue, which evokes and institutionalises hierarchies, and invites citizenship-, culture- and class-related comparisons, has a significance beyond itself.[12] Even the airport baggage reclaim, which seems to invite little more than a comparison of suitcases, may potentially be a rich source of class- and taste-related comparisons liable to become entwined with comparisons made in other locations.

An extension of the sites of everyday social encounter represents just one of the relevant consequences of transnational integration. Potentially of greater political significance is the way it invites Type 3 social comparison, involving the evocation of those with whom there are no moments of co-presence. The evocation of these hypothesised or 'imagined' comparators is fostered first by the standardisation of experience which system integration entails. With the development of the EU, Europeans have been exposed to common legislation (where there are harmonised EU rules) or to legislation which, though different from one country to the next, is designed to meet common objectives. Common quality standards on consumer goods, or the single currency, are obvious examples. Insofar as legal integration entails an extension of (imagined) common experiences before the law, it seems likely to foster the conditions in which comparison presents itself as plausible, and to foster the conjuring of comparators abroad whose experiences bring those of the subject into relief. In the absence of a larger common framework, the social world beyond the nation-state presents itself as 'apples' to the nation's 'oranges', and therefore as an inappropriate target of comparison. Legal harmonisation changes this.[13] Moreover, system integration makes possible not just one or a series of unrelated dimensions of comparison, but dimensions which present themselves in *clusters*. One of the best established findings in social comparison research is that individuals are most inclined to compare their personal circumstances with those of people they consider broadly similar to themselves, as judged on secondary factors presumed relevant to the dimension in question (Festinger 1954). For example, a comparison of earnings is likely to be of interest to an individual only if there is perceived similarity with the comparator on related dimensions (e.g. age, job type or level of education), something which requires that for every one dimension (Z) it will be possible to imagine other dimensions plausibly in correlation with it. By making several of these susceptible to measurement on single, pan-European scales, EU integration invites them to be invoked in conjunction with each other, thus raising the appeal of any single comparative dimension.

---

12. Cf. Urry 2007: 151 and Aaltola 2005 as cited.

13. The plausibility of comparison is likely to be deemed all the stronger where *interdependence* between subject and comparator is assumed: where, in other words, the circumstances of the comparator are considered not just *equivalent* to those of the subject but *connected*.

Of course, transnational integration does not *necessarily* produce these out-comes, since it also has countervailing dynamics. One of its consequences, before the effects of common legislation are felt, may be to expose people to greater extremes. Think, for instance, of the migrant labourer who changes his reference groups while living abroad, and who unwittingly provides material for a new reference group both for those in the host society, and those in the country of origin. For criteria of comparison such as wages or living conditions, such individuals may introduce new levels of variation. At best this may produce an assertion of difference – albeit one that supposes, as noted, sufficient similarity to apply the common metric by which difference can be observed. Just as plausibly it may encourage a retreat into narrower forms of comparison and a rejection of those that highlight wide discrepancies. We shall return to this point in due course.

The mere *presumption* on the subject's part that the experiences of distant strangers are of relevance is likely to be strongest where it has a basis in fact. The question then is whether transnational integration comes accompanied by the availability of information which can give foundation to comparisons. One thinks for instance of quantitative data of the kind which evokes social groups across European space as statistical categories – the kind of anonymous comparators one can associate with Type 3 comparison.[14] There is a wide range of criteria for which cross-national data can be collected: data which affords comparison for instance, of prices and purchasing power, of earnings across different employment sectors, of taxation rates for different income groups, of public spending in different policy sectors, of crime trends, and so on. Information of this kind is collected by countries around the world, and the possibility of drawing on it to make cross-national comparisons is hardly a novel phenomenon. But as comparativist social scientists have often been the first to discover, making cross-national comparisons on the basis of data aggregated separately in different countries can be highly problematic, since the methods used to collect it in different places may be quite dissimilar, and the categories used to organise it may have quite different thresholds of inclusion. The measurement of poverty and inequality is a classic instance: those classed as 'poor' in one country may be very much better off than those classed as poor in another (Fahey 2010).[15] What presents itself as a single criterion of comparison may in fact therefore be a compound of two, and while such data may continue erroneously to be drawn on for comparison purposes, when their limitations become known they are likely to be rejected and perhaps

---

14. While quantitative data especially lends itself to this, there may be plenty of *qualitative* empirical comparisons to be made too, e.g. of the fortunes of different party families from one country to the next.

15. Cf. Fahey (2010: 12): 'in the UK, a single person household with an income of 11,000 PPS would be counted as poor (just below the UK poverty threshold of 11,366), while a similar household with the same income in Poland would be counted as well off in that they would have almost double the Polish median of 5,703 PPS. Many of the poor in Britain thus have higher living standards than the Polish middle classes, not to mind the Polish poor, so that it might reasonably be asked whether there is any sense in which the extent and nature of poverty in these two contexts might need to be captured somewhat differently.'

the very possibility of comparison questioned. One of the interesting implications of EU integration is the possibility it holds for the collection of data organised at a transnational level using a pan-European scale – a possibility the EU has sought to take advantage of as it makes moves to replace a series of national benchmarks with an indicator of material deprivation expressed in pan-EU terms. An ongoing debate in social-policy research concerns whether the European frame of reference is the most appropriate or whether the national should remain the default one – a question which can be answered with appeal to a variety of criteria, including policy relevance, the observer's assessment of what is objectively valid, and the standards that citizens themselves use (Whelan and Maître 2009; Fahey 2010). This is no definitive answer – each is an act of interpretation, as well as a move with political implications – but let us simply note that where the European option is chosen it provides a further knowledge resource for those tempted to engage in practices of cross-national comparison.

Clearly, where factual information of this kind is taken up in the media, its public diffusion is likely to be greater. Relevant instances are not difficult to find. As a country low on 'European identity', Britain makes a critical case. Its print media shows a willingness to run stories based entirely on how Britain compares to specific other European countries or a European average along a particular dimension, in some cases drawing directly on Eurostat data, in others cases on private sources. Many of these stories have a 'bad news' flavour, with the article's key point being that Britain does worse than its comparator(s) with respect to the criterion in question – that it 'tops the league', be it the 'jobless league',[16] the 'crime league'[17] or the 'divorce league'.[18] Likewise an article in the German media which, drawing on Eurostat data, reports 'Bad Marks for Germany on Women's Pay'.[19] Even that most euro-sceptic of outlets, the British *Daily Mail*, has run stories premised on the relevance of cross-national comparisons and well stocked with empirical data on the 'European average': 'Let's all go to France!', was one writer's suggestion, 'British quality of life can't compare to the continent'.[20] Note that the subject of these comparisons continues to be framed in national terms: it is 'Britain', 'Germany' etc. which is being compared to other countries, not particular sub-groups with other sub-groups – even if the comparisons could easily be reframed in these terms (as in the case of gender disadvantage).[21] Note also the

---

16. www.independent.co.uk/news/uk/home-news/britain-tops-jobless-league-table-2103407.html

17. www.telegraph.co.uk/news/uknews/1541699/Britain-tops-European-crime-league.html

18. www.independent.co.uk/news/uk/this-britain/divorce-rate-falls-but-uk-still-tops-european-league-673779.html

19. www.spiegel.de/international/europe/0,1518,476658,00.html

20. www.dailymail.co.uk/news/article-1314112/France--Lets-British-quality-life-compare-continent.html.

21. Nonetheless, one can find examples which, even if still based on cross-national comparison, are *not* focused on the experience of one particular nation in comparison to others. See for example a different kind of reporting of Europe's 'gender pay gap' in the *Guardian* (www.guardian.co.uk/money/2007/jul/18/pay.business) and BBC (http://news.bbc.co.uk/1/hi/6904434.stm). See also

imagery of the 'league', which invites the dimension of comparison to be seen in purely relational terms without an anchoring ideal standard.

There have been fairly few studies of whether lay practices of social comparison amongst Europeans are likewise prone to include cross-national elements. Some researchers have attempted to explore this with opinion polls, notably (Delhey and Kohler 2006), where the focus is on levels of life satisfaction. Their research finds that, amongst the population groups studied (Turkey, Hungary, Western and Eastern Germany), 75 per cent of respondents, when asked to assess their own standard of living, made cross-national comparisons in addition to those with friends, neighbours and co-nationals. The possible range of comparators was set by the survey designers in advance: they do not include all EU and European countries, nor do they feature countries beyond Europe (the list being: Switzerland, Netherlands, Sweden, France, Poland, Spain, Italy, Hungary and Germany). While this limits what we can infer about the *content* of cross-national comparisons – in particular, whether the respondent wishes to emphasise circumstances in specifically these countries, and how far one can speak of a 'europeanisation' of reference groups rather than a few targeted, 'bilateral' references to specific country groups – it nonetheless suggests an assumption of the national boundedness of comparison practices is problematic.

The point comes through also in qualitative research.[22] In a study conducted by the author (White 2009, 2011), group interviews with citizens in Germany, Britain and the Czech Republic concerning a range of everyday problems (e.g. high and rising prices, low wages) produced a number of spontaneous cross-national comparisons. One of the study's suggested findings is that, in line with the above, the range of comparators is likely to vary according to the criterion of comparison (i.e. where Z changes, so one can expect Y to change). Whereas economic issues tend to produce comparisons with neighbouring European countries (but not necessarily Europe as a whole), issues to do with intergroup relations (e.g. the ability to successfully integrate immigrants) tend to provoke a wider range of comparators more broadly associated with the 'West'. Issues of law and order, by contrast, tend to produce few cross-national comparisons – probably because such issues are seen as local in their origins and effects. At least for the medium term, rather than a generalised trend towards Europe-wide practices of comparison, it seems most plausible to expect a series of spheres whose extension varies from one issue domain to the next.

---

the *Guardian*'s 'Europe season' (from 14th March 2011), which encouraged readers to learn how their 'neighbours', Germany, France, Spain and Poland respond to a common set of everyday social and political challenges (www.guardian.co.uk/world/2011/mar/13/germany-guardian-new-europe-series).

22. For an interesting study of how the EU is taught in French schools, see Bozec 2010, including p.168 for observations on how teacher-led initiatives to establish pen-pal links with schools in Poland, Germany and Spain led to practices of cross-national social comparison amongst pupils. See also the autobiographical narratives of Europe's highly mobile 'eurostars' in Favell 2008, many of which display elements of social comparison (see Chapter One for early examples).

Implications of an enlarging scope of comparison

So far we have examined the formal structure of social comparison, some of the reasons to expect its evolution to include cross-national dimensions, and the existing research that has looked into this. Insofar as such developments are real, what implications might they hold for social integration in Europe more generally, beyond the widening horizons of awareness and perceived relevance that social comparison signals? What are the likely consequences of an enlarging scope of comparison? We shall tackle this question at the level of lay citizens, though clearly a parallel line of research would involve posing it at the level of political and economic elites. In either case, what interests us is to identify some of the patterned sequences social comparison may give rise to, even if – as with social mechanisms generally – these are various, possibly contradictory, and the pre-eminence of one over another is not to be determined ex ante.

Evidently one likely consequence of wider comparison is the recalibration of people's sense of their own social position. System integration introduces a whole new range of comparators. Exposed to a wider variety of human experiences in Europe, people may come to rethink how they stand relative to others. Those who see themselves as of low economic or social status, confronted with the yet worse circumstances of those elsewhere, may come to rethink themselves as part of a 'comfortable middle'. Those of high status in a local setting (e.g. the provincial businessman, or the stand-out student of the local university) may come to question their superiority. In other words, by offering new points of comparison, the cross-national context prompts revisions to existing practices of comparison. The proverbial big fish may be recast as modest fare, just as the small fish is revealed to be not so minor after all.[23] This may be a disorienting and distressing process for some, as a sudden reappraisal can prompt feelings of humiliation, but in principle one would expect it to be a positive experience for others. New feelings of relative deprivation might be counter-balanced by new feelings of 'relative gratification' as it has been called (Pettigrew 2002). This twin dynamic is foreseeable even at the intra-personal level, as shifts on one dimension of comparison are compensated by shifts on another. If this process of reappraisal were engaged in by all equally, one would expect something approaching an overall balance in the numbers of those who came to reassess themselves positively or negatively – the process would be 'zero-sum' in its reallocation of self-worth.[24]

---

23. Note also that European integration has the potential to generate *new* criteria of comparison (Z) which produce new scales of advantage and disadvantage – e.g. to do with the ability to access the benefits of integration itself. The very novelty of these dimensions may give them added levels of public resonance.

24. For an overview of different emotional responses to social comparison, see Smith (chap. 10) in Suls and Wheeler 2000, esp. 176, which describes four basic variants: downward-assimilative comparisons (producing shared concerns and sympathy), downwards-contrastive (with contempt / Schadenfreude / self-satisfaction), upward-contrastive (with envy / depression) and upward-assimilative (with admiration / inspiration / optimism).

But here lies the crux: such symmetry of practice seems unlikely. Social comparison, it has been suggested, is pursued with most urgency by those who sense or fear that in relative terms they are not doing well. Those who are comfortably off (by whatever criterion) may be less aware of their advantage, and less concerned to verify it, than are those less well off.[25] The latter have added incentive to engage in comparison, whether to learn more about their predicament or to console themselves with the knowledge that it is shared, perhaps even experienced more severely elsewhere.[26] This would suggest a preponderance of cross-national comparisons amongst those who, in the existing order, feel aggrieved or insecure – e.g. the poor in a wealthy, west-European country, or the poor and middle classes in a medium-to-poor central- / east- or south-European country. It would likewise suggest particular attentiveness to those dimensions (Z) on which the subject is thought to fare badly (an impulse which the league-table examples above seem to appeal to). Furthermore, 'upward' comparisons – those which establish or are premised on the superiority of the comparator's circumstances over those of the subject – may be the ones which lodge themselves most firmly in the subject's imagination. If there is asymmetry in the comparisons pursued, it would seem to suggest the following proposition:

1) Cross-national social comparisons tend at the aggregate level to increase perceptions of relative deprivation without a corresponding increase in perceptions of relative advantage.

European integration would, in other words, make Europeans on balance feel a little bit worse about themselves.[27]

Let us leave aside the normative issues this raises – whether for example popular dissatisfaction of this kind, based on relative rather than absolute appraisal, is something one should want to avoid or whether it can be a source of inspiration for positive political change and thus a valuable component of citizenship. Let us focus instead on the sufficiently complex political-sociological dimensions. If heightened perceptions of relative deprivation are a predictable outcome of cross-national social comparison, one might infer two plausible but opposed conclusions. On the one hand one might see comparisons as generative of heightened levels of individual stress for which individual solutions are sought. Such an outcome could take several forms: it could entail feelings of resentment towards those whom comparisons reveal to be advantaged; efforts to rationalise the discrepancy e.g., by appeal to notions of merit, moves to close the gap through individual adaptation; an inclination to retreat from wider social commitments so as to minimise the

---

25. Cf. Walker and Smith (2002: 137) on the idea that the advantaged tend to take their advantage for granted, and tend to be weakly inclined to see themselves as part of an advantaged group.

26. This point needs to be balanced against the fact that expectations may be higher amongst high-status groups (and disappointments thus correspondingly stronger), as well as the likelihood that factual knowledge about other locations is higher amongst these groups.

27. This will be all the more true if there is a dynamic dimension to the appraisal, such that 'our' condition is said not just to be bad but deteriorating.

adverse feelings they produce; or a tendency to deny the feasibility of cross-national comparison, or to switch the dimension of comparison (Z) so as to produce more favourable results (e.g., to renounce a prosperity criterion in favour of a morality one – 'they' are rich, but 'I' / 'we' are good).[28] One is reminded of Elster's description of the 'sour grapes' phenomenon, a classic strategy for coping with dissatisfaction (Elster 1985). In the short to medium term, cross-national comparisons would then seem to have few destabilising political consequences. Indeed, insofar as they relativise experiences (e.g., of poverty) by showing how there is 'always someone worse off', they may produce apathy and prove actively immobilising.[29] Still, in the longer term, this tendency could be expected to have subversive consequences, as it might easily entail the slow ebbing of support for the very institutional frameworks which prompt these unfavourable comparisons. The EU's political legitimacy would, in this way, be weakened.

Yet there is a counter-tendency one might also foresee: an emergent awareness of personal disadvantage spurring moves to seek out others who share in this predicament, perhaps so as to make common cause. The initial act of social comparison which reveals relative disadvantage, and which therefore has an unsettling character, would thus be coupled with a second one that re-embeds the individual in a larger collective and forms the basis for an enlarged sense of 'we'. In this scenario, social comparison fosters the emergence of new bonds of solidarity and cross-national subjecthood. It enables moves towards the emergence of classes *for* themselves, as the familiar terminology has it (though classes in the broad, not necessarily economic, sense). This way lies the transnationalisation of social cleavages and potentially their politicisation at a European level. Insofar as these forms of subjecthood translate into specific political demands, one could expect them to impinge on the institutional structure of the EU and its legal order in the form of pressure for its redesign – i.e. to have fairly immediate consequences for system integration. Protest movements, including contemporary ones against the 'austerity' programmes being pushed by governments across Europe, involve efforts to evoke a popular sense of equivalence with precisely such goals in mind, and when their organisers acknowledge the inspiration of counterparts abroad they themselves are testifying to the mobilisatory capacity of the comparative logic.[30]

Again, for clarity's sake, we can express these alternatives in propositional form:

---

28. A retreat from social comparison may be accentuated insofar as integration exposes individuals to those whose preferred criteria of assessment are different from their own, and who thus serve to undermine the validity of the reference criteria hitherto invoked – a variation of Durkheim's *anomie*.

29. This effect is accentuated insofar as integration exposes individuals to those prioritising criteria of assessment different from their own, and who thus undermine the validity of the reference criteria hitherto invoked.

30. On British student protesters taking inspiration from Spain, see http://www.guardian.co.uk/world/2011/jun/20/student-walkouts-public-sector-strikes.

2a) The adaptation thesis: when cross-national social comparisons heighten perceptions of relative deprivation, citizens will look for narratives that can rationalise this, and/or make individual efforts to change their relative standing, and / or resist the making of comparisons, and/or seek to restructure them in more favourable ways.

2b) The mobilisation thesis: when cross-national social comparisons heighten perceptions of relative deprivation, citizens will seek out and make common cause with those revealed to be similarly disadvantaged.

Here is not the place to settle the matter, but perhaps the following can be noted. Scholars of relative deprivation make a potentially relevant distinction concerning how the comparison subject (figure X in our typology) comes to be articulated. When a speaker presents their sense of comparative disadvantage using the first person singular, 'I', this may be referred to as *personal* deprivation: it is as an individual that the subject feels deprived. When a speaker presents the matter using the first person plural 'we', this may be thought of as *group* deprivation: it is as part of a collective that the subject feels deprived (Walker and Smith 2002).[31] Both can be a basis for comparison, but the consequences of the first are likely to be mainly psychological and local – e.g. individual displeasure, and perhaps an individual effort to improve relative standing – rather than an organised effort to find a collective voice. The consequences of the second on the other hand, may be wider in scope and more likely to bring social change: comparisons formulated in this way suggest that individual responses are inappropriate, and suggest the possibility of a common cause. This would suggest that, as a minimum condition for orchestrated efforts at wider change, the subject's comparison of their circumstances with those of cross-national others must take the form of a comparison of 'people like us', not merely of 'individuals like me'. In contemporary Europe, this disposition hardly seems extinguished, but must contend nevertheless with a tendency in public discourse to individualise the citizen, and to acknowledge political demands primarily in the form of individual rights (White 2009, 2010).

Much is also likely to depend on whether the discrepancies which social comparison reveals are held to be remediable or unavoidable. For even where there is a sense of collective deprivation, this may produce no more than silent acquiescence if it is felt to be rooted in immutable conditions.[32] There needs to be the sense that tomorrow can be better than today. The implications of social comparison are inseparable from the wider political narratives by which those comparisons and their meaning are shaped (White 2011). There is an interesting interplay here between social comparison and perceptions of agency. On the one hand, it is through

---

31. Runciman 1966, 31ff., makes a related distinction between egoistic and fraternalist deprivation.

32. Note the fourth dimension of Runciman's definition (1996: 10): '[...] A is relatively deprived of X when (i) he does not have X, (ii) he sees some other person or persons [...] as having X (whether this is or will be in fact the case), (iii) he wants X, and (iv) he sees it as feasible that he should have X.'

comparisons that the space for agency can be opened, since those which highlight the variety of human experience show the ways in which things could be different – e.g., the different ways in which public services can be organised and financed. Encouraging comparisons is one way of affirming the possibility of alternatives and reducing political acquiescence. On the other hand, comparisons unaccompanied by a narrative about the possibility of *realising* these alternatives, 'here' as much as 'there', may rather provoke envy or demoralisation. In all these aspects one sees the dimension of power: those who shape these wider narratives, be they partisan actors in the parliamentary sphere or the media, have considerable influence over the extent to which the fruits of comparison are resignation or agitation. Their ability to 'nudge' people towards a certain comparator (Thaler and Sunstein 2008), and to influence how the comparison act is interpreted, is a notable source of power.

Conclusion

This chapter has examined how processes of system integration at the transnational level present new opportunities for the practices of social comparison. By generating diverse social encounters, new information resources, and an extension in the scope of common legislation, these processes invite citizens to compare their daily experiences with those of people further afield and to evoke reference groups outside their country of residence. Conceptions e.g., of economic hardship – who experiences it, who escapes it – have the potential thereby to draw in reference-points beyond the boundaries of the nation-state. Drawing on findings from recent research, the chapter has discussed how far, and when, such possibilities are likely to be realised, and the potential political significance of these practices.

To what extent should the comparison act be seen as a contribution to social integration? Clearly we are dealing with something much less demanding than is implied by notions of common identity. The structure of social comparison asserts the fact that the subject and comparator are ontologically separable, even if deemed to be similar – and any assertion of similarity is always specific to a particular metric of comparison. At the same time social comparison may form the basis for the emergence of thicker ties. Stronger bonds of collectivity may well demand the prior recognition of an equivalence of social position, as well as the motivation to find common cause that a sense of injustice promotes. By widening public conceptions of social and political space, and underscoring similarities and discrepancies of experience, comparisons offer an enabling context for this. They offer the basis on which further political narratives may draw. However, though they may be a necessary condition of deeper social integration, they are hardly a sufficient one. In some forms they may have the opposite effect of causing political disengagement and the rejection of the institutional arrangements that enable them. Comparisons can be divisive as well as integrative. Their ultimate contribution will depend as much on the *kind* of comparisons citizens are invited to make and the conclusions they are encouraged to draw – factors inseparable from larger efforts to shape the contours of political commonsense.

Let us conclude with some observations on what cross-national comparison implies for the continuing hold of the nation-state as the reference-point for popular self-understanding. As we have indicated, the subject (X) and comparator (Y) of social comparison need in no way be denominated using national categories: numerous alternatives are possible (professional, gender-based, generational, etc.), and when these are invoked there is no reason to suppose their frame of reference will be domestic to the national sphere. Social comparison thereby reduces the salience of national boundaries, even without putting them in question. Where comparisons do refer to the national unit (think of the league-tables mentioned), a twin process is at work: the relevance of the national unit is reaffirmed, yet it is simultaneously placed in a larger frame, inviting the citizen to step back to adopt a broader perspective. National boundaries remain a landmark, but no longer form the horizon. Social comparison thus effects a shift in their status. In doing so, it may also put strain on some varieties of nationalist thought. Social comparison can have an unsettling quality, placing established ideas of status in question, and undermining notions of the privileged self. It makes a precarious underpinning for national pride. Furthermore, as we have seen with parts of the British media, comparisons may come more easily with those neighbouring European countries held in little affection than with those more distant countries (e.g. the US) with whom such outlets actively promote popular identification. Such discrepancies are logically tenable, but require a double gaze that may be difficult to sustain. They remind, at the same time, that there is a multi-dimensionality to even the most Eurosceptic orientations, one that would be missed if one focused exclusively on practices of identification.

References

Aaltola, M. (2005) 'The international airport: the hub-and-spoke pedagogy of the American empire', *Global Networks* 5(3): 261–78.

Bozec, G. (2010) 'L'Europe au tableau noir: Comment les instituteurs français enseignent-ils l'Union européenne aujourd'hui?', *Politique Européenne* 30: 153–86.

Delanty, G. and C. Rumford (2005) *Rethinking Europe: Social theory and the implications of Europeanization,* London: Routledge.

Delhey, J. and Kohler, U. (2006) 'From nationally bounded to Pan-European inequalities? On the importance of foreign countries as reference groups', *European Sociological Review,* 22(2): 125–140.

Domingues, J. M.(1995) *Sociological Theory and Collective Subjectivity,* London: Macmillan.

Elster, J. (1985) *Sour Grapes: Studies in the subversion of rationality,* Cambridge: CUP.

— (1989) *Nuts and Bolts for the Social Sciences,* Cambridge: CUP.

— (2007) *Explaining Social Behaviour: More nuts and bolts for the social sciences,* Cambridge: CUP.

Fahey, T. (2010) 'Poverty and the two concepts of relative deprivation', *UCD School of Applied Social Science Working Paper Series* WP10/1.

Favell, A. (2008) *Eurostars and Eurocities: Free movement and mobility in an integrating Europe,* Oxford: Blackwell.

Feinberg, J. (1974) 'Non-Comparative Justice', *The Philosophical Review,* 83(3): 297–338.

Festinger, L. (1954) 'A theory of social comparison processes', *Human Relations* 7: 117–140.

Gartrell, C. D. 'The Embeddedness of Social Comparison' in I. Walker and H. Smith (eds) (2002) *Relative Deprivation*: Specification, development and integration, Cambridge: CUP, pp. 164–84

Guimond, S. (ed.) (2006) *Social Comparison and Social Psychology: Understanding cognition, intergroup relations and culture,* Cambridge: CUP.

Hedström, P. and Swedberg, R. (eds) (1998) *Social Mechanisms: An analytical approach to social theory,* Oxford: OUP.

Joas, H. and Knöbl, W. (2009) *Social Theory: Twenty introductory lectures,* Cambridge: CUP.

Lockwood, D. (1964) 'Social Integration and System Integration', in G. K. Zollschan and H. W. Hirsch (eds) *Social Change: Explorations, Diagnoses and Conjectures,* Cambridge MA: Schenkman, pp.244–257.

Masters, J. and Smith, W. (eds) (1987) *Social Comparison, Social Justice, and Relative Deprivation: Theoretical, empirical, and policy perspectives,* Hillsdale, N.J.: Lawrence Erlbaum Associates.

Mouzelis, N. (2008) *Modern and Post-Modern Social Theorizing,* Cambridge: CUP.

Pettigrew, T. F. (1998) 'Intergroup contact theory', *Annual Review of Psychology* 49: 65–85.

—— (2002) 'Summing Up: Relative deprivation as a key social psychological concept', in I. Walker and H. Smith (eds) *Relative Deprivation,* Cambridge: CUP, pp.351–373.

Runciman, W. G. (1996) *Relative Deprivation and Social Justice: A study of attitudes to social inequality in twentieth-century England,* London: Routledge & Kegan Paul.

Sigalas, E. (2010) 'Cross-border mobility and European identity: the effectiveness of intergroup contact during the ERASMUS year abroad', *European Union Politics* 11(2): 241–265.

Suls, J. and Wheeler, L. (eds) (2000) *Handbook of Social Comparison: Theory and research,* New York: Kluwer Academic/Plenum.

Thaler, R. H. and Sunstein, C. R. (2008) *Nudge: Improving decisions about health, wealth and happiness,* New Haven: Yale UP.

Urry, J. (2007) *Mobilities,* Cambridge: Polity.

Walker, I. and Smith, H. (eds) (2002) *Relative Deprivation: Specification, development and integration,* Cambridge: CUP.

Whelan, C. T. and Maître, B. (2009) 'The "Europeanisation" of reference groups', *European Societies* 11(2): 283–309.

White, J. (2009) 'Thematization and collective positioning in everyday political talk', *British Journal of Political Science* 39(4): 699–709.

—— (2010) 'European Integration by daylight', *Comparative European Politics* 8 (1): 55–73.

—— (2011) *Political Allegiance after European Integration,* Basingstoke: Palgrave Macmillan.

chapter eleven | constructing european citizens? evaluating the integrative force of teaching history

Stefan Seidendorf

This chapter analyses experiences with the common, Franco-German history text-book. The straightforward research question is why this book is only, to a limited extent, used in classes in France and in Germany. In an attempt to explain the obstacles to a wider use of the book, I will touch upon some more far-reaching conceptual and theoretical questions: Why do citizens use or not use the oppor-tunities provided by the process of European integration? As we will see, an easy answer would advance the role of 'national identity' as an analytical concept. The chapter will show that in order to properly explain the obstacles to a wider use of the textbook, we have to open the 'black box of national identity' and differentiate between economic, utilitarian, institutional and social constructivist elements that might explain the book's limited success. In combining these elements, we could find more general answers to the question of when, and under what conditions, citizens accept and utilise the opportunities provided by European integration.

The chapter starts out with some general considerations on the role of a com-mon textbook within the process of European integration. It is completed by a presentation of some empirical elements that are important in order to understand the role of the common textbook. It goes on by introducing the research design, establishing preliminary hypotheses and presenting some evidence. Finally, I dis-cuss results and link them back to some more far-reaching questions on the pro-cess of integration and our way of studying it.

A common textbook within the process of european integration

The symbolically loaded task of producing a common history textbook immedi-ately brings up some far-reaching questions: can and should the teaching of his-tory in school, traditionally one of the 'engines of integration' of citizens into nineteenth century nation-states (Harp 1998: 115), take on a similar role in today's Europe (for an overview see Barton and Levstik 2004)? In favour of this approach, we can argue that France and Germany are commonly seen as the advocates of European integration, as the 'couple' whose 'reconciliation' was a necessary con-dition *for,* and at the same time the rationale *of,* the process of European integra-tion. Whilst the two countries never really discussed the question of *finalité,* of the *telos* of the whole integration project, their efforts still led to an impressive number of initiatives relating to all aspects of social, political and economic life. A common textbook as an 'engine of integration' thus may be seen as a far-reaching further step in socialising citizens into a state-like European Union.

Contrary to this argument, it can be said that both countries retain traditional aspects of nation-state behaviour on the international scene, and some commentators argue that the seemingly idealistic process of European integration, 'in reality' (meaning: read in a 'realist' perspective) obscures the 'rescue of the nation-state' (Milward 1992). Even if there are no clear indicators that allow the question of *finalité* to be resolved, we still have to concede that writing a common history textbook constitutes, both politically and symbolically, a highly significant act. However, it would be too easy to attribute to this book the role of nineteenth century history books in fostering 'collective identity constructions' via compulsory schooling.

Historical evolution: teaching national or european history?

Whereas 'teaching history' used to be seen as a deliberate method of integrating citizens into nineteenth century nation-states, particularly in the unitary French Republic,[1] this is less true today. During the nineteenth century, compulsory schooling was seen as an instrument of fostering a nation 'with a common education, a common set of allegiances, and a common language' (Bell 2001: 201), different from *other* nations through a particular history. The current Franco-German case is more complicated. At the outset, we can perceive an absent elite consensus on the *telos* of the integration process, on the final aim of European integration. This means that the core history to be taught in a common textbook is not self-evident: it could be the common history of a 'European nation', as it could be the history of a 'Franco-German nation', and finally, one could envisage a text that retains separate entities, yet tells their conflictual (and at times consensual) relationship in history.

In the case of France and Germany, the first initiatives for a common history textbook can be traced back to the 1930s, when a group of professors defined elements for a common history book (Riemenschneider 1998; Alexandre 2006). With Hitler's arrival in power in Germany in 1933, the initiative came to an abrupt end. Shortly after the Second World War, a second attempt was politically more successful. The plan was completed in 1952, during the euphoria surrounding the first successful step towards European integration, the European Coal and Steel Community which was proposed in 1950 and launched in 1952. By establishing a common reading of Franco-German history, both attempts aimed to 'take away conflict potential' in textbooks. They were, however, not interested in establishing a history of a common Franco-German entity. The results of both endeavours never found the approval of public authorities for use in classes (on media reactions in 1952 see Seidendorf 2007: 111–113).

This changed with the 2003 initiative that lies behind the current Franco-German textbook. During the festivities to commemorate the 40th anniversary of

---

1.   In France, the first detailed curriculum in history dates from 1838, see Picard in de Cock and
     Picard 2009: 22.

the Franco-German *Elysée*-Treaty of 1963, a 'Franco-German Youth-Parliament' came up with proposals that were presented to the French president, Jacques Chirac and the German chancellor, Gerhard Schröder. Both agreed 'spontaneously' to politically endorse the idea of having a common Franco-German history textbook. The creation of the three volumes is described elsewhere (Claret 2006; Monnet 2006; Francois 2007; Le Quintrec 2007; Dubois 2010). Suffice to say that identical versions of the three volumes exist in two languages (French and German) and cater roughly for 15–18 year-old students, starting three years before *baccalauréat* and *Abitur*, the final school examinations that correspond to British A-levels. The volumes cover the post-war period (vol. I), the time-span 1815–1945 (vol. II), and finally Europe and the world before 1815 (vol. III).[2]

Considering these historical preliminaries, we may surmise that the current project had to overcome two main challenges: (a) concerning the content side ('which perspective to adopt?'), and (b) concerning institutional and administrative obstacles ('how to receive accreditation by public authorities?') (Geiss 2006: 98–100; Le Quintrec 2007: 5–7).

Empirical elements: what kind of history textbook?

Both challenges can be further differentiated in order to present the 'solutions' found by the textbook's authors. Regarding (a), there are three elements:

(i) How to overcome divergences on historical events? In particular, controversies along a national, Franco-German cleavage-line come to mind.

(ii) The discussion around the underlying perspective of the book (which elements should be contained, and how should they be presented?).

(iii) The methodological approach of the book (how to bring together two seemingly very different pedagogical models)?

Concerning the first point (i) it is remarkable that all the authors and contributors contacted, as well as the (sometimes very critical) reviewers (Krieger 2006; Raether 2008) agree that there were no fundamental historiographical divergences on facts and interpretation (Geiss 2006: 98; Le Quintrec 2007: 6; Defrance and Pfeil 2010: 102). This appears also in analyses based on the content of the book and seems to confirm studies that see a long-term trend towards an increasingly coherent Franco-German image of the past (Henri 2009).

(ii) Finding a compromise on the second item, the underlying perspective of the book, proved more difficult, mainly due to the necessity of covering two different national curricula in order for the book to be accredited in both countries. A closer look shows that there was enough 'common' content for a common history textbook in both national programmes. In fact, both curricula largely contain the same historical events, which should not come as a surprise: if national (French or German) history is contextualised in space and time, it is hardly possible to create

---

2.   Complete bibliographic details in appendix.

a nationally isolated narrative. According to one interviewee, the only divergences were on the importance of two particular elements: French colonial history was difficult for the Germans to accept, and Eastern European history during the Cold War seemed less important to the French side. Both agreed nevertheless, to integrate these items into the book. The result is not a book that tries to construct the history of a 'European nation', nor a narrative seeking to establish a 'Franco-German' nation. It is rather a classical 'national' textbook, focusing on France and Germany, to be used in France and Germany, yet building on a new 'transnational perspective' (Geiss 2006).

The last point (iii) proved most difficult. Indeed, both sides vigorously defended their respective pedagogical models and believed they were incompatible with any other approach to the teaching of history (Le Quintrec 2007: 6). The book tried to integrate both approaches by proposing both ('French' and 'German') forms of exercises and different elements (sources, maps, graphics) on the content side. To conclude, however, compromises were found on each one of the three items.

With regard to administrative and institutional challenges (b), the first observation concerns the link between public authorities and the accreditation that textbooks need in order to be used in public schools. In both countries, only textbooks accredited by the public authorities are allowed to be used in classes. In the German case, this accreditation is accorded at the *regional* level of the *Bundesländer*, with sixteen different regional procedures and programmes. In the French case, political and administrative actors are united in the ministry of national education. The challenge thus again, can be broken down into three parts:

(i) Both countries have a well institutionalised procedure on how school books are developed, bringing together editors, authors and regional or national authorities (themselves consisting of administrative and political actors). The challenge thus was to find a working method that would successfully integrate the two (or rather seventeen: sixteen regional German and one national French) administrative styles.

(ii) This raised, amongst other problems, the issue of how to integrate sixteen regional history programmes in Germany (questions of education are decided at a regional level in the German federal system) in order to obtain the accreditation of the sixteen regional states and

(iii) Finally, how to comply with the very detailed French programme d'histoire while still managing to meet the demands of the sixteen German agreements?

To solve the first point (i) academics, teachers and civil servants from foreign ministries and ministries of education and representatives of the two publishers (*Nathan* in France, *Klett* in Germany) created a mixed Franco-German steering committee. The members developed detailed descriptions of the project that were then handed to the authors. Each chapter was written by a bi-national team, which reported back to the steering committee, which in turn oversaw the compatibility with national and regional programmes (Defrance and Pfeil 2010: 98).

In this way it was possible (ii) to constantly bear the obligation to conform to national and regional programmes in mind. However, enormous political will was necessary to allow for the final accreditation in the sixteen German regional states. In fact, so far this is the first and only successful coordination of the sixteen curricula in one discipline. Political pressure behind the project also suggests that accreditation occurred, despite at times obvious lacunae in the history book with regard to regional programmes (Defrance and Pfeil 2010: 97).

The same (iii) is not true for the French case. Here, the centralised system has its advantages, insofar as the *Ministère de l'éducation nationale* could, from the very beginning, establish a close symbiosis between the actors in the steering committee and the civil servants dealing with the new curriculum in the ministry. However, this advantage – of a more centralised, and thus more efficient process in terms of output-considerations – soon turned into a disadvantage, when President Sarkozy's government decided to cut the huge budget of the national education system. This went along with a reduction (or even elimination) of history teaching in the final school year. These reforms necessitated a new curriculum in history, adapted to the described changes. Consequently, the Franco-German textbook is already out of date.

This is the basic setup and background for the study presented here. The following section will show that even if the main reason for the textbook's lack of success in classes seems obvious, the lack of coherence with regional/national curricula, the challenges lie deeper. Is 'lacking coherency with public programmes' rather a convenient excuse used by actors unwilling to use the textbook, but hiding behind regional and national authorities?

Research design: how to analyse?

Existing studies on the textbook mainly concentrate on the content side of the book[3]. They compare its content to that of 'national' predecessors and are, even if not explicitly, searching for a presumed influence of the 'French' or 'German' model in the three volumes (Frenkel 2008; Körber 2008, an exception is Gitton 2007). This study, interested in the use and experiences with the textbook, thus has to start from an explorative setting in order to identify actors, institutional and structural forces behind the choice for or against its use.

I started from the preliminary assumption that in both countries the final decision which textbook to choose lies with teachers. To understand why the book is not used, we thus have to explain teachers' reticence when making their choice. Teachers, of course, make their choices within a social and political environment that should be taken into account. Even if teachers are, in principle, free to decide which book to use, generally all teachers of the same discipline confer and agree on one textbook in order to establish coherence within a school. Along with the described coordination amongst colleagues, the choice of a book takes place

---

3.   See the special issue of *Dokumente*, 62:5 (2006) on 'The Franco-German history book analysed'.

under the influence of political and administrative actors. In both countries, only books 'accredited' by public authorities can be used in schools. In the case at hand, a highly symbolic and politicised project, we must expect that political and administrative actors have their own agenda and may try to influence teachers' choices. Finally, we have a group of 'experts', authors and members of the Franco-German textbook steering committee, but also academics and publishers' consultants concerned with the didactics and content of history teaching. They influence the reception of the textbook through advice, consultancy and their role within an institutionalised field (academia).

The different groups of actors are, of course, in contact with each other. The group of experts in particular, has very close and institutionalised contacts with each of the other two. Furthermore, as researchers and academics, these actors have a markedly 'reflexive' position, coming up with 'their own reasons' why the book is, or is not, successful. In this constellation, and with no precise theoretical background to deduce hypotheses, a common problem in social scientific studies comes up. Asking the identified actors about the causes why the textbook is poorly used, I cannot be sure of finding out their 'real' or 'true' intentions. It is even possible that they themselves do not exactly know *why* they chose (or chose not) to work with the new textbook. To pursue this aspect via surveys at this state of the study, thus made little sense. Insight gained by observing the situation (the actors, institutions, structures and issues at stake) was not necessarily a better alternative either. For example, I may well observe institutional constraints that are not relevant for a teacher's ultimate decision etc.

Under these circumstances, and before further refining the framework of the study, I decided to combine both approaches and to draw conclusions by comparing results. I observed and reconstructed the situation leading to the approval or rejection of a textbook (cf. Bray 2008). These observations, combined with some general social science reasoning, led to four preliminary hypotheses. Operationalising theses hypotheses allowed me to conduct thirteen in-depth semi-structured interviews (cf. Weiss 1995). After having identified three groups of actors (civil servants, teachers, experts), I decided to ask each one of them similar questions, in relation to the four hypotheses. Finally, regrouping and comparing the results allowed me to reduce and refine hypotheses, which could be used for a further, large-scale study.

Before presenting the interviews and the results, the observation of the case allows us to describe particular interests and utility functions of the different actor-groups (a). This will be used to deduce four tentative hypotheses (b). Finally, interview results will be presented according to the four hypotheses (c).

a) Institutional and structural constraints of the actors and their interests

The actor groups are the *civil servants* working at the interface between administrative and political level, *teachers* deciding on the use of the textbook, and finally academics working as *experts* in what can be described as an intellectual field.

With regard to the *civil servants* working at the interface between the administrative and political levels, a split between discourse and policy could be observed. As mentioned above, the idea of the Franco-German textbook was, from the outset, symbolically loaded and political pressure worked in favour of using it in class (Defrance and Pfeil 2010: 97). On the other hand, this contrasted with the rather incoherent behaviour of those responsible for history curricula. In France and in Germany, changes in curricula occurred during and shortly after the publication of the first two of the three volumes of the textbook (see details below). The political situation was thus ambivalent. Whereas in public discourse no critical or negative arguments could be found against the widespread use of the textbook, regional and national administrations were not unanimous in their support.

Concerning the second group of actors, *teachers*, a similar paradox could be found. Again, all actors welcomed the initiative *in principle*. Yet if we look at the institutional and structural constellation, teachers could for a number of reasons, also be *against* the use of the textbook. For a teacher a new book with new content (for German teachers, 'French' history) meant more work. If the new elements also included methodological and pedagogical aspects alongside new content, the challenge for a teacher would be even greater. At the same time, within the 'social' constellation of a school, an informal hierarchy between teachers of a particular discipline existed. A young and ambitious teacher could use the new textbook, bringing the social capital of public praise, to challenge this informal hierarchy. Investing in this new resource might allow a teacher to overthrow existing informal constellations and to climb up in the internal hierarchy. Once again, we can observe different structural constraints and new opportunity structures created through the existence of the new textbook.

Finally, the same point is also valid for the group of *experts*. On the one hand, those involved in the Franco-German project were naturally in favour of the use of this book and denied the relevance of criticism. On the other hand, there was a whole social field consisting of academics working as consultants for the educational administration, civil servants in the ministries, and the publishing houses that produced new textbooks. To justify this potentially economically and socially advantageous development, expert actors developed a case based on 'new' pedagogical or methodological standards (or the 'defence' of established standards). This line of reasoning was used in documents of considerable influence: once agreed upon by administrative and political actors, the documents served as a basis for the establishment of history curricula, methodology and didactics. Actors in this field would, of course, do everything to criticise any content, approaches or documents that would question or disqualify the existing social field (see as an example Körber 2008, and the critique of his perspective by Bendick 2009).

b) Establishing preliminary hypotheses

The information gained by observing the structural and institutional patterns and actor-constellations of the textbook-case, when linked to more general social science theory approaches, allows for four preliminary hypotheses. Alone or combined, they may explain the success (or lack of success) of the textbook. The four hypotheses will be presented along their basic argument, followed by their application to the case at hand. The hypotheses follow an (i) economic, (ii) utilitarian, (iii) institutionalist and (iv) social constructivist reasoning.

(i) Economic reasoning

If economic reasoning was to explain the limited success of the textbook in classes, we should find cost arguments. These could be in absolute (price of changing existing textbooks against new, 'Franco-German' ones) or relative terms (price of the new book compared to other new textbooks). The argument could work on the individual level of pupils (parents) or teachers, or on the institutional level (subventions by local or regional authorities etc).

(ii) Utilitarian reasoning

Utilitarian reasoning would also put forward a cost-benefit-analysis (Esser 1991), but not related to the material/economic costs, pupils or institutions. Instead, the utilitarian argument concerns teachers. They, individually, decide against or in favour of using the textbook in class, and the aggregate of their behaviour provides the observed result. In utilitarian reasoning, teachers weigh up their personal benefit in using the new book, and the costs they would have to endure. This could be operationalised as 'extra work for teachers', in comparison to the usual textbooks. Benefits could reside mainly in accrued social recognition, but also in material support for individual teachers or classes using the manual.

(iii) Institutionalist reasoning

The institutionalist argument, based on 'new institutionalism' (Hall and Taylor 1996), puts forward the existence of a transformed opportunity function due to the existence of an institutional order. The changed opportunity function can be explained by processes of social learning (sociological institutionalism), path dependency (historical institutionalism) or a cost-benefit-structure, modified again due to an existing institutional setting (rational-choice institutionalism). Operationalised, this would mean in the case of the textbook:

- For 'sociological institutionalism', the fact that the 'social learning' of a particular way to teach history is complicating the use of the Franco-German textbook. The same effect with the opposite result could be found amongst teachers of bilingual classes. Their 'social learning' processes prepared them to deal with 'foreign' methods and materials in a more positive way, favourable to the use of the textbook.
- For 'historical institutionalism' (Steinmo 2008), a similar argument could be made, yet relying more on historically path-dependent decisions to institutionalise a certain school administration, certain curricula and pedagogical principles. Here, we could find the prescription of a particular method in official documents, the role of the officially decided school curricula in history, or else the institutional order of school education (regional divergences vs. a centralised system).

- For 'rational-choice institutionalism', the argument would be that an existing institutional order acts in favour/against the use of the textbook in class, and that individual teachers follow (as a majority) this opportunity structure, leading to the use (or not) of the textbook. Concretely, there could be political pressure and reward to use the textbook, or, linked to the economic argument above, subventions for using one particular textbook.

(iv) Social constructivist reasoning

Finally, social constructivists would argue that the textbook has difficulties making headway because of deeply entrenched cultural or social habits that are difficult to change (Checkel 2007). They could be subsumed as 'national identity' in the sense that they cover collective patterns of social order that are not (completely) at the disposal of individual actors. This does not exclude their transformation and modification over time.

Operationalising this criterion is most difficult. In order not to essentialise socially constructed processes, while at the same time differentiating between social and historical institutionalism, I propose the following 'evidence' for the identity-hypothesis: References by interviewees to a 'German' or 'French' model, seen as the 'good' or 'right' way to teach history (cf. Le Quintrec 2007: 6). The 'German' model, as it turns out from documents, conversation and the interviews, aims to foster students' 'ability for critical evaluation'. During class, a number of 'open questions', introduced by keywords, which are part of the taxonomy of objectives used in German teaching (such as: 'discuss critically', 'interrogate'...[4]), encourage students to discuss historical questions critically and to develop their own capacity for evaluation.[5] This reflection on history is, according to the German approach, helpful for civic orientation nowadays. The 'German model' is criticised for the lack of knowledge and small factual basis pupils draw upon, while permanently mixing up contemporary (normative) concerns with historical constellations.

In comparison, the 'French approach' is said to be strong on factual knowledge that has to be presented by students in the particular French essay form of a *dissertation*. Students are evaluated on their knowledge of facts, of interpretations, and of their capacity to present both in convincing form. By applying the underlying methodology of the *dissertation*, they should, in principle, be able to develop a 'reasoned opinion' on any social, political or economic fact. Critics point out that

---

4. In *Baden-Württemberg*, for example, classified along three dimensions: I: 'name', 'work out', 'describe', 'characterise', II: 'analyse', 'order', 'argue', 'explain', 'compare', III: 'investigate', 'judge', 'assess', 'examine', 'design', http://www.schule-bw.de/unterricht/faecher/geschichte/operatoren (accessed 30th October 2010).

5. 'Requirements specifications III (*Abitur*) comprise the development of a reflexive capacity, in order to deal with newly introduced topics, newly applied methods, and results that are gained, aiming at autonomous and sovereign reasoning, conclusion, interpretation, and evaluation (reflexive and problem-solving)', catalogue of unified requirements to be met in the final examinations (*Abitur*) in history, www.kmk.org/doc/beschl/196–13_EPA-Geschichte-Endversion-formatiert.pdf, accessed 30th October 2010).

in practice, learning a number of facts 'by heart' takes on a greater importance than training the methodological capabilities of students. With regard to different interpretations and their presentation in a dissertation, this is more an exercise to show knowledge than the ability for independent reflection.

c) Results of the interviews – what the actors say

From a total of thirteen interviews, eleven were conducted by phone and two, as face to face interviews (all with preliminary e-mail contact that announced the aim of the study and contained the structure of the interviews). They took place between the 15th August and 15th October 2010 and lasted between 45 and 90 minutes. As I was at the same time interested in gaining broad *and* deep inside-knowledge, I chose interviewees that currently (or had previously) belonged to more than one actor-group. This meant, for example, that they were teachers now working in administration; or that they came from the ministry of education and had been delegated to the expert steering group; or that they work as history-teachers but cooperate with the editors on the writing of the Franco-German textbook etc. I attributed the interviewees to one of the three actor-groups according to their current employment and to the role they chose themselves in the interviews (i.e.: speaking as 'teacher', 'expert' or 'civil servant'). Finally, I obtained interviews with five teachers, five experts and three civil servants. As only two of the thirteen (one expert/teacher, one expert/civil servant) were French, I decided to use their contribution as a corrective to claims of 'German' actors (instead of analysing the French case on the basis of only two interviews). To allow for more coherence, I concentrated (although not exclusively) on actors in southwest Germany (the regional state of *Baden-Württemberg*) and the French region of *Alsace*. These regions are commonly considered to be particularly involved in Franco-German cooperation, both at an ideological level as well as in practical politics. Actors of these regions should thus, in theory, be particularly open to the use of the new textbook. Finally, as I cannot exclude that my interviewees might experience political pressure as a result of the highly politicised and symbolic textbook project, I granted them anonymity, giving them numbers instead of names.

The interviews followed a semi-structured script. They started out with a section on the dissemination and use of the textbook, with questions on personal experience and an assessment of the distribution of the book. A second part dwelt on the four preliminary hypotheses. The final section contained questions on the process that led to the development of the book, on the interviewees' personal appreciation of the initiative, its advantages and disadvantages.

A first result thus concerns the success of the book. Both publishers chose not to react directly to my questions. However, several of the expert actors estimated that 40,000 copies had been sold in France and roughly the same number in Germany.[6] Behind these numbers, a qualitative approach revealed that very few

---

6.   This has to be read in relation to the political support of the project (see the discussion below on

'normal' classes actually use the book. Most users are to be found amongst 'bi-na-tional' Franco-German classes, in France amongst the '*AbiBac*'-classes.[7] Indeed, none of the interviewed actors could precisely identify a case where the textbook would have been used as a regular course book in a normal class. The book is used as supplementary material, especially in bi-national classes. In this context, it is not only used in history, but also in French and German lessons. Eventually, I was able to identify one French *lycée* in Rennes (Brittany), where one class uses the Franco-German textbook within their normal history lessons.

A second result concerns the structure of the arguments found in the interviews. This largely correlates with actors' current background: teachers blame civil serv-ants in the administration (for changing the curriculum, thus rendering the use of the Franco-German book difficult), and civil servants blame teachers (for being too narrow-minded, fearing extra work and not accepting the intellectual challenge of this new kind of history book). Finally, the expert group is divided: those involved in one way or another with the development of the Franco-German textbook de-fend their *oeuvre*, whilst those experts *not* directly involved defend established na-tional pedagogical, methodological or didactic standards. One's *own* standards are seen as objectively 'right' and 'good'. As they are institutionalised (as 'documents of reference' upon which the administration builds its programmes, curricula, and teaching modalities), no further argumentative legitimacy is needed. On the other hand, arguments are advanced criticising the *foreign* standards, which lack official recognition; the foreign model thus is not refuted simply because it is foreign.

In this situation, after two preliminary interviews and finding the same constel-lation in the third interview, I decided to add a fourth section to the interviews, confronting actors with the apparent incoherency in the different accounts and inviting them to 'change roles'. This can be understood as a sort of 'counterfactual analysis': 'if you (a civil servant) were a teacher, what could the reasons be *not* to use the textbook?', 'if you (a teacher) were an expert (of the group involved with the textbook), what elements would you put in the textbook?'. Based on this dou-ble strategy, I still found evidence for all four hypotheses, yet am able to qualify this evidence.

---

the numbers of copies distributed free of charge). Furthermore, one actor qualifies the number of sold copies for the French market: about 350,000 students require textbooks in the final *lycée* (high school) year. A textbook is seen as a success from 100,000 sold copies onward.

7.   Based on a bilateral agreement between France and Germany. Participating schools not only teach French or German as a foreign language, but choose to teach several disciplines (partly) in the respective 'foreign language'. The final examination after eight years of secondary schooling, leads to both a French *baccalauréat* and a German *Abitur*, hence the name 'AbiBac'. A non-language discipline (history, mathematics, sport…) is taught in 1083 classes in German, in 2081 in French. A total number of c. 200,000 students are in these classes (all languages together) (see Gitton 2007: 2).

Concerning the economic hypothesis

Ample evidence was found for political support for the project, translating into free distribution of copies of the textbook by public authorities. We thus find the *Baden-Württemberg* regional government offering two copies of the book to every *Gymnasium*. Furthermore, all bilingual (Franco-German) classes in *Baden-Württemberg* were issued with a set of textbooks. The regional government of *Alsace* bought 3,000 copies of the book and distributed it to schools in the region, as did the *Académie de Grenoble* and the regional government of Lower Saxony, which bought and distributed 2,000 copies. Thus a clear political will to promote the use of the book translated into an economic argument in favour of the book. This is, however, not a one-way or coherent picture. For example in *Baden-Württemberg*, the Association of German Cities and Towns (*Städtetag*), concerned with the rising cost of textbooks, asked schools in 2009 and 2010 to refrain from buying new textbooks – including the Franco-German history book. This message of course is opposed to the regional government's promotion of the book. It seems as if the economic argument can be used in both directions, to argue in favour or against the use of the textbook. Alone, however, it cannot explain the limited success of the book.

Concerning the utilitarian hypothesis

As mentioned above, the administrative and expert actors were accusing teachers of not using the textbook for utilitarian reasons. The Franco-German book is different from other history books in that there is no teachers' manual. Usually, a teacher's manual provides background information and complementary material. Not having access to this material could thus be a reason *not to use* the book (No.2, p. 3). Although all interviewed teachers claimed to 'know French history' (No.2, p.3) and to be able to teach it, two of them did acknowledge that a complementary teachers' manual would be helpful, even 'necessary' for the successful use of the Franco-German textbook (No.3, p. 2). Furthermore, the argument was advanced that the 'strange exercises' in the book made it hard to use the German keywords (see above), This should be contrasted with the convincing line of argument put forward by two interviewed experts engaged in the development of the Franco-German textbook. They both claim that the keywords were duly integrated into the book, without which it would have failed to gain regional accreditation in Germany (No. 10, p. 3; No. 11, p. 2). The experts present the 'strange' exercises as the particular added value of the textbook, integrating German *and* French methodology, thus giving access to a larger spectrum of pedagogical traditions[8].

---

8. The French editor of the textbook Guillaume Le Quintrec is even more affirmative: 'We aimed at overcoming these [Franco-German methodological] differences, in taking the best of each pedagogical tradition. Finally, Germans appreciate a certain French 'rigor' and the particular importance we put on iconographic documents (the methodology for analyzing images is less developed on the other side of the Rhine). The French appreciated the accent Germans put on

With regard to the opposite argument, 'using the common textbook as a social resource' in order to climb the internal hierarchy within a school, no direct evidence could be found in interviews. However, the only *unconditional* support for the textbook came from teachers in bilingual classes. These teachers, with high personal motivation to overcome obstacles in the still experimental Franco-German classes, and profiting from political support, actually could be examples for actors that gain social esteem by using the new book. This interpretation is further confirmed if we link it to two critical claims: One actor criticised the 'political pressure' to use the book – which according to him resulted in the opposite effect among 'normal' teachers, 'refusing to use the book' and 'jealously observing who' actually uses it amongst the colleagues (No.1, p. 1). Furthermore, one experienced teacher/expert, specialised in training young bilingual teachers, heavily criticised the textbook's usability in class. This person attributed the above-mentioned younger colleagues' support for the book as 'idealism', in contrast to his 'overview' on negative experiences with the book. It seems that the utilitarian hypothesis has to be retained and further refined in more large-scale studies, especially when linked to sociological institutionalist reasoning (see below).

Concerning the institutionalist hypotheses

Sociological institutionalism: Linked to processes of social learning, one could argue that only those actors experienced with, and having learned to use 'foreign' resources and 'foreign' pedagogical approaches, are able to successfully use the common textbook. This corresponds to the (relative) success of the book in bilingual classes and at the same time to the criticism from teachers with a 'normal' background. Their criticism scarcely touches on the historical content of the book, but is mainly based on the methodological, didactic and pedagogical elements of the book (cf. Körber 2008). More generally, teachers perceive an underlying 'French model' (No.2, p.2; No.3, p.1; No.4, p. 1; No.8, p. 2). This is not seen as negative per se, but as incongruent and irreconcilable with German regional education standards (No.8, p.2, 3). 'Normal' teachers do not question the German standards; they are unquestionably seen as the 'right' way of teaching.

Historical institutionalism: Of course, these standards can be seen as resulting from a historically path-dependent evolution that started in Germany after (and as a result of) the Second World War. Creating the standards of an educational system capable of producing critical citizens took place within a social field. It brought together academics, civil servants and teachers and produced pedagogical and methodological choices difficult to revoke or abolish without threatening the existence of the social field and its actors as a whole.

Amongst the interviewed teachers in particular, an important and recurring criticism was the 'incoherency' of the book with regard to 'German standards'

---

concepts, historiographic debates and different ways of examining the documents' (Le Quintrec 2007: 6, author's translation).

and the 'poor' or 'too short' (No.3, p. 2; No.8, p. 1) presentation of factual elements in the textbook. At the same time they criticised the 'too complicated', 'too dense' language, no longer accessible to 'today's school children' (No.2, p. 3). This argument ties in with the heavy criticism advanced by teachers and experts of the modification of school curricula by governments and administration: 'Because of' these changes, the Franco-German textbook is 'no longer' usable. The two French experts put this argument forcefully: France is in the process of completely changing its history curriculum between 2009/10 and 2012/13. The curriculum had already been modified in 2004/05 when the textbook was developed. Yet the same is true in Germany for Lower Saxony, where the compulsory topics for the final *Abitur* examination were changed shortly after the publication of the first and second volume of the common textbook. For one interviewed teacher, 'this made the Franco-German textbook useless' (No.8, p. 1).

This contrasts with the fact that the book, even after modified curricula, is still used in *AbiBac*-and bilingual classes, especially in Baden-Württemberg. These classes, however, are governed by different guidelines,[9] with some leverage regarding the officially fixed standards. At the same time, the 'liberal' use of compulsory standards could again be the result of a process of social learning amongst those teachers that had to adapt existing standards and pedagogical materials to the situation of bilingual teaching. An interviewee (No.4, p.1) explained that 'no textbook exists for these [bilingual] classes. Therefore we use the Franco-German book'. Whereas there is thus some evidence for the historical institutionalist argument, it seems important to qualify this evidence by the fact that it is only advanced by teachers – and constitutes a welcome argument for them *not* to use the new book. In this, it is linked to rational-choice-institutionalism.

Rational-choice institutionalism: Here, only indirect evidence can be found. In a social constellation favourable to the new textbook, with politicians publicly claiming it to be a 'success story', it would be difficult for teachers to claim (even in an anonymous interview) that they are not using the book for 'selfish' reasons. No teacher will admit to being 'too lazy' or 'not motivated' enough to use the new book. However, the heavy and at times exaggerated criticism of the content, the methodological and pedagogical standards of the book point in another direction: teachers may 'hide' behind the criticism of 'poor standards' and 'changed curricula' in order to deflect from their own reticence to use the book in class.

In the current, as yet unrefined state of the hypotheses, it seems as if all three institutionalisms can claim some evidence, especially if linked to other arguments. However, we can already ascertain that the 'linking element' can be found in social processes taking place within particular groups, in established 'social fields'. If the Franco-German textbook challenges these constellations, then actors of these groups point to the lacunae of a textbook that is perceived as 'foreign'. This argument is even stronger if we turn to social constructivist reasoning.

---

9. The 'standards' that apply to Franco-German classes in Baden-Württemberg: www.bildung-staerkt-den-menschen.de/service/downloads/bildungsstandards/Gym/Gym_G_bilingual_2010–11_bs.pdf (accessed 30th October 2010).

Concerning the social constructivist hypothesis

As mentioned above, both in France and Germany 'other' models of teaching history have been constructed. In both cases, this is linked to the perception of an 'own' model, constructed in opposition to the 'other' one. If an outside observer may easily have the impression that both approaches are mutually compatible and complement each other (Miard-Delacroix 2006: 34–35; Le Quintrec 2007: 6), the interviews show that this is absolutely not the understanding of the teachers and experts involved on both sides.

In seven interviews of teachers and experts, the recurrent argument came up that the textbook is 'better used in the French context' as it is 'conceptualised along the lines of French books of *première* and *terminale*'. This was underlined by pointing out the 'poor quality of the authors' texts and choice of sources' when applied to the needs of a German final year class. Yet the same author points to the 'very demanding, dense and complicated' texts, too difficult for his (German) pupils to grasp (No.2, p. 1, 4; also No. 8, p. 1; No.9, p. 2). An expert and teacher (No.9) mentions, Franco-German differences of 'methodological-didactic nature' cannot be solved in one book. He explicitly advances that

> French students have to learn to develop a plan but not to give their opinion. For the French, developing a plan means reproducing things learnt by heart. In France, they use the author's text and the sources, illustrating the author's text and 'legitimising' it. In Germany, we want to make students aware of problems. We may even reproduce sources contradicting the author's text. An autonomous judgement is extremely important in Germany (No.9, p. 3).

Asked if both approaches could not be combined, the interviewee changes his role and now criticises as an 'expert' his German colleagues:

> Yes, you could combine, certainly [...] of course, you could, well, if they [Germans] cannot find their keywords, they won't be able to. If they had to transform normal questions into questions introduced by keywords, that would already be too much for [...] an average German history teacher does not know about French history. Learning French history and liberating it from keywords, that is too much...(No.9, p. 5).

Finally, asked about the importance of didactic standards and the use of keywords, this person points to

> the role played by educationalists. People working in that field, eh, are not accepted by their colleagues, err, in universities. You know, these people [educationalists] have to defend their position [...] if they give up their standards they give up, give up their position (No.9, p.5).

This evidence again contrasts with the appreciation coming from bilingual or French contacts. A 'bilingual' teacher (No.4, p. 2) and a French expert-teacher (No. 10, p. 4) claim that, didactically speaking, the book is 'successfully realised'. A civil servant dealing with experiences of teachers in the bilingual programme mentions the 'regular positive feedback [from teachers in bilingual classes] on the book's presentation, the many photos, illustrations and graphics. In particular, the very thoroughly crafted pages with methodological content and the broad number of topics covered' (No.13, p. 1) are positively mentioned. The same person argues that this is 'due to the French programme, it corresponds more to their programme' – but inherently turns this argument into a *positive* one. In a next, 'reflexive' step, he advances: 'well this is, err, probably, what makes them use it less, well, in normal classes, they do not use it, it is too far away from our programme, they do not find the keywords and cannot adapt the exercises, eh the questions to the exercises' (No.13, p.2).

It is interesting that both French (No. 10, p. 2; No. 6, p. 1) and German (No.13, p. 1) interviewees claim that 'there is much more in it [the book] that can only be used on the other [German/French] side', yet this claim leads to different assumptions, depending on the interviewee's background. What seems after all quite normal for a book that is supposed to accommodate two (or 17) different curricula is then given as evidence for its perceived German [French] character. The perceived 'national' character of the book (in fact perceived in all those elements that seem 'not normal') is seen as a 'good' or 'bad' thing, depending on the social context in which the book is used (normal versus bilingual class). Most interviewees agree with the experts who were not involved in the development of the textbook, who claimed that 'a lack of coherence in the 17 plus 1 curricula leads to a lack of coherence in the book' (No.8, p. 2; No.9, p. 1). However, all of my interviewees did not see this as a problem. Those working in bilingual classes maintained that the 'lack of coherence' could easily be compensated for if the teacher 'knows what she wants' (No. 4, p. 1).

In conclusion, the implicit reference to a 'national model' of teaching history is the reason most often evoked for the Franco-German textbook's lack of success. While this argument comes in different shades (lacking coherency with new or reformed programmes, lacking pedagogical or didactic standards etc.), there is a split between teachers able to deal with these incoherencies and those who refuse this challenge. The cleavage line separates teachers in 'normal' classes from those in 'bilingual' classes. It is astonishing to find, at times, the same evidence presented in favour or against the use of the common textbook, depending on the arguments it is linked to. The task, therefore, is to better understand the constellation or set of conditions behind these outcomes. The question is which conditions are decisive for a teacher, to see the new textbook as a burden, a challenge or an opportunity?

Discussing the results

How should the results of this study be evaluated? Clearly, the presented evidence, so far, only allows for a very general picture. Yet based on this picture, more systematic studies are needed. One main criticism concerns the small number of cases. At this stage of the study, it is still possible that more cases will lead to very different findings. At the same time, my approach allowed for an in-depth analysis, differentiating some 'standard' arguments. It should be clear by now that a 'single explanation' or purely structural or actor-based approaches will not be enough. Instead, a thick contextualisation within social and institutional environments is necessary. In this respect, the differentiation along national lines is clearly not sufficient. In Germany we find both constellations, in favour or against the use of the textbook, at times referring to the same observed evidence, yet using it in different arguments. Here, the social differentiation between the elite group of teachers in bilingual classes and the 'normal' teachers is the main cause for variance in the responses. What gives rise to these differences?

Apparently, 'normal teachers' perceive the school book in 'national' terms – meaning a 'French' versus a 'German' textbook with their underlying methodologies, pedagogical and didactic approaches, necessarily different and incompatible. In contrast, bilingual teachers see the school book as a welcome enhancement to the standard programme, as an opportunity that has to be seized. Even if they still perceive the school book in terms of national, 'French' and 'German' models, this does not translate into an identity conflict for them. The question then arises which further resources they have at their disposal that allow them to positively react to the changed opportunity structure?

This question is a broader one: Under what conditions do individual citizens perceive a changed opportunity structure in a positive way? If we assume that the change of the opportunity structure originates in the process of European integration, we may even be able to tackle the question of individual positive or negative perceptions of, and behaviour towards, European integration.

For the case of the textbook, 'normal' teachers are struck by the 'strange' methodology applied in the book. This methodology, if it is not seen as 'strange', is assumed to be 'French'. Yet the introduction of the textbook provides a different picture.[10] The manual, as its introduction states, builds on a new methodology. It has,

> an understanding of history that leaves as much room for facts as for interpretations. Based on these fundamentals, the manual aims to overcome the national perspective and to guide attention towards similarities, differences, and interactions as linchpins for a comparative observation of developments in France and Germany, analysed in an at first European and then more and

---

10. See also the editors and authors of the book discussing 'overcoming the national regard' (Le Quintrec 2007), 'multi-perspectivity and complementarity' (Geiss 2006) and 'transnational knowledge – the nation-state principle in the common history book' (Lange 2008).

more global context. This approach gives students the key for understanding a complex world (Henri *et al.* 2008: 3, author's translation).

The underlying aim, presented as the added value and great advantage of the new book, is to learn to deal with and to integrate different views, with the intention of helping students understand a more complex world. It can help 'change one's perspective on the other and on oneself'. This new perspective is explicitly defined:

> Its characteristic feature is the change of perspective that underlines the enmeshment of historical lines of development, the common as the contested memories and the multiple and different accesses to one and the same reality – as well as the differences between words, meanings, perceptions and their reception. In that sense, this is a Franco-German book on history and not a book on Franco-German history (Henri *et al.* 2008: 3, author's translation).

Of course, this perception is in stark contrast to what 'national history' has tried to do since the end of the nineteenth century. In pretending that an 'objective' historical 'science' is possible, it claimed that the nation's history, and therefore its existence as a group, 'objectively existed'. From that standpoint, the Franco-German textbook looks strange and disturbing. Yet building a methodology able to integrate two perspectives, accepting both of them equally as relevant and legitimate, is surely a valuable tool to deal with today's European constellation in a larger sense. Those able to employ this tool have the resources to succeed in today's European Union. Those chained to their model of the nation-state will have difficulties accepting the underlying challenge of a binational history textbook.

Appendix: List of Interviews

Interview number	Date	Role	Region	Country
1	09.09.2010	Expert, consulting French schools on 'German' topics	Lorraine and Alsace	France / Germany
2	31.08.2010	Teacher, bilingual	Baden-Württemberg	Germany
3	10.09.2010	Teacher, bilingual	Baden-Württemberg	Germany
4	09.09.2010	Teacher, bilingual	Baden-Württemberg	Germany
5	16.09.2010	Teacher, co-author of the textbook		Germany
6	01.10.2010	Administration	Alsace	France
7	04.10.2010	Expert	Lower Saxony	Germany
8	05.10.2010	Teacher, Expert	North Rhine-Westphalia	Germany
9	05.10.2010	Teacher, expert	Baden-Württemberg	Germany
10	07.10.2010	Teacher, expert	Alsace	France
11	09.10.2010	Expert	Saxony	Germany
12	14.10.2010	Expert, regional administration	Baden-Württemberg	Germany
13	15.10.2010	Regional administration, bilingual classes	Baden-Württemberg	Germany

References

Alexandre, P. (2006) 'Zur Vorgeschichte einer deutsch-französischen Geschichtsschulbuchrevision', http://www.france-blog.info/pdf/ Alexandre_250906.pdf (accessed 30th October 2010).

Barton, K. C. and Levstik, L. S. (2004) Teaching History for the Common Good, Oxford: Routledge.

Bell, D. A. (2001) The Cult of the Nation in France: Inventing nationalism, 1680–1800 Cambridge, MA: Harvard University Press.

Bendick, R. (2009) 'Das deutsch-französische Schulgeschichtsbuch. Die Möglichkeit zum binationalen Geschichtsunterricht und die nationalen Reserven der deutschen Geschichtsdidaktik', Eckert: Beiträge, 4.

Bray, Z. (2008) 'Ethnographic Methods', in M. Keating and D. della Porta (eds) Methodologies in the Social and Political Sciences, Cambridge: Cambridge University Press, pp. 296–314.

Checkel, J. T. (2007) 'Constructivism and EU politics', in K. E. Jørgensen, M. A. Pollack and B. Rosamond (eds) Handbook of European Union Politics, London: Sage, pp. 57–76.

Chilosi, D. (2007) 'Old wine in new bottles: civic nation-building and ethnic nationalism in schooling in Piedmont, ca. 1700–1861', Nations and Nationalism 13(3): 417–436.

Claret, F. (2006) 'Le manuel franco-allemand d'histoire, de l'utopie à la réalité', Lendemains 122/123: 235–240.

De Cock, L. and Picard, E. (2009) La fabrique scolaire de l'histoire, Marseille: Agone.

Defrance, C. and Pfeil, U. (2010) 'Historischer Perspektivenwechsel. Das deutsch-französische Geschichtsbuch: Vorgeschichte und Realisierung', in F. Baasner (ed.) Frankreich-Jahrbuch 2009. Französische Blicke auf das zeitgenössische Deutschland, Wiesbaden: VS-Verlag, pp. 95–113.

Droit, E. (2007) 'Entre histoire croisée et histoire denationalisée: le manuel franco-allemand d'histoire', Histoire de l'éducation, Paris: Service, pp. 151–162.

Dubois, J.-P. (2010) 'Le manuel d'histoire franco-allemand: travail de mémoire et projet d'avenir', Revue des deux mondes, March: 156–165.

Esser, H. (1991) Alltagshandeln und Verstehen: zum Verhältnis von erklärender und verstehender Soziologie am Beispiel von Alfred Schütz und 'Rational Choice', Tübingen: Mohr.

François, E. (2007) 'Le manuel franco-allemand d'histoire. Une enterprise inédite', Vingtième Siècle, Revue d'histoire 94: 73–86.

Frenkel, C. (2008) 'Vichy Waschi. Der Zweite Weltkrieg im binationalen Geschichtsbuch', Dokumente 64(4): 25–28.

Garcia, P. and Leduc, J. (2004) L'enseignement de l'histoire en France de l'Ancien Régime à nos jours, Paris: Armand Colin.

Geiss, P. (2006) 'Multiperspektivität und Komplementarität. Das deutsch-französische Geschichtsbuch als Herausforderung für Autoren und

Herausgeber', *Dokumente* 62(5): 97–102.

Geiss, P. and Le Quintrec. G. (eds) (2006) *Histoire /Geschichte: L'Europe et le monde depuis 1945, manuel d'histoire franco-allemand. Terminale L/ ES/S*, Paris: Nathan.

Gitton, R. (2007) 'Le manuel franco-allemand à l'épreuve de la classe', *Histoire@ Politique 2*, available at http://www.histoire-politique.fr/documents/02/ autresArticles/pdf/HP2-Gitton-tap-def.pdf (accessed 30th October 2010).

Hall, P. A. and Taylor, R. C. R. (1996) 'Political Science and the Three New Institutionalisms', *Political Studies* 44: 936–957.

Harp, S. (1998) *Learning to be Loyal: Primary Schooling as Nation Building in Alsace and Lorraine*, DeKalb, Illinois: Northern Illinois University Press.

Harvey, D. A. (2001) *Constructing Class and Nationality in Alsace, 1830–1945*, DeKalb, Illinois: Northern Illinois University Press.

Henri, D. (2009) 'Gemeinsame Geschichtsbücher, gemeinsame Geschichte?', Eckert: *Das Bulletin*, 5: 28–31.

Henri, D., Le Quintrec G. and Geiss, P. (eds) (2008) *Histoire/Geschichte. Europa und die Welt vom Wiener Kongress bis 1945*, Stuttgart & Leipzig: Klett, *Histoire /Geschichte. L'Europe et le monde du congrès de Vienne à 1945, Manuel d'Histoire franco-allemand. Histoire 1ère L-ES-S*, Paris: Nathan.

Hobsbawm, E. (1992) 'Ethnicity and nationalism in Europe today', *Anthropology Today* 8(1): 3–8.

Körber, A. (2008) 'The Franco-German History Textbook from the Perspective of Specialist Didactics', available at http://www.gei.de/publikationen/ eckert-dossiers/europa-und-die-welt/fachdidaktik/didactics.html. (accessed 30th October 2010)

Krieger, W. (2006) 'Wirtschaftliche, gesellschaftliche und kulturelle Entwicklungen – Mangelndes sozioökonomishces Verständnis – zu Teil 4', *Dokumente*, 62(5): 76–87.

Lange, U. (2008) 'Transnationales Wissen: das nationalstaatliche Prinzip im gemeinsamen Geschichtsbuch', *Dokumente*, 64(4): 21–24.

Le Quintrec, G. (2007) 'Le manuel franco-allemand: une écriture commune de l'histoire', *Histoire@Politique 2*, available at http://www.histoire-politique.fr/documents/02/autresArticles/pdf/HP2-Le_Quintrec-tap-def. pdf (accessed 30.10.2010)

Le Quintrec, G. and Geiss, P. (eds) (2006) *Histoire /Geschichte. Europa und die Welt seit 1945, Deutsch-französisches Geschichtsbuch. Gymnasiale Oberstufe*, Stuttgart & Leipzig: Klett.

Miard-Delacroix, H. (2006) 'Das gemeinsame Geschichtsbuch. Eine erste Reaktion auf die französische Prüfauflage', *Dokumente* 62(4): 32–35.

Milward, A. (1992) *The European Rescue of the Nation-State*, Oxford: Routledge.

Monnet, P. (2006) 'Un manuel d'histoire franco-allemand', *Revue historique* 639: 409–422.

Raether, M. (2008) 'Un revers de deux médailles?', *Francia. Forschungen zur westeuropäischen Geschichte* 35: 585–590.

Riemenschneider, R. (1998) 'Transnationale Konfliktbearbeitung. Die deutsch-französischen und die deutsch-polnischen Schulbuchgespräche im Vergleich, 1935–1997', *Internationale Schulbuchforschung* 20: 71–80.

Seidendorf, S. (2007) *Europäisierung nationaler Identitätsdiskurse? Ein Vergleich französischer und deutscher Printmedien*, Baden-Baden: Nomos.

Steinmo, S. (2008) 'Historical Institutionalism', in M. Keating and D. della Porta (eds) *Methodologies in the Social and Political Sciences*, Cambridge: Cambridge University Press, pp. 118–137.

Weiss, R. S. (1995) *Learning From Strangers: The art and method of qualitative interview studies*, New York: Free Press.

index

Balanyá, B. 55
Ball, P. 7
Balme, R. 28, 32, 40, 55
Banchoff, T. F. 203
Barroso Commission 54
Barroso, J. M. *24*, 25, 66
Bartelson, J. 121
Bartolini, S. 203
Barton, K. C. 243
Basaran, T. 121
Basilien-Gainche, M.-L. 55
Bates, E. 149
Baudrillard, J. 199
Bauman, Z. 111, 121
BBC 233 n.21
Beauvallet, W. 8
Becker, H. 56, 82, 83
Beckfield, J. 1
Beetham, D. 202, 204
Belgium 151
    EU attitudes and 168, 169 n.2, 174,
        175, 181, 186, *199*
Bell, D. A. 240, 244
Bélot, C. 166
Bendick, R. 249
Bendix, R. 19
Benford, R. D. 34, 35
Berezin, M. 203, 214
Berger, P. 5, 86 n.10
Best, H. 3, 11, 169 n.3
Beyers, J. 56
Bieler, A. 29, 42 n.7
Bigo, D. 3, 10, 120, 121, 122, 191
Billet, S. 54
Billig, M. 26, 215
Binnema, H. 166
Blanchard, P. 10, 57, 86
Blavoukos, S. 55
Bocco, R. 120
Bodin, J. 118
Bohman, J. 26
Bolkestein directive 24, 25, 30, 36,
    40–1, 42, 43
Boltanski, L. 64
Bonditti, P. 122, 123

Boomgaarden, H. G. 171, 208
borders 111–102
    as barrier, myth of 101–2
    control of 112, 115–16, 120, 121–2
        identity and 112, 115, 119, 122
        Schengen system and 196 n.4
    European Union and 118, 193
        Schengen Agreement and 118
        space-sets, concept of and 193
        system/social integration, use of
            concepts 224
    function of 116–17
    globalisation, effect on 119
    narratives of 117-, 119
        alternative discourses119–120
        as politics of order 111, 116, 118,
            120, 121, 122
    national identity and 115, 116
    as networks 119, 123
    notion of 111–14
        geographical sense of 111, 112,
            113–14, 118, 119
        sovereignty and 112, 113, 114,
            115–16, 117, 118
        territory and 112, 113, 114, 116,
            117, 118, 122
    social construction of 112–13
    surveillance and 121
    transnationalism and 112
    see also citizens and citizenship
        (EU); migration; transnational-
        ism, EU integration and
Bourdieu, P. 3, 148
    transnational fields and 148
Bourdin, J. 128, 130, 131
Bozec, G. 234 n.22
Braibant, G. 156
Braun, M. 196
Bray, Z. 248
Brazil 195
Broqua, C. 83, 86 n.10, 87, 97, 99
Brücker, H. 196
Bruter, M. 204
Bulgaria *197*
    EU attitudes and 169 n.2, 175, 186

Savino, M. 132
Sawicki, F. 82
Saxenian, A. 193
Sayad, A. 194
Scharpf, F. 203
Schattschneider, E. E. 57
Scheeck, L. 154
Scheepers, P. 208
Scheingold, S. 204
Scherrer, A. 121
Scheuer, A. 202
Scheve, K. 204
Schiltz, M.-A. 64
Schmidt, V. A. 215
Schmitt, C. 115, 117
Schmitt, H. 9, 206, 214 n.11
Schneider, B. 86 n.10
Schröder, G. 245
Scholz, E. 206, 214 n.11
Schumaker, P. D. 22
SEAP 59, 66, 67, 68, 70, 71
Seidendorf, S. 3, 11, 244
sequence analysis (SA) 4, 10, 82–3,
    84, 87
    multiple 83, 84–5, 87
    see also Aides, SMO case study
Serres, M. 111
Sewell, W. H. 21
Sigalas, E. 9, 11, 230 n.11
Sikkink, K. 19, 25, 42
Silva, F. 19, 43
Siméant, J. 82
Simpson, A. W. B. 151–2
Single European Act (1986) 31
Sinnott, R. 202
Sitter, N. 167
Sloterdijk, P. 115
Slovakia 175, 183, 196, *197*
Slovenia *197*
Smith, A. 57
Smith, H. 226 n.7, 236 n.25, 238
Smith, J. 20, 27, 31, 39
Smith, M. P. 31, 203
Smith, W. 225
Snow, D. A. 34, 35

social comparison research 224, 225-
    concept of 225–7
    cross-national dimensions of 232–4,
        235, 239–40
        criteria of comparison and 232,
            240
        data collection and 232–3
        media, role in 233–4, 239
        national boundedness of 234,
            240
    European integration and 229–34,
        235
        cross-national comparison and
            234–9
        EU mobility and 230
        new bonds of solidarity and 237,
            238, 239
        political effects of 237, 238
        relative deprivation, perception
            of and 236–8
        system integration and 230, 231,
            235, 239
    politics, use in 227
    see also transnationalisation, EU
        integration and
social movement organisations (SMO)
    1, 4, 9, 19, 23–45
    action strategies 39–41, *44*, 45
    'Another Europe' campaign 21, 38
    cultural and symbolic dimensions
        9, 20, 38
    effects, analysis of 21, 22–3
        policy change and 22, 23
        political opportunities and 21,
            25, 26
        resource mobilisation and 21, 23,
            26, 27, 30–1, 33
    European transnational study 19,
        20, 21, 22, 23–45
        actions strategies in 40–3, *44*
        allies, influence of and 29–30
        Bolkestein Directive campaign
            24, 25, 30, 36, 40–1, 42, 43
        chemicals legislation (REACH)
            campaign 23–4, 29, 33, 37, 41

www.ingramcontent.com/pod-product-compliance
Lightning Source LLC
Chambersburg PA
CBHW072100040426
42334CB00041B/1520